STRUCTURED READING

Seventh Edition

Lynn Quitman Troyka

Queensborough Community College,
The City University of New York

Joseph Wayne Thweatt

Southwest Tennessee Community College

PEARSON
Prentice
Hall

Upper Saddle River, New Jersey 07458

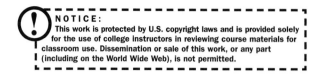
Editorial Director: Leah Jewell
Senior Editor: Vivian Garcia
Editorial Assistant: Deborah Doyle
Full Service Production Liaison: Joanne Hakim
Operations Specialist: Christina Amato
Marketing Manager: Lindsey Prudhomme
Marketing Assistant: Jessica Muraviov
Creative Director: Jayne Conte
Cover Design: Bruce Kenselaar
Cover Photo: Siri Stafford/Getty Images Inc.
Permissions Specialist: Warren Drabek

Director, Image Resource Center: Melinda Patelli
Manager, Rights and Permissions: Zina Arabia
Manager, Visual Research: Beth Brenzel
Manager, Cover Visual Research & Permissions: Karen Sanatar
Image Permission Coordinator: Frances Toepfer
Photo Research: Nancy Tobin
Full-Service Project Management: John Shannon/Pine Tree Composition
Composition: Laserwords Private Limited
Printer/Binder: Edwards Brothers, Inc.

Dictionary extracts reproduced with permission from *Webster's New™ World Collection Dictionary, Fourth Edition.* Copyright © 2001 IDG Books Worldwide Inc. Reprinted by permission of John Wiley & Sons.

Credits and acknowledgments borrowed from other sources and reproduced, with permission, in this textbook appear on appropriate page within text or on pages 427–428.

Pearson Education LTD., London
Pearson Education Singapore, Pte. Ltd
Pearson Education, Canada, Ltd
Pearson Education–Japan
Pearson Education Australia PTY, Limited

Pearson Education North Asia Ltd
Pearson Educación de Mexico, S.A. de C.V.
Pearson Education Malaysia, Pte. Ltd
Pearson Education, Upper Saddle River, New Jersey

PEARSON
Prentice
Hall

10 9 8 7 6 5 4 3 2 1

Contents

*New for this edition.

Exercises:

Exercises:

Exercises:

Exercises:

Preface

In writing *Structured Reading*, Seventh Edition, we remained convinced that students learn best from guided, hands-on experience with complete, not partial, reading selections. We believe, too, that the best approach starts with detailed instruction in the separate skills areas that ensure movement to college-level reading abilities, followed by extensive, repeated practice with many complete reading selections that comprise five-sixths of this book.

In flight training, student pilots spend some instructional time in a training simulator. But within a short time, the instructors move students from the simulator to the cockpit of the airplane to give the students hands-on practice in flying the plane. Few passengers would fly with a pilot who had only simulator experience. Most want a pilot who has logged many hours of real flight time in the cockpit. Likewise, we want students to move quickly from the skills (the simulator) to actual reading (the cockpit) for extended practice. This method has worked well since the first edition of *Structured Reading* and is evidenced by its continued use by hundreds of teachers and thousands of students in the United States and Canada.

This new edition of *Structured Reading* builds on the techniques and strategies that have been the backbone of our previous editions. We've learned from our reviewers and teaching colleagues that Part One, which includes instruction in the separate college-level reading skills students need ("Central Theme and Main Ideas"; "Major Details"; "Inferences"; "Critical Reading"; and "Reader's Response") is exactly what students are seeking from a reading textbook. This Seventh Edition features an expanded, comprehensive Part One, "Skills for Reading," that has adapted to the evolving needs of college-level readers. This fourteen-chapter part explains and demonstrates each of the primary reading skills covered in previous editions and includes much-needed instruction on building vocabulary through structural analysis, writing summaries, identifying audience, tone and purpose, and reading visuals. Each chapter also offers extensive skills-based exercises to prepare students for their hands-on experience with the twenty-nine complete reading selections in Parts Two through Six.

Our commitment to meeting the evolving needs of our students is also reflected in the topics of the reading selections. College students live in a world dominated by visual images, and gaining proficiency in reading these alternate texts is imperative in their efforts to become critical readers. As a result, we've also added a selection solely devoted to reading pictures, illustrations, charts, and graphs. This is in addition to the six reading selections we've replaced with new selections on more current, absorbing issues that students will find engaging.

Here are the major features of *Structured Reading*, Seventh Edition:

• Part One, "Skills for Reading" explains the reading process. Using an FAQ approach, it gives students down-to-earth advice—with lots of chances for practice—about how to improve reading speed, expand vocabulary, make useful predictions during reading, read "on, between, and beyond" the lines, find central themes and main ideas, identify major and minor details, make inferences, read critically, and respond to ideas.

• **NEW**! We've expanded Chapter 5, "How Can I Improve My Vocabulary?" to include instruction on strengthening vocabulary acquisition through structural analysis using roots, prefixes, and suffixes. Now students have not only the tools to use contextual clues to understand new vocabulary, but also the additional capability to use basic word parts to grasp meaning.

• **NEW**! We've developed a chapter on identifying the author's strategies of audience, tone, and purpose. As a critical reader, it is necessary to question and analyze an author's craft and purpose in writing. In fact, many state-mandated tests for preparatory reading courses require mastery of these elements of crtical reading, and now Chapter 12 of the Seventh Edition addresses this need. The exercises after the readings in Parts Two through Six reflect this additional focus.

• **NEW**! We've added a chapter on summary to support students' ability to recall and comprehend what they read. Here, students are given the essentials on how to write and identify a summary that captures the essential message of a reading selection. Again, the exercises after the readings in Parts Two through Six now include a question on summary, which will assess students' strength in this area.

• **NEW**! We've integrated into Chapter 9 a disscussion on how to read visual images (pictures, illustrations, charts, and graphs) using the same reading strategies students learn to read text. This is followed by Selection 30 in Part Six, which provides a variety of visuals accompanied by exercises that evaluate a student's ability to read the visual both literally and inferentially.

Twenty-nine reading selections, with six new for this edition, represent our desire to offer an instructive, stimulating balance of readings from books, magazines, newspapers, and textbooks in disciplines across the curriculum. The final mix represents both male and female writers, as well as writers from a variety of ethnic groups.

• "Thinking: Getting Started" sections, another unique feature of *Structured Reading*, open Parts Two through Six to help students engage in predictive reading. This Seventh Edition features new, engaging posters, photographs, advertisements, cartoons, and other visuals to prepare students for the topics to come.

• **NEW**! Exercises are deliberately structured to promote analytic and critical reasoning. Indeed, our structured sequences of exercises following every reading selection are the key feature that teachers and students have been praising from the first edition of *Structured Reading*: "Vocabulary," "Central Theme and Main Ideas," "Major Details," "Inferences," and "Reader's Response." New to this Seventh Edition is an expanded focus on

"Critical Reading," which now includes exercises on "The Author's Strategies," and "Summary" in addition to "Fact vs. Opinion." All in all, the structured sequence presented here demands concentrated work in **reading for literal meaning, for inferential meaning, and for critical thinking**. This approach, used repeatedly, leads students to internalize successfully complex reading and thinking skills.

• The answer options for our structured exercises may look to some like multiple-choice items, but the similarity stops there. *Structured Reading* exercises are unique, which can be seen as soon as anyone looks beneath the surface. We've written the incorrect answers (called "distracters") to propel students into close reading and active analysis. They're forced to marshal their higher-order reasoning powers to think through mental challenges. Students' powers of persistence and focus can become habit when teachers require them not only to identify a correct answer (called "the key") but also to analyze and articulate why other choices are incorrect.

• Complete, authentic dictionary entries accompany each reading selection to help students tackle the more difficult words in the piece. This unique, popular feature of *Structured Reading* provides students hands-on experience with dictionary use. We have again been fortunate to offer entries from *Webster's New World College Dictionary*, Fourth Edition. Our Appendix, "Guide to Dictionary Use," helps students—in plain English—retrieve information from dictionary entries.

• The book has six parts. Part One teaches the reading process and its college-level skills. Parts Two through Six contain reading selections with increasingly difficult readability levels (see the *Instructor's Edition* of *Structured Reading*), and with short-to-longer selections within each part.

Here are highly useful supplements for our Seventh Edition:

• The *Instructor's Edition* (ISBN 0-13-047512-2) of our Seventh Edition of *Structured Reading* marks another milestone on behalf of teachers. For the first time, we provide instructors with a special edition that includes answers to all exercises right on the student text pages, along with a 45-page "Instructor's Guide" found at the back of the text. The "Instructor's Guide" contains additional teaching strategies, readability levels for the thirty Reading Selections, and tips on using *Structured Reading* in either a classroom setting or a self-paced lab. We hope this special edition will help new teachers along with their more experienced colleagues. It is available to instructors at no additional cost.

• An *Instructor's Resource Manual* (ISBN 0-13-188727-0) provides additional material for instructors as they prepare for class. This manual contains transparency masters, comprehension boosters, extra vocabulary exercises, and supplementary dictionary exercises. We have designed these materials to support instructors and lab tutors as they work with students. It is available to instructors at no additional cost.

• *MyReadingLab* is an online learning system that helps students improve both their reading skills and their reading level. *MyReadingLab* includes interactive tutorial exercises. All of *MyReadingLab*'s practice exercises and tests include tutorials and models for extra help at point of use, and they offer helpful feedback when students enter incorrect answers. The readings are engaging and include a combination of textbook and popular sources for optimum student interest. Readings provided in the *Reading Skills* practice area are organized around a popular road trip theme. Skill areas are connected to locations throughout the United States. Photos, points of interest, and readings all reflect a particular location. Readings provided in the *Reading Level* practice area are organized by topic and were selected from textbooks and popular readings. Students can choose from the readings provided based on their personal interests. *MyReadingLab* also has a study plan for self-paced learning. The *Study Plan* is the heart of the site where all the student activities and tests are found. *MyReadingLab* can generate a personalized study plan for each student based on his or her diagnostic test results, and the study plan links directly to interactive, tutorial exercises for topics the student has not yet mastered. Instructors can ask their Prentice Hall sales representative to create a package with *MyReadingLab*.

• The Prentice Hall Reading Skills Test Bank contains 100 exercises on each of eleven different reading skills. Available online, designed for use with any text, this test bank has over 1,000 exercises, covering word analysis, context clues, stated main idea, implied main idea, tone and bias, details, major versus minor details, style, study reading, reading rate, and visual aids. Questions are multiple-choice, matching, or true/false. The test bank is available in printed format or electronically. ISBN (printed): 0-13-041249-X. Instructors can contact their Prentice Hall representative to request the electronic version. It is available to instructors upon adoption at no additional cost.

• Free dictionary offer: Students can receive the *New American Webster Handy College Dictionary* packaged with their text at no additional cost when instructors adopt *Structured Reading*, Seventh Edition. This dictionary has over 1.5 million Signet copies in print with over 115,000 definitions, including current phrases, slang, and scientific terms. It offers more than 1,500 new words, with over 200 not found in any competing dictionary, and it features boxed inserts on etymologies and language. It also includes foreign words and phrases and an international gazetteer with correct place-name pronunciations. Instructors can ask their Prentice Hall sales representative for the ISBN of the package.

ACKNOWLEDGMENTS

The advice of our colleagues across the United States has helped our continuing quest to make each edition of *Structured Reading* the best it can be. With their active participation, our Seventh Edition has evolved with the dynamic changes in theory and practice.

For their invaluable reviews of our Sixth Edition as we prepared our revision plan for this Seventh Edition, we thank Jennifer Campbell, Villa Maria College of Buffalo; Judy Hubble, Austin Community College; Sharon Lagina, Wayne County Community College District; Judith Resnick, Borough of Manhattan Community College; Ruth Sowell, Southwest Tennessee Community College; Chae Sweet, Hudson Community College; Sharon Taylor, Western Wyoming Community College; and Katherine Winkler, Blue Ridge Community College. As is true for all authors, any lapses you discover on these pages are ours.

We started this revision when Craig Campanella was Senior Editor for Developmental English, and we finished it when Vivian Garcia moved into that role. Both of them lent us their invaluable guidance and support. Most of all, Vivian recommended to us Chae Sweet, Hudson County Community College, as a talented and delightful partner in completing the Seventh Edition, especially the revision of Part One; we are fortunate to have worked with someone who cares enthusiastically about students of reading.

On a personal level, we thank Ida Morea, Administrative Assistant to Lynn Quitman Troyka, for her excellent organizational skills and always-supportive disposition. Lynn Quitman Troyka also thanks her husband, David, for being her chief cheerleader, indispensable consultant, and beloved companion. Joseph Wayne Thweatt thanks his wife, Marilyn, for her ever-ready willingness to listen, respond, and provide consistently wise counsel throughout the writing process and Professors Donna Overstreet and Jean McDonald at Lambuth University in Jackson, Tennessee, for the opportunities to field-test *Structured Reading* material in their reading classes.

Lynn Quitman Troyka

Joseph Wayne Thweatt

Part 1

Skills for Reading

A s a college student, why do you need a textbook called *Structured Reading*? After all, you already know how to read. Yet, a placement test score or an academic advisor says you need a course to show you how to read successfully at a college level. Our purpose in writing this textbook is to provide you with a concrete, structured method—with lots of opportunity for practice—that can ensure that you reach your goal.

Reading is a challenge for many people. As a college student, however, you're more advanced than the 90 million Americans who are unable to read well enough to function productively in today's world. Over 40 million adults cannot fill out a simple form. Another 50 million are unable to read newspapers or magazines. College students aren't in these groups. Rather, they need to master reading strategies needed for college success.

In *Structured Reading*, we draw on excellent, convincing research about how adults improve their reading skills most efficiently. The best approach involves a structured system of skill building that is applied repeatedly to complete, whole reading selections. Part One, the section you're now reading, explains the overall approach of *Structured Reading*, introducing you to the structured reading strategies that successful adult readers use. Part One also gives you much initial practice, with each skill presented separately.

Parts Two through Six of *Structured Reading* provide you with multiple opportunities to combine all the skills introduced in Part One. After each of the twenty-nine complete reading selections, you'll find structured questions that reinforce the strategies you've learned. The whole selections are representative of material that adults encounter in books, newspapers, magazines, and textbooks. Within Parts Two through Six, the reading selections get longer. Also, each successive part increases in difficulty. (In Part One, we include some short excerpts so that you can practice initially with isolated skills.)

SETTING *YOUR* GOALS

Now that we, the authors of *Structured Reading,* have set our goals, we invite you to set yours. Please list below what you consider your strengths as a reader before starting your college-level reading class. Then, please list the areas in which you'd like to improve as a reader. These are your personal lists, so make them informal and honest.

WHAT ARE MY STRENGTHS AS A READER?

In what areas would I like to improve as a reader?

Chapter 1

What Is Your Personal Reading History?

Everyone has a history of learning to read and of being a reader. By recalling the details of that history, people can come to understand their strengths and weaknesses as readers. Here's a questionnaire that prompts you to remember and analyze your reading history.

ACTIVITY A   MY READING HISTORY

Think about and answer these questions.

1. Before you started to read as a child, did family members or other adults read to you? _____ If yes, did you enjoy it? _____ Why or why not? _____

2. What's your first memory of starting to read (if you recall your approximate age at the time, give it)? _____

   _____

3. What's the title (or story outline) of one of the first books you read as a young child? _____

4. When you were in school (1st through 12th grades), did you encounter any difficulties with reading? _____ If yes, what were they? _____

5. What's the title (or story) of your favorite book when you were in elementary school? _____What did you like about it?

   _____

6. What's the title (or theme) of one of the best books you've ever read?

   _____

7. In general, as you were growing up, if you could choose between watching television or reading for pleasure, which did you choose? _____ Why? _____

8. What's your estimate of the number of complete books you were assigned to read in school? _____ Did you enjoy most of them? _____ Why or why not? _____

9. How often did you read for your own pleasure (fill in the table below)?

SCHOOLS YEARS	almost daily	once a week	once a month	once or twice a year	never
Elementary					
Middle					
High					

10. How often do you currently read for your own pleasure? _____ Do you read newspapers? _____ magazines? _____ books? _____

11. Other memories or comments: _____

As you reflect on your answers, what do they suggest about your current reading ability? Your answers might hold a clue about why you're enrolled in a college-level reading class. For example, people who've had many reading experiences in childhood tend to be better adult readers. These people had many chances to practice regularly. If you didn't have such chances, the reading class you're enrolled in offers you the chance to start catching up. Anything you do well requires continued, disciplined practice—whether it is participating in a sport, playing a musical instrument, or cooking a favorite dish.

Chapter 2

What Is the Reading Process?

Reading is not just looking at words. Reading is a complex, diverse process. The reading process, like many other processes, involves a number of distinct, yet connected, stages. An often overlooked stage in the reading process is preparing to read—preparing both your mind and your surroundings—so that you are able to concentrate on the material. Another stage in the reading process involves your eyes (looking at the page) working together with your memory (accessing the store of information you already know). To learn new material by reading, you "hook" it to what's in your memory. Knowledge builds on knowledge. To build the knowledge base required in college, you need to marshal your self-discipline so that you actively engage with all interactions between your eyes and your memory. This chapter will discuss three primary stages in the reading process and show you how to make them an active part of your reading process.

CONCENTRATING DURING THE READING PROCESS

The ability to use the reading process skillfully takes concentration and self-discipline. Before you start a reading session, seek out places where, and times of day when, you'll not be interrupted or distracted by people or noise. Never mislead yourself into thinking you can concentrate adequately when you're in a room where people are talking, or the TV is on, or music is playing loudly, or when you're expecting phone calls. If you are uncomfortable with silence, as some people tend to be, experiment *honestly* with what gives you comfort: soft, nondistracting music, a clock that ticks reassuringly, or other options. If there's little private time where you live, schedule yourself to read in a quiet corner of the library or a spot in a park or public building with minimum human traffic. Check out which college classrooms are empty during off-peak class hours.

Aside from external influences on your concentration, internal factors can also get in your way. These include daydreams, personal problems, anxiety, and failure to stick with what you set out to accomplish. Concentration takes your total mental immersion in what you're doing. Developing an outstanding ability to concentrate is a major challenge facing college students. At all times, try to work with fierce determination to concentrate and focus with razor-sharp intensity. This is a learned ability. It doesn't come to most people automatically. The good news is that everyone can learn to concentrate and focus. You'll find that the more you practice, the stronger and more stubborn becomes your refusal to tolerate distractions, either external or internal.

One way to monitor your powers of concentration is to place a short stroke (vertical mark) on a sheet of paper each time your mind wanders. Doing this reminds you that you're not concentrating. At the end of the page or article, count the number of strokes you have accumulated. The next time you read, compete with yourself. Reduce the number of strokes you make per page or article. Soon, with practice, you can decrease the number of strokes.

Use the following paragraph to test your powers of concentration. Place a short stroke (vertical line) within the lines each time your mind wanders. Then, count the strokes as your baseline to measure your progress toward reducing the number of strokes as you read. The paragraph is from a student essay about the homeless in *Steps in Composition*, Seventh Edition, by Lynn Quitman Troyka and Jerrold Nudelman.

> The largest group of homeless people consists of families with children. To save on the cost of labor, many companies have downsized their operations or moved them out of the United States. The companies' stockholders may have benefited, but the companies' workers have not. For example, May and Joe Kalson, who lost their jobs when General Motors closed its factory in New York, had to live on welfare after their unemployment insurance ran out. But the payments did not cover all of their expenses. When the Kalsons no longer could pay their rent, they piled into their old Chevy and headed for Detroit in search of work in an automobile factory. But there were no job openings. Their first night in Detroit the family stayed in a homeless shelter, where some of their clothing was stolen while they slept. The Kalsons now sleep in their car. According to the U.S. Conference of Mayors, over half of all the homeless people in this country are families like the Kalsons.

PREVIEWING IN THE READING PROCESS

The overview of this chapter highlighted the idea that learning involves your "hooking" new knowledge to old. Because of this, you read best when you already know something about the topic at hand. Even a little helps. Thus, your first concern when beginning a reading selection is to determine your level of prior knowledge about the topic. To check your prior knowledge about a topic, use the technique called *previewing*. For example, would you go to a movie without knowing something about it? Most likely, no—unless you specifically want to be totally surprised. Perhaps you have heard people say good things about the movie, you have read a review of it, or you know one of the actors. If you have an idea about the movie, you can predict in a broad sense what to expect.

The same holds tenfold for reading. Before you read, you need some knowledge of what you're about to read. By engaging in the act of previewing, you establish all-important connections between what you already know and what's new to you. And once you have some basic information about the reading, you can begin to make predictions about that information. As you will see, the act of previewing and predicting will give you a platform on which to stand as you dive into the reading process.

To preview, do these three things (to yourself or aloud):

1. Based on your looking over the material, consciously predict what the topic and its development are likely to be about.
2. Ask yourself consciously what you already know about the topic.
3. Predict what your reading the material will add to what you already know.

It is also important to keep in mind that no one previewing method works for all material. Writers present material in a huge variety of ways. Here are guidelines for other approaches to try out—and to adapt to your needs and preferences.

- For an essay or article, read the opening and closing paragraphs, where main ideas are often found. Then, stop to decide what you predict the essay or article is about. Next, read the first lines of the paragraphs (as you become more skilled, you can skip some paragraphs if a few seem to cluster around one idea). Then, stop to revisit your first prediction and modify it, if necessary.
- For a textbook chapter, read the title, the first paragraph or introduction, the subheadings (often appearing in **boldface print** or *italics*), and the conclusion or summary. Then, stop to decide what you predict the textbook material will cover.

Students often avoid previewing and predicting because they aren't willing to take the time to do it. Yes, previewing and predicting take time, but the payoff is tremendous. Without previewing and predicting as you start each reading selection, you float in an open sea without oars and a compass.

The discipline for, and skill of, predicting as you read is so important that the next section discusses how effective readers continue to predict even after the previewing stage of the reading process.

PREDICTING IN THE READING PROCESS

Predicting is a continuous, active part of reading. This means that your mind is always ahead of where your eyes are on a page. You're actively wondering, guessing, and forecasting what's next. At the same time, you're actively deciding whether your predictions were correct or incorrect compared to what you found and adjusting future predictions in light of that. Practicing and polishing your predicting skills upgrade not only your comprehension but also your reading speed.

In working to read at a college level, you want to make conscious what is largely a preconscious human mental process. To master the art of predicting, you need to be aware of your thinking as you read. Stop occasionally to predict to yourself what you think will come next. As you move along, revise your predictions according to what you encounter. No one, not even the most skilled reader, always predicts accurately. The more you practice predicting, the easier and more useful it will become for you. If at first this activity slows you down, rest assured that you'll catch on soon.

Here's a description of the predicting process in action. It's based on Selection 4 in this textbook. Turn to it now, and keep your finger there so that you can flip easily to it as you read this paragraph. Immediately, you see that the title is "Darkness at Noon." In thinking quickly about those words, you can reasonably predict that the essay will be about (1) an eclipse of the sun; (2) a blackout caused by loss of electricity; (3) a tragedy of some sort; or (4) because each person's predictions are personal, anything else that comes to your mind. Next, read beyond the title and get a general impression of the essay through surveying—looking over—the piece. Then, scan the first and last few paragraphs, and you'll find that predictions 1, 2, and 3 are way off the mark. Adjust your thinking accordingly. Once you know what "Darkness at Noon" is about, you continue predicting as you go through the rest of the material.

In *Structured Reading*, each of Parts Two through Six starts with a collection of visual items called "Thinking: Getting Started." We have designed those sections to prompt you to start your predicting process concerning the reading selections in each part. Use the cartoons, advertisements, and posters—and the thought-provoking questions that tie each visual item to a reading selection—to get ready for your reading.

When you read a textbook, the process of predicting is central to your being able to study and remember information. The next chapter (Chapter 3) shows you how prediction operates as part of a structured reading and study technique. Often referred to as *SQ3R*, its first two steps (*S* and *Q*) involve active predicting during reading.

ASSESSING *YOUR* SKILL WITH PREDICTING

You might already be skilled in making predictions as you read. Or you might do well with only one aspect of making predictions. Choose a chapter (or a four- to five-page section of a chapter) in one of your textbooks other than *Structured Reading* and apply the techniques of prediction in this chapter. Then, record below the title of the book and chapter (or section) you read, and write a brief summary of what you discovered about your skill with predicting.

Chapter 3

What Is the Role of "SQ3R" When Reading to Study?

SQ3R stands for *Survey*, *Question*, *Read*, *Recite*, and *Review*. It's a study technique to help you maximize your comprehension while minimizing your reading time. Learning how to use these principles will help you master textbook material—that is retaining information over the long term, learning information to the point of recall, and understanding the facts and how they fit together. Try applying this five-step process to the textbook excerpts in this textbook (Selections 27 and 28). The investment of your time is worth the benefits. You'll notice improvement in your concentration, comprehension, and reading rate. The following box describes the SQ3R technique.

SQ3R for Studying

S = Survey Before you read closely, look over the title, headings, and subheadings. Look also at the captions under pictures, charts, graphs, or maps. Consciously predict what you think the topics will be.

Q = Question Turn each heading and subheading into a question using the *"five W's and one H"*: *who, what, when, where, why,* and *how*. By asking questions, you prepare your mind to read for the answer.

R = Read Read closely, keeping in mind the questions you've already asked about the material. Strive to hook any new material onto what you already know. Come to understand the material.

R = Recite After you've read two or more pages, go back to whatever headings, subheadings, or boldface words you used to form questions during the Q part of SQ3R. Cover up the specific paragraphs, and in your own words, say aloud or to yourself what the material is about.

R = Review Look over the material again. Move somewhat slowly and take special notice of key spots: the title, main headings, subheadings, and important paragraphs. As you review, you might highlight key areas with a see-through marking pen—but be careful to highlight only major ideas. If you fill a page with highlighter pen, you need to work harder on separating minor material from key points. Next, think through whether your predictions made during your survey were correct. The review is intended to pull together all the pieces as if you're working on a jigsaw puzzle.

Following are a few paragraphs about the giant panda, from a publication of *The Healthy Planet*. Practice applying the SQ3R technique as you read it.

Evidence of the Giant Panda in Ancient Times

For more than three million years, the Giant Panda lived in remote, forested areas of China. Numerous fossil remains provide evidence that the mammal known to the Chinese as daxiong mao (dah-sh-WING, MAH-oo) which means, "large cat-bear," lived in more than 48 different localities throughout China as well as one site in Burma.

The Giant Panda has appeared in Chinese books about literature, medicine and geography for more than 2,000 years. At one time, the mammal was hunted for its beautiful and unusual coat because superstitions thought it to possess the power of prediction and protection: It was believed that having a good night's sleep on a panda pelt indicated good fortune, while the pelt itself was thought to keep ghosts at bay. Today, the Giant Panda is the much respected national symbol of China.

An Appealing Pace of Life

A slow metabolism makes the panda an energy-conserving animal, which means it uses a minimal amount of energy to find its next food source. If it didn't have to, the panda would probably not move at all. In the wild, the Giant Panda will plunk itself down in the midst of a bamboo forest and simply pull at the shoots it can reach.

Using its unique wrist bone that acts as an opposable thumb, the panda can grasp bamboo. The animal peels the bamboo like a banana by holding it between its five fingers and its wrist knob. An especially tough esophagus helps the panda swallow the fibrous bamboo.

Chapter 4

What Is the Role of Speed During Reading?

Research indicates a close relation between speed and understanding. But that connection is not what you might assume it to be. Speed-reading, even though various commercial sources claim to teach it, isn't the major skill you need to read college-level material. Rather, you need the mental flexibility to adjust your reading pace according to your purpose for reading—just as you adjust your speed in a car to the terrain, such as hills or curves or flat roadway. A fast look at words in complex material isn't suited to understanding and remembering new information. Conversely, too slow a pace for fairly simple, straightforward information tends to distract your concentration. You can usually pick up your speed with information that confirms what you already know. Expect, however, to slow down as you encounter new information.

RELATING SPEED TO PURPOSES FOR READING

Always expect to adjust your reading speed to your purpose for reading. The following box lists the major reading purposes and the relative speeds they usually demand.

If you're like many college students, you're probably holding down a full- or part-time job. With classes, work, and family commitments, you might have little time left over for studying—not to mention a social life. To meet the demands on your life, and to fit in well-used study time, you want to call on the most effective reading strategies available. This effort starts with becoming aware of the relativity of reading speed according to your purposes for reading.

The average college student reads between 250 and 300 words per minute (wpm) with at least 70 percent comprehension on fiction and nontechnical materials. Textbook material, especially that involving complex ideas in the social sciences and in mathematics and science, demands a slower pace. That rate might go down to 100 or 150 wpm for difficult material. Your reading speed is influenced by many factors, including your desire to improve, your willingness to try new techniques, and your motivation to practice.

Purposes for Reading

Casual Reading *Reading for relaxation, amusement.* Casual reading means catching the basics without worrying about minor details, though sometimes you might find the reading is so pleasurable that you prefer not to miss anything. You adjust your speed according to how much you want to retain the material.

Scanning *Reading for specific information, such as a telephone number, street address, or the time of an event.* Scanning requires you to move quickly through the material with a specific word or phrase in mind.

Skimming *Reading for the overall idea or gist of the material.* Skimming is accomplished by omitting unnecessary words, phrases, and sentences. This method is useful for getting an overview of a topic or for reviewing major ideas and concepts after you have studied the material. You adjust your speed according to your goals, sometimes speeding ahead and sometimes slowing down.

Study *Reading for a thorough understanding of central themes, main ideas, supporting details, and inferences.* Reading to learn and remember takes time. The pace is slow, not because you read word by word, but because you need to think about the material and consciously associate it with knowledge that you already have. Often, you need to read the material a few times. This is what college-level readers do.

USING RAPID WORD DISCRIMINATION

If you find yourself daydreaming as you read, you actually may need to increase your rate of movement through words. The Rapid Discrimination Drills coming up show you how to push yourself to read more quickly when necessary. They demand that you look at words and pick out, at very rapid rates, those that are alike or different. Using a watch or clock with a second hand, note the time you begin on a sheet of paper. Then note the time you finish. Subtract the time you began from the time you finished to determine the total time you read. Then go back and carefully check to see if your responses are correct. Give yourself five points for each correct answer.

ACTIVITY B   RAPID DISCRIMINATION DRILL 1

Circle the word that is different *in each line. (Answers on page 86.)*

Key Word	1	2	3	4
1. fight	fight	fight	light	fight
2. side	side	side	side	site
3. than	then	than	than	than
4. sail	nail	nail	nail	nail
5. foot	food	foot	foot	foot
6. ride	ride	hide	ride	ride
7. flood	flood	flood	floor	flood
8. hump	bump	hump	hump	hump
9. tool	fool	fool	fool	fool
10. hold	hold	hold	hold	sold
11. sack	rack	sack	sack	sack
12. took	book	book	book	book
13. real	seal	seal	seal	seal
14. cook	cook	cool	cook	cook
15. maps	maps	maps	maps	mops
16. bore	bore	bore	tore	bore
17. lamp	lamp	lump	lamp	lamp
18. trick	trick	trick	track	trick
19. mail	mail	mail	mail	nail
20. cave	cave	cove	cave	cave

ACTIVITY C   RAPID DISCRIMINATION DRILL 2

Circle the word that matches *the key word in each line. (Answers on page 86.)*

Key Word	1	2	3	4	5
1. pore	tore	bore	pore	gore	more
2. jack	sack	jack	tack	pack	rack
3. cake	take	make	bake	fake	cake
4. hats	hats	cats	mats	pats	rats
5. call	fall	mall	tall	call	pall
6. hide	hide	ride	side	tide	wide
7. rap	cap	sap	map	tap	rap
8. hook	cook	took	hook	book	look
9. mart	cart	mart	tart	part	dart
10. park	bark	dark	hark	park	lark
11. tear	bear	tear	fear	sear	hear
12. chide	pride	hide	tide	side	chide
13. tan	can	man	tan	fan	pan
14. rash	cash	rash	mash	bash	sash
15. mold	sold	fold	told	mold	bold
16. kill	fill	kill	pill	till	bill
17. tone	tone	bone	cone	done	lone
18. take	make	take	cake	bake	fake
19. leach	beach	reach	teach	peach	leach
20. sunny	puny	runny	sunny	funny	bunny

ACTIVITY D   RAPID DRILL DISCRIMINATION 3

Circle the word that is different in each line. (Answers on page 86.)

Key Word	1	2	3	4
1. stove	cove	stove	stove	stove
2. their	their	their	their	there
3. hall	hall	hall	fall	hall
4. belief	belief	relief	belief	belief
5. redo	redo	undo	redo	redo
6. unless	unless	unless	unless	unlock
7. confine	confide	confine	confine	confine
8. trestle	trestle	trestle	bustle	trestle
9. ladder	madder	ladder	ladder	ladder
10. truck	truck	truce	truck	truck
11. flip	flip	flip	slip	flip
12. cable	cable	cable	cable	table
13. tricycle	tricycle	tricycle	tricycle	bicycle
14. clammer	clammer	clammer	hammer	clammer
15. bee	see	bee	bee	bee
16. toil	toil	foil	toil	toil
17. flow	flow	flow	blow	flow
18. tip	hip	tip	tip	tip
19. liking	liking	liking	liking	hiking
20. carry	carry	marry	carry	carry

Scanning at appropriate speeds is another essential discrimination technique for reading. Without scanning, imagine how long using the dictionary, telephone directory, or encyclopedia would take. People do not want to start at the beginning of such reference works and look at every entry until they find what they're seeking. Here's an activity to involve you in a scanning situation that many people need for everyday life.

ACTIVITY E   SCANNING A COMMUTER TRAIN SCHEDULE

For this activity, accuracy is more important than speed. Look at the commuter train schedule on page 16 that shows the times for trips from Little Neck to Penn Station on weekdays and on weekends and holidays. Answer the questions placed after the schedule. Before you begin, scan the timetables, getting used to the variety of column headings. Each of the smaller column headings names a train station between Little Neck and Penn Station. Next, figure out how to determine the days of operation and the times of departures and arrivals. To determine those times, move your eyes across each row. (Answers on page 86.)

15

TO WOODSIDE AND NEW YORK — MONDAY TO FRIDAY EXCEPT HOLIDAYS

Morning Service

Note	Leave Little Neck	Leave Douglaston	Leave Bayside	Leave Flushing	Arrive Woodside	Arrive Penn Station
	12:51	12:53	12:56	1:05	1:14	1:24
	1:38	1:40	1:43	1:52	2:00	2:10
	3:35	3:37	3:40	3:49	3:57	4:06
	5:21	5:23	5:26	5:36	5:42	5:52
Peak	5:48	5:50	5:53	6:02	6:10	6:20
Peak	6:30	6:32	6:35	6:44	6:52	7:03
Peak	6:40	6:42	6:45	6:55	7:03	7:14
Peak	.....	.....	7:02	.....	.....	7:24
Peak	7:23	7:26	7:30	.....	.....	7:55
Peak	7:55	7:57	8:00	.....	.....	8:26
Peak	8:07	8:10	8:14	.....	8:26	8:38
Peak	8:32	8:35	8:38	8:41	.....	9:02
	8:41	8:43	8:46	8:55	9:03	9:14
	9:01	9:03	9:06	9:15	9:23	9:34
	9:29	9:31	9:34	9:43	9:50	10:01
	9:52	9:54	9:57	10:03	10:12	10:22
	10:21	10:23	10:26	10:33	10:42	10:52
	10:52	10:54	10:57	11:03	11:12	11:22
	11:21	11:23	11:26	11:33	11:42	11:52
	11:52	11:54	11:57	12:03	12:12	12:22

Afternoon and Evening Service

Note	Leave Little Neck	Leave Douglaston	Leave Bayside	Leave Flushing	Arrive Woodside	Arrive Penn Station
	12:21	12:23	12:26	12:33	12:42	12:52
	12:52	12:54	12:57	1:03	1:12	1:22
	1:21	1:23	1:26	1:33	1:42	1:52
	1:52	1:54	1:57	2:03	2:12	2:22
	2:21	2:23	2:26	2:33	2:42	2:52
	2:52	2:54	2:57	3:03	3:12	3:22
	3:21	3:23	3:26	3:33	3:42	3:52
	3:52	3:54	3:57	4:03	4:12	4:23
	4:19	4:21	4:24	4:32	4:39	4:51
	4:49	4:51	4:54	5:02	5:10	5:23
	5:12	5:14	5:17	5:26	5:35	5:45
	5:46	5:48	5:51	5:57	6:04	6:17
	6:23	6:25	6:27	6:36	6:44	6:55
	6:47	6:49	6:52	6:58	7:05	7:15
	7:21	7:23	7:26	7:35	7:42	7:53
	7:51	7:53	7:56	8:05	8:12	8:23
	8:21	8:23	8:26	8:35	8:42	8:53
	8:51	8:53	8:56	9:05	9:12	9:22
	9:21	9:23	9:26	9:35	9:42	9:52
	9:51	9:53	9:56	10:05	10:12	10:22
	10:21	10:23	10:26	10:35	10:42	10:53
	10:51	10:53	10:56	11:05	11:12	11:22

TO WOODSIDE AND NEW YORK — SATURDAY, SUNDAY, AND HOLIDAYS

Morning Service

Note	Leave Little Neck	Leave Douglaston	Leave Bayside	Leave Flushing	Arrive Woodside	Arrive Penn Station
	12:51	12:53	12:56	1:05	1:14	1:24
	1:51	1:53	1:56	2:05	2:14	2:24
	3:51	3:53	3:56	4:05	4:14	4:24
	5:51	5:53	5:56	6:05	6:14	6:24
	6:51	6:53	6:56	7:05	7:14	7:24
	7:51	7:53	7:56	8:05	8:14	8:24
	8:51	8:53	8:56	9:05	9:14	9:24
	9:51	9:53	9:56	10:05	10:14	10:24
	10:51	10:53	10:56	11:05	11:14	11:24
	11:51	11:53	11:56	12:05	12:14	12:24

Afternoon and Evening Service

Note	Leave Little Neck	Leave Douglaston	Leave Bayside	Leave Flushing	Arrive Woodside	Arrive Penn Station
	12:51	12:53	12:56	1:05	1:14	1:24
	1:51	1:53	1:56	2:05	2:14	2:24
	2:51	2:53	2:56	3:05	3:14	3:24
	3:51	3:53	3:56	4:05	4:14	4:24
	4:51	4:53	4:56	5:05	5:14	5:24
	5:51	5:53	5:56	6:05	6:14	6:24
	6:51	6:53	6:56	7:05	7:14	7:24
	7:51	7:53	7:56	8:05	8:14	8:24
	8:51	8:53	8:56	9:05	9:14	9:24
	9:51	9:53	9:56	10:05	10:14	10:24
	10:51	10:53	10:56	11:05	11:14	11:24
	11:51	11:53	11:56	12:05	12:14	12:24

1. To take a train on a weekday at Douglaston Station to go to Penn Station, what's the earliest time you can leave after 6 a.m.? _____

2. How many stops are scheduled between Douglaston Station and Penn Station leaving at the earliest time after 6 a.m.? _____

3. To leave from the Little Neck Station to meet a friend at Penn Station at noon on Saturday, what time do you need to leave the Little Neck Station? _____

4. To reach Penn Station on a weekday between 6 and 7 a.m., what time would you leave from Little Neck? _____

5. What is the beginning of the peak departure time at Little Neck? The ending time of the peak departure time at Little Neck?

   _____ _____

6. If you depart Flushing on a weekday at 8:41 a.m., would you make any stops before you reach Penn Station? _____

7. If you depart Douglaston on a weekend at 10:53 p.m., what time would you arrive at Penn Station? _____

8. Is there any nonstop service from Bayside to Penn Station on Saturday, Sunday, and holidays? _____

9. How many trains run on a weekday between 7:50 a.m. and 9 a.m. from Bayside Station to Penn Station? _____

10. To leave from Little Neck Station to go to Penn Station on a weekday, what time does the train depart from Little Neck to reach your destination by 7:10 a.m.? _____

Chapter 5

How Can I Improve My Vocabulary?

English is a rich language with over 1,000,000 words. Yet, the average English-speaking adult has a vocabulary of only 40,000 to 50,000 words. And sadly, most of us use about 500 words in our everyday speech.

When you possess a large vocabulary, you can express and think about fine shades of meaning. You can think with precision. For example, unless you're a sailor, you probably refer to all the various lines on a sailboat as "ropes." *Ropes*, however, is a basic, generic term suitable only for armchair discussion. When the wind is blowing a gale, and the waves are covering the deck with solid sheets of water, you want to yell out to your crew something more specific than "tighten the rope." Sailors say such exact phrases as "harden the jib sheet," "ease the boom vang and rig a starboard preventer," or "mind the dingy painter while we back down on the anchor rode." Such phrases communicate clearly at a mature level. Whether you're reading, writing, or speaking at the college level about sailing or science, about football or philosophy, about literature or sociology, a strong vocabulary is essential.

As a young child, you learned words very quickly. You imitated adults and older children. When you grew old enough to start school, your vocabulary acquisition slowed down. By middle and high school, you had to work to enlarge your vocabulary. Teachers gave you vocabulary lists, perhaps ten words a week, and then tested you. Often what happened after the test was that unless you used the words, you forgot them. Now that you've reached college, your vocabulary has fossilized in a sense. The good news is that every adult, no matter what age, is capable of learning and using new vocabulary words. The simple truth is that you'll remember new words only when you make up your mind to use them as often as possible. Memorization without usage is ineffective.

USING CONTEXT CLUES

Success in college, and in certain jobs, depends heavily on vocabulary. One of the best ways to learn new words is to discover them in your reading. Push yourself to try to guess the meaning of a word from the way it is used in a sentence. This method calls for using *context clues*. With context clues, you try to determine the meaning of an unfamiliar word by looking for evidence in the sentence that contains the word, in the sentences that precede the word, and even in the sentences that follow the word. Context clues can be divided into four categories:

- Restatement context clues
- Definition context clues
- Example context clues
- Contrast context clues

USING RESTATEMENT CONTEXT CLUES

For a **restatement context clue,** look for a thought that's repeated in different words in the same or a nearby sentence. Sometimes, the restatement enlarges or limits the original thought. When writers repeat a thought, often taking the form of a synonym, you need simply to think about the shared meaning of the original and the restatement. For example, what does *fray* mean in the following sentence:

- He jumped into the **fray** and enjoyed every minute of the fight.

Perhaps a reader would guess that *fray* means either "fight" or "audience." After thinking of those two possibilities, the reader would note the words *jumped into* earlier in the sentence. Those words suggest an energetic entering, rather than a passive joining. *Fight* would be the correct choice.

Sometimes a restatement is set off by punctuation, which makes the reader's job easy. For example,

- Fatty deposits on artery walls combine with calcium compounds to cause **arteriosclerosis** (hardening of the arteries). [**Here the restatement appears in parentheses** *after* **the difficult word.**]
- The upper left part of the heart—the left **atrium**—receives blood returning from circulation. [**Here the restatement appears in dashes** *before* **the word.**]

ACTIVITY F   RESTATEMENT CONTEXT CLUES

Using restatement context clues, circle the best meaning for the italicized *words in the sentences below. (Answers on page 86.)*

1. In searching for food, homeless people often have to *scavenge* in dumpsters.

   Scavenge means   a. sleep.   b. hunt.   c. hide.

2. Sir Edmund Hillary and his climbing partner, Sherpa Temzing Norgay, were famous *alpinists*. In fact, they were the first to reach the top of Mt. Everest in 1953.

   Alpinists means   a. balloonists.   b. mountain climbers.   c. parachutists.

3. An *adroit* boxer—one who can dodge, jab, and avoid being knocked out—is generally not the type of fighter a crowd wants to see.

   Adroit means   a. entertaining.   b. nervous.   c. skillful.

4. Era had the *audacity* to break line in front of me in the school cafeteria. Then she had the nerve to ask me to loan her a dollar to pay for her lunch.

   Audacity means   a. impoliteness.   b. opportunity.   c. boldness.

5. At first, I was *dubious* whether I could complete the course. After the first major test, however, I was not as doubtful.

   Dubious means   a. unsure.   b. discouraged.   c. devastated.

6. The basketball players made a *simultaneous* jump for the ball. This concurrent movement resulted in a collision.

   Simultaneous means   a. at different times.   b. at the same time.   c. at conflicting times.

7. We have informed the guests about the *postponement*. The ceremony will not take place until a later date.

   Postponement means   a. cancellation.   b. advancement.   c. delay.

8. I am glad you were able to *alleviate* Kathie's fear of airplanes. Your suggestions made it easier for her to fly.

   Alleviate means   a. lessen.   b. increase.   c. free.

9. George Washington Carver was a famous *botanist*. He developed literally hundreds of uses for the peanut.

   Botanist means one who studies   a. animals.   b. plants.   c. fish.

10. On a movie set, *surrogates* often stand in for the real stars while technicians adjust the lights and camera angles.

    Surrogates means   a. professionals.   b. amateurs.   c. substitutes.

USING DEFINITION CONTEXT CLUES

A **definition context clue** means that the word is formally defined in the same sentence. Formal definitions are direct and easy to spot.

- To say that my misunderstanding your instructions caused me **chagrin** would be like saying my daily appetite is satisfied by a grain of sugar. The Tenth Edition (2000) of *Merriam Webster's Collegiate Dictionary* defines **chagrin** as "distress of mind caused by humiliation, disappointment, or failure." Replace *distress* with *agony* and *misery* in that definition, and perhaps you can better imagine my feelings.

Some definition clues are less direct. For example, a difficult word might be defined by a detailed description rather than a formal definition. Descriptive definitions are less obvious than formal ones, but once you become aware of the descriptive approach, you can use them to your advantage.

- The most **overly aggressive** people I know are also the most successful in business. They possess great stores of energy, never hesitate to take the lead and make quick decisions, interrupt conversations, and tell others what to do.

ACTIVITY G   DEFINITION CONTEXT CLUES

Following are ten sentences, each of which defines the italicized word. Use the clues in the definition sentences to fill in the answers to items 1–10 that follow. (Answers on page 86.)

- *Polyester* is generally characterized as a wrinkle-resistant fabric.
- A *skeptical* thinker is one who questions beliefs or concepts.
- *Phi, theta,* and *kappa* are Greek letters meaning *wisdom, aspiration,* and *purity.*
- A street that curves and bends best describes a *sinuated* road.
- To feel *chagrin* is to be embarrassed or annoyed.
- A paragraph has *coherence* when the sentences are arranged in a clear, logical order.
- *Geriatrics* is the diagnosis and treatment of diseases associated with the elderly.
- A breed of powerful sled dogs developed in Alaska is the *malamute.*
- An *ambiguous* answer to a simple question is unclear because it can mean at least two different things.
- A person who talks without changing the pitch of the voice speaks in a *monotone.*

1. Your explanation of your actions is _____ because it can be taken in two ways.

2. I fell asleep listening to his _____ voice.

3. We need an expert in _____ to explain my grandparents' health.

4. A city apartment is no place for a dog as large as a _____.

5. My philosophy professor was _____ about whatever she read in newspapers.

6. I felt deep _____ when I realized that I had forgotten my best friend's birthday.

7. We couldn't understand the scientist's explanation of nanoseconds because it lacked _____.

8. The spot where the old country road goes up a hill and starts to _____ has been the site of many serious car accidents.

9. The Greek letter for wisdom is _____, for aspiration is _____, and for purity is _____.

10. Fabric made of _____ saves ironing time.

USING CONTRAST CONTEXT CLUES

A **contrast context clue** means you can figure out an unknown word when its opposite—or some other type of contrast—is mentioned close by.

- We feared that the new prime minister would be a *menace* to society, but she turned out to be a great peacemaker.

This sentence suggests that *menace* means *threat* because the contrast is that "she turned out to be a great peacemaker."

As you read, watch for words that signal contrasts. Such words include *but, however, nevertheless, on the other hand, unlike, in contrast,* and others.

ACTIVITY H   CONTRAST CONTEXT CLUES

Use contrast context clues to select the best meaning for the italicized *words in the following sentences. (Answers on page 86.)*

1. Even though Raleigh insisted that she hadn't passed a red light, the police officer's videotape of her doing so was *irrefutable* proof.
   Irrefutable means   a. undeniable.   b. unrealistic.   c. questionable.

2. After a ten-mile hike to reach Pike's Peak, I thought I would be *ravenous*. Yet, I was so relieved that the hike was over I couldn't eat a thing.
   Ravenous means   a. highly excited.   b. extremely lazy.   c. very hungry.

3. The Marshes enjoyed their country house on Creve Coeur, and so they found it difficult to adjust to *urban* life in St. Louis.

   Urban means   a. expensive.   b. city.   c. secluded.

4. Unlike my wife, who does not approve of our children eating between meals, I *sanctioned* their eating fruit if it keeps them from crying.

   Sanctioned means   a. ignored.   b. approved of.   c. discouraged.

5. This week my bosses assigned me to the *tedious* task of proofreading every one of the ninety-four letters they wrote last week.

   Tedious means   a. envious.   b. complex.   c. boring.

6. Greg was *gregarious*, but his twin brother, Rory, was shy.

   Gregarious means   a. distrustful.   b. sociable.   c. outspoken.

7. An abridged dictionary, not an *unabridged* dictionary, has been shortened.

   Unabridged means   a. complete.   b. incomplete.   c. blended.

8. Although Michelle *somnambulates*, Veronica, her sister, never walks in her sleep.

   Somnambulates means   a. snores in her sleep.   b. talks in her sleep.   c. strolls around while asleep.

9. Dee's whistle was *inaudible* to me; however, my puppy could hear it.

   Inaudible means   a. not seen.   b. not heard.   c. not recognizable.

10. Although a tuition increase of 15 percent has been approved, the college does not expect an *attrition* in enrollment.

    Attrition means   a. decrease.   b. growth.   c. renewed interest.

USING EXAMPLE CONTEXT CLUES

You are looking at an **example context clue** when an unfamiliar word is followed by an example that reveals what the unknown word means.

> They were *conscientious* workers, never stopping until they had taken care of every detail so that everything was done correctly and precisely.

The words *never stopping until*, *taken care of every detail*, and *done correctly and precisely* clue you to the meaning of *conscientious*. It means responsible, thorough, and reliable.

Often, an example context clue is introduced with signal words like *such as, for example, for instance,* and *including.*

ACTIVITY I   EXAMPLE CONTEXT CLUES

Select the best meaning of the word shown in italics *in the following sentences.*
(Answers on page 86.)

1. *Adversities*, such as poverty, poor grades, and a weak family background, can be overcome with effort.

   Adversities means   a. obstacles.   b. pleasures.   c. responsibilities.

2. Andrew had a reputation for doing *perilous* activities. For example, he loved to ride a racing bike without a helmet, climb mountains without a safety rope, and ride in a speedboat without a life preserver.

   Perilous means   a. thrilling.   b. dangerous.   c. remarkable.

3. *Pungent* odors, including those of perfume, room deodorizers, and household cleansers, can cause allergic reactions in some people.

   Pungent means   a. mild.   b. sharp.   c. weak.

4. An *obituary* generally includes the person's age, occupation, survivors, and funeral arrangements.

   Obituary means   a. death notice.   b. sermon.   c. will.

5. Brothers and sisters sometimes like to play a harmless *prank* on one another. For example, a sister might make up the idea that their mother wants the brother to do a messy household chore.

   Prank means   a. joke.   b. assignment.   c. request.

6. I could see by Carlos's *visage* he was upset. He had an angry frown on his face, and his eyes were wide with fury.

   Visage means   a. actions.   b. personality.   c. appearance.

7. *Pachyderms*, such as the rhinoceros, the hippopotamus, and the elephant, are mammals that live in Africa.

   Pachyderms means   a. sensitive.   b. hostile.   c. thick-skinned.

8. That mole on your arm is a dark color; you need to see a doctor who specializes in *dermatology*.

   Dermatology relates to   a. heart.   b. skin.   c. feet.

9. Servers in restaurants depend on customers to leave a *gratuity* for their services. Without tips, waiters couldn't make a living.

   Gratuity means   a. money.   b. compliment.   c. recommendation.

10. To avoid encountering fans, Mankind and The Rock of the World Federation Wrestlers, agreed to a *rendezvous* at 12 midnight at Main Street and Broadway.

    Rendezvous means   a. exhibition.   b. match.   c. meeting.

24

USING STRUCTURAL ANALYSIS

Another strategy for understanding and learning new vocabulary involves using structural analysis. Structural analysis is using the parts of a word—roots, prefixes, and suffixes—to determine the meaning of a word.

Understanding the parts of a word is useful in defining unfamiliar vocabulary, although it is most effective when used in conjunction with the strategies for using context clues. Word parts, in the many combinations that you will find them, make up over 50 percent of the English language; so knowing the more common roots, prefixes, and suffixes can make a huge impact in your ability to expand your vocabulary. Here are some of the common word parts that you will encounter in the readings in *Structured Reading* and elsewhere.

USING ROOTS

Many words in the English language have their origins in Latin and Greek. These Latin and Greek roots allow you to know the basic meaning of many English words of which they are a part. Review the following list of common roots and notice the ways the root is used to form various words.

Root	Basic meaning	Example words
-anthrop-	human	misanthrope, philanthropy, anthropomorphic
-dem-	people	democracy, demography, demagogue, endemic, pandemic
-derm-	skin	dermatology, epidermis, hypodermic
-dict-	to say	contradict, dictate, diction, edict, predict
-duc-	to lead, bring, take	deduce, produce, reduce
-gress-	to walk	digress, progress, transgress
-ject-	to throw	eject, inject, interject, project, subject
-ped-	child, children, foot	pediatrician, pedagogue, pedestrian, pedestal
-pel-	to drive	compel, dispel, impel, repel
-pend-	to hang	append, depend, impend, pendant, pendulum

Root	Basic meaning	Example words
-philo-, -phil-	having a strong affinity for; love for	philanthropy, philharmonic, philosophy
-phon-	sound	polyphonic, cacophony, phonetics
-port-	to carry	deport, export, import, report, support
-scrib-, -script-	to write	describe, description, prescribe, prescription, subscribe, subscription, transcribe, transcription
-tract-	to pull, drag, draw	attract, contract, detract, extract, protract, retract, traction

USING PREFIXES

A prefix is a word part that is added at the beginning of a word to change the meaning. Review the list that follows and notice the many ways prefixes are used to create new words.

Prefix	Basic meaning	Example words
a-, an-	without	achromatic, amoral, atypical, anaerobic
anti-, ant-	opposite; opposing	anticrime, antipollution, antacid
auto-	self, same	autobiography, automatic, autopilot
bio-, bi-	life, living organism	biology, biophysics, biotechnology, biopsy
co-	together	coauthor, coedit, coheir
de-	away, off; reversal or removal	deactivate, defrost, decompress, deplane
dis-	not, separate	disbelief, discomfort, discredit, disrepair
ex-	from, beyond, former	exclude, exhale
fore-	before (in time or place)	forerunner, forecast

Prefix	Basic meaning	Example words
hyper-	excessive, excessively	hyperactive, hypercritical, hypersensitive
inter-	between, among	international, interfaith, intertwine, interject
ir-, in-, il-, im-	not	irregular, irreplaceable, illegal, imperfect
micro-	small	microcosm, micronucleus, microscope
mono-	one, single, alone	monochrome, monosyllable, monoxide
non-	not	nonessential, nonmetallic, nonresident
post-	after	postdate, postwar, postnasal, postnatal
pre-	before	preconceive, preexist, prepay
re-	again; back, backward	rearrange, rebuild recall, rerun, rewrite
sub-	under	submarine, subway, subhuman
thermo-, therm-	heat	thermal, thermometer, thermostat
trans-	across, beyond, through	transatlantic, transpolar

USING SUFFIXES

A suffix is added to the end of a word to change the meaning or to change the part of speech of a word. For example, by adding the suffix "-ion" to the verb *create* you will change it to *creation*, which is a noun. Observe the various ways the following common suffixes are used and the types of words they form.

Suffix	Basic meaning	Example words
-able, -ible	forms adjectives and means "capable or worthy of "	likable, flexible
-ation	forms nouns from verbs	creation, civilization, speculation, information

Suffix	Basic meaning	Example words
-fy, -ify	forms verbs and means "to make or cause to become"	purify, acidify, humidify
-ism	forms nouns and means "the act, state, or theory of "	criticism, optimism, capitalism
-ize	forms verbs from nouns and adjectives	formalize, jeopardize, legalize, modernize
-logue, -log	speech, discourse; to speak	monologue, dialogue, travelogue
-logy	science, theory, study	phraseology, biology, dermatology
-ment	forms nouns from verbs	entertainment, amazement, statement, banishment
-ty, -ity	forms nouns from adjectives	subtlety, certainty, cruelty, frailty, loyalty, royalty; eccentricity, electricity, peculiarity, similarity

After reviewing these lists, you may notice that many roots, prefixes, and suffixes are used in combination. For example, the word *dermatology* combines the root *derm* with the suffix *-logy* to form a word that means the study of the skin. It is useful to keep in mind that structural analysis is only one strategy for understanding unfamiliar vocabulary. Used in combination with the other strategies discussed in this chapter, knowing roots, suffixes, and prefixes will greatly expand your ability to decipher new words.

ACTIVITY J   STRUCTURAL ANALYSIS

Use context clues and structural analysis to select the best meaning for the italicized words in the sentences that follow. (Answers on page 86.)

1. Animals have been known to use *nonverbal* signals to let both other animals and humans know what they want.

   Nonverbal means   a. not loud.   b. with aggression.   c. without sound.

2. Mike's behavior is *inconsistent* with who he is, and I will have a talk with him to find out why.

   Inconsistent means   a. unfriendly.   b. changeable.   c. odd.

3. The young man talked to everyone at the party *except* the woman he really liked.

   Except means   a. not included.   b. especially.   c. mostly.

4. The woman couldn't wait for the *disbursement* from the bank to arrive in the mail.

    Disbursement means   a. letter.   b. payment.   c. package.

5. After Lucy brought the dress back to the store with a ragged tear, it was not *salable*.

    Salable means   a. able to be returned.   b. able to be worn.   c. able to be sold.

6. The two brothers shared the car, so they had a *rotation* schedule they both followed.

    Rotation means   a. rule.   b. consistent.   c. regular change.

7. After John *transferred* to the new high school, he was unable to make new friends.

    Transferred means   a. failed.   b. joined.   c. moved.

8. Rachel wasn't going to deal with a boyfriend who didn't believe in *monogamy*.

    Monogamy means   a. gift buying.   b. religion.   c. fidelity.

9. There is no way a neat person like Jake will be able to *cohabitate* with someone as messy as Mike.

    Cohabitate means   a. to share.   b. to live with.   c. to be friends with.

10. The cyclist stared after the speeding car in utter *astonishment*.

    Astonishment means   a. shock.   b. anger.   c. sadness.

LEARNING AND REMEMBERING NEW WORDS

So that you do not have to rediscover a new word repeatedly, you want to work at reviewing and remembering new words all the time. How can you learn to remember new words? A personal method of vocabulary study that fits your learning style will work. Here's a good method to try—or to adapt to be most effective for you.

Learning New Words: The PWRA System

P = Pick Look and listen for new words you would like to add to your vocabulary. Choose selectively so that you concentrate on the words that will serve you best. Each word that is new to you will require thorough, repeated study. Most people can learn about ten new words at a time.

W = Write Use a 3 × 5 index card for each word you want to learn. On the front side of the card, write the word. On the backside of the card, write the definition.

→

Learning New Words: The PWRA System, continued

Below the definition, write an original sentence using the word. Here's a sample card for the word *avocado*:

avocado

Front side

a pear-shaped tropical fruit

An avocado is sometimes mashed and combined with onion, lemon juice, etc. to make a dip.

Back side

Learning New Words: The PWRA System, continued

R = Review Stack your 3 × 5 cards so that you see each card only on the side showing the word alone. Look at the word and try to recall the definition on the back. After you have been through the entire stack, turn over the cards so that you now see the sides with the definitions. This time look at the definition and your sentence to recall the word on the other side. As you work through your cards, divide them into two stacks: "know" and "don't know." Then, review the cards in your "don't know" stack. This intensifies your concentration. Before you end your study session, go through both stacks of cards again.

A = Apply Once you have learned a word, apply it. Actively use the word in your speaking and writing. Push yourself to find occasions that allow you to fit in the word. To reinforce your mastery of the word, hold it in the front of your mind, thinking about its definition and appropriate use. Only when you're certain that you "own" the word—that is, it's in your active vocabulary—can you move it to your list for every-two-weeks or monthly review. If you've forgotten the word, put it back on your daily study list.

In *Structured Reading*, we give you actual dictionary entries for the more challenging words in each reading selection. They are from *Webster's New World College Dictionary, Fourth Edition.* Having the entries readily accessible gives you hands-on experience with a first-class dictionary. We designed this resource so that you can become familiar with dictionary entries. Dictionary entries can look more complex than they are. Take apart the sections of a dictionary entry:

- Pronunciation guide for the word
- Material at the beginning of many entries, which tells how to pronounce the word and the origin of the word if it's derived from languages other than modern English
- Sequence of definitions for words with more than one meaning (most-to-less frequently used? oldest use to newest? other?)
- Various forms the word can take, such as a noun that can be adapted for use as an adjective

Along with the complete dictionary entries, *Structured Reading* offers you various types of vocabulary practice exercises. They include context clues, fill-ins, multiple choices, and crossword puzzles. Working with vocabulary exercises in this textbook gives you hands-on opportunities to master your knowledge of words. Your goal is to "own" the new words.

Chapter 6

What Is Reading On, Between, and Beyond the Lines?

Reading **on, between,** and **beyond** the lines means reading closely. You can get intensive and extensive practice by reading closely all the exercises that follow each reading selection in *Structured Reading*.

Reading **on the lines** means understanding the stated meaning of the material. Here you look for the exact, literal meaning of what's written. In *Structured Reading*, three kinds of exercises have been designed especially to help you develop your ability to read on the lines: "Vocabulary" (explained in Chapter 5 in Part One), "Central Theme and Main Ideas" (Chapter 7), and "Major Details" (Chapter 8).

Reading **between the lines** means understanding what's implied but not stated outright. When ideas are implied, you need to read between the lines to figure out what's not said directly, but is meant for the reader to realize nevertheless. To do this, look for these underlying assumptions or attitudes:

- Attitude toward you, the reader (respectful, condescending, playful, etc.), as reflected in the writing
- Assumptions concerning what you, the reader, are expected to know before you begin reading the material
- Attitude toward the topic (objective, biased, passionate, etc.)

To figure out authors' assumptions and attitudes, depend on how the authors express what they say. What words and phrases hint at something that's not stated? What alternatives of word choice were at the authors' disposal, and why did the authors choose the words used? Also, how do authors use evidence? Do they distort facts and information only to make their point? What line of reasoning do the authors use? Does the writer tell a story or make an argument? Your answers to such questions provide a portrait of the author's tone. Just as you can tell how people feel about a topic from their tone of voice, so can tone also emerge from the writing. In *Structured Reading*, a number of exercises have been designed especially to give you practice with reading between the lines: "Inferences" (Chapter 10) and "Critical Reading" (Chapters 11, 12, and 13).

Reading **beyond the lines** means you develop informed opinions about the subject being discussed in the material you're reading. To do this, come to your own conclusions based on what's been stated (on the lines) and what has been implied (between the lines). In *Structured Reading,* "Reader's Response" exercises (Chapter 14) offer you opportunities to think and talk about your personal point of view about the subject of what you're reading. The subjects vary so that you can practice in diverse realms of thought.

In Parts Two through Six, every reading selection in *Structured Reading* provides you structured practice with reading on, between, and beyond the lines. The entire purpose of *Structured Reading*'s exercises is *not* merely to test whether you've read a selection. That would be a simplistic waste of time. Rather, the purpose of all the exercises is to guide you along a structured path that leads to your being comfortable and skilled with reading at a college level.

The driving force behind the structure and content of the exercises is this: "If a person can't make a mistake, that person can't make anything." The learning moment is at hand if you choose a wrong answer to a question. Seize that moment! Figure out *why* your answer is wrong. If your answer is incorrect, examine your personal line of reasoning to figure out what you misunderstood. The exercises in *Structured Reading* are designed so that students learn as much, if not more, from an incorrect answer than from a correct one. Did the misunderstanding come from forgetting to read closely, with your full focus? Did the misunderstanding result from having missed what's implied but not stated?

Learning the reading habits and thinking strategies for college-level performance takes time. Don't get discouraged, and don't give up. *Structured Reading* challenges you to grow as a reader by deliberately asking you to stretch beyond what you're used to as your personal reading method. The ultimate goal is for you to make giant strides toward upgrading your reading ability.

Chapter 7

What Are "Central Theme" and "Main Ideas"?

In *Structured Reading*, the term **central theme** refers to what an entire reading selection is about. The term **main idea** refers to what a paragraph or group of paragraphs is about. To identify a reading selection's central theme and main ideas, you usually need to "read on the lines"—see Chapter 6 in Part One. Sometimes, however, a central theme or the main ideas aren't stated outright. They're implied, which calls for you to "read between the lines," explained in Chapter 6. To figure out the central theme and main ideas of a passage, you need to read closely and give yourself the time to reflect on what you've read.

FINDING A CENTRAL THEME

The **central theme** of a reading selection is your answer to the question "What's the key point here?" A central theme is the key, the core, the significant message of a reading selection. To get to the central theme, try imagining this scene: A close friend stops by to visit you for a few minutes on the way to work. You invite him in and ask him to sit down. He glances briefly at the headlines on the front page of the newspaper lying on the floor. Not having time to hear all the details, he asks, "What's this about?"

The summary you give—neither too long nor too short—is a statement of the central theme, in this case of the newspaper article. For example, a good statement of a central theme would be "A high school coach is accused of receiving $200,000 for convincing one of his players to sign with a nearby college."

FINDING MAIN IDEAS

The **main idea** is the key message in a paragraph or several paragraphs. The main idea is the thesis, the topic, the subject of a subsection of paragraphs within a whole piece of reading. For example, what's the topic in the following paragraph?

Many students believe teachers can prevent cheating. In other words, cheating would not be a problem if teachers took certain steps to prevent it. For example, students believe that cheating could be prevented if teachers announced tests early and the material to be covered on the test. They believe that in small classes teachers who work with students in a personal manner discourage cheating. Seating arrangements can also aid in combating cheating. They also believe that cheating could be prevented if penalties were made clear and firmly enforced. In short, cheating is perceived to be a teacher's responsibility, not a student's responsibility.

To find the main idea do this: First, locate one or two words that represent what the paragraph is about. In the preceding paragraph, the word is *cheating*. Using *cheating* as your key word, ask yourself *what* the paragraph says about cheating. The answer is the main idea: "Many students believe teachers can prevent cheating." (By the way, usually you need to state the main idea in your own words, even though here a quotation is appropriate.)

A good way to think of a main idea in a paragraph is to think about the design of an umbrella. Main ideas are "umbrella ideas." The main idea can be compared to the fabric covering an umbrella. All the major details are the supporting ideas—reasons, examples, names, statistics, and other material that support the main idea—make up the metal spines of the umbrella. The diagram on the next page shows the relationship between a main idea and its supporting details.

Main ideas usually appear at the beginning of paragraphs, especially in textbooks, articles, and essays. Yet, many times, authors place the main idea at the end of a paragraph so that they can lead up to a small climax. Sometimes, writers put the main idea in the middle of the paragraph so that related material can surround it.

A main idea stated at the beginning of a paragraph is illustrated by the passage about cheating, shown earlier in this chapter. Here's a paragraph with the main idea stated in the final sentence. It's from "Dr. Ice Cream," in the *Washington Post*.

Since Wendell Arbuckle retired, he has worked as a consultant—often traveling to ice cream factories to taste what they produce and evaluate it, much as tea tasters taste tea and wine tasters, wine. The tasting usually is done with two spoons, Arbuckle said, one for scooping the ice cream out of the package, the other for putting it into his mouth. Arbuckle said he usually stands over a sink, and spits out each sample without swallowing. "Sometimes I sample 90 batches a day," he said. "If I swallowed just a little bit of each one that would be too much." He evaluates the ice cream not only for flavor but also for texture as well, and gives advice on how to improve it.

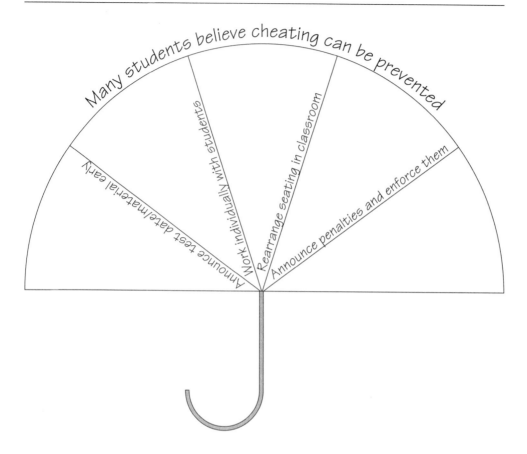

Here's a paragraph with the main idea implied, not stated directly. It's from "Things Are Seldom What They Seem," in *Pageant* magazine.

> Just because a body's in a hearse or on a body cart covered with a sheet in a funeral home doesn't mean it's dead, although the casual onlooker has every right to think so. However, policemen in Fresno, California, being of more suspicious mind, detected breathing coming from the bodies and arrested the two suspects they had been pursuing. Both were very much alive.

You need to "read between the lines" to determine when main ideas are implied, not stated. You want to identify the main point from the reasons, examples, and other details mentioned in the passage. In the paragraph from *Pageant* magazine, the author comments about appearance versus reality. What appeared to be two dead bodies were actually two fugitives who had tried to elude the police.

OBSERVING CENTRAL THEMES AND MAIN IDEAS IN ACTION

Structured Reading provides two types of practice in finding central themes and main ideas. One type asks you to select the correct statement of a central theme or main idea from among four options (multiple choice). Read the choices closely and think about them so that you're ready to justify why you chose what you did and why you rejected what you did. Reasons for not choosing an option are as important as reasons for choosing. Here's an example from *Black Belt* magazine:

> Lookout Mountain School for boys in Colorado is a school for boys who will not stay, voluntarily, at other places. They've been in trouble, in some cases deep trouble, with society. But the school, like other confining institutions, can't always offer total rehabilitation programs. The boys develop a certain amount of social retardation, being retained and confined. As one counselor puts it, "They can't function in society so they come here. Then we try to teach them to function in society." It's a tough job because, as he says, "The question remains: How can we teach them to function in society when they can't go out there?"

_____ 1. What's the main idea of this paragraph?
   a. Because Lookout Mountain School is a confining institution, it can't offer a total rehabilitation program.
   b. There's no attempt to rehabilitate the boys at Lookout Mountain School.
   c. Most boys at Lookout Mountain School are too "hardened" to be rehabilitated.
   d. Teaching delinquent boys to function in society is a tough job.

Answer: *a*

The second type of practice for finding central themes and main ideas is *open ended.* This type asks you to state a central theme or main idea in your own words. Here's an example from "People Are the Attraction," by Bill and Sonia Freedman. (Another passage from this essay appears in Chapter 8 in Part One.)

> Among the Pennsylvania Dutch, married couples travel in covered horse-drawn buggies. Unmarried ones drive in open carts without a roof. You guessed it: so the entire community can see that no hanky-panky is going on. On top of which, Mama sees to it that instead of hooks-and-eyes, daughter's dress is fastened with straight pins—sharp ones placed in strategic locations. It may be a coincidence, but it is rumored any bachelor worth his salt always wears three or more Band-Aids on his pinkies.

In your own words, give the main idea of the preceding paragraph.

_____

_____

Answer: In your own words, convey this idea: Among the Pennsylvania Dutch, the romantic morals of an unmarried couple are watched over all the time.

PRACTICING WITH CENTRAL THEMES AND MAIN IDEAS

ACTIVITY K   CENTRAL THEME AND MAIN IDEAS 1

Read the following paragraphs and answer the questions that follow them. (Answers on page 87.)

From "Dealing with Unhappy and Difficult Customers," by Eric Tyson

(1) Some people say, "The customer is always right." In other words, even if a customer is being a jerk and trying to take advantage of you or is just being all-around difficult, you should bend over backward to please a customer.

(2) I don't buy this way of thinking. You should give the benefit of the doubt to customers because they can do lots of good for your business if you keep them happy and lots of harm if you don't. But some customers are a major pain in the posterior and impossible to please. Trying to keep them happy can be a time-consuming, costly process.

(3) Difficult people often don't have many friends so you probably won't get referrals anyway, and those customers they do refer to you may be as difficult as they are.

(4) If your business didn't do right by a customer, apologize, and bend over backward to make the customer happy. Offer a discount on the problem purchase or, if possible, a refund on product purchases. Also, be sure that you have a clear return and refund policy. Be willing to bend that policy if doing so helps you satisfy an unhappy customer or rids you of a difficult customer.

_____ 1. What's the central theme of "Dealing with Unhappy and Difficult Customers"?
   a. A business's customers are always right, so it's wise business practice to please them no matter how difficult they are.
   b. Some customers can never be pleased, no matter what you do, because they enjoy being unhappy and making others miserable.

    c. Business benefits when customers are happy, but getting rid of some difficult customers can help a business sometimes.

    d. Because of their never-can-be-satisfied personalities, difficult customers probably have few friends—or potential customers—to refer to you.

_____ 2. What's the main idea of paragraph 2?

    a. The author thinks that pleasing customers, even when they're difficult, is a bad idea.

    b. A business must give customers the benefit of the doubt, no matter how difficult they become.

    c. Unhappy customers can cause trouble for a business by spreading their opinions to other people.

    d. Keeping difficult customers happy can be a time-consuming, costly, frustrating process.

_____ 3. What's the main idea of paragraph 4?

    a. If your business has clear policies—with room to make exceptions—for handling complaints, most customers are usually satisfied.

    b. Clear policies for handling complaints help a business get rid of impossibly difficult customers without making the matter seem personal.

    c. Most businesses are better off without impossibly difficult customers, even if official policy says all customers must be satisfied.

    d. When a business can offer discounts and refunds, unhappy and difficult customers alike can be satisfied.

ACTIVITY L   CENTRAL THEME AND MAIN IDEAS 2

Read the following paragraphs and answer the questions that follow them. (Answers on page 87.)

From *Direct from Dell,* by Michael Dell with Catherine Friedman

    (1) Dell is the kind of company where everyone rolls up his sleeves and gets personally involved. We may be an $18 billion company, but our entire management team, myself included, is involved in the details of our business every day. This is, in fact, how we got to be successful: As managers, it's not enough to sit around theorizing and reviewing what those who report to us do. We frequently meet with customers and attend working-level meetings about products, procurement, and technology, to tap into the real source of our company's experience and brainpower.

    (2) Why bother? It's a way to get close to our people, for certain. But that's not all. Our day-to-day involvement in the business

helps us establish and allows us to maintain one of Dell's critical competitive advantages: speed. In this case, "staying involved in the details" allows for rapid decision making because we know what's going on.

(3) For example, when a problem crops up, there's no need for us to do more research or assign someone the job of figuring out what the issues are. Because we often have all the information at our fingertips, we can gather the right people in one room, make a decision, and move forward—fast. The pace of business moves too quickly these days to waste time noodling over a decision. And while we strive to always make the right choice, I believe it's better to be first at the risk of being wrong than it is to be 100 percent perfect two years late.

_____ 1. What's the central theme of this excerpt from *Direct from Dell*?
   a. Dell's managers stay involved in day-to-day issues so that they can make informed decisions.
   b. Almost everyone at Dell likes being part of an $18 billion company.
   c. The pace of most businesses today is slower than the pace at Dell, a fact that makes many people uncomfortable.
   d. Dell is successful because its managers do the theorizing and reviewing without having to consult its customers.

2. What's the main idea of paragraph 1?

   _____

   _____

_____ 3. What's the main idea of paragraph 3?
   a. Problems are solved more easily when research has been completed.
   b. It's important for people to have information at their fingertips.
   c. Making decisions quickly is more valuable than making correct decisions.
   d. Today's rapid pace of business makes quick decision making important.

ACTIVITY M CENTRAL THEME AND MAIN IDEAS 3

Read the following paragraphs and answer the questions that follow them. (Answers on page 87.)

From *Catfish and Mandala*, by Andrew X. Pham

(1) The engine was running, but the sea had us in its palm. Our poor fishing vessel bobbed directionless, putting no distance between us and the mysterious ship in pursuit. The crew

looked defeated. Mom muttered that it was terrible luck. First, the net fouling the propeller, now this. She said to Dad, "How could this be?" The calendar showed today to be auspicious. All the celestial signs were good—clear sky, good wind. She shook her head, looking at her Japanese flag, a patch of red on a white sheet, flapping noisily. Our hopes were pinned on that fraudulent banner.

(2) We waited. Time sagged. I counted the waves beneath our keel. There was nothing to do. The men's lips were moving, mumbling prayers. Eyes closed. Mom had her jade Buddha in her palms. Miracle. Miracle. Our boat seemed to plead with the ocean. Please send a miracle.

(3) It happened. The men stirred, but no one uttered a word. They looked hopeful, fearing that saying something might jinx whatever was happening. Another minute I could tell that the ship was veering away from us. They cheered. Tai instructed us to stay hidden, knowing that the ship had us in its binoculars. Mom was shaking with relief. Eventually, the ship went over the horizon and the men celebrated with a meal.

_____ 1. What is the central theme of this excerpt from *Catfish and Mandala*?
   a. A family hiding on a fishing vessel prays they will not be discovered.
   b. A family hidden by a boat's crew experiences several instances of terrible luck.
   c. People hiding on a fishing vessel are relieved when a crew from another ship chooses not to investigate them more closely.
   d. A ship's crew mistakes an illegal fishing vessel as Japanese.

_____ 2. What's the main idea of paragraph 1?
   a. The fishing vessel is not Japanese, even though it's flying the Japanese flag.
   b. The people hiding on the disguised ship are unhappy about their terrible luck.
   c. The people on the fishing vessel are strong believers in good luck and bad luck.
   d. The two examples of bad luck are the net fouling the propeller and a pursuing ship.

_____ 3. What's the main idea of paragraph 3?
   a. The men celebrate when a pursuing ship turns away.
   b. Tai, as the captain of the fishing vessel, gave the orders and everyone obeyed.
   c. The men stayed silent as the "miracle" happened before their eyes.
   d. The author's mother shook with relief when the ship went over the horizon.

ACTIVITY N   CENTRAL THEME AND MAIN IDEAS 4

Read the following paragraph and answer the questions following it. (Answers on page 87.)

From *Fish for All Seasons*, by Kitty Crider

(1) There is a lot of hoopla in the summer about wild salmon, especially the Copper River fish, which has had a highly successful marketing program in recent years. And it's a fine fish, to be sure.

(2) But the thing about salmon today is that it's like a strawberry. You can buy it fresh any time of the year, from somewhere. Salmon is no longer a seasonal item, found only in the wild. It's also farm-raised—in about 40 countries—and shows up on plates in the middle of the desert as well as near the coasts.

(3) Salmon illustrates how much the fresh-fish platter has changed in the past 10 years, primarily because of improved airline distribution and farm raising of more species. Fish that were once available only near their waters have become frequent fliers. And species that were only eaten in certain areas or months are being farmed in a variety of locations for year-round distributions.

1. What's the central theme for "Fish"?

_____

_____

_____ 2. What's the main idea for paragraph 2?
   a. Salmon is like a strawberry because both decay quickly.
   b. People almost anywhere can buy fresh salmon any time of the year.
   c. Salmon is farm-raised in about 40 countries.
   d. People can eat fresh fish, even in the desert.

_____ 3. What's the main idea of paragraph 3?
   a. All kinds of fresh fish can be flown to almost anywhere in the world.
   b. Fish farming in a variety of locations means year-round salmon distribution.
   c. Fresh fish can be found in the wild and on fish farms in 40 countries.
   d. Fast airline distribution and fish farming have led to increased availability of salmon.

Chapter 8

What Are "Major Details"?

Major details support and develop a main idea. They emerge as you read "on the lines," a concept discussed in Chapter 6. Being able to tell the difference between a major detail and a minor detail is an important reading skill. Major details are the metal spines in the umbrella diagram shown on page 36. If you view all details as equally important, you'll become overloaded by details. To remember efficiently, you want to sort out the major details from the rest. Minor details can be interesting, but they're not basic to the understanding of the material you're reading.

FINDING MAJOR DETAILS

Differentiating between major and minor details takes practice. You can make such judgments only in the context of a complete reading selection. Depending on the framework in which the major detail is used, the same detail can be major or minor. For example, a person's age can be a major detail if the material is about the person's tragic, early death. On the other hand, a person's age can be a minor detail if the material is about the person's thoughts on global warming. Outlining (explained in Chapter 9) can help you figure out what's major, because it must be written on the outline, and what's minor, because it can be skipped without losing the main drift of the material.

Another way to identify major details is to look for words of transition such as *first, one, next, moreover, another, furthermore, in addition, also,* and *finally.* You are more likely—but not positively—looking at a minor detail when it follows words such as *for example, to illustrate, in particular,* and *for instance.* (For a complete list of words of transition, see Chapter 14 in Part One.)

Categories for Major Details: REFS-NNDQ

- **R = Reasons**
- **E = Examples**
- **F = Facts**
- **S = Senses** ((sight, hearing, touch, smell, taste)
- **N = Names**
- **N = Numbers** (statistics)
- **D = Definitions**
- **Q = Quotations**

Yet another method for deciding what are major details is this formula: **REFS NNDQ** (hint: pronounce REFS, and name the letters NNDQ). Be aware, however, that this formula doesn't include the more obscure categories for major details.

Many writers depend solely on major details to imply the main idea of their material. For example, in the following paragraphs, details accumulate and build to give the whole picture. They explain why the doctor has recommended that his patient's leg be amputated. As you read this passage from *Mortal Lessons: Notes on the Art of Surgery,* by Richard Selzer, M.D., underline each detail.

> I invited a young diabetic woman to the operating room to amputate her leg. She could not see the great shaggy black ulcer upon her foot and ankle that threatened to encroach upon the rest of her body, for she was blind as well. There upon her foot was a Mississippi Delta brimming with corruption, sending its raw tributaries down between her toes. Gone were all the little web spaces that when fresh and whole are such delights to loving men. She could not see her wound, but she could feel it. There's no pain like that of the bloodless limb turned rotten and festering. There's neither unguent nor anodyne to kill such a pain yet leave intact the body.
>
> For over a year, I trimmed away the putrid flesh, cleansed, anointed, and dressed the foot, staving off, delaying. Three times each week, in her darkness, she sat upon my table, rocking back and forth, holding her extended leg by the thigh, gripping it as though it were a rocket that must be steadied lest it explode and scatter her toes about the room. And I would cut away a bit here, a bit there, of the swollen blue leather that was her tissue.
>
> At last we gave up, she and I. We could no longer run ahead of the gangrene. We had not the legs for it. There must be an amputation in order that she might live—and I as well. It was to heal us both that I must take up knife and saw, cut it off. And when I could feel it drop from her body to the table, see the blessed space appear between her and that leg, I too would be well.

OBSERVING MAJOR DETAILS IN ACTION

Structured Reading provides you with three types of practice for finding major details. The first type asks you to decide if a listed detail is major or minor *in the context of the entire reading selection.* As you read the following example from *Read Magazine,* identify each detail and then decide whether it's major or minor. Be ready to defend your choice each time.

> Where he lives, the air is so clean that sunsets are never red, not even purple. There's simply not enough dust in the atmosphere to break up the light. Instead, the purple evening sky is tinged with green from the forests below. Where he lives, the mountain slopes tumble downward from the sky, picking up trees as they go along and ending in the rush of a clear and unpolluted river. Eagles soar high above on the swirling air currents. Bighorn sheep bounce with sure hooves along the mountain peaks. Bears, deer, elk, and mountain lions roam the lower slopes. Where he lives is America, as it existed long before the coming of white settlers. He lives where Five Mile Creek flows into The River of No Return in a country named Light on the Mountains. He is one-sixteenth Apache but most of his forbearers came to America 300 years ago and kept moving westward in a search for freedom and elbowroom. Even his name is appropriate—Sylvan Hart. Sylvan comes from a Latin root meaning "forest," and a hart is one of nature's most elusive creatures, the male red deer.

_____ 1. Where Sylvan Hart lives, eagles soar high above on the swirling air currents.

_____ 2. Sylvan Hart lives in the rugged north central section of Idaho.

_____ 3. Sylvan Hart is one-sixteenth Apache.

_____ 4. Sylvan comes from a Latin root meaning "forest."

Answers: 1. minor; 2. major; 3 minor; 4. minor

TRUE, FALSE, or NOT DISCUSSED is a second type of exercise for Major Details. This type asks you to decide whether a listed detail is true, false, or isn't discussed in the material. To decide whether a major detail is *true* or *false*, read and reread carefully so that your concept of what the author wrote is clear. Only with close reading can you avoid jumping to the wrong conclusions. To decide whether an item is *not discussed* in the material, avoid allowing your mind to add in what's missing, no matter how much sense it makes. As you answer each question, be prepared to point to the source of each of your decisions.

Here's an example of a TRUE/FALSE/NOT DISCUSSED exercise for Major Details. It's from "People Are the Attraction" by Sonia and Bill

Freedman. (Another passage from this essay appears in Chapter 7 in Part One.)

> In most places that tourists go to, things are the attraction—cathedrals and museums and pyramids and the like. In Pennsylvania Dutch country, it is the people. The Mennonites and Amish and Dunkers doggedly and picturesquely manage to live 17th-century lives in the 20th century. You've seen pictures of them: bearded men in black clothes, always hatted, and regardless of what *Esquire* says, holding their trousers up with suspenders. The women are no less severely clad, usually in black, but never without a white, frilled cap on their heads. They are stern looking, perhaps even dour, but in five minutes flat, you'll find out that they are the friendliest, most sincere people you have ever met.

Decide whether each detail is true (T), false (F), or not discussed (ND).

_____ 1. Pennsylvania Dutch country is located in Lancaster County, Pennsylvania.

_____ 2. The Pennsylvania Dutch consists of Mennonites, Amish, and Dunkers.

_____ 3. The Pennsylvania Dutch women do not wear severe clothes.

_____ 4. The Pennsylvania Dutch people look stern, but they are friendly.

Answers: 1. ND; 2. T; 3. F; 4. T

FILL-INS are the third type of practice with major details. By filling in the missing words in a statement, your mind works to retrieve accurate information. As you work with fill-ins, be prepared to point to the material that led you to complete the statements the way that you did. (Consider a close synonym of the answer given to be correct.)

Here's an example of a fill-in exercise for Major Details. It's from a newspaper article published by United Press International.

> Kim Jung-Sup's tragic man-against-mountain saga has made him a bitter man. He says he will find no peace until he conquers the Himalayan peak that killed two of his brothers. "I am a sick man, badly sick, sick with Mt. Manaslu," said the 42-year-old veteran climber. "I cannot fall asleep, haunted by the snow-covered mountain that keeps beckoning me. Unless it is conquered, I can never feel free." Kim has just returned home from his third unsuccessful attempt to scale the 26,915-foot-high Manaslu and was soaking his frostbitten feet in a bowl of medicated water. But his five-year battle against the mountain is not over, he said. He will

try again next year. One of his two dead brothers still lies in a crevasse, his body in plain sight. The body of the other has never been found. Korean expeditions have lost 16 persons in Manaslu, including a Japanese cameraman and 10 Nepalese Sherpa guides.

Fill in the word that correctly completes each statement.

1. Kim Jung-Sup wants to conquer Mt. _____ in the _____ mountain range.

2. The mountain is _____ feet high.

3. Kim's battle against the mountain was unsuccessful _____ times.

4. Of Kim's dead brothers, the body of one has never been found, and the body of the other lies at the bottom of a _____ on the mountain.

Answers: 1. Manaslu/Himalayan; 2. 26,915; 3. three; 4. crevasse

PRACTICING WITH MAJOR DETAILS

ACTIVITY O   MAJOR DETAILS 1

Read the following paragraph and answer the questions that follow it. (Answers on page 87.)

From *Learn Horseback Riding in a Weekend*, by Mark Gordon Watson

Learning how to behave with your horse is the first step towards building a good working relationship with him. A well-treated horse is trusting but a frightened horse can be very strong and dangerously unsafe. Always speak calmly. Horses are sensitive to tone of voice, so never shout. Avoid noises like road drills or motorbikes. Don't move suddenly or carelessly when around horses. Use persuasion to encourage your horse. Horses never forget a bad experience, but you can use their memory to your advantage, as they will also remember praise and rewards. Horses work best when they are in a happy environment and they like routine.

Fill in the word that correctly completes each statement.

1. Use a _____ tone when speaking to a horse.

2. Horses can become frightened by shouting and other loud _____

3. Horses work best when in a routine, _____ environment.

ACTIVITY P   MAJOR DETAILS 2

Read the following paragraphs and answer the questions that follow them. (Answers on page 87.)

"Diamonds" in *Mammoth Book of Fascinating Information*, by Richard B. Manchester

(1) "Diamonds in the rough" are usually round and greasy looking. But diamond miners are in no need of dark glasses to shield them from the dazzling brilliance of the mines for quite another reason: even in a diamond pipe, there is only one part diamond per 14 million parts of worthless rock. Approximately 46,000 pounds of earth must be mined and sifted to produce the half-carat gem you might be wearing. No wonder diamonds are expensive!

(2) After diamond-bearing ore is brought up from the mine, it is crushed into smaller rocks no larger than one-and-a-quarter-inches in diameter, and then washed to remove loose dirt. At the recovery plant, the ore is spread on tables covered with grease and sprayed with water. The water moves the rocks off the table, but the diamonds adhere to the grease. Then the grease is boiled off, leaving "rocks" of quite another sort.

Decide whether each detail is true (T), false (F), or not discussed (ND).

_____ 1. Out of 14 million parts of certain rocks, only a small part is diamond.
_____ 2. A diamond's worth is determined by how many carats it has.
_____ 3. No one has ever found a diamond larger than $1\frac{1}{4}$ inches in diameter.
_____ 4. Radioactive substances are used to separate the diamonds from the ore.

ACTIVITY Q   MAJOR DETAILS 3

Read the following paragraph and answer the questions that follow it. (Answers on page 87.)

The Cake Mix Doctor, by Anne Byrn

In addition to their shortening preparation time, cake mixes are a reliable friend. Cakes "from scratch" require some practice to pull off, and you fuss over the ingredients—the right flour, room-temperature butter. Yet, the doctored-up mixes are easily assembled using the dump method in which all ingredients are mixed in one bowl. And they bake up looking pretty, time after time. Plus, cake mixes adapt to new ingredients, be it a can of cherry pie filling or a handful of fresh strawberries. Tweak them with the right number of eggs and a suitable amount of fat and liquid, and they bake up not only into cakes, but also into bars, cookies, cheesecakes, crisps, pies, even a gingerbread house.

Decide whether each detail is MAJOR or MINOR based on the context of the reading selection.

_____ 1. Doctored-up cake mixes are easily assembled.
_____ 2. Baked cake mixes look pretty, time after time.
_____ 3. Pie fillings can be a can of cherries.
_____ 4. Cake mixes can be used to make bars, cookies, cheesecakes, crisps, and pies.

ACTIVITY R   MAJOR DETAILS 4

Read the following paragraphs and answer the questions that follow them. (Answers on page 87.)

Careers and Occupations, by Catherine Dubiec Holm

(1) A variety of information is available on the Internet, including job listings and job search resources and techniques. Internet resources are available 7 days a week, 24 hours a day. No single network or resource will contain all information on employment or career opportunities, so be prepared to search for what you need. Job listings may be posted by field or discipline, so begin your search using key words.

(2) A good place to start your job search is America's Job Bank <http://www.ajb.dni.us/>. America's Job bank, run by the U.S. Department of Labor's Employment and Training Administration, provides information on preparing resumés and using the Internet for job searches, as well as trends in the U.S. jobs market and approximately 1.4 million openings. The Internet is completely unregulated, so if you come across a job offer that seems too good to be true, it probably is.

Fill in the word that correctly completes each statement.

1. Job listings are available at any time on the _____.

2. _____ from a field or discipline can help you search for information about jobs.

3. America's Job Bank is an Internet resource provided by the U.S. Department of _____.

Chapter 9

How Can Maps, Outlines, and Visuals Help with Reading?

Drawing maps and making outlines are two very effective ways for you to comprehend and remember what you're reading. Using the visuals that accompany a reading selection is another method to support you in determining the author's message and to further your understanding of the material.

MAPPING OF CONTENT

Mapping creates a visual diagram of a topic's major points and subpoints. Mapping, also called *clustering* or *webbing*, is a structured method to draw ideas on paper. This visual technique helps readers clarify what they are reading, comprehend larger chunks of material, and more easily remember what they have read. Maps demonstrate relationships between ideas by showing how they play themselves out spatially. The technique of mapping doesn't appeal to everyone, but try it a few times to get used to it. Then, you can decide whether to put mapping into your store of reading strategies.

To map, you begin at the center of a blank sheet of paper, which you can consider the center or nucleus. Draw a circle at the center into which you write the central topic of the article or essay. Next, drawing out from the center circle, make lines that spread out in various directions. End each line with a blank circle. In each of these new circles, write a main idea that's connected to the central topic of the material—this forms "branches" off the central topic. After this, work outward from each main idea by drawing shorter lines ending with circles into which you write supporting details for each main idea. As you work out from the center of the sheet of paper in all directions, you generate a growing, organized structure of what you're reading, which is composed of key words and phrases. Adapt this technique to what you're reading or rereading. Maps can be drawn in all sorts of patterns and shapes, so you can decide how you prefer to display it on a map.

ACTIVITY S   MAPPING 1

Read this paragraph twice. First, read it for its meaning. Second, reread it with an eye toward drawing a map of it.

Elephants are the largest animals that live on land. There are two chief kinds of elephants: African and Asiatic. African elephants live only in Africa south of the Sahara. Asiatic elephants live in parts of India and Southeast Asia. An African elephant is about the same height at the shoulder and rump. Its back dips slightly in the middle. However, an Asiatic elephant has an arched back that is slightly higher than the shoulder and the rump. The ears of an African elephant measure as wide as four feet and cover their shoulders while the ears of an Asiatic elephant are about half as large as those of the African elephant and do not cover the shoulders. The forehead of an Asiatic elephant forms a smooth curve, but the Asiatic elephant has two humps on its forehead just above the ears. The trunk of an African elephant has two finger-like knobs of flesh on the tip; whereas, the trunk of an Asiatic elephant has only one

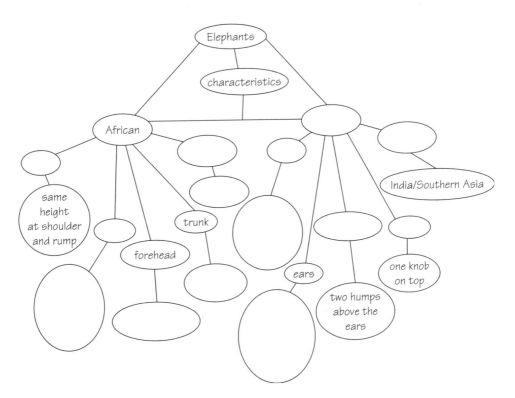

fingerlike knob on the tip. The trunk provides a keen sense of smell, and elephants depend on this sense more than on any other.

Fill in this map of the paragraph about elephants. Some answers are provided to get you started. (Answer on page 88.)

ACTIVITY T   MAPPING 2

Read this paragraph twice. First, read it for its meaning. Second, reread it with an eye toward drawing a map of it.

From "You Are How You Eat" by Enid Nemy

As for chocolate eaters, there are three main varieties, at least among those who like the small individual chocolates. A certain percentage pop the whole chocolate into their mouths, crunch once or twice and down it goes. Others pop the whole chocolate into their mouths and let it slowly melt. A smaller number hold the chocolate in hand while taking dainty little bites.

Peanuts and popcorn are a completely different matter. Of course, there are always one or two souls who actually pick up single peanuts and popcorn kernels, but the usual procedure is to scoop up a handful. But even these can be subdivided into those who feed them in one at a time and those who sort of throw the handful into the open mouth, then keep on throwing in handfuls until the plate, bag or box is empty. The feeders-in-one-at-a-time are, needless to say, a rare breed with such iron discipline that they probably exercise every morning and love it.

Candies like M&M's are treated by most people in much the same way as peanuts or popcorn. But there are exceptions, among them those who don't start eating until they have separated the colors. Then they eat one color at a time, or one of each color in rotation. Honestly.

Fill in this map of the paragraphs about eating methods. Some answers are provided to get you started. (Answer on page 89.)

Many people like to work at understanding ideas by using mapping techniques. These people report that mapping feels like drawing a picture. They let their hand glide across the page, capturing ideas within circles. Many "mappers," who often prefer not to write outlines, say that they relax and think better when they map. Many other people, however, feel that a map seems cluttered, unorganized, and difficult to use to identify the main and subpoints. They prefer to outline.

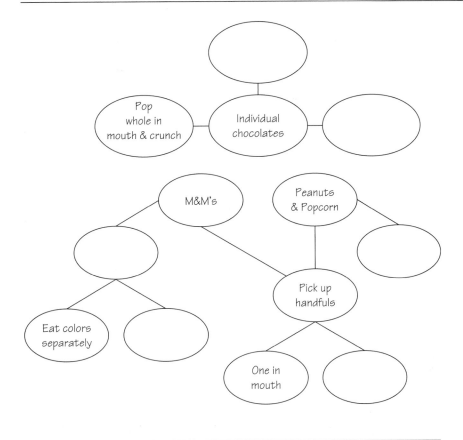

OUTLINING

Outlining is a structuring process that helps you organize, understand, and remember information. You might find that outlining isn't appropriate for everything you read (for example, fiction), but it can assist you particularly well when you need to master a sizable amount of material. Two common methods of outlining are creating informal and formal outlines.

CREATING AN INFORMAL OUTLINE

An informal outline breaks down material into sections that correspond roughly to different parts of the material. Its purpose is to increase your awareness of the separate parts of what you've read. No strict format exists for informal outlines. Writers often use informal outlines to create their working plans, a way to lay out the major parts of an essay. Readers can imagine an informal outline when they read a selection. Here's an informal outline for an essay about weight lifting for women.

Informal Outline

<u>weights/how to use</u>

safety is vital

free weights

    don't bend at waist

    do align neck and back

    do look straight ahead

weight machines—safety is easier

CREATING A FORMAL OUTLINE

A formal outline takes the concept of an informal outline a few steps further. It adheres to strict format requirements, using Roman numerals, letters, and numbers to show how ideas relate to another. Roman numerals identify main ideas. Letters identify major details. Numbers identify minor details if they're necessary to include. Here's a formal outline for an essay about weight lifting for women. Following it is a box that summarizes guidelines for creating formal outlines.

Formal Outline

      Title: Weight Lifting for Women

  I. Avoiding massive muscle development

    A. Role of women's biology

    B. Role of combining exercise types

      1. Anaerobic (weight lifting)

      2. Aerobic (swimming)

 II. Using Weights Safely

    A. Free weights

    B. Weight Machines (built-in safeguards)

Guidelines for a Formal Outline

FORMAT

  I. First main idea

    A. First major detail

    B. Second major detail

      1. First minor detail

      2. Second minor detail

        a. First smaller detail

        b. Second smaller detail

Guidelines for a Formal Outline, continued

II. Second main idea
    A. First major detail
    B. Second major detail

RULES

- *Groupings:* Numbers, letters, and indentations identify groupings and levels of importance. Roman numerals (I, II, III) signal major subdivisions of the topic. Indented capital letters (A, B) signal the next level of generality. Even more indented Arabic numbers (1, 2, 3) show the third level of generality. And, finally, if absolutely necessary, indented lowercase letters (a, b) show the fourth level. Remember, all subdivisions must be at the same level of generality. For example, a main idea can't be paired with a supporting detail.
- *Levels:* Each level *must* have more than one entry. Don't enter a *I* unless there's a *II*; don't enter an *A* unless there's a *B*; don't enter a *1* unless there's a *2*; don't enter an *a* unless there's a *b*. If only one entry is possible, that entry is part of the heading in the next higher level.

    NO   A. Free weights
           1. Safe lifting technique
        B. Weight machines
    YES A. Free weights
        B. Weight machines
    YES A. Free weights
           1. Unsafe lifting techniques
           2. Safe lifting techniques
        B. Weight machines

- *Headings:* Headings don't overlap. For example, whatever is covered in subdivision 1, must be distinct from whatever is covered in subdivision 2.

    NO   A. Free weights
           1. Unsafe lifting techniques
           2. Not aligning head and neck
    YES A. Free weights
           1. Unsafe lifting techniques
           2. Safe lifting techniques

- *Parallelism:* Entries are grammatically parallel (all items start with a verb, or with a noun, or with any other word form). For example, all start with the *-ing* forms of verbs (*Helping, Assisting, Guiding*).

    NO   A. Free weights
        B. Using weight machines
    YES A. Using free weights
        B. Using weight machines

- *Capitalization and Punctuation:* The first word of each entry is capitalized, and proper nouns are always capitalized. The items in a sentence outline end with a period (or a question mark, if needed). The items in a topic outline don't end with punctuation.
- *Introductory and Concluding Paragraphs:* These aren't part of a formal outline.

Your outline form itself depends on the material you're reading, your purpose in reading it, and how much you want to recall. If you're reading for a class or a test, your outline should include all the important main points and their supporting details. If you're reading for general recall only, your outline requires less detail. Although you will not always outline everything you read, you might want to practice the technique so that it becomes an easy way for you to make notes when thorough recall is important.

USING VISUALS

Mapping and outlines are techniques you do yourself to improve your understanding of what you've read. **Visuals** are images, charts, and graphs that are provided by the author. Visuals, which can include words as in cartoons or a caption beneath a photograph, are actually alternate texts that both enhance the author's written text and stand alone to make their own statement. The good news is that reading visuals is not so different from reading texts.

READING IMAGES

Images are visual representations provided by the authors to enhance the message they want their material to deliver. Images may be photographs, posters, cartoons, drawings, film or video, and artwork, for example. Images are as open to being "read" as words are. You can begin to read any one of these images using the techniques you are developing to read written material. When you look at an image, you are *reading on the line*. You are observing what is clearly stated visually. Ask yourself, what is it that I'm viewing? Literally describe the image presented. What does the image communicate to you? Next, if there are words accompanying the visual, what do they say? Are the words in contrast to the image, or do they support and create further curiosity about the image? If the image is included with a piece of writing, how does it relate to that writing?

As you may have already noticed, the questions you ask about an image are similar to those you ask of written texts. Ultimately, your goal is to determine what the author intended to communicate to you, the reader, by using the image. Sometimes, the intention is very specific—to shock, to puzzle, to inform—and other times it may simply be interesting. To practice reading images, turn to Selection 23 in Part 5 of this book. Read "Mute in an English-Only World" and examine the image included with the essay. What is the central theme of the reading? Look at the picture, and then describe it. What are the main images? What message does the image communicate? Does it help you grasp what the reading is about?

READING CHARTS AND GRAPHS

Charts and graphs are visual representations that present large amounts of information clearly and quickly. The well-known quotation, "A picture is worth a thousand words," explains much about an author's choice to use charts and graphs. In your academic and personal reading, you may encounter a variety of types of graphs and charts. The most common types are bar graphs, line graphs, and pie charts. A **bar graph** compares values. A **line graph** indicates changes over a period of time. A **pie chart**, often called a pie graph, shows the relationship of parts to a whole.

Reading graphs and charts is not harder than reading text or images, but you need to be aware of certain characteristics. Bar and line graphs are presented on a *grid* that show the scale by which the graph is interpreted. They also have two *scales* that display what is being measured and how it is being measured. A pie chart, on the other hand, is presented as a circle and is usually represented in percentages. All three of the graphs/charts discussed may use a *key* to describe the elements being measured. The title of the graph/chart tells you what is being shown. The purpose of any one of these graphs/charts is to relate a large amount of information to the reader clearly and efficiently. When you use the basic elements just discussed along with your ability to understand what's stated, reading graphs and charts can be no more difficult than reading plain text. In Selection 30 (Part 6) of *Structured Reading*, you will have an opportunity to practice reading pictures, charts, and graphs. The activity that follows reflects the types of questions you will answer about graphs and charts in Selection 30.

ACTIVITY U   GRAPHS/CHARTS

Read the graphs/charts and answer the questions that follow. (Answers on page 87.)

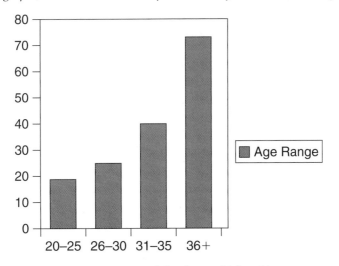

Figure 9.1—Percentage of Graduates Living Alone

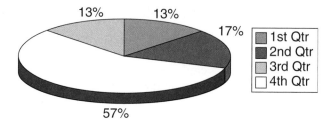

Figure 9.2—Percentage of Earnings per Quarter

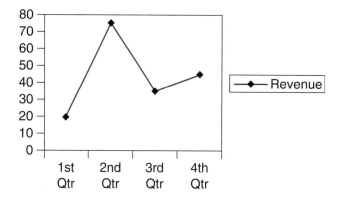

Figure 9.3—Increase in Earnings per Quarter

_____ 1. According to Figure 9.1, which age range is most likely to live with other people?

_____ 2. In Figure 9.2, what is being measured by the pie chart?

_____ 3. According to Figure 9.3, which quarter had a decrease in earnings from the previous quarter?

Chapter 10

What Are "Inferences"?

To make an **inference** in reading is to "read between the lines," a concept discussed in Chapter 6 in Part One. To make an inference, you arrive at a decision or opinion by drawing on what's said "on the lines," such as facts or evidence, to infer what isn't said but is nevertheless intended to be understood.

MAKING INFERENCES

In everyday life, everyone makes inferences. When we deal with people, ride in a car, or watch television, we make inferences. We use the five senses—sight, sound, touch, taste, and smell—to figure out what's going on. For example, when people smile sincerely, the look on their faces implies that they're happy or pleased. When you walk into a kitchen or restaurant filled with delicious smells, the scent implies that the person cooking is an excellent chef.

Here are more examples of your making inferences all the time:

- On your way to a classroom, you wave to a friend, but she does not wave back. You may infer that she is angry, that she is displeased with you, that her mind is on something else, or that she did not see you.
- As you're driving home, you come to a traffic light. On the side of the road sits an unshaven man wearing wrinkled, dirty clothes. He holds a sign that says, "Will work for food." You might infer that he is homeless, has no job, and is hungry. Or you might infer that this is a rip-off. Rather than passersby offering him a job, the man expects people to give him a couple of dollars to buy food.
- You turn on the television to watch a program. The announcer mentions rolling blackouts, nuclear power, and conservation. You know that all the guests are environmentalists, so you infer that the program will be about an energy plan.

Making inferences is as natural for everyone as being human is. To use inference making in reading, however, isn't as automatic. In reading, you think about what the author says "on the lines" to lead you to make an inference about what the author doesn't say outright.

The ability to make inferences while you read is a learned skill. To make inferences, you take hints from what's stated and then fill in the gaps. You need to practice consciously so that you can easily understand more than what is said. Here are questions to keep in mind as you look for inferences:

- What does the author take for granted that I already know on the subject?
- What does the author take for granted about my attitudes toward the subject? Is the author's assumption accurate? Does the author give me room to have an open mind?
- What is the tone of the material? That is, how does the author say what's said? Are the words chosen to make the material clear or complicated? Honest or manipulative? Respectful or superior sounding? When humor is used, is the goal to help me understand the material or to distract me from thinking seriously about the subject?
- Does the author demonstrate a bias toward the material and try to make me accept the same bias?
- What unstated assumptions or conclusions does the author expect me to come to from reading the material?

To make correct inferences, a clear understanding of exactly what the author states is essential. You don't want to draw incorrect conclusions because you understood only part of the information given. Also, to make correct inferences, you are expected to draw on your prior knowledge. For example, if an author names a famous person without giving any details about him or her, the author is assuming that you know who the person is. Without that knowledge, you'll likely miss the message of the material. Therefore, you'll want to do research about the person so that the author's point is clear.

College-level readers dislike being manipulated by an author. For example, suppose an author seeks to convince readers that elderly parents should be put in nursing homes rather than cared for at home. You want to ask yourself whether the author is an expert on family life, on the elderly, or related areas. The answer should affect your reaction to the material. Perhaps the author is the owner of a nursing home, which means the author wants people to give him business by placing their elderly parents in his facility. This means that the author is biased and is trying to manipulate readers. Or, suppose that the author is a health-care professional, such as a doctor of internal medicine, a psychiatrist, or a rehabilitation specialist. You would want to see whether that professional provides only a medical view of the elderly without consideration of life in a nursing home from a resident's standpoint. Of course, sometimes information about the author is not revealed by what the writer says or implies. In such cases, especially if you're being influenced to change your mind on an issue, you want to do research about the author so that you'll be well informed.

OBSERVING INFERENCES IN ACTION

Often, the basic understanding of the main point of a piece depends on your ability to make good inferences. In "How to Stay Alive," Reading Selection 13 in this textbook, the author begins this way:

> Once upon a time, there was a man named Snadley Klabberhorn who was the healthiest man in the whole wide world. Snadley wasn't always the healthiest man in the whole wide world. When he was young, Snadley smoked what he wanted, drank what he wanted, ate what he wanted, and exercised only with young ladies in bed.

Much in the preceding paragraph implies that the author is using exaggeration and humor to drive home a point about some people's excessive concern with their health. The hints include the opening storybook phrase, "Once upon a time ... "; the unusual, deliberately humorous name "Snadley Klabberhorn"; and the exaggerated statement that Snadley was the "healthiest man in the whole wide world." It takes reading inferentially to catch the message of the material. Also, if you happen to have prior knowledge about the author, Art Hoppe, you know that he usually writes humorous satire, poking fun at the problems and whims of human life. That's a further clue about the spirit of the essay.

Here are two examples of drawing inferences for you to observe. Both contain paragraphs from "Coretta Scott King: A Woman of Courage," by Paul Taylor. The message concerns Mrs. King's inner strength and courage in her devotion to her husband and the civil rights movement.

> Shortly before Dexter was born, Coretta again feared for her husband's life. He was arrested for leading a sit-in at a lunch counter in Atlanta. For this minor offense, the judge handed down a harsh sentence of 6 months hard labor at the State Penitentiary. Coretta was terribly upset. The penitentiary was 300 miles from the Kings' home in Atlanta. Pregnant and with two small children, she could rarely make the 8-hour trip to visit her husband. She knew how black prisoners were treated in southern jails. Martin might be beaten— or worse.

Which of these statements can you infer from the preceding paragraph?

Coretta Scott King knew that black prisoners were poorly treated in southern jails because

    a. black prisoners complained more than white prisoners about poor food and health care in prison.

    b. the guards resented the civil rights movement and took out their anger on black prisoners.

c. Coretta Scott King had been in jail and therefore knew that black prisoners were mistreated.

d. The U.S. South had a long history of mistreatment of blacks both in and out of prison.

Answer: d

Here's another paragraph from the same source as the preceding paragraph.

> Before lawyers had time to appeal the judge's decision, Martin was roughly dragged from his Atlanta jail cell. He was chained and handcuffed. In the middle of the night, he was taken to the penitentiary. When Coretta heard what had happened, she was distraught. Just as she was about to give up hope, the telephone rang. "Just a moment, Mrs. King," the long-distance operator said, "Senator John F. Kennedy wants to speak to you." "How are you, Mrs. King?" a warm voice inquired. After chatting a few minutes about her family and the new baby they were expecting, Senator Kennedy told Coretta he was concerned about Martin's arrest. "Let me know if there's anything I can do to help," he told her. The next day, Martin was released.

Which of these four statements can you infer from the preceding paragraph?

Coretta Scott King was about to give up hope because she felt that

a. the lawyers were not very capable and therefore were unable to help her husband.

b. the lawyers were secretly plotting with the judge to make sure that her husband was in jail.

c. after the rough treatment given her husband in the Atlanta jail, there was almost no hope he could survive the even tougher world of the penitentiary.

d. she would not be allowed to visit her husband while he was in the penitentiary.

Answer: c

PRACTICING WITH INFERENCES

Structured Reading offers much practice in the art of drawing inferences from reading. Following are four practices for you to try your skill at inference making. Then, every reading selection in the rest of this textbook includes a structured exercise to guide you into the patterns of thought that make someone a college-level reader.

ACTIVITY V   INFERENCES 1

Read the following paragraph and answer the questions that follow it. (Answers on page 87.)

Travels with Lizbeth, by Lars Eighner

I find it hard to believe that anyone would have thought I had anything of much value. My clothes, besides being worn, would not fit many other people, and this should have been obvious to look at me. The little radio was of no appreciable value. Besides my papers, most of the bulk of what was taken was the remainder of Lizbeth's food and the bedding, which was warm enough, but could not have been sold. Other than a few dollars in postage, nothing could have been readily converted to cash. I was left with what I was wearing, a football practice jersey and my most ragged pair of jeans.

_____ 1. Read the paragraph again. What happened to the author's belongings?
   a. They were destroyed in a fire.
   b. They were borrowed but never returned.
   c. They were stolen.
   d. They were thrown out.

_____ 2. Read the paragraph again. Why does the author remark, "My clothes [. . .] would not fit many other people, and this should have been obvious to look at me"?
   a. The author wants people to look at him so he can show off his unusual appearance.
   b. By saying his size is unusual, the authors implies he's hugely obese.
   c. Only a fool would be interested in the author's clothes.
   d. The author is happy to be rid of his ill-fitting, ragged clothes.

ACTIVITY W   INFERENCES 2

Read the following paragraph and answer the questions that follow it. (Answers on page 87.)

Let's Get Well, by Adelle Davis

A study of the eating habits of individuals who could not reduce showed that they ate little throughout the day, obtained most of their food at dinner and during the evening, and had no appetite for breakfast. Anyone who has tried to reduce knows this pattern only too well. In the morning while the blood sugar is still high from food eaten the night before, will power is strong and resolutions firm. One vows he is going to stop feeling like the anchor on the *Queen Mary* and thinking of himself as a baby blimp; hence he forgoes or merely samples breakfast and lunch. As the bright star of success begins to glitter brilliantly before him, his blood sugar drops and he becomes exhausted, irritable, and starved. His undoing was not that he ate too much, but that he ate too little.

Decide whether each statement below can be inferred (YES) or cannot be inferred (NO) from the reading selection.

_____ 1. People need to eat three meals a day.
_____ 2. Fasting helps build moral character in people.
_____ 3. Lunch is the most important meal of the day.
_____ 4. Bad moods can be caused by low blood sugar.

ACTIVITY X   INFERENCES 3

Read the following paragraph and answer the questions that follow it. (Answers on page 87.)

From "Saint Valentine's Day" in the *New Yorker*

> There are at least two saints after whom Saint Valentine's Day may have been named. One, known as "the lover's saint," was a third-century Italian bishop. In defiance of an edict of Claudius II, abolishing marriage, on the ground that it made restless soldiery, the good bishop secretly officiated at a number of wedding ceremonies, was pitched into jail, and died there. Or (there are a couple of other versions of his end) he was burned at the stake, at the behest of a Roman senator who objected to his marrying the senator's son to the daughter of an impoverished miller; or he choked to death on a fishbone. The other Saint Valentine was beheaded in 270 A.D., for refusing to renounce Christianity. While awaiting execution, he is supposed to have dashed off a farewell message to his jailer's blind daughter, signed "From Your Valentine." How he expected a blind girl to read the note the story doesn't say.

Decide whether each following statement can be inferred (YES) or cannot be inferred (NO) from the reading selection.

_____ 1. The saint who inspired Saint Valentine's Day might never be identified.
_____ 2. A Roman senator was held in greater respect than was a miller.

_____ 3. One requirement for sainthood is to have died by execution.

_____ 4. One Saint Valentine was in love with a jailer's daughter.

ACTIVITY Y   INFERENCES 4

Read the following paragraph and answer the questions that follow it. (Answers on page 87.)

From _Computers_, by Larry Long and Nancy Long

At the Skalny Basket Company, in Springfield, Ohio, Cheryl Hart insisted on daily backups of the small family-owned company's accounts receivables files [records of who owed money to the company]. The backups were inconvenient and took 30 minutes each day. Cheryl took the backup home each day in her briefcase, just in case. On December 23, she packed her briefcase and left for Christmas holidays. Five days later, Skalny Basket Company burned to the ground, wiping out all inventory and its computer system. The company was up in smoke, all except for a tape cassette that contained records of $600,000 accounts receivables. Cheryl said, "We thought we were out of business. Without the tape, we couldn't have rebuilt."

_____ 1. Read the paragraph again. What do the authors mean when they say, "Cheryl took the backup home each day in her briefcase, just in case"?
   a. Cheryl worried that someone would steal the information from the office.
   b. Cheryl wanted an extra copy of the files in case of disaster.
   c. Cheryl was considering stealing the company's files and escaping to Canada.
   d. Cheryl intended to work on the company's files while she was at home.

_____ 2. Read the paragraph again. Why did having the files of accounts receivables mean the company could rebuild?
   a. The accounts receivable had the original floor plans for the company's building.
   b. Cheryl Hart held all details of the company's inventory and operations in her head.
   c. The company had fire insurance, so there would be money to reconstruct its building.
   d. By knowing whom to bill for purchased baskets, the company's income wouldn't stop.

Chapter 11

What Is "Critical Reading"?

Critical reading calls for "reading between the lines," a concept explained in Chapter 6 in Part One. Here the concept has a different focus: the one needed for making inferences (explained in Chapter 10 in Part One). Reading critically means analyzing how each author presents the ideas in each piece of writing. Critical reading is much like critical thinking. Both require you to *question, compare,* and *evaluate.* The three most important areas for critical reading are (1) being able to tell the difference between a fact and an opinion, so that the material doesn't manipulate you; (2) being able to determine the author's strategies, so as to understand the audience, purpose, and tone of a reading selection; and (3) being able to state in one or two sentences the primary message of a reading. This chapter and Chapters 12 and 13 will discuss the strategies that will support you in mastering these areas of critical reading.

CRITICAL READING: DECIDING BETWEEN FACT AND OPINION

As a reader, you're often called on to make judgments about whether the material is objective rather than subjective, or whether it's honest or distorted. Here are two statements, one a fact and the other an opinion, each followed by a critical analysis.

- Rebecca is the friendliest contestant in the pageant. [**"Friendliest" is an opinion. Being friendly means something different to each of us. Even if you happen to agree that Rebecca is the friendliest contestant, your assessment is still an opinion.**]
- Rebecca's peers elected her as the friendliest contestant in the pageant. [**"Friendliest" is not the issue here. Rather it's the fact that Rebecca has been *voted* the friendliest contestant in the pageant. The vote is a fact.**]

Test for Facts: E R O

E = Experiment For example, "The Glaser study showed that elder residents of retirement homes in Ohio who learned progressive relaxation and guided imagery enhanced their immune function and reported better health than did the other residents."

R = Research For example, "According to the Americans' Use of Time Project, when we don't have to do anything else, most Americans mainly watch television."

O = Observation For example: "After a perfectly miserable, aggravating day, a teacher comes home and yells at her children for making too much noise. Another individual, after an equally stressful day, jokes about what went wrong during the all-time most miserable moment of the month. [...] The first is displacing anger onto someone else. The second uses humor to vent frustration."

Facts are statements that can be verified. You can "test" whether a statement is a fact or opinion by applying to it the three tests listed in the box. If the statement passes any one of the three tests, it's a fact. The examples in the box are from "A Personal Stress Survival Guide," which is Reading Selection 28 in this textbook.

Opinions are statements of personal beliefs. They contain ideas that can't be verified or confirmed. As such, opinions are open to debate. Opinions often contain abstract ideas, information that can't be proven, and/or emotionally charged words.

Sometimes an opinion is written so that it appears to be a fact. This is especially true when a quotation is involved. A quotation isn't automatically a fact. True, someone made the statement, but whether the content of the quotation expresses a fact or an opinion is what counts. For example, an author might quote a horse owner as follows: "Having a healthy horse to ride, work, show, or even keep as a pet is a rare privilege." The content of the quotation expresses an opinion, one certainly not shared by all. In contrast, the following quotation expresses a fact: A horse owner reports, "It costs me $600 a year to feed my horse."

OBSERVING FACT AND OPINION IN ACTION

Sometimes, even without doing any reading, you can decide whether a statement is a fact or an opinion.

Write F or O in the blank.

_____ 1. Health investigators have not found the cause of illness that affected two dozen workers at a hazardous waste processing plant.

_____ 2. Last year Jarred and Jossie missed school nine days.

_____ 3. Sometimes the best way to judge a truck is to look under one.

_____ 4. Nothing is better on a cold, winter day than a warm bowl of soup or stew—except maybe a loaf of homemade bread.

_____ 5. Bull sharks are common along beaches in the South.

_____ 6. "You have to love mushrooms to work here," says the owner of Oakhaven Mushroom Farm.

_____ 7. When I was a youngster, my grandfather used to bring me rusty bicycles, old rope, and broken toys he found in the junkyard.

_____ 8. In *Bon Appetit* magazine's fourth annual reader survey, cheesecake topped the list of dessert favorites.

_____ 9. Clark LaGrange, drama director at ECS, will be remembered for his enthusiasm, sense of humor, and patience under production pressure.

_____ 10. No healthy child is going to suffer because Shelby County Schools are turning the thermostat down to 68 degrees.

Answers: 1. F; 2. F; 3. O; 4. O; 5. F; 6. O; 7. O; 8. F; 9. O; 10. O.

Now try reading a passage and then deciding whether the statements following are facts or opinions. These paragraphs, published in *The Washington Post*, speak about Wendell Arbuckle, who was an expert on ice cream, who wrote a major book on the topic, and who served as an ice cream consultant throughout the world.

(1) During the past four years, he has been doing this sort of tasting throughout the United States, but also in Germany, France, Switzerland, Britain, and Japan. He also has done consulting work by mail with firms in about 20 countries [. . .] all of which, he said, signals an "explosion of interest" around the world in American-style ice cream.

(2) He refused to say, though, which brand of ice cream he likes best. "It depends on what people want," he said. "They all can be good for you." His own favorite flavor, he said, is plain vanilla. "It's the basis of the industry and it goes with almost everything."

Decide if the content of each statement, whether or not it's a quotation, is a fact or an opinion. Write F or O in the blank.

_____ 1. *From paragraph 1:* During the past four years he has been doing this sort of tasting throughout the United States, but also in Germany, France, Switzerland, Britain, and Japan.

_____ 2. *From paragraph 2:* "He refused to say, though, which brand of ice cream he likes best."

_____ 3. *From paragraph 2:* All brands of ice cream "can be good for you," according to Arbuckle.

Answers: 1. F; 2. F; 3. O.

PRACTICING WITH FACT OR OPINION

ACTIVITY Z CRITICAL READING: FACT OR OPINION 1

Read the following paragraph and answer the question that follows it. (Answers on page 87.)

From *Warriors Don't Cry*, by Melba Pattillo Beals

I don't remember life without Grandmother India. Mother and Daddy had lived with her in North Little Rock even before I was born. When they purchased our Little Rock house, Grandma came with them. Unlike Mother, who was delicate and fair, Grandma was tall and copper-skinned. She had pronounced cheekbones and huge deep-set almond-shaped eyes that peered at me from behind wire-rimmed spectacles. She had a regal posture and a fearless attitude. My happiest evenings were spent listening to her read aloud from the Bible, from Archie comic books, or from Shakespeare. I sometimes gave up my favorite radio programs like the *Edgar Bergen and Charlie McCarthy Show*, *Our Miss Brooks*, and *The Aldrich Family* to hear her read to me.

Decide whether the content of each statement, even if it's a quotation, is a FACT or an OPINION.

_____ 1. "Mother and Daddy had lived with her in North Little Rock even before I was born."

_____ 2. "She had a regal posture and a fearless attitude."

_____ 3. Grandma wore wire-rimmed spectacles.

_____ 4. "My happiest evenings were spent listening to her read aloud."

ACTIVITY AA   CRITICAL THINKING: FACT OR OPINION 2

Read the following paragraph and answer the questions following it. (Answers on page 87.)

From *Words Still Count with Me,* by Herbert Mitgang

Octavio Paz, poet-diplomat, won the Nobel Prize in literature in 1990—the first Mexican writer to achieve the high honor. Since many authors and civilians consider the Nobel political and geographical, I thought it would not be impolite to ask him if the prize was for him or for his country. He didn't seem surprised, and his answer was philosophical: "To me, a poet represents not only a region but the universe. Writers are the servants of language. Language is the common property of society, and writers are the guardians of language. A writer has two loyalties. First, he belongs to the special tribe of writers. Then he also belongs to a culture, to his own country. Mine is Mexico."

Decide whether the content of each statement, even if it quotes someone, is a FACT or an OPINION.

_____ 1. Octavio Paz was the first Mexican writer to win the Nobel Prize in literature.

_____ 2. "A poet represents not only a region but the universe."

_____ 3. "Writers are the servants of language."

_____ 4. Writers should be loyal to the tribe of writers and to their cultures.

ACTIVITY BB   CRITICAL READING: FACT OR OPINION 3

Read the following paragraph and answer the questions following it. (Answers on page 87.)

From *Hispanics,* "Top Ten Cities for Hispanics," by Diana A. Terry-Azios

Tampa, located on Florida's West Coast, just 84 miles from Orlando, is an ideal location for outdoor activities. *Runner's World* magazine named it one of the top ten cities for runners, and more than 200 species of fish, including sport fish, inhabit the bay. The climate is semi-tropical; temperatures average 62 degrees during the winter and 81 degrees in the summer. The Meyers Group, of Irvine, California, ranked Tampa thirteenth of the nation's top twenty hottest real estate markets. Although Tampa is one of the nation's oldest cities, its residents make it one of the youngest cities, with the median age around 35. The crime rate is higher than average in Tampa, but the cost-of-living is relatively low. And with jobs, transportation, recreation and climate receiving top-tenth percentile ratings, Tampa offers the best in quality-of-life.

Decide if the content of each statement, whether or not it's a quotation, contains a FACT or an OPINION.

_____ 1. *Runner's World* magazine named Tampa one of the top ten cities for runners.
_____ 2. The median age of Tampa's residents is around 35.
_____ 3. "Tampa offers the best in quality-of-life."
_____ 4. For someone interested in outdoor activities, Tampa is ideal.

ACTIVITY CC   CRITICAL READING: FACT OR OPINION 4

Read the following paragraph and answer the questions that follow it. (Answers on page 87.)

Total Television, 4th edition, by Alex McNeil

Because of its impact on American audiences and on the style of television comedy, *All in the Family* is perhaps the single most influential program in the history of broadcasting. In terms of production techniques, the series added nothing new; in some ways, it represented a return to the old days of television: one basic set, a small cast, and little reliance on guest stars. *I Love Lucy*, TV's first smash hit sitcom, was the first to be filmed before a live audience; *All in the Family* was the first sitcom to be video-taped, and unlike the vast majority of sitcoms of the 1960s, it was performed before a live audience.

Decide if the content of each statement, whether or not it quotes someone, contains a FACT or an OPINION.

_____ 1. *All in the Family* is perhaps the single most influential program in the history of broadcasting.
_____ 2. *I Love Lucy* was the first sitcom to be filmed before a live audience.
_____ 3. *All in the Family* was the first sitcom to be videotaped and performed before a live audience.

Chapter 12

Critical Reading: What Are "The Author's Strategies"?

The author's strategies refer to the approaches the author uses to relate information to the reader. There are three primary elements of an author's strategies that you will need to gain an accurate understanding of a piece of writing. The elements that you will focus on are audience, purpose, and tone.

THE AUTHOR'S STRATEGIES: AUDIENCE, PURPOSE, AND TONE

To begin, let's look at audience. When authors begin to write, they often have an intended audience in mind. The intended **audience** is the group of people who will most likely be interested in and read the material. Your task as the critical reader is to determine for what group of people the material seems to be written. To do this, you may look at certain choices the author has made, such as the way the material is presented (narrative or comparison and contrast, for example), the information the author has included and the information the author assumes the reader knows, the choice of language, and the purpose of the piece of writing. Examining these factors will lead you to determine who the intended audience of the material is. Here are a few examples of the types of audiences a writer may gear his or her writing toward:

- A general audience, intended to reach a wide population of readers
- A specific audience, from a particular historical era or cultural background, for example
- A skeptical or unsupportive audience, who are generally opposed to the author's points or beliefs
- A sympathetic audience, who are generally accepting of the author's points or beliefs
- A specific audience, such as an editor or politician
- A specific individual, such as a letter to X (and ask yourself who is X?)

Sometimes determining the audience can be quite easy. For example, if you are reading a magazine for car enthusiasts, you can assume the articles in the magazine are geared toward people who are interested in cars. At other times, determining the audience may be less obvious, and you will need to examine the level of the language, the author's presentation of information, and the point conveyed by the author.

Determining the intended audience is a practice that is often used in conjunction with determining the author's purpose. Once you have determined who the author is speaking to, you can begin to consider what the author intends to say to that audience. Thus, the **author's purpose** is the reason he/she is presenting the material and what the author intends to accomplish in presenting it. There are five major purposes for writing, although authors may take differing approaches to accomplishing a purpose. The five major purposes are to narrate, to describe, to inform or expose, to entertain, and to persuade or argue.

Here is an overview of the five purposes of writing and the characteristics that can help you identify the purpose.

To Narrate	Tells a story Uses chronological order Main idea is generally not stated Contains the who, what and where of an event or incident
To Describe	Uses descriptive language Paints a verbal picture Main idea is generally not stated Describes using the five senses
To Inform/Expose	Explains and discusses ideas Presents information objectively Gives examples Gives definitions or characteristics Analyzes or questions ideas Shows both sides of an issue
To Entertain	Uses humor Amuses
To Persuade/Convince	Advocates the author's opinion Tries to alter or influence the reader's viewpoint or course of action Evaluates or judges Praises, admires, or gives honor to

Using the characteristics will aid you in determining an author's reason for writing. Sometimes, the purpose is easily identifiable. Take the case of an editorial in a daily newspaper where a writer states, "The use of cell phones on public transportation must be kept to a minimum." From this statement, you can determine that the writer's purpose is to convince readers to support his position. Other times, the purpose of the material must be inferred using the characteristics implicit in the material. Overall, you must keep in mind that determining the author's purpose will increase your understanding of the material being read.

The third element of an author's strategies that you will need to pay attention to is the tone. The **tone** can be defined as the author's attitude and mood toward the subject being written about and the approach taken toward the audience. One way to consider tone is to think of how you hear people when they are speaking to you. Not only do you hear the words the people say, but you also hear the emotional impact of *how* they say it. Consequently, both elements, the words spoken and the way the words are spoken, contribute to the ultimate meaning you get from a person's statement. In the same way, authors use the words written and the attitude or mood implicit in the words to express tone to readers. Tone is described using the range of words used to explain human emotions. For example, the tone of a reading can be sarcastic, joyful, resigned, straightforward, angry, nostalgic, or admiring.

To determine the author's tone, examine the author's audience, purpose, and language. When examining the author's language, pay particular attention to a word's denotation, the dictionary definition of a word, and a word's connotation, which includes the emotional weight of a word. For example, if a writer says that someone is "unhappy," the statement seems mostly objective. On the other hand, if the writer describes the person as "pitiful," the statement carries a negative judgment. Thus, when determining tone, view both *what* the author says and *how* the author says it.

OBSERVING THE AUTHOR'S STRATEGIES IN ACTION

Questions about an author's strategies are best answered after you've finished your first pass at reading the material. To guide you in determining the audience, purpose, and tone of a reading, *Structured Reading* provides multiple-choice questions that ask you to select the correct answer from among four. Here's an example from "My World Now" by Anna Mae Halgrim Seaver.

> This is my world now; it's all I have left. You see, I'm old. And, I'm not as healthy as I used to be. I'm not necessarily happy with it, but I accept it. Occasionally, a member of my family will stop in to see me. He or she will bring me some flowers or a little present, maybe a set of slippers—I've got eight pair. We'll visit for awhile and then they will return to the outside world and I'll be alone again. Oh, there are other people here in the nursing home. Residents, we're called. The majority are about my age. I'm 84. Many are in wheelchairs. The lucky ones are passing through—a broken hip, a diseased heart, something has brought them here for rehabilitation. When they're well, they'll be going home.

Most of us are aware of our plight—some are not. Varying stages of Alzheimer's have robbed several of their mental capacities. We listen to endlessly repeated stories and questions. We meet them anew daily, hourly, or more often. We smile and nod gracefully each time we hear a retelling. They seldom listen to my stories, so I've stopped trying.

_____ 1. The main audience for "My World Now" is
   a. nursing home employees being trained for their jobs.
   b. people who are interested in what life is like for a nursing home resident.
   c. people who are in nursing homes.
   d. people who have put someone in a nursing home.

_____ 2. The author's main purpose in this essay is to
   a. inform.
   b. entertain.
   c. frighten.
   d. persuade.

_____ 3. The author's tone in this reading is
   a. irrational.
   b. nostalgic.
   c. sad.
   d. objective.

Answers: 1. b; 2. a; 3. c.

PRACTICING WITH THE AUTHOR'S STRATEGIES

ACTIVITY DD   CRITICAL READING: THE AUTHOR'S STRATEGIES 1

Read the following paragraphs and answer the questions that follow them. (Answers on page 87.)

From "You Are How You Eat" by Enid Nemy

The most irritating of all ice cream eaters are the elegant creatures who manage to devour a whole cone with delicate little nibbles and no dribble. The thermometer might soar, the pavement might melt, but their ice cream stays as firm and as rounded as it was in the scoop. No drips, no minor calamities—and it's absolutely not fair, but what can you do about it?

Some of the strangest ice cream fans can be seen devouring sundaes and banana splits. They are known as "layer by layer" types. First they eat the nuts and coconut and whatever else is sprinkled on top. Then they eat the sauce; then the banana, and finally the ice cream, flavor by flavor. Some might feel that they are eating ingredients and not a sundae or a split, but what do they care?

_____ 1. The main audience for "You Are How You Eat" is
      a. people who eat a lot of ice cream.
      b. the general reading public.
      c. anyone who likes watching other people eat.
      d. people who read magazines about ice cream.

_____ 2. The author's purpose in writing this reading is to
      a. inform.
      b. narrate.
      c. describe.
      d. entertain.

_____ 3. The author's tone in this reading is
      a. annoyed.
      b. nostalgic.
      c. humorous.
      d. frustrated.

ACTIVITY EE CRITICAL READING: THE AUTHOR'S STRATEGIES 2

Read the following paragraph and answer the questions that follow it. (Answers on page 87.)

From "Home" in *Steps in Composition*, by Lynn Quitman Troyka and Jerrold Nudelman

These days Americans of all ages lead such hectic lives that home is often little more than a place to sleep and change clothes. Family members see each other in passing; they seldom share activities, let alone a daily meal. In the morning, Mom and Dad rush off to work at 7:30 and the children leave for school a half hour later. At 3:30, Betty goes directly from school to her part-time job at Burger King. After returning to an empty house, Jason goes out to play for a while and then eats dinner alone. When his parents arrive home at 6:30, he is in his bedroom doing his homework. When Betty comes in the door a few hours later, she yells a quick hello to her parents, grabs some leftovers from the refrigerator, and heads for her room to eat and relax. Because the family members have different schedules, they have little chance to spend time with each other.

_____ 1. The main audience for "Home" is
   a. people who miss their families.
   b. people who have never married.
   c. people who are interested in American families.
   d. people who have a busy family life.

_____ 2. The author's purpose in writing this reading is to
   a. inform.
   b. persuade.
   c. entertain.
   d. argue.

_____ 3. The author's tone in this reading is
   a. angry.
   b. humorous.
   c. annoyed.
   d. straightforward.

ACTIVITY FF   CRITICAL READING: THE AUTHOR'S STRATEGIES 3

Read the following paragraphs and answer the questions that follow them. (Answers on page 87.)

From "American Schools Should Take a Lesson from Japan" in *Steps in Composition*, by Lynn Quitman Troyka and Jerrold Nudelman

> It is a widely accepted fact that many of America's schools are doing a poor job of educating the nation's young people. Research studies indicate that about 30 percent of American high school students drop out before graduating. In some high school systems, fewer than half of the students who enter ever graduate. We should not be surprised, then, that one in four Americans is illiterate—unable to read and write at the most basic level. What can be done? American schools should take a lesson from Japan, where strict rules of behavior, very demanding school schedules, and high academic standards have produced nearly 100 percent literacy.

_____ 1. The main audience for this reading is
   a. people who believe American schools should lower graduation standards.
   b. people who believe American schools are working.
   c. people who are interested in American schools.
   d. people who are interested in Japanese schools.

_____ 2. The author's purpose in writing this reading is to
   a. expose.
   b. narrate.
   c. entertain.
   d. describe.

_____ 3. The author's tone in this reading is
   a. concerned.
   b. naïve.
   c. pessimistic.
   d. hopeless.

ACTIVITY GG   CRITICAL READING: THE AUTHOR'S STRATEGIES 4

Read the following paragraphs and answer the questions that follow them. (Answers on page 87.)

From *Baseball Anecdotes*, by Daniel Okrent and Steve Wulff

A baseball reporter once asked a coach of long and varied experience what were his fondest memories of a lifetime in the game. The coach was removing his uniform after a spring training workout, an aging man whose shrunken chest and loose-fitting skin made him seem—to anyone but an experienced denizen of baseball clubhouses—incredibly out-of-place in that world of speed and muscle and skill. Yet, at the same time, the entire history of baseball seemed to reside in the gray stubble on his face, the wrinkles in his neck, the dry flesh on his arms and legs.

"Which stories do you want?" he asked the reporter. "The true ones or the other ones?"

_____ 1. The main audience for "From *Baseball Anecdotes*" is
   a. people who are curious about baseball coaching.
   b. people who believe coaches should be athletic.
   c. people who are interested in baseball.
   d. people who read magazines about athletes and coaches.

_____ 2. The author's purpose in writing this reading is to
   a. argue.
   b. narrate.
   c. inform.
   d. describe.

_____ 3. The author's tone in this reading is
   a. objective.
   b. sentimental.
   c. surprised.
   d. admiring.

Chapter 13

Critical Reading: What Is a "Summary"?

A **summary** is the process by which you compress and restate the author's central theme and main ideas using your own words. A summary is objective and meant to convey the gist of the author's message. It is not an evaluation, explanation, or response to what the author said. Being able to summarize effectively develops after you have successfully navigated the other stages of the reading process, including identifying central theme and main ideas and making inferences. As a result, when you are able to write and identify appropriate summaries, you are well on your way to having mastered the reader's process to reading effectively.

WRITING A SUMMARY

Writing a summary is an important addition to your arsenal of reading strategies. Summary writing is especially important in the college classroom, as you will be required to read and understand numerous texts for writing and research projects. Summary writing reflects your ability to efficiently "sum up" the main message of a piece of writing—and in doing so, demonstrate your comprehension of the material. To compose effective summaries, ask yourself these questions:

- What is the central theme?
- What are the stated and implied main ideas?
- What details are necessary to include?
- What is the author's purpose?

Once you have answered these questions, you are ready to begin drafting your summary. To draft your summary, look at the responses you wrote down for the preceding questions. How can you bring together the central message as presented in your responses? Write several versions of your summary. Write as many versions as it takes to find the summary that most effectively captures the author's message. Keep in mind these tips:

- Summaries are brief.
- Restate the author's ideas, not your response to those ideas.

- Use your own words.
- Avoid unnecessary details.

There are some stumbling blocks on the way to writing effective summaries. For many students, summary writing is often mistaken for writing a synthesis. A **synthesis** is when you bring together the author's message and connect it with your own experience and other sources to produce an alternate view of the original topic. As noted earlier, a summary does not add anything to the author's point. Another stumbling block that you may encounter is writing a paraphrase rather than a summary. A **paraphrase** is a restatement of the author's ideas in your own words. However, a summary is a condensed restatement of the author's *central or main* ideas. So, although paraphrasing and summary both include restating the author's point in your own words, the type of information restated is the key difference.

OBSERVING SUMMARY IN ACTION

The type of summary exercise you will encounter after the reading selections in *Structured Reading* will ask you to identify the appropriate summary of a piece of writing. How do you know what is an appropriate summary? To start, reflect on the questions you would ask yourself if you were writing the summary. What are the author's main ideas? What details need to be included? Then, based on your answers to these questions, determine which of the suggested summaries most effectively conveys the author's message. Here is an excerpt from "Collegians Predisposed to Road Rage" by Andrew J. Pulskamp to practice identifying the best summary of a passage.

> Age isn't the only factor in aggressive driving. James' research also shows that being a road hog has a lot to do with gender and what kind of car a person drives. James says, in general, men are more aggressive drivers than women. And as far as cars go, if the highways were oceans then sports cars, trucks, and sports utility vehicles would be the sharks, whereas economy cars, family cars, and vans would be the angel fish. There are no hard-line explanations as to why different cars are driven more or less aggressively, but James thinks most likely there are multiple factors at play. It might have to do with the idea that more aggressive people are drawn to certain cars, and it could also mean that certain vehicles make drivers feel more aggressive. After all, it's easier to feel like the king of the road when one is cruising around in a Ford Explorer rather than a Dodge Neon.

_____ 1. What is the best summary of this passage?
   a. In general, women tend to be safer drivers than men, who are often considered aggressive drivers.
   b. People who drive certain vehicles are more aggressive drivers, especially if they drive a sports car or an SUV.
   c. Aggressive drivers, for the most part, do not drive economy cars, family cars, and vans.

ANSWER: 1. b.

PRACTICING WITH SUMMARY

ACTIVITY HH   SUMMARY 1

Read the following excerpt from "Houses to Save the Earth" by Seth Shulman and select the summary that best conveys the author's message. (Answers on page 87.)

Despite the sound of it, the house doesn't look newfangled or avant-garde. In fact, without Loken's animated descriptions, a visitor would never guess the origins of the materials—a feature he says was important when he set out in 1990 to build his "recycled" house. "I wanted to show that you could use recycled building materials without making any compromises on the type of house most Americans want," says Loken, 45. "This meant that the place had to look like any other house if the ideas behind it were going to catch on." Since his house was completed in 1992, Loken's efforts have caught on in ways he never imagined, helping to spawn one of the country's hottest trends in house construction. In fact, over the past few years, Loken has become something of a guru to an alternative-materials movement among builders. He travels the country regularly giving lectures about his building techniques. So far, 12,000 people, including architects and builders from around the world, have made the pilgrimage to his Missoula home.

_____ 1. What is the best summary of this passage?
   a. Recycled materials can be used to build houses that most Americans like without compromising any of the features they want.
   b. Loken is an expert in the field of alternative materials and built a house in Missoula to showcase his knowledge.
   c. After Loken built his house of recycled materials, he now travels the country to share his ideas and techniques with others about using recycled materials.
   d. Using alternative building materials became a new option for builders and architects after Loken completed his "recycled house" in 1992.

ACTIVITY II   SUMMARY 2

Read the following excerpt from "In Praise of the F Word" by Mary Sherry and select the summary that best conveys the author's message. (Answers on page 87.)

Tens of thousands of 18-year-olds will graduate this year and be handed meaningless diplomas. These diplomas will not look any different from those awarded their luckier classmates. Their validity will be questioned only when their employers discover that these graduates are semiliterate.

Eventually a fortunate few will find their way into education-repair shops—adult-literacy programs, such as the one where I teach basic grammar and writing. There, high school graduates and high school dropouts pursuing graduate-equivalency certificates will learn the skills they should have learned in school. They will also discover they have been cheated by our educational system.

_____ 1. What is the best summary of this passage?
   a. High schools are graduating many students who haven't done the work to learn the basic skills.
   b. Some high school dropouts are going to get their diplomas or equivalency certificates.
   c. Employers are discovering that high schools are not teaching students what they need to know.
   d. Students are graduating from high school with a diploma but lack the basic skills that high schools are meant to teach.

ACTIVITY JJ   SUMMARY 3

Read the following excerpt from "A Lady's Life in the Rocky Mountains" by Isabella L. Bird and select the summary that best conveys the author's message. (Answers on page 87.)

I had gone to sleep with six blankets on, and a heavy sheet over my face. Between two and three I was awakened by the cabin being shifted from underneath by the wind, and the sheet was frozen to my lips. I put out my hands, and the bed was thickly covered with fine snow. Getting up to investigate matters, I found the floor some inches deep in parts in fine snow, and a gust of fine, needlelike snow stung my face. The bucket of water was solid ice. I lay in bed freezing till sunrise, when some of the men came to see if I "was alive," and to dig me out. They brought a can of hot water, which turned to ice before I could use it. I dressed standing in snow, and my brushes, boots, and etceteras were covered with snow.

_____ 1. What is the best summary of this passage?

    a. A woman describes the conditions she went through while living in the Rocky Mountains.

    b. A woman complains about how she suffered during her stay in the Rocky Mountains.

    c. A woman describes how quickly water freezes in the Rocky Mountains.

    d. A woman gives examples of how cold the weather is in the Rocky Mountains.

ACTIVITY KK   SUMMARY 4

Read the following excerpt from "Every Kid Needs Some Manual Arts" by William Raspberry and select the summary that best conveys the author's message. (Answers on page 87.)

Today's youngsters, except for those deemed slow enough to be consigned to shop class, are unlikely to be taught even how to make a shoeshine box or replace a frayed lamp cord. My prep school children are innocent of any such household skills and uninterested in acquiring them. But it isn't just prep school children who are deprived of the chance to learn rudimentary manual skills. Probably most academically gifted youngsters are hustled into "academic" tracks whose focus is almost entirely on courses that will help them to get into college. One result is that those who don't go on to college are likely to leave high school unable to earn a decent living. It's a mistake, and not just for the boys. A small part of the reason is cost. Shop classes large enough to accommodate all the children at a school take too much space and too much money. But a larger part is our either/or mentality with regard to academic and manual training. Smart kids do books; dumb kids do tools.

_____ 1. What is the best summary of this passage?

    a. Boys should be required to enroll in shop classes so that they can get good jobs after high school graduation.

    b. The author believes his prep school children could not make a shoebox or repair a frayed lamp cord.

    c. All students should have the opportunity to take shop classes and learn a manual skill whether they plan to attend college or not.

    d. If students are not given training in a manual skill, they will not be able to earn enough money when they graduate high school.

Chapter 14

What Is "Reader's Response"?

Reader's response means that you are expected to express your own opinions by answering three open-ended questions. Based on what you've read, your previous experience, and your best reasoning, here's the opportunity for *your* response, *your* opinion, *your* thinking. This is the realm of questions with no right or wrong answers. They express *your* point of view. Of course, if your peers or instructor challenges your viewpoint, you want to be ready to explain your line of reasoning and defend your conclusion.

Whether you express your responses through discussion or writing, always start by restating the question. Doing this reminds your listeners or readers what has prompted your response. Follow immediately with a clear one- or two-sentence statement of your point of view (in writing, called a "topic sentence"). Next, support your opinion with specific details in the form of facts, examples, names, incidents, and other concrete material.

If you supply more than one supporting detail, tie your presentation together with transitional words so that your audience knows what's coming next. Just as a driver watches for traffic signals and road signs to anticipate what's ahead, listeners and readers need directional signals (in the form of transitional words) to know what's coming next. Here's a list of frequently used transitional words and phrases.

Transitional Expressions

Relationship	Expressions
ADDITION	also, in addition, too, moreover, and, besides, furthermore, equally important, then, finally
EXAMPLE	for example, for instance, thus, as an illustration, namely, specifically
CONTRAST	but, yet, however, nevertheless, nonetheless, conversely, in contrast, still, at the same time, on the one hand, on the other hand

	Transitional Expressions, continued
COMPARISON	similarly, likewise, in the same way
CONCESSION	of course, to be sure, certainly, granted
RESULT	therefore, thus, as a result, so, accordingly
SUMMARY	hence, in short, in brief, in summary, in conclusion, finally
TIME ORDER	first, second, third, next, then, finally, afterwards, before, soon, later, meanwhile, subsequently, immediately, eventually, currently
PLACE	in the front, in the foreground, in the back, in the background, at the side, adjacent, nearby, in the distance, here, there

SUMMARY OF PART ONE

The goal of *Structured Reading* is to give you structured strategies for upgrading your reading skills to a college level. Part One has two purposes. First, Chapters 1 through 5 explain how the reading process works. They offer you information about previewing a reading, predicting during reading, reading speed, developing a college-level vocabulary, and the *SQ3R* method for reading and remembering textbook material.

Second, Chapters 6 through 14 get you working on the seven specific approaches to reading that research shows can greatly upgrade your reading ability. They are understanding "reading on, between, and beyond the lines"; finding central themes and main ideas in reading; making inferences while reading; telling the difference between facts and opinions in reading; identifying the author's strategies; writing summaries; and bringing your personal, informed response to what you've read. There is also a chapter on making maps and/or outlines after reading to support you in comprehending and remembering what you read and using visuals while you read to enhance and expand the information provided to you by the author.

Throughout Part One, *Structured Reading* provides many opportunities for you to apply what you're learning by practicing each separate skill. Then, in Parts Two through Six, each of twenty-nine whole—never abridged or excerpted—reading selections is followed by exercises that allow you to combine the separate skills. By using all your structured reading skills together, repeatedly, you'll have upgraded your ability to read successfully at a college level.

Answers to Activities in Part One

Activity A: No right or wrong answers here.

Activity B: These are the mismatched words: 1. light; 2. site; 3. then; 4. sail; 5. food; 6. hide; 7. floor; 8. bump; 9. tool; 10. sold; 11. rack; 12. took; 13. real; 14. cool; 15. mops; 16. tore; 17. lump; 18, track; 19. nail; 20. cove.

Activity C: 1. three; 2. two; 3. five; 4. one; 5. four; 6. one; 7. five; 8. three; 9. two; 10. four; 11. two; 12. five; 13. three; 14. two; 15. four; 16. two; 17. one; 18. two; 19. five; 20. three.

Activity D: 1. cove; 2. there; 3. fall; 4. relief; 5. undo; 6. unlock; 7. confide; 8. bustle; 9. madder; 10. truce; 11. slip; 12. table; 13. bicycle; 14. hammer; 15. see; 16. foil; 17. blow; 18. hip; 19. hiking; 20. marry.

Activity E: 1. 6:32; 2. 3; 3. 10:51 a.m.; 4. 5:48 a.m.; 5. 5:48 a.m./9:01 a.m.; 6. No; 7. 11:24 p.m.; 8. No; 9. 4; 10. 6:30 a.m.

Activity F: 1. b; 2. b; 3. c; 4. c; 5. a; 6. b; 7. c; 8. a; 9. b; 10. c.

Activity G: 1. ambiguous; 2. monotone; 3. geriatrics; 4. malamute; 5. skeptical; 6. chagrin; 7. coherence; 8. sinuate; 9. phi, theta, kappa; 10. polyester.

Activity H: 1. a; 2. c; 3. b; 4. b; 5. c; 6. b; 7. a; 8. c; 9. b; 10. a.

Activity I: 1. a; 2. b; 3. b; 4. a; 5. a; 6. c; 7. c; 8. b; 9. a; 10. c.

Activity J: 1. c; 2. b; 3. a; 4. b; 5. c; 6. c; 7. c; 8. c; 9. b; 10. a.

Activity K: 1. c; 2. b; 3. a.

Activity L: 1. a; 2. Answers will vary; here's one possibility: Dell's secret of success is that all managers get personally involved in the details of the business; 3. d.

Activity M: 1. c; 2. b; 3. a.

Activity N: 1. Answers will vary; here's one possibility: Salmon is now available for year-round distribution; 2. b; 3. d.

Activity O: 1. calm; 2. noises; 3. happy.

Activity P: 1. T; 2. ND; 3. ND; 4. F.

Activity Q: 1. major; 2. major; 3. minor; 4. major.

Activity R: 1. Internet; 2. key words; 3. Labor.

Activity S: See p. 88.

Activity T: See p. 89.

Activity U: 1. 20–25; 2. earnings; 3. 3rd quarter.

Activity V: 1. c; 2. c.

Activity W: 1. Yes; 2. No; 3. No; 4. Yes.

Activity X: 1. Yes; 2. Yes; 3. No; 4. No.

Activity Y: 1. b; 2. d.

Activity Z: 1. fact; 2. opinion; 3. fact; 4. fact.

Activity AA: 1. fact; 2. fact; 3. opinion; 4. opinion.

Activity BB: 1. fact; 2. fact; 3. opinion; 4. opinion.

Activity CC: 1. opinion; 2. fact; 3. fact.

Activity DD: 1. b; 2. d; 3. c.

Activity EE: 1. c; 2. a; 3. d.

Activity FF: 1. c; 2. a; 3. a.

Activity GG: 1. c; 2. d; 3. a.

Activity HH: 1. c.

Activity II: 1. d.

Activity JJ: 1. a.

Activity KK: 1. c.

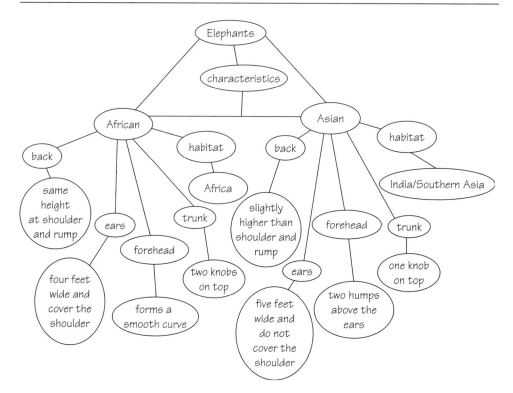

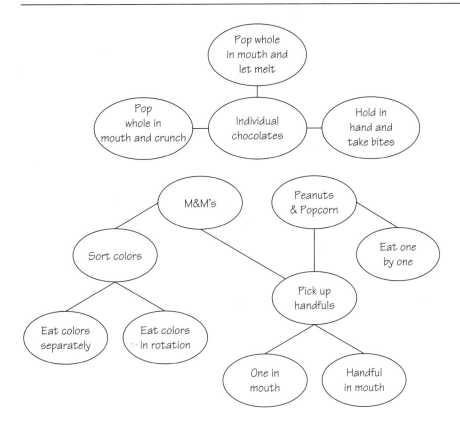

Part 2

THINKING: GETTING STARTED

Reading is an active process. It is also a visual process. At any given moment, your eyes are carrying visual information to your brain, which then begins to process that information. Most often when you think of "reading" you are probably thinking of reading words on the page. Yet, there are many more types of "reading" that you do—for example, reading images, situations, and facial expressions. What all these types of reading have in common is that your eyes take in the information, and then your brain sorts it out and gives meaning to it. If you really think about it, reading—in the broader sense—is how you make sense of the world.

To use your capacity to read and understand most effectively, you can apply the previewing techniques described in Chapter 2 (Part 1) of this book. Previewing allows your mind to "hook" new information being presented to what's already in your memory, your prior knowledge. Previewing gives you a foundation on which to build—you actually create a place to store the new information you are reading. Creating a foundation from your prior knowledge will allow you to get more out of your reading. With that in mind, the next three pages of visual material are offered to help you start thinking about your prior knowledge on the subjects in the reading selections in Part 2 of this book.

In what situations might someone's gentle, quiet voice be heard as a shout? (See "Tyranny of Weakness.")

What obstacles might prevent a child from pursuing his dream? (See "Don't Sell Your Ambition Short to 'Keep It Real'. "?)

Never before has this nation
had a greater need for educated minds . . .
to help solve problems of energy,
the economy, equal rights,
employment, and the environment.
Higher education must be a higher priority
because educated people solve problems.
Support our colleges and universities!

Why do so many people assume that if a person has a physical handicap, that person is also mentally limited? (See "Darkness at Noon.")

What would you do if you caught a neighbor stealing? (See "To catch a Thief.")

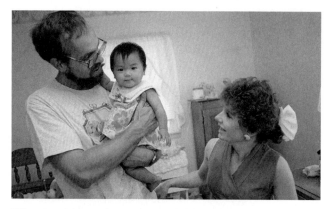

Why should warnings about child abuse be widely pub-
licized? (See "Real Loss.") Why would a birth mother
give up her child for adoption? (See "Seoul Searching.")

A Real Loss

Fern Kupfer

(1) I was sitting in back of a little girl flying as an unaccompanied minor, put on the plane by a mother who placed a Care Bear in her arms and told her to remind Daddy to call when she got to California. The girl adjusted her seat belt and sniffed back a tear, bravely setting her jaw.

(2) As we prepared for takeoff, the man next to the girl asked her the name of her bear and nodded in approval, saying Furry was a good name for a bear. When the little girl told him she was 6 years old, the man replied that he had a daughter who was 6 years old. His daughter was missing the same teeth, in fact. He asked how much money the tooth fairy was giving out in New York these days.

(3) By the time we were in the air, the man and the little girl were playing tic-tac-toe, and she revealed to him the names of her favorite friends. Somewhere over Ohio, I fell asleep, awakened by my mother instinct when I heard a child announce that she had to go to the bathroom.

(4) "It's in the back, right?" I heard the girl say to the man. She looked tentative. The flight attendants were busy collecting lunch trays.

(5) "Do you want me to take you there?" the man asked, standing.

(6) At once my antennae were up and, leaning into the aisle, I craned my neck, practically knocking heads with the woman in the seat across from me. For one moment our eyes locked. She had been listening, too, and both of us had the same idea. Would this man go into the bathroom with the child? I held my breath as he held open the bathroom door. Suddenly, he became transformed in my eyes—the dark business suit looked sinister, the friendly smile really a lure to something evil.

(7) Then the man showed the little girl how the lock worked and waited outside the door. The woman and I sighed in relief. She said, "Well, you can't be too careful these days."

(8) I've thought about that man on the plane since then, and the image of him and the little girl always leaves an empty sorrow. I know that a new heightened consciousness about child molestation is in itself a good thing. I know that sexual abuse of children is awful, and that we must guard against it. But it saddened me that I looked at someone who understood a child's fear and saw a child molester.

(9) These are trying times for men. We women say how we want men to be sensitive and nurturing, to be caring and affectionate. But my sense is that now these qualities cannot be readily displayed without arousing

suspicion. Perhaps there is some sort of ironic retribution for all those years of accepting the male stereotypes. But there is a real loss here for us all when we must always be wary of the kindness of strangers.

(498 words)

Here are some of the more difficult words in "A Real Loss."

antennae
(paragraph 6)

an·tenna (an ten′ə) *n.* ⟦L, earlier *antemna*, sail yard⟧ **1** *pl.* **··nae** (-ē) or **··nas** either of a pair of movable, jointed sense organs on the head of most arthropods, as insects, crabs, or lobsters; feeler: see INSECT, illus. **2** *pl.* **··nas** *Radio, TV* an arrangement of wires, metal rods, etc. used in sending and receiving electromagnetic waves; aerial

craned
(paragraph 6)

crane (krān) *n.* ⟦ME < OE *cran:* akin to Du *kraan,* Ger *kranich* < IE **gr-on* < base **ger-:* see CROW[1]⟧ **1** *pl.* **cranes** or **crane** *a)* any of a family (Gruidae) of usually large gruiform wading birds with very long legs and neck, and a long, straight bill *b)* popularly, any of various unrelated birds, as herons and storks **2** any of various machines for lifting or moving heavy weights by means of a movable projecting arm or a horizontal beam traveling on an overhead support **3** any device with a swinging arm fixed on a vertical axis /a fireplace *crane* is used for holding a kettle/ —*vt., vi.* **craned, cran′·ing 1** to raise or move with a crane **2** to stretch (the neck) as a crane does, as in straining to see over something

heightened
(paragraph 8)

heighten (hīt″n) *vt., vi.* ⟦< prec. + -EN⟧ **1** to bring or come to a high or higher position; raise or rise **2** to make or become larger, greater, stronger, brighter, etc.; increase; intensify —*SYN.* INTENSIFY —**height′·ener** *n.*

ironic
(paragraph 9)

ironic (ī rän′ik) *adj.* **1** meaning the contrary of what is expressed **2** using, or given to the use of, irony **3** having the quality of irony; directly opposite to what is or might be expected **4** marked by coincidence or by a curious or striking juxtaposition of events: regarded by many as a loose usage Also **iron′i·cal** —**iron′i·cally** *adv.*

irony[1] (ī′rə nē, ī′ər nē) *n., pl.* **··nies** ⟦Fr *ironie* < L *ironia* < Gr *eirōneia* < *eirōn,* dissembler in speech < *eirein,* to speak < IE base **wer-,* to speak > WORD⟧ **1** *a)* a method of humorous or subtly sarcastic expression in which the intended meaning of the words is the direct opposite of their usual sense /the *irony* of calling a stupid plan "clever"/ *b)* an instance of this **2** the contrast, as in a play, between what a character thinks the truth is, as revealed in a speech or action, and what an audience or reader knows the truth to be: often **dramatic irony 3** a combination of circumstances or a result that is the opposite of what is or might be expected or considered appropriate /an *irony* that the firehouse burned/ **4** *a)* a cool, detached attitude of mind, characterized by recognition of the incongruities and complexities of experience *b)* the expression of such an attitude in a literary work **5** the feigning of ignorance in argument: often called **Socratic irony** (after Socrates' use of this tactic in Plato's *Dialogues*) —*SYN.* WIT[1]

molestation
(paragraph 8)

mo·lest (mə lest′, mō-) *vt.* ⟦ME *molesten* < OFr *molester* < L *molestare* < *molestus,* troublesome < *moles,* a burden: see MOLE[3]⟧ **1** to annoy, interfere with, or meddle with so as to trouble or harm, or with intent to trouble or harm ☆**2** to make improper advances to, esp. of a sexual nature **3** to assault or attack (esp. a child) sexually —**mo·les·ta·tion** (mō′les tā′shən, mäl′əs-) *n.* —**mo·lest′er** *n.*

nurturing
(paragraph 9)

nur·ture (nur′chər) *n.* ⟦ME < OFr *norreture* < LL *nutritura,* pp. of L *nutrire,* to nourish: see NURSE⟧ **1** anything that nourishes; food; nutriment **2** the act or process of raising or promoting the development of; training, educating, fostering, etc.: also **nur′·tur·ance 3** all the environmental factors, collectively, to which one is subjected from conception onward, as distinguished from one's nature or heredity —*vt.* **·-tured, ·-tur·ing 1** to feed or nourish **2** *a*) to promote the development of *b*) to raise by educating, training, etc. —**nur′·tur·ant** *adj.* or **nur′·tural** —**nur′·turer** *n.*

retribution
(paragraph 9)

ret·ri·bu·tion (re′trə byōō′shən) *n.* ⟦ME *retribucioun* < OFr *retribution* < LL(Ec) *retributio* < L *retributus,* pp. of *retribuere,* to repay < *re-,* back + *tribuere,* to pay: see TRIBUTE⟧ punishment for evil done or reward for good done; requital —**re·trib·u·tive** (ri trib′yoo tiv) *adj.* or **re·trib′u·to·ry** (-tôr′ē) —**re·trib′u·tive·ly** *adv.*

sinister
(paragraph 6)

sin·is·ter (sin′is tər) *adj.* ⟦ME *sinistre* < L *sinister,* left-hand, or unlucky (side), orig. lucky (side) < IE base **sene-,* to prepare, achieve > Sans *sániyān,* more favorable: early Roman augurs faced south, with the east (lucky side) to the left, but the Greeks (followed by later Romans) faced north⟧ **1** *a*) [Archaic] on, to, or toward the left-hand side; left *b*) *Heraldry* on the left side of a shield (the right as seen by the viewer) (opposed to DEXTER) **2** threatening harm, evil, or misfortune; ominous; portentous [*sinister* storm clouds] **3** wicked, evil, or dishonest, esp. in some dark, mysterious way [a *sinister* plot] **4** most unfavorable or unfortunate; disastrous [met a *sinister* fate] —**sin′·is·terly** *adv.* —**sin′·is·ter·ness** *n.*

SYN.—**sinister,** in this connection, applies to that which can be interpreted as presaging imminent danger or evil [a *sinister* smile]; **baleful** refers to that which is inevitably deadly, destructive, pernicious, etc. [a *baleful* influence]; **malign** is applied to that which is regarded as having an inherent tendency toward evil or destruction [a *malign* doctrine]

tentative
(paragraph 4)

ten·ta·tive (ten′tə tiv) *adj.* ⟦LL *tentativus* < pp. of L *tentare,* to touch, try: see TENT[2]⟧ **1** made, done, proposed, etc. experimentally or provisionally; not definite or final [*tentative* plans, a *tentative* explanation] **2** indicating timidity, hesitancy, or uncertainty [a *tentative* caress] —**ten′·ta·tively** *adv.* —**ten′·ta·tive·ness** *n.*

transformed
(paragraph 6)

trans·form (trans fôrm′; *for n.* trans′fôrm′) *vt.* ⟦ME *transformen* < L *transformare* < *trans-,* TRANS- + *formare,* to form < *forma,* FORM⟧ **1** to change the form or outward appearance of **2** to change the condition, nature, or function of; convert **3** to change the personality or character of **4** *Elec.* to change (a voltage or current value) by use of a transformer **5** *Linguis.* to change by means of a syntactic transformational rule **6** *Math.* to change (an algebraic expression or equation) to a different form having the same value **7** *Physics* to change (one form of energy) into another —*vi.* [Rare] to be or become transformed —*n. Math.* the process or result of a mathematical transformation —**trans·form′·able** *adj.* —**trans·form′a·tive** *adj.*

SYN.—**transform,** the broadest in scope of these terms, implies a change either in external form or in inner nature, in function, etc. [she was *transformed* into a happy girl]; **transmute,** from its earlier use in alchemy, suggests a change in basic nature that seems almost miraculous [*transmuted* from a shy youth into a sophisticated man about town]; **convert** implies a change in details so as to be suitable for a new use [to *convert* an attic into an apartment]; **metamorphose** suggests a startling change produced as if by magic [a tadpole is *metamorphosed* into a frog]; **transfigure** implies a change in outward appearance which seems to exalt or glorify [his whole being was *transfigured* by love] See also CHANGE

wary
(paragraph 9)

wary (wer′ē) *adj.* **war′i·er, war′i·est** ⟦< WARE[2] + -Y[2]⟧ **1** cautious; on one's guard **2** characterized by caution [a *wary* look] —*SYN.* CAREFUL —**wary of** careful of

1A   VOCABULARY

From the context of "A Real Loss," explain the meaning of each of the vocabulary words shown in boldface in the following sentences.

1. *From paragraph 4:* She looked **tentative.**

   hesitant

2. *From paragraph 6:* At once my **antennae** were up and, leaning into the aisle, I **craned** my neck.

   sense organs at the top of my head/stretched

3. *From paragraph 6:* Suddenly, he became **transformed** in my eyes—the dark business suit looked **sinister.**

   changed in appearance/evil

4. *From paragraph 8:* I know that a new **heightened** consciousness about child **molestation** is in itself a good thing.

   increased/improper advances toward

5. *From paragraph 9:* We women say how we want men to be sensitive and **nurturing.**

   to promote the development of others

Name   Date

6. *From paragraph 9:* Perhaps there is some sort of **ironic retribution** for all those years of accepting the male stereotypes.

that which has happened is the opposite of what was actually

intented/deserved punishment

_____

_____

7. *From paragraph 9:* But there is a real loss here for us all when we must always be **wary** of the kindness of strangers.

on our guard against

_____

1B CENTRAL THEME AND MAIN IDEAS

Choose the best answer.

  d   1. What is the central theme of "A Real Loss"?
   a. These are trying times for men because all the media attention on child molestation has made even their simple kindnesses toward children appear to be evil.
   b. The author felt sorry for the little girl who had to fly from New York to California by herself, but at the same time the author admired the child's bravery.
   c. Child molesters can find victims everywhere, even on airplanes, so all travelers should be suspicious of anyone who is kind to children flying alone.
   d. Because of her increased awareness that some people are child molesters, the author now realizes that she has become suspicious of people who are kind to children they do not know.

  c   2. What is the main idea of paragraph 6?
   a. Airplane passengers often listen to other people's conversations and exchange glances about what is said.
   b. Becoming suspicious, the author leaned far into the aisle and nearly bumped heads with another watchful woman.
   c. As she waited to see what the man would do, he suddenly changed in her eyes into an evil person.
   d. The man opened the bathroom door for the little girl as the author held her breath.

1C   MAJOR DETAILS

Decide whether each detail is MAJOR or MINOR based on the context of the reading selection.

MAJOR   1. The author was sitting in back of a little girl who was flying alone.

MINOR   2. The little girl's mother placed a Care Bear in the girl's arms.

MINOR   3. The little girl was going to California.

MINOR   4. The little girl knew how to adjust her seat belt.

MINOR   5. The bear's name was Furry.

MAJOR   6. Both the girl and the man's daughter were six years old.

MAJOR   7. The little girl announced that she had to go to the bathroom.

MAJOR   8. At that moment, the flight attendants were busy collecting lunch trays, so the man offered to take the girl to the bathroom.

MAJOR   9. The man showed the girl how the lock worked, and then he waited for her outside the door.

MINOR 10. The other woman sighed in relief.

MAJOR 11. The author's image of the man and the little girl on the plane left her with a feeling of loss.

MAJOR 12. A new heightened consciousness about child molestation is in itself a good thing.

1D   INFERENCES

Choose the best answer.

____b____ 1. *Read paragraph 1 again.* Why did the little girl's mother tell her to remind Daddy to call?
   a. The mother did not want to spend the money to call California herself.
   b. The mother wanted to know that the girl had arrived safely after the long trip.
   c. The father was not considerate of the woman's feelings, so he had to be reminded to call.
   d. The mother wanted to know that the girl's father was in good health.

Name   Date

___c___ 2. *Read paragraph 2 again.* Why did the man say Furry was a good name?
   a. He had once had a bear named Furry.
   b. He wanted to make the little girl settle down so that she would not bother him and he could rest or read quietly.
   c. He wanted to make her feel comfortable and secure.
   d. The bear was very fluffy, and so Furry seemed an appropriate name.

___d___ 3. *Read paragraph 3 again.* Why did the little girl's announcement that she had to go to the bathroom wake up the author?
   a. The child was speaking very loudly and moving around in her seat, indicating that she was very uncomfortable.
   b. The author was afraid the little girl might have an accident unless someone took her to the bathroom right away.
   c. As a mother, the author thought she should be the one asked to take the little girl to the bathroom if the flight attendants were busy.
   d. As a mother, the author was used to listening—even in her sleep—for children's calls for help.

___c___ 4. *Read paragraph 7 again.* By saying "Well, you can't be too careful these days," the woman was communicating that she was
   a. annoyed at the flight attendants for being too busy to take the little girl to the bathroom.
   b. angry that the little girl had asked the man for help instead of turning to a nearby woman.
   c. slightly embarrassed that she had worried about what the man might do to the little girl.
   d. somewhat worried that the girl was too little to learn how to use the bathroom lock.

___a___ 5. *Read paragraphs 8 and 9 again.* What does the author mean when she says, "there is a real loss here for us all when we must always be wary of the kindness of strangers"?
   a. Constant suspicion is a poisonous feeling, preventing people from enjoying some of the pleasanter moments in life, such as watching a man being kind to a child.
   b. Because rarely is there a way of telling who might be evil, people stop talking to strangers and miss chances to make friends.
   c. Years ago fewer child molesters existed, so children's lives were safer, and their parents had peace of mind that now has been lost.

      d. Because people today are constantly on the lookout for child molesters, nice people like the author are afraid to be kind to strangers' children for fear of being suspected of molestation.

<u> a </u> 6. The word *loss* used in the title refers to the
      a. author's loss of trust of adults who are kind to children.
      b. little girl's having to leave her mother behind.
      c. negative effect on children when divorced parents live long distances apart.
      d. man's missing his own little girl who was also six years old.

1E   CRITICAL READING: FACT OR OPINION

Decide whether each statement, even if it quotes someone, contains a FACT or an OPINION.

<u>FACT</u> 1. *From paragraph 1:* "The girl adjusted her seat belt and sniffed back a tear [. . .]."

<u>FACT</u> 2. *From paragraph 2:* "He asked her how much money the tooth fairy was giving out in New York these days."

<u>FACT</u> 3. *From paragraph 3:* "[. . .] she revealed to him the names of her favorite friends."

OPINION 4. *From paragraph 4:* "She looked tentative."

<u>FACT</u> 5. *From paragraph 6:* "[. . .] he became transformed in my eyes [. . .]."

OPI<u>NION</u> 6. *From paragraph 6:* "[. . .] the dark business suit looked sinister."

<u>FACT</u> 7. *From paragraph 7:* "The woman and I sighed in relief."

OPINION 8. *From paragraph 7:* "[. . .] you can't be too careful these days."

OPINION 9. *From paragraph 8:* "[. . .] a new heightened consciousness about child molestation is in itself a good thing."

OPI<u>NION</u>10. *From paragraph 9:* "These are trying times for men."

1F   CRITICAL READING: THE AUTHOR'S STRATEGIES

Choose the best answer.

<u> b </u> 1. The main audience for "A Real Loss" is
      a. anyone who lets young children travel alone.
      b. anyone who identifies with the loss of trust in our society.
      c. anyone who has a fear of child molesters.
      d. anyone who has been sexually abused.

             Name   Date

_c_ 2. The author's purpose in writing this reading is to
   a. persuade.
   b. argue.
   c. inform.
   d. entertain.

_d_ 3. The author's tone in this reading is
   a. angry.
   b. unsure.
   c. bitter.
   d. sad.

1G   READER'S PROCESS: SUMMARIZING YOUR READING

_b_ 1. What is the best summary of "A Real Loss"?
   a. A woman explains her feelings about a conversation she over-heard on a cross-country flight to California.
   b. A woman explains how our fears of child molesters affect the way we view innocent men when they are around children.
   c. A woman explains her feelings about men who talk to chil-dren who are traveling alone.
   d. A woman explains how she and other women feel about men who sexually abuse children.

1H   READER'S RESPONSE: TO DISCUSS OR WRITE ABOUT

1. Why do some people consider it "unmanly" when men are kind, con-siderate, and wholesomely affectionate toward children?

2. Traditionally, American society has not encouraged men to be especially affectionate, even toward their own children. But attitudes seem to be changing. Discuss the benefits for men, for women, and for children when men are free to express wholesome affection.

HOW DID YOU DO?

1 A Real Loss

SKILL (number of items)	Number Correct		Points for each		Score
Vocabulary (11)	_____	×	2	=	_____
Central Theme and Main Ideas (2)	_____	×	6	=	_____
Major Details (12)	_____	×	3	=	_____
Inferences (6)	_____	×	2	=	_____
Critical Reading: Fact or Opinion (10)	_____	×	1	=	_____
Critical Reading: The Author's Strategies (3)	_____	×	2	=	_____
Reader's Process: Summarizing Your Reading (1)	_____	×	2	=	_____

(Possible Total: 100) *Total* _____

SPEED

Reading Time: _____ Reading Rate (page 411): _____ Words Per Minute

Selection 2
Tyranny of Weakness

Eda LeShan

(1) If I were to ask you who are the most aggressive people you know, chances are you would describe someone who tells other people what to do, bosses people around, has a great deal of energy—a forceful personality.

(2) Wrong! The most aggressive, the strongest people we know are the weak ones. They are people who want someone else to take care of them and have somehow managed to convince those around them that they are too sick, too weak, too helpless, too incompetent to do anything for themselves. They are not really sick or helpless at all, but they have found a way to control the world that is fool-proof.

(3) I suppose it begins in childhood when a child realizes that helplessness is a way of controlling parents and teachers and other kids. And anyone who chooses such techniques may very well believe they really are unable to function.

(4) I recall a time when I had been on a book publicity tour for 10 days and came home to face preparing Thanksgiving dinner for 14 people. I asked a friend who did not work if she could bring a salad and she said she was too tired. Or there is a man who was sure he wanted a quiet, shy helpless wife because his mother had been aggressive, competent and somewhat overpowering. So he has spent his life taking care of a wife who "gets sick" at every family crisis and takes to her own bed if a child gets sick, if the family has to move, if her husband is in a car accident.

(5) Often people who have been strong and competent become helpless after some major emotional trauma. A friend told me, "I have a full-time job and three school-age kids, and when my father died, my mother, who had always been a competent person, suddenly turned into an infant. She expected me to take her shopping, cook for her, stay at her house, drive her everywhere, listen to her endless complaints. I became so exhausted that it began to dawn on me that she wasn't weak and helpless, she was a tyrant!

(6) Weakness and helplessness can be a form of aggression. But its origins may start with feelings of incompetence, fear, lack of self-esteem.

(7) When we meet with the tyranny of weakness, we need to help the person discover strengths, ways of accepting the challenges of life.

(8) One husband, married 40 years, told me "I don't know what happened, except I finally realized my wife had made me her slave—not by yelling at me or ordering me around, but by appearing to be helpless. I was getting a few aches and pains of my own, I guess, and it wasn't fun anymore

feeling I was 'The Big Man' who could do everything. Finally, one day when she told me to mop the kitchen floor because she needed to take a nap, I said, 'Do it yourself or leave it dirty!' I thought she'd faint from the shock, but it did her a world of good. It seemed to break a pattern that was bad for both of us."

(9) It's a very good idea to keep in mind that it is not only the strong who push us around, but very often it is the person who appears to be weak and helpless.

(563 words)

Here are some of the more difficult words in "Tyranny of Weakness."

Vocabulary List

aggressive
(paragraph 1)

ag·gres·sive (ə gres'iv) *adj.* **1** aggressing or inclined to aggress; starting fights or quarrels **2** ready or willing to take issue or engage in direct action; militant **3** full of enterprise and initiative; bold and active; pushing **4** *Psychiatry* of or involving aggression — **ag·gres'sive·ly** *adv.* —**ag·gres'sive·ness** *n.* —**ag·gres·siv·ity** (ag'res iv'ə tē, ə gres'-) *n.*

SYN.—aggressive implies a bold and energetic pursuit of one's ends, connoting, in derogatory usage, a ruthless desire to dominate and, in a favorable sense, enterprise or initiative; **militant** implies a vigorous, unrelenting espousal of a cause, movement, etc. and rarely suggests the furthering of one's own ends; **assertive** emphasizes self-confidence and a persistent determination to express oneself or one's opinions; **pushing** is applied derogatorily to a forwardness of personality that manifests itself in officiousness or rudeness

competent
(paragraph 4)

com·pe·tent (-tənt) *adj.* [ME < OFr < L *competens,* prp. of *competere:* see COMPETE] **1** well qualified; capable; fit [a *competent* doctor] **2** sufficient; adequate [a *competent* understanding of law] **3** permissible or properly belonging: with *to* **4** *Law* legally qualified, authorized, or fit —*SYN.* ABLE —**com'pe·tently** *adv.*

incompetent
(paragraph 2)

in·com·pe·tent (in käm'pə tənt) *adj.* [Fr *incompétent* < LL *incompetens:* see IN-² & COMPETENT] **1** without adequate ability, knowledge, fitness, etc.; failing to meet requirements; incapable; unskillful **2** not legally qualified **3** lacking strength and sufficient flexibility to transmit pressure, thus breaking or flowing under stress: said of rock structures —*n.* an incompetent person; esp., one who is mentally deficient —**in·com'pe·tence** *n.* or **in·com'pe·tency** —**in·com'pe·tently** *adv.*

personality
(paragraph 1)

per·son·al·ity (pur'sə nal'ə tē) *n., pl.* **-ties** [ME *personalite* < LL *personalitas* < *personalis,* personal] **1** the quality or fact of being a person **2** the quality or fact of being a particular person; personal identity; individuality **3** *a)* habitual patterns and qualities of behavior of any individual as expressed by physical and mental activities and attitudes; distinctive individual qualities of a person, considered collectively *b)* the complex of qualities and characteristics seen as being distinctive to a group, nation, place, etc. **4** *a)* the sum of such qualities seen as being capable of making, or likely to make, a favorable impression on other people *b)* [Informal] personal attractiveness; engaging manner or qualities **5** a person; specif., *a)* a notable person; personage *b)* a person known for appearances on TV, radio, etc. **6** [*pl.*] remarks, usually of an offensive or disparaging nature, aimed at or referring to a person — *SYN.* DISPOSITION

self-esteem
(paragraph 6)

self-esteem (-e stēm') *n.* **1** belief in oneself; self-respect **2** undue pride in oneself; conceit —*SYN.* PRIDE

techniques
(paragraph 3)

tech·nique (tek nēk′) *n.* ⟦Fr < Gr *technikos:* see TECHNIC⟧ **1** the method of procedure (with reference to practical or formal details), or way of using basic skills, in rendering an artistic work or carrying out a scientific or mechanical operation **2** the degree of expertness in following this *[a pianist with good technique but poor expression]* **3** any method or manner of accomplishing something

trauma
(paragraph 5)

trauma (trô′mə, trä′-) *n., pl.* **··mas** or **··mata** (-mə tə) ⟦ModL < Gr *trauma* (gen. *traumatos*): for IE base see THROE⟧ **1** *Med.* a bodily injury, wound, or shock **2** *Psychiatry* a painful emotional experience, or shock, often producing a lasting psychic effect and, sometimes, a neurosis —**trau·ma′·tic** (-mat′ik) *adj.* —**trau·mat′i·cally** *adv.*

tyrant
(paragraph 5)

ty·rant (tī′rənt) *n.* ⟦ME *tirant* < OFr *tiran, tirant* (with *-t* after ending *-ant* of prp.) < L *tyrannus* < Gr *tyrannos*⟧ **1** an absolute ruler; specif., in ancient Greece, etc., one who seized sovereignty illegally; usurper **2** a cruel, oppressive ruler; despot **3** any person who exercises authority in an oppressive manner; cruel master **4** a tyrannical influence

Vocabulary List

2A   VOCABULARY

Using the vocabulary words listed on pages 106–107, fill in the blanks.

1. ___Competent___ employees will earn not only a bonus but also praise from their employers.

2. The president of the company, while appearing to be a ___tyrant___, was actually loved by his employees.

3. Research shows that ___aggressive___ behavior in a younger child is often learned from an older sibling.

4. A ___personality___ disorder should be diagnosed and treated by a trained professional.

5. Art students study various artists and their ___techniques___ in order to develop their own styles.

6. The teacher was judged to be highly ___incompetent___ when her students failed to learn to read.

7. Constant criticism by a spouse is likely to damage one's ___self-esteem___ .

8. The parents went into shock after the ___trauma___ of seeing their only child struck by a car.

2B   CENTRAL THEME AND MAIN IDEAS

Choose the best answer.

___a___ 1. What is the central theme of "Tyranny of Weakness"?
   a. The strongest people we know are often those who appear weak and helpless.
   b. Children should always give in to the demands of parents.
   c. A wife should be able to expect household help from her husband when she is tired.
   d. Weak people often take advantage of their good-natured friends.

___c___ 2. What is the main idea of paragraph 5?
   a. Mothers should help adult daughters who have full-time jobs and children of their own.
   b. The roles of parent and child may be reversed as the parent ages.
   c. Often an emotional trauma will turn a strong individual into a helpless one.
   d. Medical studies claim that women who lose their husbands are no longer able to take care of themselves.

___b___ 3. What is the main idea of paragraph 8?
   a. After 40 years of marriage, a husband should willingly help his wife.
   b. It is never too late in a marriage to reverse an undesirable behavior pattern.
   c. After many years of marriage, a husband will become tired of being "The Big Man."
   d. Unwillingness by a husband to help his wife may signal the beginning of the end of the marriage.

2C   MAJOR DETAILS

Decide whether each detail is MAJOR or MINOR based on the context of the reading selection.

MAJOR 1. Children learn early in life that helplessness can be a controlling technique.

MINOR 2. The author's friend was too tired to bring a salad for Thanksgiving dinner.

MAJOR 3. A man who marries a woman opposite in personality to his mother is trading one set of problems for another.

MAJOR 4. The intent of the incompetent individual is often to control family and friends.

Name   Date

MAJOR 5. Sudden helplessness in a healthy, competent individual may have been triggered by an emotional trauma.

MAJOR 6. A person may display aggressive behavior because of feelings of low self-esteem or even fear.

2D INFERENCES

Decide whether each statement that follows can be inferred (YES) or cannot be inferred (NO) from the story.

NO 1. Aggressive behavior is bad manners.

YES 2. People who appear to be incompetent and helpless may actually be very controlling.

NO 3. A friend who will not help cook Thanksgiving dinner is not a true friend.

NO 4. An only child will feel more responsibility toward a weak, helpless parent than toward a competent one.

YES 5. Refusing to cooperate with a spouse's helpless behavior will "cure" the spouse.

NO 6. A man should marry a woman whose personality is the opposite of his mother's personality.

NO 7. A person who has behaved in a certain way toward a spouse for many years will not be able to change.

2E CRITICAL READING: FACT OR OPINION

Decide whether each statement, even if it quotes someone, contains a FACT or an OPINION.

OPINION 1. *From paragraph 2:* "The most aggressive, the strongest people we know are the weak ones."

OPINION 2. *From paragraph 3:* "I suppose it begins in childhood when a child realizes that helplessness is a way of controlling parents [. . .]."

FACT 3. *From paragraph 4:* "The man wanted a quiet, shy, helpless wife because his mother had been aggressive and overpowering."

FACT 4. *From paragraph 4:* "[. . .] she said she was too tired."

OPINION 5. *From paragraph 5:* "A competent mother will turn into a weak, helpless widow."

OPINION 6. *From paragraph 8:* "It seemed to break a pattern that was bad for both of us."

2F CRITICAL READING: THE AUTHOR'S STRATEGIES

Choose the best answer.

__b__ 1. The main audience for "Tyranny of Weakness" is
a. anyone who is weak enough to be controlled by others.
b. anyone who is interested in learning more about human behavior.
c. anyone who needs advice on handling a controlling husband or wife.
d. anyone who is confused about how to handle aggressive people.

__d__ 2. The author's purpose in writing this reading is to
a. describe.
b. narrate.
c. entertain.
d. inform.

__a__ 3. The author's tone in this reading is
a. reflective.
b. sad.
c. angry.
d. aloof.

2G READER'S PROCESS: SUMMARIZING YOUR READING

__a__ 1. What is the best summary of "Tyranny of Weakness"?
a. The writer shares her insights about the hidden side of people who appear to be weak.
b. The writer shares several experiences she has had with people who took her for granted.
c. The writer shares advice on how to handle people who are controlling.
d. The writer shares her experiences with people who learned helplessness in childhood.

2H READER'S RESPONSE: TO DISCUSS OR WRITE ABOUT

1. "The most aggressive, the strongest people we know are the weak ones" (paragraph 2). Explain what you think is meant by this statement. Provide at least one example to support your explanation.

Name   Date

2. Describe someone you know personally or have observed in the television or motion picture media who tyrannizes in the way described in this essay.

HOW DID YOU DO?
2 Tyranny of Weakness

SKILL (Number of Items)	Number Correct		Points for each		Score
Vocabulary (8)	_____	×	2	=	_____
Central Theme and Main Ideas (3)	_____	×	4	=	_____
Major Details (6)	_____	×	4	=	_____
Inferences (7)	_____	×	4	=	_____
Critical Reading: Fact or Opinion (6)	_____	×	2	=	_____
Critical Reading: The Author's Strategies (3)	_____	×	2	=	_____
Reader's Process: Summarizing Your Reading (1)	_____	×	2	=	_____

(Possible Total: 100) *Total* _____

SPEED

Reading Time: _____ Reading Rate (page 411): _____ Words Per Minute

Selection 3

Don't Sell Your Ambitions Short to "Keep It Real"

Leonard Pitts Jr.

(1) An open letter to African-American kids. The other day, I used a big word in this column. The word was brobdingnagian; it's from a book called *Gulliver's Travels* by Jonathan Swift, a fantasy about a man whose adventures take him to a number of strange lands. One of those lands was Brobdingnag, where the people were all giants. Thus, "brobdingnagian" is a big word that means, well . . . big. (I like using it because it's odd and kind of ugly-sounding.)

(2) Anyway, some guy e-mailed me about it. Here's what he said: "Uncle Tom: Stop trying to act like the white man and mastering his culture. . . . I mean, bro, your [sic] using white man words like Brobdingnabian [sic] or whatever. I never hear talk like that on Black Entertainment Television. For us homeys, keep it real. If you want to describe something as big, say 'Shaq-size.'" My middle son thought it had to be somebody's idea of a joke. And it might be. But there are some rather . . . odd people out there, so I'm not sure. Not that it matters. Whether it was meant as a joke or not, it made me laugh out loud.

(3) Then I thought about you. It occurred to me: You hear stuff like that all the time, don't you? Seems like everybody has an idea of what you can and cannot do, whom you can and cannot be friends with, how you ought and ought not speak, where you can and cannot go, if you want to "keep it real." If you want, in other words, to be considered truly black. I've heard the story a hundred times, guys. I've heard it from your teachers, heard it from my own kids, and even heard it from some of you. Like a girl I knew who said black kids ostracized her because she spoke standard English and liked a white boy band.

(4) You know the crazy part? When white people prejudge us, when they say blacks can't do this, that or the other, when they demand that we conform to their expectations of what black is, we have no problem calling them on it. But when black people do the same thing, we're more apt to soul-search about why we don't fit in. You have to wonder at that. Should it really matter whether it's a white person or a black one who presumes us to be less than we are? Doesn't the presumption stink either way?

(5) I'm going to tell you something you might not want to hear. If you have a goal in this life, something you want to be, you have to realize that the road between here and there might get narrow sometimes. There may be parts you have to walk alone because there's no space for all your friends; there's only room for one. Maybe you enjoy opera, maybe you

want to be an astronaut, and maybe you'd like to be a surgeon. And maybe some black people tell you "we" don't do those kinds of things.

(6) They'll say they're keeping it real. But the only thing they're keeping is some old lies that date all the way back to slavery. White people—many, not all—have told us those lies every day for four centuries, told them so constantly and so convincingly that some of us can't help but to believe. So when black people repeat those lies, when they advise you to dream the kind of dreams black kids are supposed to dream—rap star, basketball player, pimp—you have to recognize it for what it is. You have to know that Marian Anderson sang opera, Dr. Mae Jemison went into space on a shuttle, Dr. Daniel Hale Williams performed the first successful surgery on a human heart and all three were black, like you.

(7) Most of all, you have to be prepared, if need be, to walk that road alone. I won't lie: It's not easy. People—black and white—will always have expectations and when you refuse to live by those expectations, they'll call you names; they'll shut you out. It's not easy, but I guarantee that if you stay with it, you'll find that it is worthwhile. I guess what I'm telling you is this: Please have the guts to be who you are. And to dream brobdingnagian dreams.

(722 words)

Here are some of the more difficult words in "Don't Sell Your Ambitions Short to 'Keep It Real.'"

Vocabulary List

culture
(paragraph 2)

cul·ture (kul'chər) *n.* ⟦ME < L *cultura* < *colere*: see CULT⟧ **1** cultivation of the soil **2** production, development, or improvement of a particular plant, animal, commodity, etc. **3** *a)* the growth of bacteria, microorganisms, or other plant and animal cells in a specially prepared nourishing fluid or solid *b)* a colony of microorganisms or cells thus grown **4** *a)* development, improvement, or refinement of the intellect, emotions, interests, manners, and taste *b)* the result of this; refined ways of thinking, talking, and acting **5** development or improvement of physical qualities by special training or care *[body culture,* voice *culture]* **6** *a)* the ideas, customs, skills, arts, etc. of a people or group, that are transferred, communicated, or passed along, as in or to succeeding generations *b)* such ideas, customs, etc. of a particular people or group in a particular period; civilization *c)* the particular people or group having such ideas, customs, etc. —*vt.* **··tured, ··tur·ing 1** to cultivate **2** to grow (microorganisms or cells) in a specially prepared medium

fantasy
(paragraph 1)

fan·ta·sy (fant'ə sē, -zē) *n., pl.* **··sies** ⟦ME *fantasie* < OFr < L *phantasia,* idea, notion < Gr, appearance of a thing < *phainein,* to show, appear < IE base **bhā-,* to gleam, shine > OE *bonian,* to ornament⟧ **1** imagination or fancy; esp., wild, visionary fancy **2** an unnatural or bizarre mental image; illusion; phantasm **3** an odd notion; whim; caprice **4** *a)* a work of fiction portraying highly IMAGINATIVE (sense 3) characters or settings that have no counterparts in the real world *b)* such works, collectively, as a literary form; specif., those works dealing with dragons, elves, ghosts, etc. **5** *Music* FANTASIA (sense 1a) **6** *Psychol. a)* a more-or-less connected series of mental images, as in a daydream, usually involving some unfulfilled desire *b)* the activity of forming such images —*vt.* **··sied, ··sy·ing** to form fantasies about —*vi.* to indulge in fantasies, as by daydreaming —*adj.* **1** of or like a fantasy **2** of or pertaining to any of various games in which scoring is keyed statistically to the performances of actual players within a sports league, as of professional baseball or football: typically, each contestant puts together a roster of players to form an imaginary team

homeys
(paragraph 2)

homey[1] (hōm′ē) *adj.* **hom′i·er, hom′i·est** having qualities usually associated with home; comfortable, familiar, cozy, etc. —**home′y·ness** *n.*
homey[2] (hōm′ē) *n., pl.* **··eys** [Slang] HOMEBOY

ostracized
(paragraph 3)

os·tra·cize (äs′trə sīz′) *vt.* **··cized′, ··ciz′·ing** [Gr *ostrakizein,* to exile by votes written on tiles or potsherds < *ostrakon,* a shell, potsherd, akin to *osteon,* bone: see OSSIFY] to banish, bar, exclude, etc. by ostracism —*SYN.* BANISH

prejudge
(paragraph 4)

pre·judge (prē juj′) *vt.* **··judged′, ··judg′·ing** [Fr *préjuger* < L *praejudicare:* see PRE- & JUDGE] to judge beforehand, prematurely, or without all the evidence —**pre·judg′er** *n.* —**pre·judg′·ment** *n.* or **pre·judge′·ment**

presumes
(paragraph 4)

pre·sume (prē zōōm′, -zyōōm′, pri-) *vt.* **··sumed′, ··sum′·ing** [ME *presumen* < OFr *presumer* < L *praesumere* < *prae-,* before (see PRE-) + *sumere,* to take: see CONSUME] **1** to take upon oneself without permission or authority; dare (to say or do something) **2** to take for granted; accept as true, lacking proof to the contrary; suppose **3** to constitute reasonable evidence for supposing [a signed invoice *presumes* receipt of goods] —*vi.* **1** to act presumptuously; take liberties **2** to rely too much (*on* or *upon*), as in taking liberties [to *presume* on another's friendship] **3** to take something for granted —**pre·sum′·edly** (-id lē) *adv.* —**pre·sum′er** *n.*
SYN.—**presume** implies a taking something for granted or accepting it as true, usually on the basis of probable evidence in its favor and the absence of proof to the contrary [the man is *presumed* to be of sound mind]; **presuppose** is the broadest term here, sometimes suggesting a taking something for granted unjustifiably [this writer *presupposes* a too extensive vocabulary in children] and, in another sense, implying that something is required as a preceding condition [brilliant technique in piano playing *presupposes* years of practice]; **assume** implies the supposition of something as the basis for argument or action [let us *assume* his motives were good]; **postulate** implies the assumption of something as an underlying factor, often one that is incapable of proof [his argument *postulates* the inherent goodness of man]; **premise** implies the setting forth of a proposition on which a conclusion can be based See also PRESUME

sic
(paragraph 2)

sic[1] (sik) *adj.* Scot. var. of SUCH
sic[2] (sik) *vt.* **sicced** or **sicked, sic′·cing** or **sick′·ing** [var. of SEEK] **1** to set upon; pursue and attack: said esp. of or to a dog **2** to urge or incite to attack [to *sic* a dog on someone]
sic[3] (sik, sēk) *adv.* [L] thus; so: used within brackets, [*sic*], to show that a quoted passage, esp. one containing some error or something questionable, is precisely reproduced

Uncle Tom
(paragraph 2)

Uncle Tom [after the main character, an elderly black slave, in Harriet Beecher Stowe's antislavery novel, *Uncle Tom's Cabin* (1852)] [Informal] a black whose behavior toward whites is regarded as fawning or servile: a term of contempt —**Uncle Tom′·ism′**

3A VOCABULARY

Choose the best answer.

  b   1. To know the **culture** of a group, you need to understand most of its
      a. ancient civilization.
      b. ideas and customs.
      c. attitudes toward science.
      d. customs for growing foods.

___b___ 2. If a book is a **fantasy**, it is
    a. comical.
    b. imagined.
    c. childlike.
    d. realistic.

___a___ 3. **Homeys** is a slang word for homeboy, which means
    a. males from the same neighborhood as you live in.
    b. people who speak honestly and directly to each other.
    c. professional actors who appear on the Black Entertainment Television.
    d. people who behave oddly and live in your neighborhood.

___c___ 4. If your friends **ostracized** you, you would be
    a. ridiculed.
    b. appreciated.
    c. excluded.
    d. accepted.

___c___ 5. To **prejudge** is to make a judgment
    a. without consulting a public prosecutor.
    b. without the assistance of an attorney.
    c. without considering all the evidence.
    d. without a judge's recommendation.

___d___ 6. To **presume** is to
    a. assume and act on immediately without giving the information any thought.
    b. imply strongly that one racial group is more racist than another.
    c. hold rigidly to prejudices no matter what the logical or scientific evidence shows otherwise.
    d. accept automatically as true even though no evidence of accuracy or reliability exists.

___b___ 7. When [sic] is enclosed in brackets, it indicates that something has been
    a. omitted from the original source.
    b. copied exactly from the original source.
    c. reworded from the original source.
    d. replaced with a synonym from the original source.

___c___ 8. If someone is referred to as **Uncle Tom**, his behavior suggests that of
    a. an African-American supervisor who is mean-spirited.
    b. an African-American actor who plays elderly parts.
    c. an African American who acts submissive with Whites.
    d. a nonrelative who pretends to be an uncle.

3B   CENTRAL THEME AND MAIN IDEAS

Choose the best answer.

__b__   1. What is the central theme of "Don't Sell Your Ambitions Short to 'Keep It Real'"?
   a. African-American kids should not use slang if they hope to realize their ambitions.
   b. African-American kids should not let others' expectations keep them from achieving their ambitions.
   c. African-American kids should not use big words but common, everyday words understood by everyone.
   d. African-American kids should not try to imitate the white man's culture.

__d__   2. What is the main idea of paragraph 5?
   a. Some African Americans get made fun of because they do things not considered "black."
   b. African Americans should aspire to be opera singers, astronauts, and surgeons.
   c. African Americans may have to distance themselves from those who have unrealistic goals.
   d. African Americans may find the road to success narrow and lonely at times.

3C   MAJOR DETAILS

Decide whether each detail is MAJOR or MINOR based on the context of the reading selection.

MAJOR 1. Leonard Pitts used the word *brobdingnagian* in one of his columns.

MAJOR 2. Pitts received an e-mail from a reader who objected to his using big words.

MINOR 3. Pitts' son thought the e-mail was a joke.

MAJOR 4. The reader who e-mailed Pitts suggested Pitts use words that were "real."

MINOR 5. Dr. Mae Jemison went into space on a shuttle.

3D   INFERENCES

Decide whether each statement below can be inferred (YES) or cannot be inferred (NO) from the reading selection.

__NO__   1. Leonard Pitts prefers books written by white authors.

<u>NO</u> 2. The reader who e-mailed Pitts was not a college graduate.

<u>NO</u> 3. Pitts' children think he is an Uncle Tom.

<u>YES</u> 4. Pitts would support an African-American kid who dreamed of being a scientist.

<u>NO</u> 5. Pitts' letter to African-American kids will influence them to use big words, not slang.

3E CRITICAL READING: FACT OR OPINION

Decide whether each statement, even if it quotes someone, contains a FACT or an OPINION.

<u>FACT</u> 1. *From paragraph 1:* "The other day I used a big word in this column."

<u>FACT</u> 2. *From paragraph 1:* "[. . .] it's from a book called *Gulliver's Travels* by Jonathan Swift [. . .]."

OPINION 3. *From paragraph 2:* "Stop trying to act like the white man and mastering his culture."

OPINION 4. *From paragraph 3:* "[. . .] 'keep it real!' If you want, in other words, to be considered truly black."

OPINION 5. *From paragraph 3:* "[. . .] black kids ostracized her because she spoke standard English and liked a white boy band."

<u>FACT</u> 6. *From paragraph 6:* "[. . .] Dr. Daniel Hale Williams performed the first successful surgery on a human heart [. . .]."

OPINION 7. *From paragraph 6:* "White people [. . .] have told us those lies every day for four centuries [. . .]."

OPINION 8. *From paragraph 7:* "People—black and white—will always have expectations."

3F CRITICAL READING: AUTHOR'S STRATEGIES

Choose the best answer.

<u>c</u> 1. Leonard Pitts Jr.'s main audience for "Don't Sell Your Ambitions Short to 'Keep It Real'" is
   a. African-American teenagers and young adults who drop out of school and turn to a life of crime.
   b. African Americans and others who enjoy reading *Gulliver's Travels*, by Jonathan Swift, especially because of its big words.

Name   Date

    c. African Americans and others who might allow their friends to discourage them from getting a good (so-called White) education.

    d. African Americans and others who tease friends and call them names for wanting a good (so-called White) education.

<u> a </u> 2. The author's purpose in writing this reading is to
    a. inform.
    b. narrate.
    c. entertain.
    d. describe.

<u> a </u> 3. The author's tone in this reading is
    a. straightforward.
    b. insulting.
    c. humorous.
    d. sarcastic.

3G READER'S PROCESS: SUMMARIZING YOUR READING

<u> c </u> 1. What is the best summary of "Don't Sell Your Ambitions Short to 'Keep It Real'"?
    a. Leonard Pitts Jr. reacts to being called an "Uncle Tom" because he used the word "Brobdingnagian" in his newspaper column.
    b. Sometimes the road is lonely for people whose goals involve becoming an opera star, an astronaut, or a surgeon.
    c. African-American kids should always try to get the best education they can, even if some people don't like it and try to hold them back.
    d. Equal opportunity in education for all is an important goal, but old lies and prejudice lead many people to oppose the idea.

3H READER'S RESPONSE: TO DISCUSS OR WRITE ABOUT

1. In the movie *Hustle & Flow*, DJay, the central character and a street-smart philosopher, says: "Everybody's got to have a dream." Do you agree with DJay? What role do you think dreams play in someone's achieving a goal or giving it up?

2. In a column in *The Commercial Appeal*, Wendi C. Thomas wrote that several black readers had chastised her for her "bourgeois, uppity ways" when she wrote a review of *Hustle & Flow*. Do you think it is necessary to use slang or community dialect to be accepted by your peers? Why? Should you have to apologize for using standard English? Explain your response.

HOW DID YOU DO?

3 Don't Sell Your Ambitions Short to "Keep It Real"

SKILL (number of items)	Number Correct		Points for each		Score
Vocabulary (8)	_____	×	2	=	_____
Central Theme and Main Ideas (2)	_____	×	8	=	_____
Major Details (5)	_____	×	4	=	_____
Inferences (5)	_____	×	4	=	_____
Critical Reading: Fact or Opinion (8)	_____	×	2	=	_____
Critical Reading: The Author's Strategies (3)	_____	×	3	=	_____
Reader's Process: Summarizing Your Reading (1)	_____	×	3	=	_____

(Possible Total: 100) *Total* _____

SPEED

Reading Time: _____ Reading Rate (page 411): _____ Words Per Minute

Name   Date

Darkness at Noon

Harold Krents

(1) Blind from birth, I have never had the opportunity to see myself and have been completely dependent on the image I create in the eye of the observer. To date it has not been narcissistic.

(2) There are those who assume that since I can't see, I obviously also cannot hear. Very often people will converse with me at the top of their lungs, enunciating each word very carefully. Conversely, people will also often whisper, assuming that since my eyes don't work, my ears don't either. For example, when I go to the airport and ask the ticket agent for assistance to the plane, he or she will invariably pick up the phone, call a ground hostess and whisper, "Hi, Jane, we've got a 76 here." I have concluded that the word "blind" is not used for one of two reasons: Either they fear that if the dread word is spoken, the ticket agent's retina will immediately detach, or they are reluctant to inform me of my condition of which I may not have been previously aware.

(3) On the other hand, others know that of course I can hear, but believe that I can't talk. Often, therefore, when my wife and I go out to dinner, a waiter or waitress will ask Kit if "*he* would like a drink" to which I respond that "indeed *he* would." This point was graphically driven home to me while we were in England. I had been given a year's leave of absence from my Washington law firm to study for a diploma-in-law degree at Oxford University. During the year I became ill and was hospitalized. Immediately after admission, I was wheeled down to the X-ray room. Just at the door sat an elderly woman—elderly I would judge from the sound of her voice. "What is his name?" the woman asked the orderly who had been wheeling me.

Harold Krents, inspiration for the award-winning play and movie "Butterflies Are Free," died of a brain tumor twelve years after he wrote "Darkness at Noon."

New York Times Permissions

"What's your name?" the orderly repeated to me.

"Harold Krents," I replied.

"Harold Krents," he repeated.

"When was he born?"

"When were you born?"

"November 5, 1944," I responded.

"November 5, 1944," the orderly intoned.

(4) This procedure continued for approximately five minutes at which point even my saint-like disposition deserted me. "Look," I finally blurted out, "this is absolutely ridiculous. Okay, granted I can't see, but it's got to have become pretty clear to both of you that I don't need an interpreter."

"He says he doesn't need an interpreter," the orderly reported to the woman.

(5) The toughest misconception of all is the view that because I can't see, I can't work. I was turned down by over forty law firms because of my blindness, even though my qualifications included a cum laude degree from Harvard College and a good ranking in my Harvard Law School class. The attempt to find employment, the continuous frustration of being told that it was impossible for a blind person to practice law, the rejection letters, not based on my lack of ability but rather on my disability, will always remain one of the most disillusioning experiences of my life.

(6) Fortunately, this view of limitation and exclusion is beginning to change. On April 16, 1976, the Department of Labor issued regulations that mandate equal-employment opportunities for the handicapped. By and large, the business community's response to offering employment to the disabled has been enthusiastic.

(7) I therefore look forward to the day, with the expectation that it is certain to come, when employers will view their handicapped workers as a little child did me years ago when my family still lived in Scarsdale. I was playing basketball with my father in our backyard according to procedures we had developed. My father would stand beneath the hoop, shout, and I would shoot over his head at the basket attached to the garage. Our next-door neighbor, aged five, wandered over into our yard with a playmate. "He's blind," our neighbor whispered to her friend in a voice that could be heard distinctly by Dad and me. Dad shot and missed; I did the same. Dad hit the rim: I missed entirely; Dad shot and missed the garage entirely. "Which one is blind?" whispered back the little friend.

(8) I would hope that in the near future when a plant manager is touring the factory with the foreman and comes upon a handicapped and non-handicapped person working together, his comment after watching them work will be, "Which one is disabled?"

(775 words)

Here are some of the more difficult words in "Darkness at Noon."

disillusioning
(paragraph 5)

dis·il·lu·sion (dis′i lo͞o′zhən) *vt.* **1** to free from illusion or false ideas; disenchant **2** to take away the ideals or idealism of and make disappointed, bitter, etc. —*n.* DISILLUSIONMENT

enunciating
(paragraph 2)

enun·ci·ate (ē nun′sē āt′, i-; *also*, -shē-) *vt.* --at′ed, --at′ing ⟦< L *enuntiatus,* pp. of *enuntiare* < *e-,* out + *nuntiare,* to announce < *nuntius,* a messenger⟧ **1** to state definitely; express in a systematic way *[to enunciate a theory]* **2** to announce; proclaim **3** to pronounce (words), esp. clearly and distinctly —*vi.* to pronounce words, esp. clearly and distinctly; articulate —*SYN.* UTTER[2] — **enun′·cia′·tion** (-sē ā′-) *n.* —**enun′·cia·tive** (-āt′iv, -ə tiv) *adj.* —**enun′·cia·tor** *n.*

exclusion
(paragraph 6)

ex·clude (eks klo͞od′, iks-) *vt.* --clud′ed, --clud′ing ⟦ME *excluden* < L *excludere* < *ex-,* out + *claudere,* CLOSE[3]⟧ **1** to refuse to admit, consider, include, etc.; shut out; keep from entering, happening, or being; reject; bar **2** to put out; force out; expel —**ex·clud′·able** *adj.* —**ex·clud′er** *n.*

SYN.—**exclude** implies a keeping out or prohibiting of that which is not yet in *[to exclude someone from membership]*; **debar** connotes the existence of some barrier, as legal authority or force, which excludes someone from a privilege, right, etc. *[to debar certain groups from voting]*; **disbar** refers only to the expulsion of a lawyer from the group of those who are permitted to practice law; **eliminate** implies the removal of that which is already in, usually connoting its undesirability or irrelevance *[to eliminate waste products]*; **suspend** refers to the removal, usually temporary, of someone from some organization, institution, etc., as for the infraction of some rule *[to suspend a student from school]* — *ANT.* admit, include

ex·clu·sion (eks klo͞o′zhən, iks-) *n.* ⟦ME *exclusioun* < L *exclusio* < pp. of *excludere*⟧ **1** an excluding or being excluded **2** a thing excluded —**to the exclusion of** so as to keep out, bar, etc. —**ex·clu′·sion·ar′y** *adj.*

intoned
(paragraph 3)

in·tone (in tōn′) *vt.* --toned′, --ton′ing ⟦ME *entonen* < OFr *entoner* < ML *intonare:* IN-[1] & TONE⟧ **1** to utter or recite in a singing tone or in prolonged monotones; chant **2** to give a particular intonation to **3** to sing or recite the opening phrase of (a chant, canticle, etc.) —*vi.* to speak or recite in a singing tone or in prolonged monotones; chant —**in·ton′er** *n.*

invariably
(paragraph 2)

in·vari·able (in ver′ē ə bəl) *adj.* ⟦ML *invariabilis*⟧ not variable; not changing; constant; uniform —*n.* an invariable quantity; constant —**in·var′i·abil′·ity** *n.* or **in·var′i·able·ness** —**in·var′i·ably** *adv.*

mandate
(paragraph 6)

man·date (man′dāt′) *n.* ⟦L *mandatum,* neut. pp. of *mandare,* lit., to put into one's hand, command, entrust < *manus,* a hand + pp. of *dare,* to give: see MANUAL & DATE[1]⟧ **1** an authoritative order or command, esp. a written one **2** [Historical] *a)* a commission from the League of Nations to a country to administer some region, colony, etc. (cf. TRUSTEESHIP, sense 2) *b)* the area so administered (cf. TRUST TERRITORY) **3** the wishes of constituents expressed to a representative, legislature, etc., as through an election and regarded as an order **4** *Law a)* an order from a higher court or official to a lower one: a **mandate on remission** is a mandate from an appellate court to the lower court, communicating its decision in a case appealed *b)* in English law, a bailment of personal property with no consideration *c)* in Roman law, a commission or contract by which a person undertakes to do something for another, without recompense but with indemnity against loss *d)* any contract of agency —*vt.* --dat′ed, --dat′ing **1** to assign (a region, etc.) as a mandate **2** to require as by law; make mandatory —**man·da′·tor** *n.*

misconception
(paragraph 5)

mis·con·ceive (mis′kən sēv′) *vt., vi.* --ceived′, --ceiv′·ing to conceive wrongly; interpret incorrectly; misunderstand —**mis′·con·cep′·tion** (-sep′shən) *n.*

narcissistic
(paragraph 1)

nar·cis·sism (när′sə siz′əm; *chiefly Brit,* när sis′iz′əm) *n.* 〚Ger *Narzissismus* (< *Narziss,* NARCISSUS) + *-ismus,* -ISM〛 **1** self-love; interest, often excessive interest, in one's own appearance, comfort, importance, abilities, etc. **2** *Psychoanalysis* arrest at or regression to the first stage of libidinal development, in which the self is an object of erotic pleasure Also **nar′·cism′** —**nar′·cis·sist** *n.,* *adj.* —**nar′·cis·sis′·tic** *adj.*

retina
(paragraph 2)

reti·na (ret″n ə) *n., pl.* **--nas** or **--nae′** (-ē′) 〚ML, prob. < L *rete* (gen. *retis*), net < IE base **ere-*, loose, separate > Gr *erēmos,* solitary, Lith *rētis,* sieve & (prob.) L *rarus,* rare〛 the innermost coat lining the interior of the eyeball, containing various layers of photoreceptive cells that are directly connected to the brain by means of the optic nerve: see EYE, illus.

4A   VOCABULARY

Using the dictionary entries on pages 123–124, fill in the blanks.

1. The rear part of the eyeball that is sensitive to light is called the _____retina._____

2. In the United States the _____exclusion_____ of any person from employment because of his race, color, or sex is both illegal and immoral.

3. It is ____disillusioning____ when we discover that a public official has used his or her office to force people to pay bribes.

4. The diplomat spoke precisely, carefully _____enunciating_____ each word clearly for his audience.

5. Some people are so self-centered and convinced of their own importance that they can easily be labeled "_____narcissistic_____."

6. The restaurant owners decided to _____exclude_____ all smokers from the main dining room.

7. The higher court issued a _____mandate_____ that reversed the lower court's ruling concerning discrimination.

8. A person with employable skills will _____invariably_____ have better job opportunities than will a person without such skills.

9. An adult can _____disillusion_____ a child very quickly if that adult sets a bad example by breaking the law or by being cruel to people.

10. At the funeral the minister _____intoned_____ special passages from the Bible.

Name   Date

11. The tenant was acting under the serious ___misconception___ that he
could continue to occupy his apartment without paying rent.

4B   CENTRAL THEME AND MAIN IDEAS

Choose the best answer.

__d__ 1. What is the central theme of "Darkness at Noon"?
- a. The author leads a very fulfilling life as a lawyer and husband.
- b. Blind people often have difficulty finding jobs because employers prefer to hire sighted people.
- c. Handicapped people need to organize and campaign for better laws to protect them.
- d. People often assume that because blind people cannot see, they cannot hear, learn, or work.

__b__ 2. What is the main idea of paragraph 2?
- a. It is generally assumed that people who cannot see cannot hear.
- b. The way that many people behave in the presence of the blind can be described as downright "silly."
- c. Some people think that it is improper to use the word "blind" in the presence of blind people.
- d. Airline personnel use the number "76" to refer to blind people.

__a__ 3. What is the main idea of paragraph 5?
- a. The worst frustration for the author was when 40 or more law firms refused to hire him because he was blind.
- b. Many employers think that if a lawyer cannot see, he or she cannot work.
- c. The author got his undergraduate degree from Harvard College and his law degree from Harvard Law School.
- d. The rejection letters sent to the author were disillusioning.

4C   MAJOR DETAILS

Decide whether each detail is MAJOR or MINOR based on the context of the reading selection.

MAJOR   1. The author has been blind from birth.

MAJOR   2. People often shout at blind people and pronounce every word with great care.

MINOR   3. Airline personnel use a code to refer to blind people.

MINOR   4. The author goes out to dinner with his wife, Kit.

MAJOR   5. If a blind person and a sighted person are together, other people will usually communicate with them by talking with the sighted person.

MINOR   6. The author was given a year's leave of absence from his Washington law firm to study for a diploma-in-law degree at Oxford University.

MINOR   7. The author had to be hospitalized while he was studying in England.

MAJOR   8. In 1976 the Department of Labor issued regulations that require equal employment opportunities for the handicapped.

MAJOR   9. On the whole, the business community's response to offering employment to the handicapped has been enthusiastic.

MINOR 10. The author and his father played basketball in the backyard using a special system they had worked out.

MINOR 11. The author's father shot for the basket and missed completely.

MAJOR 12. The neighbor's friend was not sure if the author or his father was blind.

4D   INFERENCES

Decide whether each statement can be inferred (YES) or cannot be inferred (NO) from the reading selection.

YES   1. The title of the essay suggests that it is sighted people, not blind people, who cannot "see."

NO   2. The author feels that he is greatly admired by people who meet him.

YES   3. The author feels that he can make his point more effectively with humor than with a stern lecture.

NO   4. The author often eats in restaurants with his wife, Kit.

NO   5. The author was highly entertained by the conversation in the hospital between the elderly lady and the orderly.

NO   6. The author got good grades at Harvard Law School because he was given special privileges reserved for blind students.

NO   7. The April 10, 1976, Department of Labor regulations were enacted because the author had complained publicly about the discrimination he experienced while looking for a job.

Name   Date

NO 8. The author's father was a much better basketball player than was the author.

4E CRITICAL READING: FACT OR OPINION

Decide whether each statement contains a FACT or an OPINION.

FACT 1. *From paragraph 1:* "Blind from birth, I have never had the opportunity to see myself [. . .]."

OPINION 2. *From paragraph 2:* "[. . .] they fear that if the dread word is spoken, the ticket agent's retina will immediately detach [. . .]."

FACT 3. *From paragraph 3:* "I had been given a year's leave of absence from my Washington law firm to study for a diploma-in-law degree at Oxford University."

FACT 4. *From paragraph 5:* "I was turned down by over forty law firms because of my blindness [. . .]."

OPINION 5. *From paragraph 6:* "By and large, the business community's response to offering employment to the disabled has been enthusiastic."

FACT 6. *From paragraph 7:* "Dad shot [the basketball] and missed the garage entirely."

4F CRITICAL READING: THE AUTHOR'S STRATEGIES

Choose the best answer.

c 1. The main audience for "Darkness at Noon" is
   a. people who have been discriminated against.
   b. people who do not trust blind people.
   c. people who enjoy stories of achievement.
   d. people who have treated the disabled badly.

c 2. The author's purpose in writing this essay is to
   a. narrate.
   b. entertain.
   c. expose.
   d. describe.

d 3. The author's tone in this reading is
   a. objective.
   b. happy.
   c. arrogant.
   d. emotional.

4G READER'S PROCESS: SUMMARIZING YOUR READING

  b   1. What is the best summary of "Darkness at Noon"?
   a. Harold Krents tells how his life is frustrating because of his blindness and how the government is changing the laws to make his life better.
   b. Harold Krents tells how people discriminated against him in his everyday life and in his employment search due to his blindness and how attitudes and perceptions of the disabled are slowly changing for the better.
   c. Harold Krents tells how employers refused to hire him because of his blindness even though he graduated from Harvard.
   d. Harold Krents tells how annoying people were to him because of his blindness and how federal regulations are making his life and the lives of other disabled people much easier.

4H READER'S RESPONSE: TO DISCUSS OR WRITE ABOUT

1. How do you think physically handicapped people feel when they have to be with people who "can't see the person behind the handicap"? Using specific examples, explain your ideas fully.

2. In recent years our society has started to pay more attention to the needs of people who are physically handicapped. Do you think that society is doing enough? Using specific examples, explain your point of view.

HOW DID YOU DO?

4 **Darkness at Noon**

SKILL (number of items)	Number Correct		Points for each		Score
Vocabulary (11)	_____	×	3	=	_____
Central Theme and Main Ideas (3)	_____	×	4	=	_____
Major Details (12)	_____	×	2	=	_____
Inferences (8)	_____	×	2	=	_____
Critical Reading: Fact or Opinion (6)	_____	×	1	=	_____
Critical Reading: The Author's Strategies (3)	_____	×	2	=	_____
Reader's Process: Summarizing Your Reading (1)	_____	×	3	=	_____

(Possible Total: 100) *Total* _____

SPEED

Reading Time: _____ Reading Rate (page 411): _____ Words Per Minute

Selection 5

To Catch a Thief

Stephen Holt

(1) Several months ago, I began noticing the business section missing from my *New York Times*, which I have delivered to my home on Gramercy Park. I presumed the deliveryman was at fault and sent several indignant e-mails to customer service. I was repeatedly assured that the paper was being delivered intact. Gradually, it occurred to me that a neighbor might be stealing it.

(2) My wife suggested that I post a note in the lobby stating: "Please Stop Taking My Business Section." Although I agreed that this might deter the person, it would have done nothing to satisfy me. Since I am president of a company and an involved father of two boys, my morning train ride is one of few moments in the day that I have to read the paper, which is typically on top of a stack on a table in our lobby. I needed to confront the person depriving me of this simple pleasure. I needed justice. I decided to try a stakeout.

(3) On my third attempt, I hit pay dirt. The sanctity of my paper had been violated twice that week. From a back hallway, I watched a neighbor stop and peruse my paper before leaving. Ten minutes later he returned with dry cleaning in hand. Then, in a quick, snakelike motion, he grabbed my paper and jumped into the elevator. Prepared to confront someone exiting the building, I was not anticipating this turn of events. To catch him red-handed, I would have to race up many flights of stairs and beat the elevator to his floor. Harking back to my track years in boarding school, I took off like a rocket and reached his floor as the elevator door opened. Snatching the paper from his hands, I saw my name on the address label. Pumped with adrenaline from my sprint, I unleashed a tirade of epithets. I then produced a camera from my back pocket and snapped a picture of him. Disoriented by the sudden onslaught, he began to apologize. I said that I was going to have him evicted and that I would file charges with the police. "Isn't there something we can do to keep this between us?" he asked. I told him he was a sociopath, that this was the biggest mistake of his life.

(4) Shortly thereafter, a note appeared under my door: "I want to formally apologize for taking your newspaper this morning. It was completely careless and based totally in laziness on my part. . . . I am absolutely prepared to do whatever it takes to make amends with you. I hope we can solve this between the two of us, without the involvement of the building and/or the authorities."

(5) I knew that he could afford to buy his own newspaper. I went to the police. The next morning I wrote this response: "Thank you for your note. I believe that you are sorry about what happened. I also believe that this feeling stems more from getting caught than from a genuine sense of contrition for your actions. You wrote that taking my paper was 'careless.' I believe it was carelessness that allowed me to catch you in the act of pilfering. I would use such words as dishonest and insensitive to describe your actions. Getting on the 6 train only to find that the business section is missing *again* is an incredible aggravation.

(6) "I have met with a detective from the 13th Precinct. He informed me that I could have you arrested for misdemeanor petit larceny. He said you would be put in handcuffs and brought to the police station. I agreed to a cooling-off period. . . . There is also the option of petitioning the co-op board to have you evicted. If this were an isolated occasion, I could accept your apology at face value. That this has been a recurring problem, and the premeditated way in which I saw you take my paper, makes resolution more difficult. I welcome your suggestions."

(7) Two days later he replied: "Thank you for your note. Thank you for being open to a dialogue towards resolution to this thoughtless and utterly embarrassing incident. I want you to know that I love living in [our building]. With this exception, I have been a model tenant and solid citizen of the community. The last thing I would wish to do is foster a sense of ill will, deception or animosity in an otherwise idyllic environment. I am truly sorry. As far as resolution and restitution go . . . broken trust and loss of (potential) friendship are not easily repaired. . . . It is up to me to do everything in my power to rectify this issue. . . . I would like to purchase a new one-year subscription to *The New York Times* for you. Please accept the enclosed check for $384. I do not expect money to repair the loss of trust or respect. I hope you might view this as a good faith gesture on my part to make amends and move forward."

(8) Left with the question of how to proceed, I solicited the advice of friends. Those who had been victims of similar crimes felt I should make an example of him and pursue arrest. Others felt that the humiliation of being caught was enough and that I should cash the check and move on. I began this process, however, not for monetary gain, nor with the intention of ruining someone's life. For me, justice was found in catching the thief in the act. Restitution came in the profound humiliation he experienced. I decided to endorse his check to *The New York Times* to buy *him* a one-year subscription. He will now know that a few hundred dollars cannot erase past transgressions. His paper will be a daily reminder of his crime, and will serve as an insurance policy against future newspaper theft in our building (at least until his subscription runs out).

(986 words)

Here are some of the more difficult words in "To Catch a Thief."

Vocabulary List

animosity
(paragraph 7)

ani·mos·ity (an'ə mäs'ə tē) *n., pl.* **-ties** 〖ME *animosite* < L *animositas*, boldness, spirit < *animosus*, spirited < *animus*: see fol.〗 a feeling of strong dislike or hatred; ill will; hostility —*SYN.* ENMITY

contrition
(paragraph 5)

con·tri·tion (kən trish'ən) *n.* 〖ME *contricioun* < OFr *contrition* < LL(Ec) *contritio*, grief: see prec.〗 **1** remorse for having done wrong **2** *Theol.* sorrow for having offended God: **perfect contrition** is such sorrow arising out of pure love of God —*SYN.* PENITENCE

epithets
(paragraph 3)

epi·thet (ep'ə thet', -thət) *n.* 〖L *epitheton* < Gr, lit., that which is added < *epitithenai*, to put on, add < *epi-*, on + *tithenai*, to put, DO[1]〗 **1** an adjective, noun, or phrase, often specif. a disparaging one, used to characterize some person or thing (Ex.: "egghead" for an intellectual) **2** a descriptive name or title (Ex.: Philip the Fair; America the Beautiful) —**epi·thet'ic** *adj.* or **epi·thet'i·cal**

indignant
(paragraph 1)

in·dig·nant (in dig'nənt) *adj.* 〖L *indignans*, prp. of *indignari*, to consider as unworthy or improper, be displeased at < *in-*, not + *dignari*, to deem worthy < *dignus*, worthy: see DIGNITY〗 feeling or expressing anger or scorn, esp. at unjust, mean, or ungrateful action or treatment —**in·dig'·nantly** *adv.*

larceny
(paragraph 6)

lar·ceny (lär'sə nē) *n., pl.* **-nies** 〖ME < Anglo-Fr *larcin* < OFr *larrecin* < L *latrocinium* < *latrocinari*, to rob, plunder < *latro*, mercenary soldier, robber < Gr *latrōn* < *latron*, wages, pay < IE *lēi-*, to possess, acquire > OE *læs*, landed property〗 *Law* the taking of personal property without consent and with the intention of permanently depriving the owner of it; theft: in some states of the U.S., and formerly in England, larceny in which the value of the property equals or exceeds a specified amount is *grand larceny*, and larceny involving lesser amounts is *petit* (or *petty*) *larceny* —*SYN.* THEFT —**lar'·cenist** *n.* or **lar'·cener** —**lar'·cenous** *adj.* —**lar'·cenous·ly** *adv.*

misdemeanor
(paragraph 6)

mis·de·mean·or (mis'də mēn'ər) *n.* 〖MIS-[1] + DEMEANOR〗 **1** [Rare] the act of misbehaving **2** *Law* any minor offense, as the breaking of a municipal ordinance, for which statute provides a lesser punishment than for a felony: the penalty is usually a fine or imprisonment for a short time (usually less than one year) in a local jail, workhouse, etc.: Brit. sp. **mis'·de·mean'·our**

peruse
(paragraph 3)

pe·ruse (pə rōōz') *vt.* **··rused'**, **··rus'·ing** 〖LME *perusen*, to use up, prob. < L *per-*, intens. + ME *usen*, to USE〗 **1** [Obs.] to examine in detail; scrutinize **2** to read carefully or thoroughly; study **3** to read in a casual or leisurely way —**pe·rus'er** *n.*

restitution
(paragraph 7)

res·ti·tu·tion (res'tə tōō'shən, -tyōō'-) *n.* 〖ME < MFr < L *restitutio* < *restitutus*, pp. of *restituere*, to set up again, restore < *re-*, again + *statuere*, to set up: see STATUE〗 **1** a giving back to the rightful owner of something that has been lost or taken away; restoration **2** a making good for loss or damage; reimbursement **3** a return to a former condition or situation **4** *Physics* the recovery of its shape by an elastic body after pressure or strain is released —*SYN.* REPARATION —**res'·ti·tu'·tive** *adj.*

sociopath
(paragraph 3)

so·cio·path (sō'sē ə path', -shē-) *n.* 〖SOCIO- + (PSYCHO)PATH〗 a person suffering from psychopathic personality, whose behavior is aggressively antisocial —**so'·cio·path'ic** *adj.*

stakeout
(paragraph 2)

stake·out (-out') *n.* **1** the staking out of police, etc. in a surveillance of a location, suspected criminal, etc. **2** an area so staked out

tirade
(paragraph 3)

ti·rade (tī'rād', tī rād') *n.* 〖Fr < It *tirata*, a volley < pp. of *tirare*, to draw, fire < VL *tirare*〗 a long, vehement speech, esp. one of denunciation; harangue

transgressions
(paragraph 8)

trans·gres·sion (-gresh'ən) *n.* the act or an instance of transgressing; breach of a law, duty, etc.; sin

5A   VOCABULARY

Using the vocabulary on page 133, *fill in this crossword puzzle.*

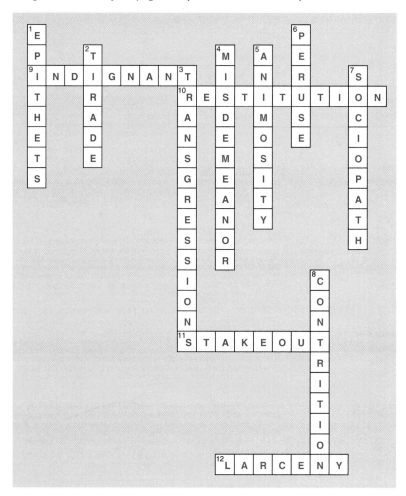

Across

9. expressing anger
10. returning what has been stolen
11. keeping a close watch on an area
12. theft

Down

1. disrespectful remarks
2. a long speech
3. breaking laws
4. a minor offense
5. hatred or ill will
6. examine closely
7. person who exhibits ill will
8. remorse for having done wrong

Name   Date

5B CENTRAL THEME AND MAIN IDEAS

Choose the best answer.

_d_ 1. What is the central theme of "To Catch a Thief"?
   a. A New Yorker steals the *New York Times* business section from the building's lobby.
   b. John Holt decides not to prosecute the neighbor for stealing the *New York Times.*
   c. The thief offers John Holt money to avoid prosecution for misdemeanor petit larceny.
   d. To get justice, John Holt sets up a stakeout, confronts the thief, and gets revenge.

_b_ 2. What is the main idea of paragraph 2?
   a. Stephen Holt's wife offers her husband a suggestion to deter newspaper theft.
   b. To see justice prevail, Stephen Holt devises a plan to catch the newspaper thief.
   c. The thief steals only the business section of the *New York Times.*
   d. Stephen Holt reads the *New York Times* on Train 6 every morning.

5C MAJOR DETAILS

Number the following details from the story according to the order in which they occurred. Number the events 1 to 11, with 1 next to the event that happened first.

_6_ 1. Stephen Holt confronts a neighbor with the stolen newspaper at the elevator door.

_2_ 2. Stephen Holt writes e-mails to customer service to complain about the missing newspaper.

_4_ 3. Stephen Holt suspects the possibility of a neighbor's stealing the newspaper.

_8_ 4. Stephen Holt meets with a detective at the 13th Precinct.

_10_ 5. The thief writes Stephen Holt a second note and includes a check for a one-year subscription to the *New York Times.*

_11_ 6. Stephen Holt endorses check and has one-year subscription to the *New York Times* sent to the thief.

_9_ 7. Stephen Holt writes a note to the thief and accuses the thief of carelessness, not remorse.

_7_ 8. Stephen Holt receives a note of apology from the neighbor who offers to make amends.

  5   9. After several attempts to catch the thief, Stephen Holt sees a neighbor steal his paper.

  3   10. The *New York Times* assures Stephen Holt that the deliveryman is not at fault.

  1   11. Stephen Holt notices the business section missing from the *New York Times*.

5D INFERENCES

Decide whether each statement can be inferred (YES) or cannot be inferred (NO) from the reading selection.

 NO 1. Stephen Holt's neighbor liked stealing newspapers.

 NO 2. Stephen Holt's neighbor stole only Holt's newspaper from the lobby.

 NO 3. Stephen Holt rode the train to his company because he did not own a car.

 YES 4. Stephen Holt felt great satisfaction in catching his neighbor with the stolen newspaper.

 YES 5. Until he was caught, the neighbor never realized the seriousness of stealing a newspaper.

 YES 6. The neighbor worried that Stephen Holt might convince the co-op board to have him evicted from the building.

 YES 7. The neighbor is unlikely to steal a newspaper from the building's lobby again.

 NO 8. Stephen Holt wrote a note of apology to customer service for mistakenly thinking the deliveryman was at fault for the missing newspaper section.

5E CRITICAL READING: FACT OR OPINION

Decide whether each statement, even if it quotes someone, contains a FACT or an OPINION.

OPINION 1. *From paragraph 2:* "I needed justice."

FACT 2. *From paragraph 3:* "On my third attempt, I hit pay dirt."

OPINION 3. *From paragraph 3:* [. . .] he was a sociopath [. . .].

OPINION 4. *From paragraph 5:* "I believe it was carelessness that allowed me to catch you in the act of pilfering."

Name   Date

<u>FACT</u> 5. *From paragraph 6:* "I agreed to a cooling off period."

<u>OPINION</u> 6. *From paragraph 7:* "With this exception, I have been a model tenant and solid citizen of the community."

<u>OPINION</u> 7. *From paragraph 7:* "[. . .] broken trust and loss of (potential) friendship are not easily repaired [. . .]."

<u>OPINION</u> 8. *From paragraph 8:* "His paper [. . .] will serve as an insurance policy against future newspaper theft in our building [. . .]."

5F CRITICAL READING: THE AUTHOR'S STRATEGIES

Choose the best answer.

  <u>c</u>   1. Stephen Holt's main audience for "To Catch a Thief" is
   a. the complaint department of his newspaper delivery service.
   b. other residents in his apartment building whose newspapers are delivered.
   c. readers of a newspaper or magazine for general readers.
   d. his newspaper-stealing neighbor and, eventually, his family.

  <u>c</u>   2. The author's purpose in writing this reading is to
   a. describe.
   b. narrate.
   c. expose.
   d. entertain.

  <u>c</u>   3. The author's tone in this reading is
   a. confused.
   b. objective.
   c. unforgiving.
   d. amused.

5G READER'S PROCESS: SUMMARIZING YOUR READING

  <u>c</u>   1. What is the best summary of "To Catch a Thief"?
   a. A man tells how he uncovers the thief of the business section of his copy of the *New York Times*, which is delivered to him daily, and then decides to report him to the police.
   b. A man tells how angry and frustrated he became over not being able to discover the identity of the person who daily has been stealing the business section of his delivered copy of the *New York Times*.
   c. A man tells how he dealt with the person in the apartment building where he lives who daily was stealing the business section of his delivered copy of the *New York Times*.

d. A man tells how he decided to write a letter to his neighbors to publicly embarrass the thief who steals the business section of his daily delivered copy of the *New York Times*.

5H   READER'S RESPONSE: TO DISCUSS OR WRITE ABOUT

1. Petit larceny is often defined as the theft of another's property or money under the value of five hundred dollars. If convicted, the person could be imprisoned (not to exceed six months) or fined (not to exceed one thousand dollars). If you had been Stephen Holt, would you have pursued prosecution of the neighbor for stealing the newspaper? If "yes," then what would be your reasons for doing so? If "no," then why would you not pursue action?

2. Until recently people could pump gasoline for their vehicles and then pay the cashier after they had filled up their tanks. Most stations today require a prepay at the pump with a credit card or a cash deposit held by the cashier. Pumping gas into a car and then driving off without paying for the gasoline is theft. Why do you think people would risk losing their drivers' licenses and receiving a fine for a tank of gas?

Name   Date

HOW DID YOU DO?

5 To Catch a Thief

SKILL (number of items)	Number Correct		Points for each		Score
Vocabulary (12)	_____	×	2	=	_____
Central Theme and Main Ideas (2)	_____	×	7	=	_____
Major Details (11)	_____	×	2	=	_____
Inferences (8)	_____	×	2	=	_____
Critical Reading: Fact or Opinion (8)	_____	×	2	=	_____
Critical Reading: The Author's Strategies (3)	_____	×	2	=	_____
Reader's Process: Summarizing Your Reading (1)	_____	×	2	=	_____

(Possible Total: 100) *Total* _____

SPEED

Reading Time: _____ Reading Rate (page 411): _____ Words Per Minute

Name   Date

Seoul Searching

Rick Reilly

(1) After 11 years and 6,000 miles, we still hadn't met our daughter's mother. We had come only this close: staked out in a van across from a tiny Seoul coffee shop, the mother inside with a Korean interpreter, afraid to come out, afraid of being discovered, afraid to meet her own flesh.

(2) Inside the van, Rae, our 11-year-old Korean adopted daughter, was trying to make sense of it. How could we have flown the entire family 6,000 miles from Denver to meet a woman who was afraid to walk 20 yards across the street to meet us? Why had we come this far if she was only going to reject Rae again? We were told we had an hour. There were 40 minutes left. The cell phone rang. "Drive the van to the alley behind the coffee shop," said the interpreter. "And wait."

(3) When a four-month-old-Rae was hand-delivered to us at Gate B-7 at Denver's Stapleton Airport, we knew someday we would be in Korea trying to find her birth mother. We just never dreamed it would be this soon. Then again, since Rae was a toddler, we've told her she was adopted, and she has constantly asked about her birth mother. "Do you think my birth mother plays the piano like I do? "Do you think my birth mother is pretty?" And then, at 10, after a day of too many stares: a teary "I just want to meet someone I'm related to." "When they start asking that," the adoption therapist said, "you can start looking."

(4) We started looking. We asked the agency that had arranged the adoption, Friends of Children of Various Nations, to begin a search. Within six months our caseworker, Kim Matsunaga, told us they had found the birth mother but she was highly reluctant to meet us. She had never told anyone about Rae. In Korea, the shame of unwed pregnancy is huge. The mother is disowned, the baby rootless. Kim guessed she had told her parents she was moving to the city to work and had gone to a home for unwed mothers.

(5) Kim told us the agency was taking a group of Colorado and New Mexico families to Korea in the summer to meet birth relatives. She said if we went, Rae's would probably show up. "The birth mothers almost always show up," she said, Almost. We were unsure. And then we talked to a family who had gone the year before. They said it would be wonderful. At the very least, Rae would meet her foster mother, who had cared for her those four months. She would meet the doctor who delivered her. Hell, I had never met the doctor who delivered me. But meeting the birth mother was said to be the sweetest. A 16-year-old Korean-American girl told Rae, "I don't know, it just kinda fills a hole in your heart." We risked it. Five plane tickets to Seoul for our two redheaded

birth boys —Kellen, 15, and Jake, 13 — Rae, me and my wife Linda. We steeled Rae for the chance that her birth mother wouldn't show up. Come to think of it, we steeled ourselves.

(6) At first, it was wonderful. We met Rae's foster mother, who swooped in and rushed for Rae as if she were her long-lost daughter, which she almost was. She bear-hugged her. She stroked her hair. She touched every little nick and scar on her tan arms and legs. "What's this from?" she asked in Korean. She had fostered 31 babies, but it was as if she'd known only Rae. Rae was half grossed out, half purring. Somebody had just rushed in with the missing four months of her life. The foster mother wept. We wept.

(7) All of us, all six American families, sat in one room at a home for unwed mothers outside Seoul across from 25 unwed mothers, some who had just given up their babies, some soon to. They looked into unmet children's futures. We looked into our unmet birth mothers' pasts. A 17-year-old Korean-American girl—roughly the same age as the distraught girls in front of her—rose and choked out, "I know it's hard for you now, but I want you to know I love my American family." Another 17-year-old adoptee met not only her birth father but also her four elder birth sisters. They were still a family—had always been one—but they had given her up as one mouth too many to feed. Then they told her that her birth mother had died of an aneurysm two weeks earlier. So how was she supposed to feel now? Joy at finding her father and her sisters? Grief at 17 years without them? Anger at being given up? Gratitude for her American parents? Horror at coming so close to and then losing her birth mother? We heard her story that night on the tour bus, went to our hotel room and wept some more.

(8) All these kids—even the three who never found their birth relatives—were piecing together the puzzle of their lives at whiplash speed. This is where you were born. This is the woman who held you. This was the city, the food, the smells. For them, it was two parts home ("It's so nice," Rae said amid a throng of Koreans on a street. "For once, people are staring at Kel and Jake instead of me") and three parts I'm-never-coming-here-again (a teenage boy ate dinner at his foster parents' home only to discover in mid-bite that they raise dogs for meat).

(9) When the day came for our visit with Rae's birth mother we were told "It has to be handled very, very carefully." She had three children by a husband she had never told about Rae, and she was terribly afraid someone would see her. And that's how we found ourselves hiding in that van like Joe Friday, waiting for the woman of a lifetime to show up. It is a very odd feeling to be staring holes in every Korean woman walking down a Korean street, thinking that your daughter may have sprung from her womb. All we knew about her was that she 1) might have her newborn girl with her, 2) was tiny—the birth certificate said she was 4 ft. 10 in.—and 3) would look slightly more nervous than a cat burglar.

(10) First came a youngish, chic woman pushing a stroller. "That might be her!" yelled Rae—until she strolled by. Then a short, fat woman with a baby tied at her stomach. "There she is!" yelled Rae—until she got on a bus. Then a pretty, petite woman in yellow with an infant in a baby carrier. "I know that's her!" yelled Rae—and lo and behold, the woman quick-stepped into the coffee shop across the street. The only problem was, she didn't come out. She stayed in that coffee shop, talking to the interpreter for what seemed like six hours but was probably only 20 minutes. We stared at the dark windows of the shop. We stared at the cell phone. We stared at one another. What was this, Panmunjom? Finally, the interpreter called Kim: Drive down the alley and wait. We drove down the alley and waited. Nothing.

(11) By this time, I could have been the centerfold for *Psychology Today*. Rae was still calm. I told her, "If she's not out here in five minutes, I want you to walk right in and introduce yourself." Rae swallowed. Suddenly, at the van window . . . and now, opening the van door . . . the woman in yellow with the baby. And just as suddenly, inside . . . sitting next to her daughter. Our daughter—all of ours. She was nervous. She wouldn't look at us, only at her baby and the interpreter. "We'll go somewhere," said the interpreter. Where do you go with your deepest, darkest secret? We went to a park. Old Korean men looked up from their chess games in astonishment to see a gaggle of whites and redheads and Koreans sit down at the table next to them with cameras, gifts and notebooks. Rae presented her birth mother with a book she had made about her life—full of childhood pictures and purple-penned poems—but the woman showed no emotion as she looked at it. Rae presented her with a silver locket—a picture of herself inside—but again, no eye contact, no hugs, no touches. The woman was either guarding her heart now the way she'd done 11 years ago, or she simply didn't care anymore, maybe had never cared.

(12) Months before, Rae had drawn up a list of 20 questions she wanted to ask at the big moment. Now, unruffled, she pulled it out of her little purse. Some of us forgot to breathe. "Why did you give me up?" Rae asked simply. All heads turned to the woman. The interpreted answer: Too young, only 19 then, no money, great shame. "Where is my birth dad?" The answer: No idea. Only knew him for two dates. Long gone. Still no emotion. I ached for Rae. How would she handle such iciness from the woman she had dreamed of, fantasized about, held on to? Finally, this one: "When I was born, did you get to hold me?" The woman's lips parted in a small gasp. She swallowed and stared at the grass. "No," she said slowly, "they took you from me." And that's when our caseworker, Kim, said, "Well, now you can." That did it. That broke her. She lurched, tears running down her cheeks, reached for Rae and pulled her close, holding her as if they might take her again. "I told myself I wouldn't cry," she said. The interpreter wept. Linda wept. I wept. Right then, right that minute, the heavens opened up, and it poured a monsoon starter kit on us, just an all-out Noah. Yeah, even the sky wept.

(13) Any sane group of people would have run for the van, but none of us wanted the moment to end. We had finally got her, and we would float to Pusan before we would give her up. We were all crying and laughing and trying to fit all of us under the birth mother's tiny pink umbrella. But the rain was so loud you couldn't talk. We ran for the van and sat in there, Rae holding her half sister and her birth mother holding the daughter she must have thought she would never see. Time was so short. Little sentences contained whole lifetimes. She thanked us for raising her baby. "You are a very good family," she said, eyeing the giants around her. "Very strong and good." And how do you thank someone for giving you her daughter? Linda said, "Thank you for the gift you gave us." The birth mother smiled bitter sweetly. She held Rae with one arm and the book and the locket tight with the other.

(14) Then it was over. She said she had to get back. She asked the driver to pull over so she could get out. We started pleading for more time. Meet us for dinner? No. Breakfast tomorrow? No. Send you pictures? Please, no. The van stopped at a red light. Somebody opened the door. She kissed Rae on the head, stroked her hair one last time, stepped out, finally let go of her hand and closed the door. The light turned green. We drove off and watched her shrink away from us, dropped off on the corner of Nowhere and Forever. I think I was still crying when I looked at Rae. She was beaming, of course, which must be how you feel when a hole in your heart finally gets filled.

(1,956 words)

Here are some of the more difficult words in "Seoul Searching."

<table>
<tr><td>aneurysm
(paragraph 7)</td><td>aneu·rysm or aneu·rism (an'yōō riz'əm, -yə-) n. ⟦ModL aneur-isma < Gr aneurysma < ana-, up + eurys, broad: see EURY-⟧ a sac formed by local enlargement of the weakened wall of an artery, a vein, or the heart, caused by disease or injury —an'eu·rys'·mal adj. or an'eu·ris'·mal (-riz'məl)</td></tr>
<tr><td>chic
(paragraph 10)</td><td>chic (shēk) n. ⟦Fr, orig., subtlety < MLowG schick, order, skill or MHG schicken, behavior, arrangement⟧ smart elegance of style and manner: said esp. of women or their clothes —☆adj. stylish in a smart, pleasing way</td></tr>
<tr><td>disowned
(paragraph 4)</td><td>dis·own (dis ōn') vt. to refuse to acknowledge as one's own; repudi-ate; cast off</td></tr>
<tr><td>distraught
(paragraph 7)</td><td>dis·traught (di strôt') adj. ⟦ME, var. of prec.⟧ 1 extremely trou-bled; mentally confused; distracted; harassed 2 driven mad; crazed —SYN. ABSENT-MINDED</td></tr>
</table>

Vocabulary List

Vocabulary List

foster
(paragraph 6)

fos·ter (fôs'tər, fäs'-) **vt.** ⟦ME *fostren* < OE *fostrian*, to nourish, bring up < *fostor*, food, nourishment < base of *foda*, FOOD⟧ **1** to bring up with care; rear **2** to help to grow or develop; stimulate; promote [to *foster* discontent] **3** to cling to in one's mind; cherish [*foster* a hope] —**adj. 1** having the standing of a specified member of the family, though not by birth or adoption, and giving, receiving, or sharing the care appropriate to that standing [*foster* parent, *foster* brother] **2** designating or relating to such care —**fos'·terer** *n.*

gaggle
(paragraph 11)

gag·gle (gag'əl) **n.** ⟦ME *gagel* < *gagelen*, to cackle: orig. echoic⟧ **1** a flock of geese **2** any group or cluster

grossed
(paragraph 6)

gross (grōs) **adj.** ⟦ME *grose* < OFr *gros*, big, thick, coarse < LL *grossus*, thick⟧ **1** big or fat and coarse-looking; corpulent; burly **2** glaring; flagrant; very bad [a *gross* miscalculation] **3** dense; thick **4** *a*) lacking fineness, as in texture *b*) lacking fine distinctions or specific details **5** lacking in refinement or perception; insensitive; dull **6** vulgar; obscene; coarse [*gross* language] **7** [Slang] unpleasant, disgusting, offensive, etc. **8** with no deductions; total; entire [*gross* income]: opposed to NET² **9** [Archaic] evident; obvious —**n.** ⟦ME *groos* < OFr *grosse*, orig. fem. of *gros*⟧ **1** *pl.* **gross'es** overall total, as of income, before deductions are taken **2** *pl.* **gross** twelve dozen —**vt., vi.** to earn (a specified total amount) before expenses are deducted —**SYN.** COARSE —**gross out** [Slang] to disgust, shock, offend, etc. —**in the gross 1** in bulk; as a whole **2** wholesale: also **by the gross** —**gross'ly adv.** —**gross'·ness** *n.*

lurched
(paragraph 12)

lurch¹ (lurch) **vi.** ⟦< ?⟧ **1** to roll, pitch, or sway suddenly forward or to one side **2** to stagger —**n.** ⟦earlier *lee-lurch* < ?⟧ a lurching movement; sudden rolling, pitching, etc.
lurch² (lurch) **vi.** ⟦ME *lorchen*, var. of LURK⟧ [Obs.] to remain furtively near a place; lurk —**vt. 1** [Archaic] to prevent (a person) from getting his fair share of something **2** [Obs.] to get by cheating, robbing, tricking, etc. —**n.** [Obs.] the act of lurching —**lie at** (or **on**) **the lurch** [Archaic] to lie in wait
lurch³ (lurch) **n.** ⟦Fr *lourche*, name of a 16th-c. game like backgammon, prob. < OFr, duped < MDu *lurz*, left (hand), hence unlucky, akin to MHG *lërz*, left, *lürzen*, to deceive⟧ [Archaic] a situation in certain card games, in which the winner has more than double the score of the loser —**leave someone in the lurch** to leave someone in a difficult situation; leave someone in trouble and needing help

monsoon
(paragraph 12)

mon·soon (män sōōn') **n.** ⟦MDu *monssoen* < Port *monção* < Ar *mausim*, a time, a season⟧ **1** a seasonal wind of the Indian Ocean and S Asia, blowing from the southwest from April to October, and from the northeast during the rest of the year **2** the season during which this wind blows from the southwest, characterized by heavy rains **3** any wind that reverses its direction seasonally or blows constantly between land and adjacent water —**mon·soon'al adj.**

petite
(paragraph 10)

pe·tite (pə tēt') **adj.** ⟦Fr, fem. of *petit*⟧ small and trim in figure: said of a woman —**SYN.** SMALL —**pe·tite'·ness** *n.*

rootless
(paragraph 4)

root·less (-lis) **adj.** having no roots or no stabilizing ties, as to society —**root'·lessly adv.** —**root'·less·ness** *n.*

6A   VOCABULARY

Using the dictionary entries on pages 144–145 , fill in the blank.

1. The model wore a _____chic_____ gown designed by the late American designer Patrick Kelly.

2. The father _____disowned_____ his wayward son so that he would not receive any of the family inheritance.

3. Because he did not know his birth parents, the child felt _____rootless._____

4. Many people are _____grossed_____ out by horror movies that show blood and guts.

5. _____Distraught_____ from grief, the young widow flung herself over-board.

6. If left untreated, an _____aneurysm_____ generally results in death.

7. The Balinese dancers are very slight and _____petite._____

8. A _____monsoon_____ generally includes strong winds and heavy rains.

9. Before children are adopted, they often live with a _____foster_____ parent.

10. A _____gaggle_____ of eager shoppers crowded outside the store, waiting for the doors to open.

11. The bicyclist _____lurched_____ forward when he hit a deep hole in the street.

6B   CENTRAL THEME AND MAIN IDEAS

Choose the best answer

__d__ 1. What is the central theme of "Seoul Searching"?
   a. The Reillys adopted a four-month-old baby girl from Korea.
   b. In Korea, having a child out of wedlock is considered a disgrace.
   c. An adoption agency arranged for a group of adopted children to meet their birth parents.
   d. At the age of eleven, Rae's constant desire to meet her birth mother came true.

Name   Date

__b__ 2. What is the main idea of paragraph 3?
   a. The Reillys picked up four-month-old Rae at Denver's Stapleton Airport.
   b. Rae's constant desire to know about her birth mother sent the Reillys back to Korea sooner than they expected.
   c. The Reillys could not answer Rae's unending questions she asked about her birth mother.
   d. From the time she was a toddler, the Reillys told Rae she was adopted.

__c__ 3. What is the main idea of paragraph 11?
   a. As the family waited in an alley, Rick Reilly was nervous, but Rae was calm.
   b. Holding a baby, a woman dressed in yellow appeared at the van window.
   c. The interpreter finally convinced the birth mother to meet the daughter she had never seen.
   d. Because she was nervous, the birth mother looked only at her baby and the interpreter.

6C   MAJOR DETAILS

Decide whether each detail is MAJOR or MINOR based on the context of the reading selection.

MAJOR   1. The Reillys flew 6,000 miles from Colorado to Korea for Rae to meet her birth mother.

MAJOR   2. Friends of Children of Various Nations began a search to find Rae's birth mother.

MINOR   3. Kim Matsanaga was the caseworker assigned to locate Rae's birth mother.

MAJOR   4. The birth mother was very reluctant to meet Rae and her adoptive parents.

MINOR   5. Rae's foster mother had looked after thirty-one babies at the home.

MINOR   6. Rae's birth mother had three other children.

MINOR   7. The interpreter was to meet the birth mother in a coffee shop.

MAJOR   8. Rae's birth mother showed no emotion when Rae began asking her questions.

MINOR   9. Rae had a list of twenty questions to ask her birth mother.

MINOR   10. A heavy rain drenched the Reillys, the birth mother, case-worker, and the interpreter as they visited in the park.

6D   INFERENCES

Decide whether each statement can be inferred (YES) or cannot be inferred (NO) from the reading selection.

NO   1. The Reillys would have preferred to adopt an American baby rather than a Korean baby.

YES   2. After eleven years, the foster mother still cared for Rae.

YES   3. Upon returning to Korea, Rae felt comfortable because she looked like most of the people around her.

YES   4. The birth mother took a great risk to meet Rae and her adopted family.

NO   5. The Reillys could see a resemblance between Rae and her birth mother.

NO   6. The birth mother's answers were not truthful.

YES   7. The birth mother regretted she was not allowed to hold her daughter at birth.

YES   8. The birth mother could never show Rae's gifts to her husband and children.

YES   9. The birth mother was glad that she met with Rae and the Reillys.

NO   10. Rae would have preferred to have been adopted by a Korean, not an American, couple.

6E   CRITICAL READING: THE AUTHOR'S STRATEGIES

Choose the best answer.

d   1. Rick Reilly's main audience for "Seoul Searching" is
   a. Korean children adopted by American families who need the courage to ask to look for either or both of their birth parents.
   b. Americans thinking of adopting Korean children who fear the children will grow up and desert their American families.
   c. Adopted people interested in the stories of how others like them found either or both of their birth parents.
   d. Families and others interested in what happens when adopted children meet either or both of their birth parents.

Name   Date

_a_ 2. The author's purpose in writing this reading is to
   a. narrate.
   b. describe.
   c. argue.
   d. entertain.

_c_ 3. The overall tone of this reading is
   a. pessimistic.
   b. joyful.
   c. heartfelt.
   d. resentful.

6F   READER'S PROCESS: SUMMARIZING YOUR READING

_a_ 1. What is the best summary of "Seoul Searching"?
   a. An American family travels with their adopted Korean daughter to Korea to help her find her birth mother.
   b. Birth mothers of adopted Korean children rarely want to be located later in the lives of those children because the mothers want to keep the adoptions secret.
   c. Instructions for arrangements need to be made in advance to hold secret meetings in Korea between adopted Korean children and their birth mothers.
   d. Families with adopted children from countries other than the United States are torn apart when the adopted children decide they want to return to their birth mothers.

6G   READER'S RESPONSE: TO DISCUSS OR WRITE ABOUT

1. Rae's birth mother gave up her daughter because in Korea an unwed mother is disowned. Do you think the birth mother made the right choice? Why or why not? How do you suppose the birth mother felt after meeting the daughter she had not seen in eleven years? Explain your response.

2. Adoption results in the birth parent's giving up parenting rights and responsibilities to another set of parents, permanently. Adoption costs can range from $2,000 for an adoption through a public agency to $30,000 for an international adoption. How much would you be willing to spend to adopt a child? If you were considering adoption, would you have conditions or requirements with regard to the child's age, race, and ethnicity; mental and physical ability; and parental background? Be specific with your answers.

HOW DID YOU DO?

6 Seoul Searching

SKILL (number of items)	Number Correct		Points for each		Score
Vocabulary (11)	_____	×	2	=	_____
Central Theme and Main Ideas (3)	_____	×	9	=	_____
Major Details (10)	_____	×	2	=	_____
Inferences (10)	_____	×	2	=	_____
Critical Reading: The Author's Strategies (3)	_____	×	3	=	_____
Reader's Process: Summarizing Your Reading (1)	_____	×	2	=	_____

(Possible Total: 100) *Total*   _____

SPEED

Reading Time: _____ Reading Rate (page 411): _____ Words Per Minute

Name   Date

Part 3

THINKING: GETTING STARTED

In today's world there are so many sources from which we draw information. You may watch the evening news, scan a daily newspaper, surf the latest magazines on the Internet, or listen to a radio broadcast to obtain information about what's happening in the world. With all these possible sources and opportunities to obtain knowledge, most readers know something—even a little bit, no matter how remote—about almost any subject they encounter. That little bit of prior knowledge can become the foundation on which you build a larger bank of learned information.

The next three pages of visuals and accompanying questions are an opportunity for you to consider what you already know about the subjects in the reading selections in Part 3 of this book. Survey the images and the readings to which they are related, and jot down the ideas and thoughts that emerge from your prior knowledge. You can refer to them later when you read the selections. You can also begin to make predictions about what the reading will reveal to you and assess your predictions when you've completed the reading. For now, review the images on the next few pages and start becoming conscious of your prior knowledge about the subjects.

What sorts of events in people's lives can drastically alter the way they look at the world? (See "Summer.")

Is a person with high intelligence admired by young adults today? (See "Brains the Ultimate See Appeal.")

Although many marriages end in divorce, many do not; and the couple stays deeply in love. What makes love so strong that it lasts forever? (See "The Girl with the Large Eyes.")

"THAT WAS VERY INTERESTING, DAD, BUT MY BIOLOGY TEACHER WANTS A REPORT ON BIRDS AND BEES."

How can a person learn parenting skills? (See "Flour Children.")

Can a child expect dreams to be fulfilled without the ability to read? (See "The Magic Words Are 'Will You Help Me?'")

Although death is a part of the cycle of life, how do people cope with the untimely death of a family member or friend? (See "Family and Friends Share Pain and Questions.")

Selection 7

Summer

Jonathan Schwartz

(1) I am running down an alley with a stolen avocado, having climbed over a white brick fence and into the forbidden back yard of a carefully manicured estate at the corner of El Dorado and Crescent Drive in Beverly Hills, California. I have snatched a rock-hard Fuerte avocado from one of the three avocado trees near the fence. I have been told that many ferocious dogs patrol the grounds; they are killers, these dogs. I am defying them. They are nowhere to be found, except in my mind, and I'm out and gone and in the alley with their growls directing my imagination. I am running with fear and exhilaration, beginning a period of summer.

(2) Emerging from the shield of the alley I cut out into the open. Summer is about running, and I am running, protected by distance from the dogs. At the corner of Crescent Drive and Lomitas I spot Bobby Tornitzer on a bike. I shout *"Tornitzer!"* He turns his head. His bike wobbles. An automobile moving rapidly catches Tornitzer's back wheel. Tornitzer is thrown high into the air and onto the concrete sidewalk of Crescent Drive. The driver, a woman with gray hair, swirls from the car hysterically and hovers noisily over Tornitzer, who will not survive the accident. I hold the avocado to my chest and stand, frozen, across the street. I am shivering in the heat, and sink to my knees. It is approximately 3:30 in the afternoon. It is June 21, 1946. In seven days I will be 8 years old.

(215 words)

Here are some of the more difficult words in "Summer."

estate
(paragraph 1)

es·tate (ə stāt', i-) **n.** ⟦ME & OFr *estat*, STATE⟧ **1** *a*) state or condition /to restore the theater to its former *estate*/ *b*) a condition or stage of life /to come to man's *estate*/ *c*) status or rank **2** [Historical] esp. in feudal times, any of the three social classes having specific political powers: the first estate was the Lords Spiritual (clergy), the second estate the Lords Temporal (nobility), and the third estate the Commons (bourgeoisie): see also FOURTH ESTATE **3** property; possessions; capital; fortune **4** the assets and liabilities of a dead or bankrupt person **5** landed property; individually owned piece of land containing a residence, esp. one that is large and maintained by great wealth **6** [Brit.] DEVELOPMENT (sense 4) **7** [Archaic] display of wealth; pomp **8** *Law a*) the degree, nature, extent, and quality of interest or ownership that one has in land or other property *b*) all the property, real or personal, owned by one

exhilaration
(paragraph 1)

ex·hila·rate (eg zil'ə rāt', ig-) **vt.** ‑‑rat'ed, ‑‑rat'ing ⟦< L *exhilaratus*, pp. of *exhilarare*, to gladden < *ex‑*, intens. + *hilarare*, to gladden < *hilaris*, glad: see HILARIOUS⟧ **1** to make cheerful, merry, or lively **2** to invigorate or stimulate —*SYN.* ANIMATE —**ex·hil'a·ra'tive** *adj.*
ex·hila·ra·tion (eg zil'ə rā'shən, ig-) **n.** ⟦LL *exhilaratio*⟧ **1** the act of exhilarating **2** an exhilarated condition or feeling; liveliness; high spirits; stimulation

ferocious
(paragraph 1)

fe·ro·cious (fə rō'shəs) **adj.** ⟦< L *ferox* (gen. *ferocis*), wild, untamed < *ferus*, FIERCE + base akin to *oculus*, EYE + ‑OUS⟧ **1** fierce; savage; violently cruel **2** [Informal] very great /a *ferocious* appetite/ —**fe·ro'·ciously** *adv.* —**fe·ro'·cious·ness** *n.*

hovers
(paragraph 2)

hover (huv'ər, häv'‑) **vi.** ⟦ME *hoveren*, freq. of *hoven*, to stay (suspended)⟧ **1** to stay suspended or flutter in the air near one place **2** to linger or wait close by, esp. in an overprotective, insistent, or anxious way **3** to be in an uncertain condition; waver (*between*) —**n.** the act of hovering —**hov'er·er** *n.*

hysterically
(paragraph 2)

hys·teri·cal (hi ster'i kəl) **adj.** ⟦prec. + ‑AL⟧ **1** of or characteristic of hysteria **2** *a*) like or suggestive of hysteria; emotionally uncontrolled and wild *b*) extremely comical **3** having or subject to hysteria —**hys·ter'i·cally** *adv.*

manicured
(paragraph 1)

mani·cure (man'i kyoor') **n.** ⟦Fr < L *manus*, a hand + *cura*, care: see CURE⟧ a trimming, cleaning, and sometimes polishing of the fingernails, esp. when done by a manicurist —**vt.** ‑‑cured', ‑‑cur'ing **1** *a*) to trim, polish, etc. (the fingernails) *b*) to give a manicure to **2** [Informal] to trim, clip, etc. meticulously /to *manicure* a lawn/

7A VOCABULARY

Match eight of the imaginary quotations with a vocabulary word listed on pages 155–156. Write "none" for the two extra quotations.

1. "If you walk too near that savage animal, it will attack you."

   <u>ferocious</u>

2. "Look at those neatly trimmed bushes and that beautifully edged lawn." <u>manicured</u>

3. "Mr. Lloyd Dexter lives in a huge house surrounded by acres of woods." <u>estate</u>

Name   Date

4. "Sometimes my doctor prescribes pain killers for my headaches."

_____none_____

5. "The young parents ran to the lifeguard in a panic when they thought their child might be drowning." ___hysterically___

6. "While the eggs are beginning to hatch, the bird is fluttering protectively over its nest." _____hovers_____

7. "I think skydivers sometimes think they can ignore the laws of gravity." ___defying___

8. "Wow! That ice cold shower certainly gives me a feeling of high spirits."

___exhilaration___

9. "What do you call that pear-shaped, yellowish-green fruit on the table?" ___avocado___

10. "No person should drive while under the influence of alcohol or drugs." _____none_____

7B MAIN IDEA AND IMAGES

Choose the best answer.

__a__ 1. Another title for this story could be
  a. June 21, 1946.
  b. Killer Dogs.
  c. My Eighth Birthday.
  d. The Alley.

__c__ 2. The main image in paragraph 1 is of a young boy
  a. climbing a white brick fence.
  b. snatching avocados.
  c. running with fear and exhilaration.
  d. defying ferocious dogs.

__b__ 3. The main image in paragraph 2 is of
  a. Tornitzer riding his bike.
  b. the playful, then horrified boy.
  c. the seven-year-old emerging from the alley.
  d. the hysteria of the woman driver.

7C   MAJOR DETAILS

Decide whether each detail is MAJOR or MINOR based on the context of the reading selection.

MAJOR 1. The seven-year-old was running from imagined ferocious dogs.

MINOR 2. The stolen avocado was still hard.

MINOR 3. The avocado tree was on an estate.

MAJOR 4. The seven-year-old froze in horror when he saw the accident.

MAJOR 5. Bobby Tornitzer was riding his bike.

MAJOR 6. A car hit Tornitzer's bike.

MAJOR 7. Tornitzer was going to die.

MINOR 8. A woman was driving the car.

MINOR 9. The street was called Crescent Drive.

7D   INFERENCES

Decide whether each statement below can be inferred (YES) or cannot be inferred (NO) from the story.

NO   1. Climbing over other people's fences is against the law.

YES 2. This experience probably left a deep emotional scar on the seven-year-old.

NO   3. The seven-year-old was being punished for stealing an avocado.

NO   4. Seven-year-old children are destructive.

YES 5. A single moment can drastically alter lives.

NO   6. The seven-year-old hated Tornitzer.

NO   7. Women are poor drivers.

NO   8. The driver was drunk.

NO   9. Tornitzer had recently arrived in America, and so he did not understand English very well.

NO 10. Tornitzer was also seven years old.

Name   Date

7E   CRITICAL READING: THE AUTHOR'S STRATEGIES

Choose the best answer.

__d__ 1. The main audience for "Summer" is
     a. young readers.
     b. readers of fiction.
     c. readers of nonfiction.
     d. readers of all ages.

__c__ 2. The author's purpose in writing this reading is to
     a. expose.
     b. persuade.
     c. narrate.
     d. describe.

__a__ 3. The author's tone in this reading is
     a. upset.
     b. hard-hearted.
     c. gentle.
     d. pessimistic.

7F   READER'S PROCESS: SUMMARIZING YOUR READING

__d__ 1. What is the best summary of "Summer"?
     a. A man tells how, at the age of seven years old, he shouted at a friend after stealing an avocado and caused the friend to be hit by a car.
     b. A man tells how, at the age of seven years old, he was responsible for the tragic death of a friend.
     c. A man tells how, at the age of seven years old, he stole an avocado and ran down the street in a state of excitement.
     d. A man tells how, at the age of seven years old, his childish act led to the tragic death of a friend who was run over by a car.

7G   READER'S RESPONSE: TO DISCUSS OR WRITE ABOUT

1. Was there a dramatic event, good or bad, in your childhood that you will never forget? Describe and discuss its effect on you.

2. What are your feelings about people who use the street rather than the sidewalk to jog, skate, or ride a bicycle? If they are hit by a car, should the driver be held responsible? Explain your point of view.

HOW DID YOU DO?
7 Summer

SKILL (number of items)	Number Correct		Points for each		Score
Vocabulary (10)	_____	×	3	=	_____
Main Ideas and Images (3)	_____	×	5	=	_____
Major Details (9)	_____	×	3	=	_____
Inferences (10)	_____	×	2	=	_____
Critical Reading: The Author's Strategies (3)	_____	×	2	=	_____
Reader's Process: Summarizing Your Reading (1)	_____	×	2	=	_____

(Possible Total: 100) *Total* _____

SPEED

Reading Time: _____ Reading Rate (page 411): _____ Words Per Minute

Name   Date

Selection 8
Brains the Ultimate Sex Appeal

Wendi C. Thomas

(1) It's a question I've been asked more than once, most recently Saturday at a dinner party. "What will it take to get kids excited about learning?" It's a good question for which there is no one answer.

(2) It will take a combination of creative and committed teachers, adequate and well-spent funding, a focused school board and administration, involved parents, disciplined students, and a supportive faith and business community. And maybe, one more thing. "We need to make being educated sexy," said Reynaldo Glover, chairman of the board at Nashville's Fisk University. His comments came last month at a gathering of black opinion writers.

(3) Learning has to become sexy. Not jump-in-bed sexy. Just "he's a hottie" sexy. Desirable, attractive, alluring. Like Glover says, "If a guy can't read, he gets nothing." Unfortunately, that's not always the way it works. Too often, young men and women are idolized for their expensive jewelry, not their extensive vocabulary. We hold high those things that are temporal and fleeting, and look with disdain on those things, like a good education, that last.

(4) So just for the record, here's what's hot: Spending more on your car than your home. Buying more clothes than books. Mangling the English language. Dropping out of high school. Bragging about getting shot, committing crimes, or being uneducated.

(5) What is sexy? A bachelor's, master's or doctorate degree. Perfect diction. Familiarity with, if not command of, another language (Ebonics and slang don't count). Being able to have an intelligent conversation about current affairs. Having favorite authors, not just favorite albums.

(6) By these criteria, Waldon Hagan, who earned his PhD at the University of Memphis, is hot. Know what brought him to Memphis from a teaching job in Florida? A book, specifically James Baldwin's *If Beale Street Could Talk*. How hot is that? It's not that Hagan, now an administrator in Fisk University's education department, came from a privileged background. He grew up in the projects, and only went to college after being rejected by the Marines.

(7) But somewhere along the way, learning changed him. Wednesday at the Memphis Cook Convention Center, the city and county will host the Learning for Success education summit. It's already a sellout, which is a good sign. The goal is to find solutions to the challenges facing public schools. The sessions scheduled are what you'd expect: on the No Child Left Behind Act, leadership development, and academic standards. Just maybe, they'll address what may be a missing link: how to make education sexy.

(415 words)

Here are some of the more difficult words in "Brains the Ultimate Sex Appeal."

alluring
(paragraph 3)

al·lur·ing (ə loor′iŋ, a-) *adj.* tempting strongly; highly attractive; charming —**al·lur′·ing·ly adv.**

criteria
(paragraph 6)

cri·teri·on (krī tir′ē ən) *n., pl.* **-ria** (-ē ə) or **-ri·ons** [< Gr *kritērion*, means of judging < *kritēs*, judge; akin to *kritikos*: see fol.] a standard, rule, or test by which something can be judged; measure of value —*SYN.* STANDARD

diction
(paragraph 5)

dic·tion (dik′shən) *n.* [L *dictio*, a speaking (in LL, word) < pp. of *dicere*, to say, orig., point out in words < IE base *deik-*, to point out > Gr *deiknynai*, to prove, Ger *zeigen*, to show, OE *teon*, to accuse, *tæcan*, TEACH] **1** manner of expression in words; choice of words; wording **2** manner of speaking or singing; enunciation

disdain
(paragraph 3)

dis·dain (dis dān′) *vt.* [ME *disdeinen* < OFr *desdaignier* < VL *disdignare*, for LL *dedignare* < L *dedignari* < *dis-*, DIS- + *dignari*: see DEIGN] to regard or treat as unworthy or beneath one's dignity; specif., to refuse or reject with aloof contempt or scorn —*n.* the feeling, attitude, or expression of disdaining; aloof contempt or scorn —*SYN.* DESPISE

idolized
(paragraph 3)

idol·ize (īd′'l īz′) *vt.* **-·ized′, -·iz′·ing** **1** to make an idol of **2** to love or admire excessively; adore —*vi.* to worship idols —**i′doli·za′·tion** *n.*

mangling
(paragraph 4)

man·gle[1] (maŋ′gəl) *vt.* **-·gled, -·gling** [ME *manglen* < Anglo-Fr *mangler*, prob. freq. of OFr *mehaigner*, MAIM] **1** to mutilate or disfigure by repeatedly and roughly cutting, tearing, hacking, or crushing; lacerate and bruise badly **2** to spoil; botch; mar; garble [to *mangle* a text] —*SYN.* MAIM —**man′·gler** *n.*
man·gle[2] (maŋ′gəl) *n.* [Du *mangel* < Ger < MHG, dim. of *mange*, a mangle < L *manganum* < Gr *manganon*, war machine, orig. deceptive device < IE base *meng-*, to embellish deceptively > MIr *meng*, deceit, L *mango*, falsifying dealer] a machine for pressing and smoothing cloth, esp. sheets and other flat pieces, between heated rollers —*vt.* **-·gled, -·gling** to press in a mangle —**man′·gler** *n.*

privileged
(paragraph 6)

privi·leged (-lijd) *adj.* **1** having one or more privileges **2** like or having the status of privileged communication; confidential **3** having special favored status **4** *Naut.* designating the vessel that has the right of way: see BURDENED

summit
(paragraph 7)

sum·mit (sum′it) *n.* [ME *sommete* < OFr, dim. of *som*, summit < L *summum*, highest part < *summus*, highest: see SUM] **1** the highest point, part, or elevation; top or apex **2** the highest degree or state; acme ☆**3** *a*) the highest level of officials; specif., in connection with diplomatic negotiations, the level restricted to heads of government [a meeting at the *summit*] *b*) a conference at the summit —*adj.* ☆of the heads of government [a *summit* parley]

temporal
(paragraph 3)

tem·po·ral[1] (tem′pə rəl, -prəl) *adj.* [ME < L *temporalis* < *tempus*, time: see TEMPER] **1** lasting only for a time; transitory; temporary, not eternal **2** of this world; worldly, not spiritual **3** civil or secular rather than ecclesiastical **4** of or limited by time **5** *Gram.* expressing distinctions in time; pertaining to tense —*n.* a temporal thing, power, etc. —**tem′·po·rally adv.**
tem·po·ral[2] (tem′pə rəl, -prəl) *adj.* [LL *temporalis* < L *tempora*: see TEMPLE[2]] of or near the temple or temples (of the head)

8A VOCABULARY

Choose the best answer.

___d___ 1. A **summit** refers to a meeting held
      a. at a satisfactory level for contestants.
      b. at the most appropriate time for participants.
      c. at an unusual location for tourists.
      d. with the highest level of officials.

___b___ 2. A **privileged** background suggests growing up with
      a. regulations.
      b. advantages.
      c. relationships.
      d. hardships.

___a___ 3. **Criteria** are standards used in making a
      a. judgment.
      b. paragraph.
      c. greeting.
      d. send-off.

___b___ 4. An **alluring** advertisement is
      a. disappointing.
      b. attractive.
      c. colorless.
      d. unpleasant.

___b___ 5. A radio announcer with good **diction** uses words that are
      a. sometimes controversial.
      b. easily understood.
      c. frequently inspirational.
      d. always convincing.

___d___ 6. **Mangling** a language is
      a. shortening the vowel sounds.
      b. speaking distinctly.
      c. using three-syllable words.
      d. tearing it apart.

___c___ 7. **Idolized** people are
      a. disliked.
      b. considerate.
      c. adored.
      d. ridiculed.

b 8. Things that are **temporal**
   a. hold up forever.
   b. last only a short time.
   c. retain their monetary value.
   d. appear in the night sky.

d 9. To show **disdain** is to
   a. exhibit preferred treatment.
   b. deny a privilege or right.
   c. show affection openly.
   d. look down on a person or thing.

8B CENTRAL THEME AND MAIN IDEAS

Choose the best answer.

c 1. What is the central theme of "Brains the Ultimate Sex Appeal"?
   a. To solve the challenges facing public schools, Memphis hosted an education summit.
   b. High school dropouts are more likely to be interested in material possessions than in an education.
   c. One possible answer to getting students interested in learning is to make it desirable.
   d. A popular topic at dinner parties is "What will it take to get kids excited about learning?"

b 2. What is the main idea of paragraph 6?
   a. Waldon Hagan worked as a teacher in Florida.
   b. A book influenced Waldon Hagan to leave Florida for Memphis.
   c. Waldon Hagan grew up in the projects.
   d. James Baldwin is the author of *If Beale Street Could Talk*.

8C MAJOR DETAILS

Decide whether each detail is MAJOR or MINOR based on the context of the reading selection.

MAJOR 1. No one specific answer exists for getting students excited about learning.

MAJOR 2. According to Reynaldo Glover, making education sexy is a possible solution to get students interested in learning.

MINOR 3. Reynaldo Glover made his comments about learning at Fisk University in Nashville.

MAJOR 4. Somewhere along the way, learning changed Waldon Hagan.

Name   Date

MINOR 5. Waldon Hagan earned his PhD at the University of Memphis.

MAJOR 6. Students often put more value on temporary, not lasting, things.

8D INFERENCES

Decide whether each statement can be inferred (YES) or cannot be inferred (NO) from the reading selection.

NO 1. The author, Wendi C. Thomas, is a public school teacher in Memphis.

NO 2. Reynaldo Glover's suggestion to make learning sexy is the best solution to resolve educational problems.

NO 3. Many Black opinion writers agree with Reynaldo Glover's proposal—to get students excited about learning, make being educated sexy.

YES 4. Students generally do not consider a college degree as "hot."

NO 5. Waldon Hagan would have attended college even if he had not been rejected by the Marines.

YES 6. Home ownership is not considered "hot" in some communities.

NO 7. One of the topics at the Learning for Success education summit was about the effect of drugs on young minds.

NO 8. Changing students' attitudes about learning begins with the parents.

8E CRITICAL READING: FACT OR OPINION

Decide whether each statement contains a FACT or OPINION.

FACT 1. *From paragraph 1*: "It's a question I've been asked more than once […]."

OPINION 2. *From paragraph 3*: "If a guy can't read, he gets nothing."

OPINION 3. *From paragraph 3*: "Learning has to become sexy."

OPINION 4. *From paragraph 3*: "Too often, young men and women are idolized for their expensive jewelry, not their extensive vocabulary."

FACT 5. *From paragraph 7*: "The goal of the Learning for Success summit is to find solutions to the challenges facing public schools."

FACT 6. *From paragraph 6*: "He grew up in the projects."

8F   CRITICAL READING: THE AUTHOR'S STRATEGIES

Choose the best answer.

  b   1. Wendi Thomas's main audience for "Brains the Ultimate Sex
        Appeal" is
        a. people who frequently attend dinner parties.
        b. general reading public, including students.
        c. teenage students and their young siblings.
        d. teachers, school board members, and school administrators.

  a   2. The author's purpose in writing this reading is to
        a. inform.
        b. narrate.
        c. describe.
        d. entertain.

  c   3. The author's tone in this reading is
        a. irrational.
        b. nostalgic.
        c. reflective.
        d. frustrated.

8G   READER'S PROCESS: SUMMARIZING YOUR READING

  d   1. What is the best summary of "Brains the Ultimate Sex Appeal"?
        a. Young people care only about what's "hot," in cars, clothes,
           and street slang, which is why so many of them drop out of
           school and never achieve success in life.
        b. Being educated with an advanced degree and a well-developed
           vocabulary is not possible for many young people because they
           are not intelligent.
        c. Taking the trouble to finish high school and get a higher edu-
           cation is a waste of time for young people today because
           impressing peers is more important.
        d. Teachers, administrators, board members, parents, and the
           local community need to work together to show students that
           being educated is "sexy."

8H   READER'S RESPONSE: TO DISCUSS OR WRITE ABOUT

  1. Motivation is probably the most significant issue educators can target
     to improve learning. If you had an opportunity to share your ideas

with a panel of educators, what suggestions would you offer to motivate students to learn in elementary school? Middle school? High school?

2. Wendi Thomas listed a number of things considered "hot." Do you agree or disagree with the list? Why? What item(s) would you drop or add to the "hot" list?

HOW DID YOU DO?

8 Brains the Ultimate Sex Appeal

SKILL (number of items)	Number Correct		Points for each		Score
Vocabulary (9)	_____	×	2	=	_____
Central Theme and Main Ideas (2)	_____	×	8	=	_____
Major Details (6)	_____	×	3	=	_____
Inferences (8)	_____	×	3	=	_____
Critical Reading: Fact or Opinion (6)	_____	×	2	=	_____
Critical Reading: The Author's Strategies (3)	_____	×	3	=	_____
Reader's Process: Summarizing Your Reading (1)	_____	×	3	=	_____
(Possible Total: 100) *Total*					_____

SPEED

Reading Time: _____ Reading Rate (page 412): _____ Words Per Minute

Selection 9
The Girl with the Large Eyes

Julius Lester

(1) Many years ago in a village in Africa, there lived a girl with large eyes. She had the most beautiful eyes of any girl in the village, and whenever one of the young men looked at her as she passed through the marketplace, her gaze was almost more than he could bear.

(2) The summer she was to marry, a drought came upon the region. No rain had fallen for months, and the crops died, the earth changed to dust, and the wells and rivers turned to mudholes. The people grew hungry, and when a man's mind can see nothing except his hunger, he cannot think of marriage, not even to such a one as the girl with the large eyes.

(3) She had little time to think of the wedding that would have been had there been no drought. She had little time to daydream of the hours of happiness she would have been sharing with her new husband. Indeed, she had little time at all, for it was her job each day to find water for her family. That was not easy. She spent the morning going up and down the river bank, scooping what little water she could from the mudholes until she had a pitcher full.

(4) One morning, she walked back and forth along the river bank for a long while, but could find no water. Suddenly, a fish surfaced from the mud and said to her, "Give me your pitcher and I will fill it with water."

(5) She was surprised to hear the fish talk, and a little frightened, but she had found no water that morning, so she handed him the pitcher, and he filled it with cold, clear water.

(6) Everyone was surprised when she brought home a pitcher of such clear water, and they wanted to know where she had found it. She smiled with her large eyes, but she said nothing.

(7) The next day she returned to the same place, called the fish, and again he filled her pitcher with cold, clear water. Each day thereafter she returned, and soon she found herself becoming fond of the fish. His skin was the colors of the rainbow and as smooth as the sky on a clear day. His voice was soft and gentle like the cool, clear water he put in her pitcher. And on the seventh day, she let the fish embrace her, and she became his wife.

(8) Her family was quite happy to get the water each day, but they were still very curious to know from where she was getting it. Each day they asked her many questions, but she only smiled at them with her large eyes and said nothing.

(9) The girl's father was a witch doctor, and he feared that the girl had taken up with evil spirits. One day he changed the girl's brother into a fly and told him to sit in the pitcher and find out from where she was getting the water. When she got to the secret place, the brother listened to the girl and the fish and watched them embrace, and he flew quickly home to tell his father what he had heard and seen. When the parents learned that their daughter had married a fish, they were greatly embarrassed and ashamed. If the young men of the village found out, none of them would ever marry her. And if the village found out, the family would be forced to leave in disgrace.

(10) The next morning, the father ordered the girl to stay at home, and the brother took him to the secret place beside the river. They called to the fish, and, when he came up, they killed him and took him home. They flung the fish at the girl's feet and said, "We have brought your husband to you."

(11) The girl looked at them and at the fish beside her feet, his skin growing dull and cloudy, his colors fading. And her eyes filled with tears.

(12) She picked up the fish and walked to the river, wondering what was to become of the child she was carrying inside her. If her parents had killed her husband, would they not kill her child when it was born?

(13) She walked for many miles, carrying her husband in her arms, until she came to a place where the waters were flowing. She knew that suffering could only be cured by medicine or patience. If neither of those relieved it, suffering would always yield to death.

(14) Calling her husband's name, she waded into the water until it flowed above her head. But as she died, she gave birth to many children, and they still float on the rivers to this day as water lilies.

(850 words)

Here are some of the more difficult words in "The Girl with the Large Eyes."

drought
(paragraph 2)

drought (drout) *n.* ⟦ME < OE *drugoth*, dryness < *drugian*, to dry up; akin to *dryge*, DRY⟧ **1** a prolonged period of dry weather; lack of rain **2** a prolonged or serious shortage or deficiency **3** [Archaic] thirst —**drought'y** *adj.* **drought'i·er, drought'i·est**

fond
(paragraph 7)

fond[1] (fänd) *adj.* ⟦ME, contr. of *fonned*, foolish, pp. of *fonnen*, to be foolish⟧ **1** [Now Rare] foolish, esp. foolishly naïve or hopeful **2** *a)* tender and affectionate; loving *b)* affectionate in a foolish or overly indulgent way **3** cherished with great or unreasoning affection; doted on /a *fond* hope/ —**fond of** having a liking for

gaze
(paragraph 1)

gaze (gāz) *vi.* **gazed, gaz'·ing** ⟦ME *gazen* < Scand, as in Norw & Swed dial. *gasa*, to stare < ON *gas*, GOOSE⟧ to look intently and steadily; stare, as in wonder or expectancy —*n.* a steady look — **gaz'er** *n.*

scooping
(paragraph 3)

scoop (skōōp) *n.* ⟦ME *scope* < MDu *schope*, bailing vessel, *schoppe*, a shovel, akin to Ger *schöpfen*, to dip out, create⟧ **1** any of various utensils shaped like a small shovel or a ladle; specif., *a*) a kitchen utensil used to take up sugar, flour, etc. *b*) a small utensil with a round bowl, for dishing up ice cream, mashed potatoes, etc. *c*) a small, spoonlike surgical instrument **2** the deep shovel of a dredge or steam shovel, which takes up sand, dirt, etc. **3** the act or motion of taking up with or as with a scoop **4** the amount taken up at one time by a scoop **5** a hollowed-out place ☆**6** [Informal] *a*) the publication or broadcast of a news item before a competitor; beat *b*) such a news item *c*) current, esp. confidential, information —*adj.* designating a rounded, somewhat low neckline in a dress, etc. —*vt.* **1** to take up or out with or as with a scoop **2** to empty by bailing **3** to dig (*out*); hollow (*out*) **4** to make by digging out **5** to gather (*in* or *up*) as if with a scoop ☆**6** [Informal] to publish or broadcast a news item before (a competitor) —**scoop'er** *n.*

surfaced
(paragraph 4)

sur·face (sur'fis) *n.* ⟦Fr < *sur-* (see SUR-¹) + *face,* FACE, based on L *superficies*⟧ **1** *a*) the outer face, or exterior, of an object *b*) any of the faces of a solid *c*) the area or extent of such a face **2** superficial features, as of a personality; outward appearance **3** AIRFOIL **4** *Geom.* an extent or magnitude having length and breadth, but no thickness —*adj.* **1** of, on, or at the surface **2** intended to function or be carried on land or sea, rather than in the air or under water [*surface* forces, *surface* mail] **3** merely apparent; external; superficial —*vt.* **--faced, --fac·ing 1** to treat the surface of, esp. so as to make smooth or level **2** to give a surface to, as in paving **3** to bring to the surface; esp., to bring (a submarine) to the surface of the water —*vi.* **1** to work at or near the surface, as in mining **2** to rise to the surface of the water **3** to become known, esp. after being concealed —**sur'·facer** *n.*

9A   VOCABULARY

From the context of "The Girl with the Large Eyes," explain the meaning of each of the vocabulary words shown in boldface.

1. *From paragraph 1:* . . . and whenever one of the young men looked at her as she passed through the marketplace, her **gaze** was almost more than he could bear.

   a steady look
   _____
   _____

2. *From paragraph 2:* The summer she was to marry, a **drought** came upon the region.

   a prolonged period of dry weather
   _____
   _____

3. *From paragraph 3:* She spent the morning going up and down the river bank, **scooping** what little water she could from the mudholes until she had a pitcher full.

   taking up with a small shovel-like utensil

4. *From paragraph 4:* A fish **surfaced** from the mud and said to her . . .

   rose to the surface or top

5. *From paragraph 7:* Each day thereafter she returned, and soon she found herself becoming **fond** of the fish.

   tender and loving toward

9B   CENTRAL THEME AND MAIN IMAGES

Choose the best answer.

  b   1. "The Girl with the Large Eyes" is a story about
  - a. a beautiful girl who feels that the purpose of her life is to give birth to water lilies.
  - b. a beautiful girl who falls in love with and marries a fish.
  - c. a father and son who want to protect the beautiful girl from disgracing herself in the village.
  - d. a fish that falls in love with and marries the most beautiful girl in the village.

  d   2. What is the moral of the underlying central theme of "The Girl with the Large Eyes"?
  - a. Love is blind.
  - b. Humans and fish have a right to marry each other.
  - c. Families have to protect their reputations.
  - d. Prejudice in all forms is destructive and cruel.

  c   3. The unexpected main image of paragraph 4 is
  - a. the girl's walking on the river bank.

Name   Date

    b. a fish that surfaced from the mud.

    c. a fish that could talk.

    d. the fish's offer to fill the pitcher.

_a_ 4. The main image in paragraph 7 is of

    a. the girl and the fish falling in love.

    b. the girl who is calling to the fish.

    c. the girl who is returning every day to see the fish.

    d. the fish's smooth colorful skin and gentle voice.

_c_ 5. The main image in paragraphs 10 and 11 is of

    a. the brother and father going to the secret place at the river.

    b. the fish's skin growing dull and cloudy.

    c. the brutal murder of the fish followed by the girl's grief.

    d. the father's ordering the girl to stay at home.

_b_ 6. The unexpected main image in paragraph 12 is

    a. the girl's picking up the dead fish.

    b. the girl's being pregnant.

    c. the girl's walking to the river.

    d. the girl's knowing that her parents killed her husband.

9C   MAJOR DETAILS

Fill in the word or words that correctly complete each statement.

1. The girl with the large eyes was the most   beautiful   girl in the village.

2. Because of the terrible drought, the girl had to spend her time   searching   for water.

3. One day a   fish   offered to bring her water.

4. On the   seventh   day, the girl let the fish embrace her, and she became his   wife   .

5. The girl's witch doctor father turned her   brother   into a   fly   so he could discover where the girl got the water.

6. The father and brother   killed   the fish and   flung   it at the girl's feet.

7. The girl was pregnant and was afraid her parents would kill the   child   when they found out.

8. The girl knew that suffering could usually be cured by medicine or
_____patience_____ rather than death.

9. The grief-stricken girl carried her dead husband to the river and waded
into it until it _____flowed_____ above her head.

10. As she died, she gave birth to many children, which to this day float
on rivers as _____water lilies_____.

9D INFERENCES

Choose the best answer.

__b__ 1. *Read paragraphs 6 and 8 again.* The girl did not tell her family about
the fish because she
a. knew the fish did not want her to say anything.
b. knew they would not approve.
c. was saving the news for a surprise.
d. was embarrassed that she loved a fish.

__d__ 2. The creation of the water lilies at the end of the story implies that
a. water lilies are part human and part fish.
b. the deaths of the girl and the fish had a purpose.
c. people should feel sad when they see water lilies.
d. the result of true love is beauty.

9E CRITICAL READING: THE AUTHOR'S STRATEGIES

Choose the best answer.

__d__ 1. The main audience for "The Girl with the Large Eyes" is
a. readers who can trace their roots to Africa.
b. readers who want to learn about African beliefs.
c. readers who like fairy tales.
d. readers who enjoy folktales that have a message.

__a__ 2. The author's purpose in writing this reading is to
a. persuade.
b. illustrate.
c. describe.
d. inform.

__c__ 3. The author's tone in this reading is
   a. amused.
   b. sincere.
   c. reflective.
   d. confused.

9F READER'S PROCESS: SUMMARIZING YOUR READING

__b__ 1. What is the best summary of "The Girl with the Large Eyes"?
   a. A beautiful village girl wants to get married to a man, but a drought sends everyone off to look for water. When a fish gives her buckets of water to take home, she falls in love with him and marries him, but her family is ashamed.
   b. A beautiful village girl falls in love with and marries a fish that gives her water for her family during a drought, but her family is so ashamed they murder her husband. The girl drowns herself in the river, where her children still live as water lilies.
   c. A beautiful village girl goes down to the river to fetch water during a drought and meets a fish who gives her clear drinking water. They fall in love, but their marriage is discovered by her family, and they become very angry.
   d. A beautiful village girl is engaged to a man, but when a drought comes to the village, she must go in search of water. Her father, a witch doctor, turns his son into a fly to sit on the pitcher and spy on her.

9G READER'S RESPONSE: TO DISCUSS OR WRITE ABOUT

1. Should two people from very different backgrounds marry? Using specific examples, explain your point of view.

2. How important is family approval when a couple decides to marry? If parents don't approve of the marriage, should the couple get married anyway? What are some problems that are likely to occur if they ignore their parents' wishes?

HOW DID YOU DO?

9 The Girl with the Large Eyes

SKILL (number of items)	Number Correct		Points for each		Score
Vocabulary (5)	_____	×	4	=	_____
Central Theme and Main Ideas (6)	_____	×	6	=	_____
Major Details* (13)	_____	×	2	=	_____
Inferences (2)	_____	×	3	=	_____
Critical Reading: The Author's Strategies (3)	_____	×	3	=	_____
Reader's Process: Summarizing Your Reading (1)	_____	×	3	=	_____

(Possible Total: 100) *Total*   _____

SPEED

Reading Time: _____ Reading Rate (page XX): _____ Words Per Minute

* Questions 4, 5, and 6 in this exercise call for two separate answers each. In computing your score, count each separate answer toward your **number correct**.

Selection 10
Flour Children

Lexine Alpert

(1) "Hey, Mister V., what are you doing dressed like that?" says a student as he enters the classroom at San Francisco's Mission High School. "I'm getting ready to deliver your baby," replies the sex education teacher, in surgical greens from cap to booties. "Do you have to take this thing so seriously?" asks another, laughing nervously as she watches her teacher bring out rubber gloves. "Yes, babies are a serious matter," he answers. As the students settle into their seats, Robert Valverde, who has been teaching sex education for four years—and "delivering babies" for three—raises his voice to convene the class.

(2) "Welcome to the nursery," he announces. "Please don't breathe on the babies. I just brought them from the hospital." The students' giggles quickly change to moans as Valverde delivers a "baby"—a five-pound sack of flour—to each student. "You must treat your baby as if it were real twenty-four hours a day for the next three weeks," he says. "It must be brought to every class. You cannot put the baby in your locker or your backpack. It must be carried like a baby, lovingly, and carefully in your arms. Students with jobs or other activities must find babysitters." To make sure the baby is being cared for at night and on weekends, Valverde calls his students at random. "If the baby is lost or broken, you must call a funeral parlor and find what it would cost to have a funeral," he says. The consequence is a new, heavier baby—a ten-pound flour sack.

(3) Valverde came up with the flour baby idea after hearing that some sex education classes assign students the care of an egg; he decided to try something more realistic. "A flour sack is heavier and more cumbersome—more like a real baby," Valverde says. To heighten the realism, he has the students dress their five-pound sacks in babies' clothes, complete with diaper, blanket, and bottle.

(4) "The primary goal is to teach responsibility," says Valverde. "I want those who can't do it to see that they can't, and to acknowledge that the students who can are doing something that is very difficult and embarrassing." After 36 classes and more than a thousand students, Valverde's project seems to be having the effect he wants. "I look at all the circumstantial evidence—the kids are talking to their parents in ways they never have before, and for the first time in their lives, they are forced to respond to an external environment. They have to fill out forms every day saying where they'll be that night and who's taking care of the baby. If their plans change I make them call me and say who's with the baby. They're forced to confront people's comments about their babies."

In "Baby Think It Over," a program designed to deter teen pregnancy, students learn parenting responsibility. Carrie takes a history test while holding a key in the baby's back to keep it from crying.

(5) Lupe Tiernan, vice-principal of the predominantly Hispanic and Asian inner-city high school, believes Valverde's class has helped to maintain the low number of teenage pregnancies at her school. "His students learn that having a baby is a novelty that wears off very quickly, and by three weeks, they no longer want any part of it," she says.

(6) At the beginning of the assignment, some students' parental instincts emerge right away. During the first week, sophomore Cylenna Terry took the rules so seriously that she was kicked out of her English class for refusing to take the baby off her lap and place it on the floor as instructed. "I said, 'No way am I putting my baby on the floor.'" Others, especially the boys, learn early that they can't cope with their new role. "I just couldn't carry the baby around," says Enrique Alday, 15. "At my age it was too embarrassing so I just threw it in my locker." He failed the class.

(7) By the second week, much of the novelty has worn off and the students begin to feel the babies are intruding on their lives. "Why does it have to be so heavy?" Cylenna Terry grumbles. "It's raining out—how am I supposed to carry this baby and open up my umbrella at the same time?" She has noticed other changes as well. "There's no way a boy is even going to look at me when I have this in my arms. No guys want to be involved with a girl who has a baby—they just stay clear."

(8) Rommel Perez misses baseball practice because he can't find a babysitter. Duane Broussard, who has helped care for his one-year-old nephew who lives in his household, learns new respect for how hard his mother and sister work at childcare. "At least this baby doesn't wake me in the middle of the night," he says. Maria Salinis says, "My boyfriend was always complaining about the sack and was feeling embarrassed about having it around. I told him, 'Imagine if it was a real baby.' It made us ask important questions of one another that we had never before considered."

(9) On the last day of the assignment, the temporary parents come to class dragging their feet. Valverde calls the students one by one to the front of the room to turn in their babies. Most, their paper skin now fragile from wear, are returned neatly swaddled in a clean blanket. But others have ended up broken and lying in the bottom of a trash bin; a half-dozen students wound up with ten-pound babies. The students' consensus is that babies have no place in their young lives. "I know that if I had a baby it would mess up my future and hold me down." "After this class, I don't want to have a baby. I couldn't handle it," says 15-year-old Erla Garcia. "It was only a sack of flour that didn't cry or scream, didn't need to be fed or put to sleep, and I still couldn't wait to get rid of it."

(1,004 words)

Here are some of the more difficult words in "Flour Children."

circumstantial (paragraph 4)	cir·cum·stan·tial (sur′kəm stan′shəl) *adj.* **1** having to do with, or depending on, circumstances **2** not of primary importance; incidental **3** full or complete in detail **4** full of pomp or display; ceremonial —**cir′·cum·stan′·tially** *adv.*
confront (paragraph 4)	con·front (kən frunt′) *vt.* ⟦Fr *confronter* < ML *confrontare* < L *com-*, together + *frons*, forehead: see FRONT¹⟧ **1** to face; stand or meet face to face **2** to face or oppose boldly, defiantly, or antagonistically **3** to bring face to face (*with*) [to *confront* someone with the facts] **4** to set side by side to compare —**con·fron·ta·tion** (kän′ frən tā′shən) *n.* or **con·front′al** —**con′·fron·ta′·tion·al** *adj.* —**con′·fron·ta′·tion·ist** *n., adj.*
consensus (paragraph 9)	con·sen·sus (kən sen′səs) *n.* ⟦L < pp. of *consentire:* see fol.⟧ **1** an opinion held by all or most **2** general agreement, esp. in opinion
consequence (paragraph 2)	con·se·quence (kän′si kwens′, -kwəns) *n.* ⟦OFr < L *consequentia* < *consequens*, prp. of *consequi*, to follow after < *com-*, with + *sequi*, to follow: see SEQUENT⟧ **1** a result of an action, process, etc.; outcome; effect **2** a logical result or conclusion; inference **3** the relation of effect to cause **4** importance as a cause or influence [a matter of slight *consequence*] **5** importance in rank; influence [a person of *consequence*] —**SYN.** EFFECT, IMPORTANCE —**in consequence (of)** as a result (of) —**take the consequences** to accept the results of one's actions
convene (paragraph 1)	con·vene (kən vēn′) *vi.* **-vened′, -ven′·ing** ⟦ME *convenen* < OFr *convenir* < L *convenire* < *com-*, together + *venire*, to COME⟧ to meet together; assemble, esp. for a common purpose —*vt.* **1** to cause to assemble, or meet together **2** to summon before a court of law —**SYN.** CALL —**con·ven′er** *n.*

Vocabulary List

cumbersome
(paragraph 3)

cum·ber·some (kum′bər səm) *adj.* hard to handle or deal with as because of size, weight, or many parts; burdensome; unwieldy; clumsy —*SYN.* HEAVY —**cum′·ber·somely** *adv.* —**cum′·ber·some·ness** *n.*

instincts
(paragraph 6)

in·stinct (in′stiŋkt′; *for adj.* in stiŋkt′, in′stiŋkt′) *n.* [< L *instinctus,* pp. of *instinguere,* to impel, instigate < *in-,* in + *stinguere,* to prick: for IE base see STICK] **1** (an) inborn tendency to behave in a way characteristic of a species; natural, unlearned, predictable response to stimuli [suckling is an *instinct* in mammals] **2** a natural or acquired tendency, aptitude, or talent; bent; knack; gift [an *instinct* for doing the right thing] **3** *Psychoanalysis* a primal psychic force or drive, as fear, love, or anger; specif., in Freudian analysis, either the life instinct (Eros) or the death instinct (Thanatos) —*adj.* filled or charged (*with*) [a look *instinct* with pity] —**in·stinc·tual** (in stiŋk′chōō əl) *adj.*

intruding
(paragraph 7)

in·trude (in trōōd′) *vt.* -·trud′ed, -·trud′·ing [L *intrudere* < *in-,* in + *trudere,* to thrust, push: see THREAT] **1** to push or force (something *in* or *upon*) **2** to force (oneself or one's thoughts) upon others without being asked or welcomed **3** *Geol.* to force (liquid magma, etc.) into or between solid rocks —*vi.* to intrude oneself —**in·trud′er** *n.*

novelty
(paragraph 5)

nov·elty (näv′əl tē) *n., pl.* -·ties [ME *novelte* < OFr *noveleté* < LL *novellitas*] **1** the quality of being novel; newness; freshness **2** something new, fresh, or unusual; change; innovation **3** a small, often cheap, cleverly made article, usually for play or adornment: *usually used in pl.* —*adj.* having characteristics that are new, unusual, atypical, etc. [a *novelty* tune]

predominantly
(paragraph 5)

pre·domi·nant (prē däm′ə nənt, pri-) *adj.* [Fr *prédominant* < ML *predominans,* prp. of *predominari:* see PRE- & DOMINANT] **1** having ascendancy, authority, or dominating influence over others; superior **2** most frequent, noticeable, etc.; prevailing; preponderant —*SYN.* DOMINANT —**pre·dom′i·nance** *n.* or **pre·dom′i·nancy,** *pl.* -·cies —**pre·dom′i·nantly** *adv.*

swaddled
(paragraph 9)

swad·dle (swäd′'l) *vt.* -·dled, -·dling [ME *swathlen,* prob. altered (infl. by *swathen,* to SWATHE[1]) < *swethlen* < OE *swethel,* swaddling band, akin to *swathian,* to SWATHE[1]] **1** to wrap (a newborn baby) in swaddling clothes, a blanket, etc. **2** to bind in or as in bandages; swathe —*n.* [ME *swathil* < OE *swethel:* see the *vt.*] a cloth, bandage, etc. used for swaddling

Name   Date

10A VOCABULARY

Using the vocabulary words on pages 179–180 fill in this crossword puzzle.

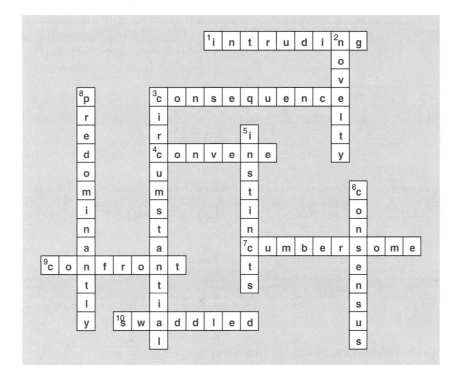

Across

1. forcing oneself on others
3. the logical result of an action
4. to call together
7. difficult to handle; heavy
9. to face or meet face to face
10. wrapped in long pieces of cloth

Down

2. something unusual
3. full or complete in detail
5. inborn tendency
6. opinion held by most people
8. most noticeably

10B CENTRAL THEME AND MAIN IDEAS

Choose the best answer.

__a__ 1. What is the central theme of "Flour Children"?
   a. Mr. Valverde hopes to teach students the responsibility involved in having children.
   b. Students learn that taking care of a baby is a 24-hour-a-day job.
   c. Students learn that babies may cause them to miss out on planned events in their lives.
   d. High school girls learn that boys are not interested in girls who have babies.

__c__ 2. What is the main idea of paragraph 2?
   a. Mr. Valverde intends to check up on his students to make sure they take the project seriously.
   b. Failure to take good care of the baby will result in a new, heavier baby.
   c. The flour babies must be treated as if they were real babies.
   d. Students do not take their flour babies seriously.

__d__ 3. What is the main idea of paragraph 8?
   a. Students often missed after-school activities to care for their "babies."
   b. Students learn that they probably don't want to have babies.
   c. Many students were embarrassed at having to care for a flour baby.
   d. The flour babies affected students' lives in different ways.

10C MAJOR DETAILS

Decide whether each detail is true (T), false (F), or not discussed (ND).

__T__ 1. Mr. Valverde takes his job teaching sex education very seriously.

__ND__ 2. For the first time students are not forced to respond to an external environment.

__T__ 3. Flour sacks instead of eggs are used because they more nearly resemble caring for an infant.

__ND__ 4. San Francisco's Mission High School Board requires this course of all students.

__ND__ 5. The students' parents have agreed to participate in the flour babies' care.

Name   Date

  T 6. Students were concerned about the embarrassment of carrying a flour baby.

  T 7. To make the babies seem more real, students must equip them with clothes, diapers, and bottles.

 ND 8. Students who communicate with their parents do well as flour baby parents.

10D   INFERENCES

Choose the best answer.

  b 1. *Read paragraph 6 again.* By refusing to put her flour sack on the floor during English, Cylenna Terry is showing that
      a. she is afraid any damage would result in getting a larger baby.
      b. she has accepted the responsibility of a baby.
      c. she knows someone would tell Mr. Valverde.
      d. she is too embarrassed to let anyone see it on the floor.

  a 2. *Read paragraph 9 again.* "The temporary parents came to class dragging their feet" indicates that they were
      a. tired of playing this game.
      b. anxious to find out if they had passed.
      c. certain they did not want to have real babies.
      d. hesitant to part with their babies after all.

10E   CRITICAL READING: FACT OR OPINION

Decide whether each statement, even if it quotes someone, contains a FACT or an OPINION.

OPINION 1. *From paragraph 1:* "Yes, babies are a serious matter […]."

 FACT 2. *From paragraph 4:* "The primary goal is to teach responsibility […]."

OPINION 3. *From paragraph 5:* "[…] [the] class has helped to maintain the low number of teen pregnancies at her school."

 FACT 4. *From paragraph 6:* "At my age, it was too embarrassing […]."

OPINION 5. *From paragraph 7:* "No guys wanted to be involved with a girl who has a baby […]."

 FACT 6. *From paragraph 9:* "[…] babies have no place in their young lives."

10F   CRITICAL READING: THE AUTHOR'S STRATEGIES

Choose the best answer.

__d__ 1. The main audience for "Flour Children" is
   a. sex education teachers.
   b. teenage parents.
   c. high school students.
   d. anyone interested in sex education for teens.

__c__ 2. The author's purpose in writing this reading is to
   a. describe.
   b. persuade.
   c. inform.
   d. narrate.

__b__ 3. The author's tone in this reading is
   a. hopeful.
   b. objective.
   c. bitter.
   d. judgmental.

10G   READER'S PROCESS: SUMMARIZING YOUR READING

__c__ 1. What is the best summary of "Flour Children"?
   a. A journalist reports on how several teenagers felt about caring for a baby after a sex education class assignment that lasts three weeks.
   b. A journalist reports on a sex education program that teaches high school students about how hard it really is to take care of a baby for three weeks.
   c. A journalist reports on a sex education program that teaches students responsibility by having them care for a sack of flour as their newborn baby for three weeks.
   d. A journalist reports on a high school sex education teacher whose students are assigned the task of caring for a five-pound "baby" for three weeks.

10H   READER'S RESPONSE: TO DISCUSS OR WRITE ABOUT

1. If you were a high school student and had the option to register for a sex education class that required students to care for flour sack babies, would you enroll? Give specific reasons for your decision.
2. From a parent's point of view, do you think sex education and parenthood classes should be taught in the public schools? Explain your point of view.

Name   Date

HOW DID YOU DO?

10 Flour Children

SKILL *(number of items)*	Number Correct		Points for each		Score
Vocabulary (11)	_____	×	2	=	_____
Central Theme and Main Ideas (3)	_____	×	4	=	_____
Major Details (8)	_____	×	4	=	_____
Inferences (2)	_____	×	4	=	_____
Critical Reading: Fact or Opinion (6)	_____	×	3	=	_____
Critical Reading: The Author's Strategies (3)	_____	×	2	=	_____
Reader's Process: Summarizing Your Reading (1)	_____	×	2	=	_____

(Possible Total: 100) *Total* _____

SPEED

Reading Time: _____ Reading Rate (page 412): _____ Words Per Minute

Selection 11

The Magic Words Are "Will You Help Me?"

Michael Ryan

(1) I had been listening to Tom Harken's life story for almost an hour when the question that had formed in my mind suddenly emerged from his lips: "How did I get from there to here?" he said in a tone of real amazement. "How did that happen?" We all have been taught that America is a land where anyone can go from rags to riches, despite whatever obstacles fate may throw at us. But as I listened to Harken, 59, I understood for the first time just how many obstacles one human being can overcome—and just how far determination and courage can carry any one of us.

(2) The man across from me was a millionaire, the owner of eight franchises of the Casa Olé restaurant chain in Texas. His office is filled with mementos of his friendships with the great and famous, from members of Congress to Supreme Court Justices, from Henry Kissinger to Norman Vincent Peale. Yet, 48 years ago, this robust man was a sickly child. And, more than that, he had a secret he was too ashamed to tell anyone.

(3) "I grew up in Lakeview, Mich.," Harken told me. "I was a sick kid. I had tuberculosis. I developed polio. One day I was riding a bicycle; the next day I was in a hospital, in an iron lung." Just a few decades ago, polio was a terrifying disease that struck tens of thousands of children and adults. Many died or were paralyzed; some lived for months in iron lungs—huge, barrel-like machines that compressed and released lungs too weak to breathe for themselves. "I was in a room the size of a gymnasium, with 35 or 40 iron lungs," Harken recalled. "Imagine being in a hospital. It looks like you're never going to get out of the darned thing, and everybody's crying all around you. I was 11."

(4) It took more than a year of therapy for Tom to recover enough to go home. "I have one leg that's shorter than the other—that's the only evidence of the illness," he said. "The day I got out of that hospital was a great day. I still remember coming home with my mom and dad." But the great day soon turned sour, because Tom also had tuberculosis, and officials worried that he might still be contagious. "The next thing I knew, I was quarantined to one room in the house for a year," he said.

(5) Harken used to tell people his life went back to normal when this second nightmare ended. He went back to school, joined the Air Force and built up his successful business career. All that is true; but, until four years ago, the story Tom Harken told people was not his whole story. And sharing it would

Tom Harken learned to read with the help of his wife, "Miss Melba."

Brian Coats

be the most difficult act of his life. "In 1992, I won the Horatio Alger Award," he told me. The award, given to men and women who have overcome adversity to achieve greatness, has been awarded to such luminaries as Gen. Colin Powell, Maya Angelou and Bob Hope. Harken was thrilled—and humbled—to be chosen to receive it. "I got really emotional while I was dictating my acceptance speech, and I started wondering whether I should talk about it," he recalled. "I'd never talked about it. Melba knew, but nobody else." "It" was Tom Harken's long-held secret: For most of his life, he had been illiterate, unable to read even the simplest sentences, to order from printed menus or to fill out a form.

(6) The origin of the problems is easy to understand: After missing years of school, Tom returned to a classroom run by a teacher who ridiculed him. "He took me up to the board and said, 'Can you spell cat?'" Harken said, "I was nervous and shy, and he said again, 'Spell cat!' He was hollering at me. Then he made me sit down." That humiliation turned Tom off to reading— and school. With his parents' reluctant permission, he dropped out. Later, he enlisted in the Air Force, where he filled in multiple-choice tests at random, unable to read the questions. While he was serving in Oklahoma, Harken had two strokes of luck: He took an after-duty job in sales and learned that he had an aptitude for business. And he met the woman he still calls "Miss Melba," now his wife of 38 years. "I had to tell her that I couldn't read or write, because I needed her to fill out the marriage license," he recalled, emotion flooding his voice. But Melba saw something in this bright young man. "He was ambitious," she said. "And he was so smart. He was so exciting to talk to that I was never afraid he wouldn't succeed."

(7) Succeed he did—with help from Melba. When he moved to Beaumont, Tex., and developed a door-to-door vacuum-cleaner sales business, she would help him write up his order each night. "I have a good memory," he said. "I would memorize names and addresses, employers and credit

information, and then Melba would write them down." Working together, they expanded into a recreational vehicle dealership and then into restaurant franchises. But the small humiliations were always there. "Whenever we went to a restaurant, I would order a cheeseburger," Harken said. "Everybody sells cheeseburgers. But one day I ordered a cheeseburger, and the waitress looked at me and said, 'What's the matter, can't you read? We don't make cheeseburgers.'"

(8) The Harkens had two sons, Tommy and Mark, both now grown and working in the family business. But Tom felt the sting of his illiteracy constantly as the boys were growing up. "They would crawl into my lap and ask me to read them something, like the Sunday comics," he said. "Melba would rescue me. She'd come over and say, 'Daddy's busy. I'll read that to you.'" A regular churchgoer, Harken recalled one occasion when he was attending Sunday school: "They passed the Scripture along, and everybody read a verse. I could feel my stomach tying itself in knots as it came closer to me, and I finally said, 'I have to go to the bathroom,' and I just left there and went home." He realized that he had to do something. He went to Melba for help. "She taught me word by word, over a course of years," Harken told me. "I was hard to teach. I got very angry sometimes." Harken worked his way through simple sentences to the point where he could read parts of the Bible aloud—as he did at the weddings of two of his employees. "That's still hard for me," he said, but Melba immediately cut him off. "You did it very well," she told him.

(9) When he was selected for the Horatio Alger Award, Harken thought about standing up in front of some of America's most important people and telling them that, until recently, he had been illiterate. Then he decided to do it. "I got teary-eyed," he told me. "Melba said I should do it and I should tell our two kids first." His sons were amazed by their father's story. "They were absolutely stunned," Harken recalled. But their reaction was nothing compared to the response of those attending the Horatio Alger awards ceremony in May 1992. They gave Harken a standing ovation. Colin Powell, the Rev. Robert Schuller and other dignitaries rushed to shake his hand.

(10) For many people, that triumphant evening would have been the end of a lifelong journey. For Harken, though, it was just a beginning. Since that night, he has given more than 300 speeches around the country, telling children and adults about the importance of literacy. After one speech, an 87-year-old woman approached him to say that she had just learned to read. "I couldn't read to my children or my grandchildren, but now I can read to my great-grandchildren," she told him. After another speech, an African-American man who was starting reading lessons told Harken that he had dispelled an onerous racist image: "He said that, before he heard me, he thought that only black people could be illiterate," Harken said. "He didn't know that illiteracy happens in every color."

(11) Harken's message is one he wants to get out to anyone who will listen: "I want people to know that they can go into any library and just say

the magic words, 'Will you help me?' Just say those words, and someone will help you learn how to read. The Literacy Volunteers of America are everywhere, and they're ready to help. Everybody should know that." It occurred to me that Tom Harken's whole life might have been changed if that one teacher had not ridiculed him. "Sure, it probably would have altered a lot of my life," Harken said. "But I'm not sure I'd want it altered. You never know your own strength until you've paid the price—and Miss Melba and I have paid the price."

(1,396 words)

Here are some of the more difficult words in "The Magic Words Are 'Will You Help Me?'"

Vocabulary List

adversity
(paragraph 5)

ad·ver·si·ty (ad vʉr′sə tē, əd-) *n*. ⟦ME < OFr *adversité, aversite* < L *adversitas* < *adversus*, prec.⟧ **1** a state of wretchedness or misfortune; poverty and trouble **2** *pl*. **-ties** an instance of misfortune; calamity

aptitude
(paragraph 6)

ap·ti·tude (ap′tə tōōd′, -tyōōd′) *n*. ⟦ME < LL *aptitudo* < L *aptus*: see APT[1]⟧ **1** the quality of being apt or appropriate; fitness **2** a natural tendency or inclination **3** a natural ability or talent **4** quickness to learn or understand —*SYN*. TALENT

dispelled
(paragraph 10)

dis·pel (di spel′) *vt*. **··pelled′, ··pel′·ling** ⟦ME *dispellen* < L *dispellere* < *dis-*, apart + *pellere*, to drive: see FELT⟧ to scatter and drive away; cause to vanish; disperse —*SYN*. SCATTER

franchises
(paragraph 2)

fran·chise (fran′chīz′) *n*. ⟦ME < OFr < *franc*, free: see FRANK[1]⟧ **1** [Archaic] freedom from some restriction, servitude, etc. **2** any special right, privilege, or exemption granted by the government, as to be a corporation, operate a public utility, etc. **3** the right to vote; suffrage: usually preceded by *the* **4** *a*) the right to market a product or provide a service, often exclusive for a specified area, as granted by a manufacturer or company *b*) a business granted such a right ☆**5** *a*) the right to own a member team as granted by a league in certain professional sports *b*) such a member team —*vt*. **··chised′, ··chis′·ing** to grant a franchise to —*adj*. designating a player on a professional team who is regarded as being essential to that team's success

illiterate
(paragraph 5)

il·lit·er·ate (i lit′ər it) *adj*. ⟦L *illiteratus*, unlettered: see IN-[2] & LITERATE⟧ **1** ignorant; uneducated; esp., not knowing how to read or write **2** having or showing limited knowledge, experience, or culture, esp. in some particular field [musically *illiterate*] **3** violating accepted usage in language [an *illiterate* sentence] —*n*. an illiterate person; esp., a person who does not know how to read or write —*SYN*. IGNORANT —**il·lit′·er·ately** *adv*.

literacy
(paragraph 10)

lit·era·cy (lit′ər ə sē) *n*. the state or quality of being literate; specif., *a*) ability to read and write *b*) knowledgeability or capability [computer *literacy*]

obstacles
(paragraph 1)

ob·sta·cle (äb′stə kəl) *n.* ⟦OFr < L *obstaculum*, obstacle < *obstare*, to withstand < *ob-* (see OB-) + *stare*, to STAND⟧ anything that gets in the way or hinders; impediment; obstruction; hindrance

SYN.—obstacle is used of anything which literally or figuratively stands in the way of one's progress /her father's opposition remained their only *obstacle*/; **impediment** applies to anything that delays or retards progress by interfering with the normal action /a speech *impediment*/; **obstruction** refers to anything that blocks progress or some activity as if by stopping up a passage /your interference is an *obstruction* of justice/; **hindrance** applies to anything that thwarts progress by holding back or delaying /lack of supplies is the greatest *hindrance* to my experiment/; **barrier** applies to any apparently insurmountable obstacle that prevents progress or keeps separate and apart /language differences are often a *barrier* to understanding/

onerous
(paragraph 10)

on·er·ous (än′ər əs, ōn′-) *adj.* ⟦ME < MFr *onereus* < L *onerosus* < *onus*, a load: see ONUS⟧ **1** burdensome; laborious **2** *Law* involving a legal obligation that equals or exceeds the benefits /onerous lease/ **—on′·er·ous·ly** *adv.* **—on′·er·ous·ness** *n.*

SYN.—onerous applies to that which is laborious or troublesome, often because of its annoying or tedious character /the *onerous* task of taking inventory/; **burdensome** applies to that which is wearisome or oppressive to the mind or spirit as well as to the body /*burdensome* responsibilities/; **oppressive** stresses the overbearing cruelty of the person or thing that inflicts hardship, or emphasizes the severity of the hardship itself /*oppressive* weather, an *oppressive* king/; **exacting** suggests the making of great demands on the attention, skill, care, etc. /an *exacting* supervisor, *exacting* work/

quarantined
(paragraph 4)

quar·an·tine (kwôr′ən tēn, kwär′-) *n.* ⟦It *quarantina*, lit., space of forty days < *quaranta*, forty < L *quadraginta* < base of *quattuor*, FOUR⟧ **1** *a)* the period, orig. 40 days, during which an arriving vessel suspected of carrying contagious disease is detained in port in strict isolation *b)* the place where such a vessel is stationed **2** any isolation or restriction on travel or passage imposed to keep contagious diseases, insect pests, etc. from spreading **3** the state of being quarantined **4** a place where persons, animals, or plants having contagious diseases, insect pests, etc. are kept in isolation, or beyond which they may not travel **5** any period of seclusion, social ostracism, etc. **—vt. ··tined′, ··tin′·ing 1** to place under quarantine **2** to isolate politically, commercially, socially, etc. **—quar′·an·tin′·able** *adj.*

reluctant
(paragraph 6)

re·luc·tant (-tənt) *adj.* ⟦L *reluctans*, prp. of *reluctari*, to resist < *re-*, against + *luctari*, to struggle: see LOCK¹⟧ **1** opposed in mind (to do something); unwilling; disinclined **2** marked by unwillingness /a *reluctant* answer/ **3** [Rare] struggling against; resisting; opposing **—re·luc′·tantly** *adv.*

robust
(paragraph 2)

ro·bust (rō bust′, rō′bust′) *adj.* ⟦L *robustus*, oaken, hard, strong < *robur*, hard variety of oak, hardness, strength, earlier *robus*, prob. akin to *ruber*, RED⟧ **1** *a)* strong and healthy; full of vigor; hardy *b)* strongly built or based; muscular or sturdy **2** suited to or requiring physical strength or stamina /*robust* work/ **3** rough; coarse; boisterous **4** full and rich, as in flavor /a *robust* port wine/ **—ro·bust′ly** *adv.* **—ro·bust′·ness** *n.*

11A VOCABULARY

Using the vocabulary words listed on pages 190–191 fill in the blanks.

1. At the age of four, Tamika showed an _____aptitude_____ for playing the drums.

2. Mom was _____reluctant_____ to let Quassim play ice hockey because his temperature was 100 degrees.

3. When my sister and I received an inheritance from our grandmother, we invested the money in a pizza _____franchise._____

4. The _____robust_____ appearance of that 70-year-old woman results from years of serious exercise.

5. The greatest _____adversity_____ Dat Pham had to overcome as a college student was his deafness.

6. When I returned from overseas with my dog Hershey, she was _____quarantined_____ to make sure she had not picked up a contagious disease.

7. The cadets had to overcome many _____obstacles_____ in their outdoor survival training.

8. The Dallas _____Literacy_____ Council uses volunteers to help people of all ages learn to read.

9. Standing up and speaking in front of a class can be an _____onerous_____ burden for some students.

10. The Queen's appearance at the balcony window _____dispelled_____ the rumor that she was hospitalized.

11. People who have almost never gone to school are often _____illiterate._____

11B CENTRAL THEME AND MAIN IDEAS

Choose the best answer.

__c__ 1. What is the central theme of "The Magic Words Are 'Will You Help Me?'"
   a. Tom Harken's being belittled by a teacher drove him to drop out of school.
   b. Tom Harken's story shows that being able to read is not essential to becoming a successful businessperson.

Name   Date

     c. Tom Harken spent years covering up a secret shame until he finally asked for help.

     d. Tom Harken's success in business is the result of his wife's support and hard work.

__d__ 2. What is the main idea of paragraph 5?

     a. Tom Harken's life returned to normal when he was well enough to attend school.

     b. The Horatio Alger Award recognized that Tom Harken overcame adversity to become successful.

     c. Only Melba Harken knew that her husband could neither read nor write.

     d. In his acceptance speech at the awards ceremony, Tom Harken planned to reveal the incredible adversity he had endured all his life.

__a__ 3. What is the main idea of paragraph 11?

     a. Help in learning to read is available to anyone who asks.

     b. Tom Harken's life would have been different if a teacher had not embarrassed him.

     c. The Literacy Volunteers of America helps people learn to read.

     d. Tom Harken and his wife suffered embarrassment because he could not read.

11C MAJOR DETAILS

Decide whether each detail listed here is MAJOR or MINOR based on the context of the reading selection.

MINOR 1. Tom Harken grew up in Lakeview, Michigan.

MAJOR 2. As a child, Tom Harken had polio.

MINOR 3. Tom Harken has one leg that is shorter than the other.

MAJOR 4. Tom Harken ordered a cheeseburger every time he went to a restaurant.

MAJOR 5. Tom Harken felt humiliated at not being able to spell "cat."

MINOR 6. Tom and Melba Harken have been married 38 years.

MINOR 7. Tom Harken served in the U.S. Air Force.

MAJOR 8. Tom Harken had a good memory.

MINOR 9. Tom Harken's sons, Tommy and Mark, work in the family business.

MAJOR 10. Tom Harken asked his wife, Melba, to teach him to read.

11D   INFERENCES

Choose the best answer.

___d___ 1. *Reread paragraph 5.* Tom Harken dictated his acceptance speech because
   a. it gave his secretary something to do.
   b. it took less time than writing one.
   c. he liked to hear himself talk.
   d. he found writing a difficult activity.

___a___ 2. *Reread paragraph 6.* The teacher embarrassed Tom Harken because the teacher
   a. hoped embarrassment would force the boy to answer a question.
   b. thought embarrassment would make the boy a better speller.
   c. felt embarrassment would help the boy overcome his shyness.
   d. used embarrassment to discipline unruly students.

___c___ 3. *Reread paragraph 8.* Tom Harken felt he was "difficult to teach" because
   a. he did not study.
   b. his wife was not a trained teacher.
   c. he was impatient with his progress.
   d. he could not concentrate on anything for long.

11E   CRITICAL READING: FACT OR OPINION

Decide whether each statement contains a FACT or an OPINION.

OPINION 1. *From paragraph 1:* "America is a land where anyone can go from rags to riches [. . .]."

FACT 2. *From paragraph 3:* Many people either died or were paralyzed from polio.

FACT 3. *From paragraph 5:* Before learning to read, Tom Harken spoke to no one but his wife about his illiteracy.

FACT 4. *From paragraph 6:* Tom Harken learned that he had an aptitude for business.

FACT 5. *From paragraph 8:* Reading the Bible aloud at the wedding of some of his employees was difficult for Tom Harken.

FACT 6. *From paragraph 10:* Since his acceptance speech for the Alger Award, Tom Harken has spoken many times on the topic "Illiteracy."

OPI<u>NION</u> 7. *From paragraph 11:* The words "will you help me" are magic.

OPI<u>NION</u> 8. *From paragraph 11:* Anyone can get help learning to read by contacting the Literacy Volunteers of America.

11F CRITICAL READING: THE AUTHOR'S STRATEGIES

Choose the best answer.

<u>a</u> 1. The main audience for "The Magic Words 'Are Will You Help Me?'" is
   a. anyone needing encouragement to overcome a disability.
   b. anyone who has experienced not being able to read.
   c. anyone who works with adults who can't read.
   d. anyone seeking help in learning to read.

<u>b</u> 2. The author's purpose in writing this reading is to
   a. emphasize.
   b. inform.
   c. describe.
   d. entertain.

<u>d</u> 3. The author's tone in this reading is
   a. amused.
   b. concerned.
   c. objective.
   d. admiring.

11G READER'S PROCESS: SUMMARIZING YOUR READING

<u>d</u> 1. What is the best summary of "The Magic Words Are 'Will You Help Me?'"?
   a. A journalist tells how Tom Harken built a successful business even though he couldn't read.
   b. A journalist tells how businessman Tom Harken learned to read with the help of his wife.
   c. A journalist tells how businessman Tom Harken coped with being illiterate while building a successful business.
   d. A journalist tells how businessman Tom Harken hid the fact that he was illiterate and finally decided to reveal his shameful secret.

11H   READER'S RESPONSE: TO DISCUSS OR WRITE ABOUT

1. Have you or someone you know or have heard about ever felt humiliated privately or publicly by an incident in college, at work, or in a social setting? Being as specific as you can, explain what happened.

2. Melba Harken thought her husband, Tom, "was so smart" even though he could not read or write. Do you think someone can be smart without those skills? Using a specific experience you know about, explain why you think this is so.

HOW DID YOU DO?

11   The Magic Words Are "Will You Help Me?"

SKILL (number of items)	Number Correct		Points for each		Score
Vocabulary (11)	_____	×	2	=	_____
Central Theme and Main Ideas (3)	_____	×	5	=	_____
Major Details (10)	_____	×	4	=	_____
Inferences (3)	_____	×	1	=	_____
Critical Reading: Fact or Opinion (8)	_____	×	1	=	_____
Critical Reading: The Author's Strategies (3)	_____	×	3	=	_____
Reader's Process: Summarizing Your Reading (1)	_____	×	3	=	_____

(Possible Total: 100) *Total*   _____

SPEED

Reading Time: _____ Reading Rate (page 412): _____ Words Per Minute

Name   Date

Selection 12

Family and Friends Share Pain and Questions

Erin Sullivan

(1) Dear Max,

They played Bob Marley at your funeral, "One Love," your favorite, the one you begged the deejay at the middle school dance to play, and he did, at the end, when everyone was leaving.

(2) The cleaning crew took your Bob Marley tapestry that hung on the wall above the couch in your bedroom. Later, your 15-year-old sister, McKenzie, said she wanted the tapestry, and your older sister, Monica Sheftall, had to tell the family it was gone and they would never get it back. The corner of your room is now empty, and plaster fills the holes in your blue walls where the pellets sprayed.

(3) You killed yourself on a Sunday morning, April 17, while your mom and McKenzie were in Alabama for one of McKenzie's softball games. Your dad was at church. Monica, 26 and married with a toddler, was doing her own thing.

(4) Your dad checked on you before he left, and you were sleeping. The day before you guys had spent the afternoon washing and detailing your cars, the sun warm, listening to Earth, Wind and Fire. It was a good, good day. You told your friends how nice it was. Your dad said the same thing, that day and later. After he came home from church and called your name and found you in your bedroom with the shotgun, he called your mom, and she and McKenzie jumped in her truck and sped the four hours home, and soon the house was filled with people, while your dad kept saying how perfect Saturday afternoon had been, and how happy you had seemed, and how he didn't understand.

(5) No one understands. Maybe you opened up to someone or hinted at the depths of your sadness. If you did, that person hasn't said. Your parents knew you were going through a rough time—you skipped classes, started lying. Not mean lies, but storytelling, fibbing. That's why they transferred you from Germantown High School to St. Benedict at Auburndale your junior year. It's a tough school and strict where you had to wear a tie, keep your hair short.

(6) You were so intelligent, but you were failing. You probably were going to repeat 11th grade. Your parents got you a tutor, and you'd do the work but not turn it in. They tested you for drugs, and you always passed.

(7) Your dad took you on that ski trip to Vail right before Christmas, just the two of you. He keeps looking at the photos. There was a snowstorm on your way back, and you got a flight into Nashville, but the other planes

were grounded. You got the last rental car, a van. While your dad got the bags, you looked for a distraught face and found one, a woman with her husband and two children. You asked if they were trying to go to Memphis. They were. You told them you could take them. It was Christmas Eve.

(8) Your parents took you to see a psychologist because of the trouble in school, the storytelling. They were worried. You went for a while, but then the psychologist thought you were better, on the upswing, and said you could take a break. He's so shaken by this. He has called your parents twice, crying, apologizing. Your principal has been to the house, asking, "What did we miss?" Your parents aren't angry with the psychologist or anyone else. It's not anyone's fault. Your dad thinks there was something in your brain, a disorder not diagnosed. It might have been an impulsive thing. You were an impulsive kid. You got up that morning and ate half a pizza. Maybe you found the key to the gun box and you decided, spur of the moment, to do it. Or maybe you planned it like this.

(9) You didn't leave a note, which is strange because you were a writer. Short stories, essays, even your journals from your church trip to Kenya, in January 2004, are lyrical. You spent most of your time there in the kitchen, talking to the local women. Before you left, the women gave you an African name. This happens to few people. They named you Luambua—one born during rain.

(10) You could always talk with adults. You had an old soul. One of your favorite hangouts was the Borders Bookstore at Poplar Pike and Kirby. You'd be the 17-year-old in the center of a group of older men, talking books and philosophy and life. After you died, the father of one of your youth group friends e-mailed one of the pastors. He said you taught him not to pre-judge people. You looked like a bad kid, with magenta hair and a Mohawk and baggy pants. But you were mature, well-spoken, charming. He liked you.

(11) I went to your house in Germantown the night of April 28. There were about 20 people there, your family, your childhood friends and new ones from St. Benedict. Your parents were surprised by what the St. Benedict kids said. They knew you were lying, telling stories, but not to this extreme. The new kid, you recreated yourself. You named yourself Caesar—the kids really thought your name was Caesar Maximus Durham and that you were born in Italy. You told wild tales, and they ate it up. You said that you had a brother in the Mafia who was murdered. You said you were in gangs. You made them laugh all the time.

(12) Your girlfriend, Monica Davis, was there. She's beautiful, half-black, half-Filipino, with long dark hair you used to play with. She showed me the note you wrote during sixth period on Valentine's Day, where you said you fell in love with her on sight. She doesn't understand either. You left a message on her phone at 3:30 a.m., about eight hours before you died, and you sounded normal and happy.

(13) Chris Peterson and Johnson Lohnes were there, the guys you've known so long that they don't have a memory without you in it. A few days

later Chris told me about the depression he has battled for years. In seventh grade you took him with you on a church trip to Colorado. It was there, Chris says, that he found God. He says he wouldn't be alive if not for you.

(14) I didn't know how you died when I called your house to ask to write a story about you. I'd seen the obituary your parents wrote. They talked about your faith, your friends at martial arts, your mission trip to Africa, your laughter, and your funky dance moves that you practiced at home before showing them off at the arcade at the mall. Your father said he was proud of you for always sticking up for the underdog. Your mom signed it the way she always signed her text messages to you:

The Max Man.

You're a good man, Charlie Brown.

Love U 2 pieces,

Mom

(15) After your dad said how you died, I said I was so sorry and asked if he was sure he wanted me to do the story. He said *yes*. He and your mom want other kids, who might be thinking of killing themselves, to know that it's not the answer, and to ask for help. Your parents also want people to know not just how you died, but how you lived. There was no question of your faith in God, they said. They were so proud of you. They still are.

(16) The day after you died, hundreds of your friends gathered at the park beside Riverdale, your old school. At first they stayed in their cliques, the barriers that you seemed to glide through. The athletes. The church kids. The girls with black lipstick. The cheerleaders. They joined hands and prayed, and then they started talking, mingling, and soon you couldn't see the lines but just kids, shocked, scared kids who couldn't understand why you did what you did.

(17) Your cousin, Angela Rickman, walked around listening. She was amazed that she kept hearing the same thing: "Max was my best friend." "He was my best friend." The way you listened, the way you cared and loved made people feel special.

(18) That same day, your parents got a call from Pakistan. Somehow, news of your death reached a girl there you had protected years ago. It was the sixth grade, and she lived here. She wore traditional Muslim clothes, and kids tormented her. You walked her home from school every day. If she had to stay late, you went home, then walked back to get her. You got in many fights standing up for her. Your associate pastor, Eli Morris, recounted the story at your memorial service at Hope Presbyterian Church. He had talked with you about it because you were fighting. He said that halfway through your story he realized you were right. Those kids deserved a fight. "He wanted people to see life differently," Eli said. "He hated injustice."

(19) More than 1,000 people came to your memorial service. They lined the walls because there were no seats left. They were honest. Eli said you were

a lunatic, "unadulterated, card-carrying." "His life was like his hair," Eli said. "You never knew what you were going to get . . . but every time it was fun."

(20) Your youth pastor, Bret Spiegelman, told the story of when you kept picking pillow fights with the two small Baptist boys down the hall during one of the Colorado trips. You were sitting in your room and saw them walking past, and you shouted, "The Baptists!" and took off, pillow in hand, chasing them, the other kids following. As you ran, your baggy pants fell to your ankles, and you smacked face-first on the floor. That same trip, you ran your bike into a tree, broke your finger and got poked in the eye. You came home in a neck brace. Your mom wasn't fazed. You were clumsy, always getting hurt.

(21) All the guys said they want to be big brothers to McKenzie. You were so protective of her. After school, it was just the two of you in the house. If there were guys on the porch with her, you'd call your mom and say you were going to make the boys leave. And you would. McKenzie doesn't like coming home after school now. You're supposed to be there, and it makes her sad.

(22) The day before the funeral your family went into your room. Your dad hadn't been in there since he found you. Monica was so scared, but when she walked in, the window was open, the breeze coming in, and it was peaceful. They love you, and they always will. They're trying not to focus on why you did it, because they will never know. They just miss you and wish you were here.

(1,808 words)

Suicide Warning Signs

Seek help as soon as possible by contacting a mental health professional or by calling the National Suicide Prevention Lifeline at 1-800-273-TALK if you or someone you know exhibits any of the following signs:

- Threatening to hurt or kill oneself or talking about wanting to hurt or kill oneself
- Looking for ways to kill oneself by seeking access to firearms, pills, or other means
- Talking or writing about death, dying, or suicide when these actions are out of the ordinary for the person
- Feeling hopeless
- Feeling rage or uncontrolled anger or seeking revenge
- Acting reckless or engaging in risky activities—seemingly without thinking
- Feeling trapped—like there's no way out
- Increasing alcohol or drug use
- Withdrawing from friends, family, and society
- Experiencing dramatic mood changes
- Seeing no reason for living or having no sense of purpose in life

Source: U.S. Department of Health and Human Services Substance Abuse and Mental Health Services Administration www. samhsa. gov

Here are some of the more difficult words in "Family and Friends Share Pain and Grief."

cliques
(paragraph 16)

clique (klik, klēk) *n.* ⟦Fr < OFr *cliquer*, to make a noise: of echoic orig.⟧ a small, exclusive circle of people; snobbish or narrow coterie —*SYN.* COTERIE —**cliqu'·ish** (-ish) *adj.*, **cliqu'ey**, or **cliqu'y** (-ē) — **cliqu'·ishly** *adv.*

impulsive
(paragraph 8)

im·pul·sive (im pul'siv) *adj.* ⟦< MFr or ML: MFr *impulsif* < ML *impulsivus* < L *impulsus*, IMPULSE⟧ **1** impelling; driving forward **2** *a)* acting or likely to act on impulse *[an impulsive person] b)* produced by or resulting from a sudden impulse *[an impulsive remark]* **3** *Mech.* acting briefly and as a result of impulse —*SYN.* SPONTANEOUS —**im·pul'·sively** *adv.* —**im·pul'·sive·ness** *n.*

lunatic
(paragraph 19)

lu·na·tic (lōō'nə tik) *adj.* ⟦ME *lunatik* < OFr *lunatique* < LL *lunaticus*, moon-struck, crazy < L *luna*, the moon: see LIGHT¹⟧ **1** suffering from lunacy; insane **2** of or characterized by lunacy **3** of or for insane persons **4** utterly foolish —*n.* an insane person Term seldom used now except in hyperbolic extension

Mafia
(paragraph 11)

Ma·fia (mä'fē ə) *n.* ⟦Sicilian⟧ **1** in Sicily, *a)* [m-] an attitude of popular hostility to law and government *b)* a secret society characterized by this attitude **2** *a)* in the U.S. and elsewhere, a secret society, of Italian origin, engaged in such illegal activities as gambling, prostitution, and illicit trade in narcotics *b)* [m-] any group engaged in such activities *[the Russian mafia]* **3** [m-] any exclusive or dominating group Also **Maf'·fia**

magenta
(paragraph 10)

ma·gen·ta (mə jen'tə) *n.* ⟦after *Magenta*, town in Italy: so called because discovered about the time (1859) of the battle fought there⟧ **1** FUCHSIN **2** purplish red —*adj.* purplish-red

obituary
(paragraph 14)

obitu·ary (ō bich'ōō er'ē) *n., pl.* **-·ar'·ies** ⟦ML *obituarius* < L *obitus*: see OBIT⟧ a notice of someone's death, as in a newspaper, usually with a brief biography —*adj.* of or recording a death or deaths —**o·bit'·u·ar'·ist** *n.*

psychologist
(paragraph 8)

psy·cholo·gist (sī käl'ə jist) *n.* a specialist in psychology

unadulterated
(paragraph 19)

adul·ter·ate (ə dul'tər āt'; *for adj.,* -tər it) *vt.* **-·at'ed, -·at'·ing** ⟦< L *adulteratus*, pp. of *adulterare*, to falsify < *adulter*, an adulterer, counterfeiter < *ad-*, to + *alter*, other, another⟧ to make inferior, impure, not genuine, etc. by adding a harmful, less valuable, or prohibited substance —*adj.* **1** guilty of adultery; adulterous **2** adulterated; not genuine —**adul'·tera'·tor** *n.*

tapestry
(paragraph 2)

tap·es·try (tap'əs trē) *n., pl.* **-·tries** ⟦LME *tapsterie*, earlier *tapicerie* < MFr *tapisserie* < OFr *tapis*, a carpet < MGr *tapētion* < Gr, dim. of *tapēs* (gen. *tapētos*), a carpet, prob. < Iran, as in Pers *tāftan*, to twist, spin < IE *temp-* < base *ten-*, to stretch > THIN⟧ a heavy cloth woven by hand or machinery with decorative designs and pictures and used as a wall hanging, furniture covering, etc. — *vt.* **-·tried, -·try·ing** to decorate as with a tapestry: usually in the pp.

12A   VOCABULARY

Using the vocabulary listed on page 201, fill in this crossword puzzle.

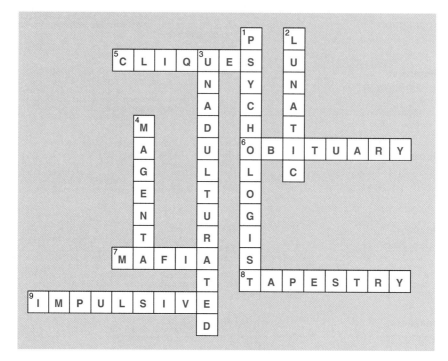

Across

5. small, exclusive circles of people
6. a notice of someone's death
7. a secret society
8. a cloth woven by hand
9. likely to act without thinking

Down

1. a specialist in dealing with the mind
2. insane
3. not inferior
4. purplish red

12B   CENTRAL THEME AND MAIN IDEAS

Choose the best answer.

  b   1. Another title for this selection could be
       a. The Last Day Was a Good Day
       b. The Life and Death of Teenager Affect Many
       c. Teenager's Fibbing and Lying Worry Parents
       d. Students Recall Max as Best Friend

Name   Date

___c___ 2. What is the main idea of paragraph 4?
   a. Before leaving home, Max Durham's father checks on his sleeping son.
   b. Max Durham and father enjoy a Saturday afternoon working on their cars.
   c. A perfect Saturday afternoon turns into a tragic Sunday morning.
   d. Max's mother and sister speed home from Alabama after learning of Max's death.

___a___ 3. What is the main idea of paragraph 8?
   a. Rather than blaming others for his death, the family tries to understand Max's impulsive action.
   b. Parents seek professional assistance of a psychologist to help their troubled son.
   c. High school principal regrets not recognizing Max's suicidal tendency.
   d. Max Durham eats half a pizza the morning he commits suicide.

___d___ 4. What is the main idea of paragraph 18?
   a. Max Durham received counseling from his minister about fighting.
   b. On learning of Max Durham's death, a Pakistani girl calls Max's parents.
   c. The memorial service for Max Durham was at Hope Presbyterian.
   d. Max Durham hated injustice and fought for justice for others.

12C MAJOR DETAILS

Decide whether each detail is true (T), false (F), or not discussed (ND).

___F___ 1. Bob Marley's "Could You Be Loved" was played at Max Durham's memorial service.

___T___ 2. Max Durham committed suicide in his bedroom.

___F___ 3. Max Durham used a pistol to commit suicide.

___F___ 4. Max Durham's parents transferred him from Germantown High School to St. Benedict because of his failing grades.

___T___ 5. At St. Benedict, Max Durham renamed himself Caesar Maximus Durham.

___T___ 6. Eight hours before he died, Max Durham left a message on his girlfriend's phone.

  ND   7. Chris Peterson and Johnson Lohnes were classmates of Max Durham at Germantown High School.

  T   8. A frequent comment by friends the day after Max Durham died was, "He was my best friend."

  F   9. The only church trip Max Durham ever went on was to Colorado.

  T   10. Besides his parents, Max Durham left two sisters, McKenzie and Monica.

12D   INFERENCES

Choose the best answer.

  c   1. *Read paragraph 5 again.* Max Durham probably told lies because
      a. he enjoyed scaring people with his stories.
      b. he knew that lying and fibbing upset his parents.
      c. he realized a pretend world was happier than the real world.
      d. he could not distinguish between the truth and a lie.

  b   2. *Read paragraph 7 again.* Max Durham's offering a family a ride to Memphis from the Nashville airport on Christmas Eve shows Max's
      a. intelligence.
      b. compassion.
      c. deceit.
      d. humor.

  c   3. *Read paragraph 7 again.* Just Max Durham and his father made a trip to Colorado because
      a. the mother and sister did not know how to ski.
      b. Max preferred to take a vacation with only his father.
      c. the father believed he needed to spend one-on-one time with Max.
      d. the family could afford a vacation for only two, not four, family members.

12E   CRITICAL READING: FACT OR OPINION

Decide whether each statement, even if it quotes someone, contains a FACT or an OPINION.

  FACT   1. *From paragraph 6:* "You were so intelligent, but you were failing."

  OPINION   2. *From paragraph 8:* "Your dad thinks there was something in your brain, a disorder not diagnosed."

Name   Date

<u>FACT</u> 3. *From paragraph 9*: "You didn't leave a note [. . .]."

<u>OPINION</u> 4. *From paragraph 10*: "You had an old soul."

<u>OPINION</u> 5. *From paragraph 13*: "He says he wouldn't be alive if not for you."

<u>FACT</u> 6. *From paragraph 18*: "You got into many fights standing up for her."

<u>OPINION</u> 7. *From paragraph 19*: "You were a lunatic"

<u>OPINION</u> 8. *From paragraph 20*: "You were clumsy [. . .]."

12F CRITICAL READING: THE AUTHOR'S STRATEGIES

Choose the best answer.

<u>c</u> 1. Erin Sullivan's main audience for "Friends and Family Share Pain and Grief," although it is a letter addressed to Max, is
   a. Max's family and friends, who she hoped would find comfort in her words.
   b. the author's English teacher, who ran a competition for the best student essay in memory of Max.
   c. Max's family, friends, and anyone in the general public who sees it.
   d. people who volunteer to be trained as counselors to talk on teenage suicide call-in help lines.

<u>d</u> 2. The author's purpose in writing this reading is to
   a. entertain.
   b. describe.
   c. argue.
   d. inform.

<u>a</u> 3. The author's tone is this reading is
   a. sorrowful.
   b. fault-finding.
   c. confused.
   d. awestruck.

12G READER'S PROCESS: SUMMARIZING YOUR READING

<u>d</u> 1. What is the best summary of "Friends and Family Share Pain and Questions"?
   a. Everyone who knew and loved Max was shocked when he killed himself with a shotgun. His friends knew he made up stories about himself, but they did not take his lies seriously because he was kind, funny, understanding, and supportive.

b. Max, sad and depressed, committed suicide with a shotgun one Sunday while he was home alone. He did not leave a note. His father was at church, and his mother and sister were out of town.

c. No one suspected that Max was so depressed that he would kill himself. His friends and family admired and loved him very much. He did many kind acts for people. For example, he protected a sixth-grade Pakistani girl tormented by other students because of her faith and traditional clothes.

d. Max, much-loved son and best friend to many, killed himself one Sunday when no one was home. His friends and relatives saw no signs of his depression, so his committing suicide shocked everyone. Family and friends have chosen to remember his loving and generous spirit.

12H   READER'S RESPONSE: TO DISCUSS OR WRITE ABOUT

1. Teen suicide is becoming more common in the United States every year. One in 10,000 teens dies from suicide. The majority of suicide attempts and deaths happen among teens with depression. Have you or someone you have known ever experienced depression? How long did the depression last? What caused the depression? How did it affect you? Was professional help needed to overcome the depression? What suggestions could you give to someone who is experiencing depression?

2. Suicide is a permanent solution to a temporary problem. More than 60 percent of teen suicide deaths happen with a gun. Is it possible Max would not have committed suicide if a gun were not so accessible? Explain your response.

Name   Date

HOW DID YOU DO?

12 Family and Friends Share Pain and Questions

SKILL (number of items)	Number Correct		Points for each		Score
Vocabulary (9)	_____	×	2	=	_____
Central Theme and Main Ideas (4)	_____	×	6	=	_____
Major Details (10)	_____	×	2	=	_____
Inferences (3)	_____	×	4	=	_____
Critical Reading: Fact or Opinion(8)	_____	×	2	=	_____
Critical Reading: The Author's Strategies (3)	_____	×	2	=	_____
Reader's Process: Summarizing Your Reading (1)	_____	×	4	=	_____

(Possible Total: 100) *Total* _____

SPEED

Reading Time: _____ Reading Rate (page 412): _____ Words Per Minute

Part 4

THINKING: GETTING STARTED

Today's world is more diverse than ever—at least that's how it appears when you turn on the television or listen to the radio. With the expanding capabilities of technology and media, it is possible to learn about and be exposed to various viewpoints regarding a wide range of social issues. The readings in Part 4 provide another opportunity for you to explore topics that you may have encountered in your experience.

Use the visuals and accompanying questions on the next three pages to begin engaging your prior knowledge. Turn also to each reading selection in Part 4 and *survey* it by looking at its title and its first and last paragraphs. What do you know about the topic already? Predict what the selection will be about. Your prediction might be off the mark—especially until you get more experienced at making predictions. Still, making a prediction focuses your mind usefully on what you will be reading.

After you *survey*, ask *questions*. This technique is explained in Chapter 3 (Part 1). You need only ask the questions, not answer them. Later, when you read with questions in mind, the answers will often seem to "jump out" from the page as you come across them. The purpose of asking questions, then, is to gear up your mind so that it actively confronts new information.

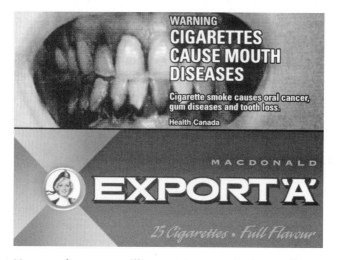

How much are you willing to give up to help you live a longer life? (See "How to Stay Alive.")

In what ways are twins born equal to each other, and in what ways do they differ? (See "Genes and Behavior: A Twin Legacy.")

Is raising a child as fulfilling an occupation as a traditional career? (See "Escaping the Daily Grind for Life as a House Father.")

What June celebration, besides Father's Day and Flag Day, is increasing in popularity? (See "Forty Acres and a Holiday.")

What memories will you treasure when you are old?
(See "My Mother's Blue Bowl.")

Some people take risks for the thrill of adventure. What
risks do immigrants take to cross the border between
Mexico and the United States? (See "From In search of
Bernabé.,")

How to Stay Alive

Art Hoppe

Once upon a time there was a man named Snadley Klabberhorn, who was the healthiest man in the whole wide world.

Snadley wasn't always the healthiest man in the whole wide world. When he was young, Snadley smoked what he wanted, drank what he wanted, ate what he wanted, and exercised only with young ladies in bed.   *5*

He thought he was happy. "Life is absolutely peachy," he was fond of saying. "Nothing beats being alive."

Then along came the Surgeon General's Report linking smoking to lung cancer, heart disease, emphysema, and tertiary coreopsis.

Snadley read about The Great Tobacco Scare with a frown. "Life is so   *10* peachy," he said, "that there's no sense taking any risks." So he gave up smoking.

Like most people who went through the hell of giving up smoking, Snadley became more interested in his own health. In fact, he became fascinated. And when he read a WCTU tract which pointed out that alcohol   *15* caused liver damage, brain damage, and acute *weltanschauung*, he gave up alcohol and drank dietary colas instead.

At least he did until The Great Cyclamate Scare.

"There's no sense in taking any risks," he said. And he switched to sugar-sweetened colas, which made him fat and caused dental caries. On realizing   *20* this he renounced colas in favor of milk and took up jogging, which was an awful bore.

That was about the time of The Great Cholesterol Scare.

Snadley gave up milk. To avoid cholesterol, which caused atherosclerosis, coronary infarcts, and chronic chryselephantinism, he also gave up meat,   *25* fats, and dairy products, subsisting on a diet of raw fish.

Then came the Great DDT Scare.

"The presence of large amounts of DDT in fish . . ." Snadley read with anguish. But fortunately that's when he met Ernestine. They were made for each other. Ernestine introduced him to home-ground wheat germ, mac-   *30* robiotic yogurt, and organic succotash.

They were very happy eating this dish twice daily, watching six hours of color television together, and spending the rest of their time in bed.

They were, that is, until The Great Color Television Scare.

"If color tee-vee does give off radiations," said Snadley, "there's no sense   *35* taking risks. After all, we still have each other."

And that's about all they had. Until The Great Pill Scare.

On hearing that The Pill might cause carcinoma, thromboses, and lingering stichometry, Ernestine promptly gave up The Pill—and Snadley.
40 "There's no sense taking any risks," she said.

Snadley was left with jogging. He was, that is, until he read somewhere that 1.3 percent of joggers are eventually run over by a truck or bitten by rabid dogs.

He then retired to a bomb shelter in his back yard (to avoid being hit by
45 a meteor), installed an air purifier (after The Great Smog Scare) and spent the next 63 years doing Royal Canadian Air Force exercises and poring over back issues of *The Reader's Digest.*

"Nothing's more important than being alive," he said proudly on reaching 102. But he never did say anymore that life was absolutely peachy.

* * *

50 CAUTION: Being alive may be hazardous to your health.

(520 words)

Here are some of the more difficult words in "How to Stay Alive."

carcinoma
(line 38)

car·ci·noma (kär'sə nō'mə) *n., pl.* **-mas** or **-mata** (-mə tə) ⟦L < Gr *karkinōma,* cancer < *karkinoun,* affect with a cancer < *karkinos,* crab: see CANCER⟧ any of several kinds of cancerous growths deriving from epithelial cells: see SARCOMA —**car'·ci·nom'a·tous** (-näm'ə təs, -nō'mə-) *adj.*

chronic
(line 25)

chronic (krän'ik) *adj.* ⟦Fr *cronique* < L *chronicus* < Gr *chronikos,* of time < *chronos,* time⟧ **1** lasting a long time or recurring often: said of a disease, and distinguished from ACUTE **2** having had an ailment for a long time [*a chronic patient*] **3** continuing indefinitely; perpetual; constant [*a chronic worry*] **4** by habit, custom, etc.; habitual; inveterate [*a chronic complainer*] —*n.* a chronic patient —**chron'i·cally** *adv.* —**chro·nic·ity** (krə nis'ə tē) *n.*
SYN.—**chronic** suggests long duration or frequent recurrence and is used especially of diseases or habits that resist all efforts to eradicate them [*chronic* sinusitis]; **inveterate** implies firm establishment as a result of continued indulgence over a long period of time [*an inveterate* liar]; **confirmed** suggests fixedness in some condition or practice, often from a deep-seated aversion to change [*a confirmed* bachelor]; **hardened** implies fixed tendencies and a callous indifference to emotional or moral considerations [*a hardened* criminal]

coronary
(line 25)

coro·nary (kôr'ə ner'ē, kär'-) *adj.* ⟦L *coronarius:* see CROWN⟧ **1** of, or in the form of, a crown **2** *Anat. a*) like a crown; encircling *b*) designating or relating to either of two arteries, or their branches, coming from the aorta and supplying blood directly to the heart muscle —☆*n., pl.* **-nar'·ies** CORONARY THROMBOSIS

DDT
(line 28)

DDT (dē'dē'tē') *n.* ⟦*d(ichloro)d(iphenyl)t(richloroethane)*⟧ a powerful insecticide ($ClC_6H_4)_2CHCCl_3$, effective upon contact: its use is restricted by law due to damaging environmental effects

emphysema
(line 9)

em·phy·sema (em′fə sē′mə; -zē′-) *n.* ⟦ModL < Gr *emphysēma,* inflation < *emphysaein,* to inflate, blow in < *en-,* in + *physaein,* to blow < IE **phus-* < base **pu-, *phu-,* echoic of blowing with puffed cheeks⟧ **1** an abnormal swelling of body tissues caused by the accumulation of air; esp., such a swelling of the lung tissue, due to the permanent loss of elasticity, or the destruction, of the alveoli, which seriously impairs respiration **2** HEAVES —**em′·phy·se′ma·tous** (-sē′mə təs, -sem′-) *adj.* —**em′·phy·se′mic** *adj., n.*

macrobiotic
(line 31)

macro·bi·ot·ics (mak′rō bī ät′iks) *pl.n.* ⟦see prec. & -BIOTIC⟧ [*with sing. v.*] the study of prolonging life, as by special diets, etc. — **mac′ro·bi·ot′ic** *adj.*

weltanschauung
(line 16)

Welt·an·schau·ung (velt′än shou′oon) *n.* ⟦Ger, world view⟧ a comprehensive, esp. personal, philosophy or conception of the universe and of human life

"How to Stay Alive" has many unusual words in it. To help you read the essay easily, here are some quick definitions.

tertiary	(line 9)	third
coreopsis	(line 9)	tickseed plant
WCTU	(line 15)	Women's Christian Temperance Union
cholesterol	(line 24)	fatty substances in the blood
atherosclerosis	(line 24)	hardening of the arteries
infarcts	(line 25)	obstruction of blood vessels
chryselephantinism	(line 25)	being overlaid with gold and ivory
yogurt	(line 31)	a fermented milk food
succotash	(line 31)	lima beans and corn cooked together
thromboses	(line 38)	blood clots
stichometry	(line 39)	practice of writing prose

13A VOCABULARY

Choose the best answer.

  b 1. If you had **emphysema**, you would
   a. be breaking the law.
   b. have trouble breathing.
   c. get frequent headaches.
   d. be unable to digest food.

    d   2. The word **weltanschauung** is closest in meaning to
  a. peptic ulcers.
  b. a passion for German opera.
  c. cruelty to children.
  d. a personal philosophy of life.

    a   3. The word **coronary** refers to
  a. the arteries leading to the heart.
  b. a medical examiner.
  c. kidney disease.
  d. the arteries leading to the brain.

    c   4. A **chronic** illness is best described as
  a. painful.
  b. extremely expensive to treat.
  c. continuing indefinitely.
  d. likely to result in death.

    b   5. **DDT** is best known as
  a. the FBI's list of "most wanted" criminals.
  b. a deadly insecticide.
  c. the cause of high blood pressure.
  d. a foreign sports car.

    a   6. Anything that is **macrobiotic** is
  a. believed to prolong life.
  b. hazardous to your health.
  c. very delicious.
  d. pornographic.

    b   7. **Carcinoma** is a medical term for
  a. tuberculosis.
  b. cancer.
  c. heart disease.
  d. measles.

13B   CENTRAL THEME

Choose the best answer.

    b   1. What is the central theme of "How to Stay Alive"?
  a. The secret of living to a ripe old age is avoiding indulgences that are hazardous to your health.
  b. Snadley Klabberhorn enjoyed life until he changed his habits in reaction to every health scare.

c. Snadley Klabberhorn's main goal was to live to 102 without giving up smoking, drinking, sweets, and color television.

d. Everyone should disregard health scares and live life to its fullest.

13C MAJOR DETAILS

Decide whether each detail is true (T), false (F), or not discussed (ND).

_T_ 1. Snadley liked to say, "Nothing beats being alive."

_T_ 2. With each new health scare, Snadley altered his life to avoid the danger.

_ND_ 3. The Great Noise Scare led Snadley to wear earplugs all the time.

_F_ 4. Snadley's wife, Ernestine, refused to give up The Pill even after hearing about its health hazards.

_F_ 5. Snadley liked to say, "Nothing beats being healthy."

_T_ 6. Snadley finally retired to his bomb shelter to avoid all hazards.

_T_ 7. By the time Snadley reached the age of 102, he no longer said that life was absolutely peachy.

13D INFERENCES

Choose the best answer.

_c_ 1. "How to Stay Alive" implies that people
   a. should avoid anything that might cause disease.
   b. should live recklessly.
   c. cannot expect to avoid all health hazards.
   d. cannot live long in today's world.

_d_ 2. *Read lines 9, 25, and 39 again.* The author uses the words "tertiary coreopsis," "chronic chryselephantinism," and "stichometry," which are not medical terms. Why does he use them?
   a. He thinks big words will impress the reader.
   b. He likes to teach his readers difficult words.
   c. He thinks that they are connected with good health and staying alive.
   d. He is poking fun at the use of big technical words to name well-known diseases.

13E   CRITICAL READING: THE AUTHOR'S STRATEGIES

Choose the best answer.

__c__ 1. The main audience for "How to Stay Alive" is
 a. people who are trying to adopt a healthier lifestyle.
 b. people who have given up worrying about their health.
 c. people who worry about medical research reports.
 d. people who haven't had a medical checkup in a long time.

__d__ 2. The author's purpose in writing this reading is to
 a. expose.
 b. describe.
 c. emphasize.
 d. entertain.

__b__ 3. The author's tone in this reading is
 a. serious.
 b. humorous.
 c. concerned.
 d. angry.

13F   READER'S PROCESS: SUMMARIZING YOUR READING

__d__ 1. What is the best summary of "How to Stay Alive"?
 a. The author suggests that we can't take medical research too seriously.
 b. The author suggests that perfect health isn't everything.
 c. The author suggests a list of foods and habits that should be avoided if one is to stay healthy.
 d. The author suggests that enjoying life is more important than living to a very old age.

13G   READER'S RESPONSE: TO DISCUSS OR WRITE ABOUT

1. Have you ever changed your habits because of health warnings? Using a specific example of a health warning, explain why you did or did not change your habits.

2. If the statement is true that you are what you eat, what are you? From your own experience, explain how who you are is a reflection of what you eat on a daily basis.

Name   Date

HOW DID YOU DO?

13 How to Stay Alive

SKILL (number of items)	Number Correct		Points for Each		Score
Vocabulary (7)	_____	×	5	=	_____
Central Theme (1)	_____	×	7	=	_____
Major Details (7)	_____	×	6	=	_____
Inferences (2)	_____	×	4	=	_____
Critical Reading: The Author's Strategies (3)	_____	×	2	=	_____
Reader's Process: Summarizing Your Reading (1)	_____	×	2	=	_____

(Possible Total: 100) *Total* _____

SPEED

Reading Time: _____ Reading Rate (page 412): _____ Words Per Minute

Name	Date

Selection 14

Genes and Behavior: A Twin Legacy

Constance Holden

(1) Biology may not be destiny, but genes apparently have a far greater influence on human behavior than is commonly thought. Similarities ranging from phobias to hobbies to bodily gestures are being found in pairs of twins separated at birth. Many of these behaviors are "things you would never think of looking at if you were going to study the genetics of behavior," says psychologist Thomas J. Bouchard, Jr., director of the Minnesota Center for Twin and Adoption Research at the University of Minnesota.

(2) Bouchard reports that so far, exhaustive psychological tests and questionnaires have been completed with approximately 50 pairs of identical twins reared apart, 25 pairs of fraternal twins reared apart and comparison groups of twins reared together. "We were amazed at the similarity in posture and expressive style," says Bouchard. "It's probably the feature of the study that's grabbed us the most." Twins tend to have similar mannerisms, gestures, speed and tempo in talking, habits, and jokes.

(3) Many of the twins dressed in similar fashion—one male pair who had never previously met arrived in England sporting identical beards, haircuts, wire-rimmed glasses and shirts. (Their photo shows them both with thumbs hooked into their pants tops.) One pair had practically the same items in their toilet cases, including the same brand of cologne and a Swedish brand of toothpaste.

(4) Although many of the separated pairs had differing types of jobs and educational levels, the investigators are finding repeated similarities in hobbies and interests—one pair were both volunteer firefighters, one pair were deputy sheriffs, a male pair had similar workshops in their basements and a female pair had strikingly similar kitchen arrangements. In one case, two women from different social classes, one of whom was a pharmacological technician and the other a bookkeeper and a high school dropout, had results on their vocational-interest tests that were "remarkably similar."

(5) Bouchard doesn't have enough information on abnormal behavior or psychopathology to make generalizations, but he has found repeated similarities. One pair of women were both very superstitious; another pair would burst into tears at the drop of a hat, and questioning revealed that both had done so since childhood. "They were on a talk show together and both started crying in response to one of the questions," says Bouchard. A third pair had

Because identical twins look alike, are their personalities usualiy alike?

the same fears and phobias. Both were afraid of water and had adopted the same coping strategy: backing into the ocean up to their knees. Bouchard took them to a shopping center one day, driving up a long, winding parking ramp to let them off. He later learned that they were both so frightened by the drive they sat on a bench for two hours to collect themselves.

(6) The most striking example of common psychopathology, however, came from a pair of fraternal twins reared apart. One had been reared by his own (poor) family; the other had been adopted into a "good solid upper-middle-class family." Both are now considered to be antisocial personalities, suffering from lack of impulse control, and both have criminal histories. Although fraternal twins share, on average, 50 percent of their genes, Bouchard suggests that the overlap is probably considerably more with this pair.

(7) Another eerie congruence that occurred in the absence of identical genes was observed in the case of two identical-twin women reared apart. Each has a son who has won a statewide mathematics contest, one in Wyoming, one in Texas.

(8) Personality similarities between the identical twins reared apart are almost as pervasive as they are with identical twins reared together, according to the results of a test developed by University of Minnesota psychologist Auke Tellegen. His personality questionnaire contains scales such as "social closeness," "harm avoidance" and "well-being." The researchers were especially surprised to find that "traditionalism"—a trait implying conservatism and respect for authority—can be inherited. In fact, says Bouchard, his and other studies have found about 11 personality traits that appear to have significant genetic input.

(9) Overall, the emerging findings of the Minnesota study constitute a powerful rebuttal to those who maintain that environmental influences are the primary shaping forces of personality. The textbooks are going to have to be rewritten, Bouchard predicts.

(694 words)

Here are some of the more difficult words in "Genes and Behavior: A Twin Legacy."

congruence
(paragraph 7)

con·gru·ence (kän′grōō əns, kän′-; kən grōō′əns) *n.* [ME < L *congruentia:* see fol.] **1** the state or quality of being in agreement; correspondence; harmony **2** *Geom.* the property of a plane or solid figure whereby it coincides with another plane or solid figure after it is moved, rotated, or flipped over **3** *Math.* the relation between two integers each of which, when divided by a third (called the *modulus*), leaves the same remainder Also **con′·gru·ency**

conservatism
(paragraph 8)

con·serva·tism (kən sur′və tiz′əm) *n.* the principles and practices of a conservative person or party; tendency to oppose change in institutions and methods
con·serva·tive (kən sur′və tiv) *adj.* [OFr *conservatif* < LL *conservativus*] **1** conserving or tending to conserve; preservative **2** tending to preserve established traditions or institutions and to resist or oppose any changes in these [*conservative* politics, *conservative* art] **3** of or characteristic of a conservative **4** [C-] designating or of the major political party of Great Britain or the similar one in Canada that is characterized by conservative positions on social and economic issues ☆**5** moderate; cautious; safe [a *conservative* estimate] **6** [C-] *Judaism* designating or of a movement that accepts traditional forms and religious ritual that have been adapted to modern life with moderation and flexibility —*n.* **1** [Archaic] a preservative **2** a conservative person **3** [C-] a member of the Conservative Party of Great Britain or of the Progressive Conservative Party of Canada —**con·serv′a·tively** *adv.* —**con·serv′·a·tive·ness** *n.*

destiny
(paragraph 1)

des·tiny (des′tə nē) *n., pl.* **-nies** [ME *destine* < OFr *destinee,* fem. pp. of *destiner:* see prec.] **1** the seemingly inevitable or necessary succession of events **2** what will necessarily happen to any person or thing; (one's) fate **3** that which determines events: said of either a supernatural agency or necessity —*SYN.* FATE

fraternal twins
(paragraph 2)

fra·ter·nal (frə tur′nəl) *adj.* [ME < ML *fraternalis* < L *fraternus,* brotherly < *frater,* BROTHER] **1** of or characteristic of a brother or brothers; brotherly **2** of or like a fraternal order or a fraternity **3** designating twins, of either the same or different sexes, developed from separately fertilized ova and thus having hereditary characteristics not necessarily the same: cf. IDENTICAL (sense 3) —**fra·ter′·nal·ism** *n.* —**fra·ter′·nally** *adv.*

genes
(paragraph 1)

☆**gene** (jēn) *n.* [< Ger *gen,* short for *pangen* (< *pan-,* PAN- + *-gen,* -GEN, after PANGENESIS)] *Genetics* any of the units occurring at specific points on the chromosomes, by which hereditary characters are transmitted and determined: each is regarded as a particular state of organization of the chromatin in the chromosome, consisting primarily of DNA and protein: see DOMINANT, RECESSIVE, MENDEL'S LAWS

genetics
(paragraph 1)

ge·net·ics (jə net′iks) *n.* [GENET(IC) + -ICS] **1** the branch of biology that deals with heredity and variation in similar or related animals and plants **2** the genetic features or constitution of an individual, group, or kind

identical twins
(paragraph 2)

iden·ti·cal (ī den′ti kəl) *adj.* [prec. + -AL] **1** the very same **2** exactly alike or equal: often followed by *with* or *to* **3** designating twins, always of the same sex, developed from a single fertilized ovum and very much alike in physical appearance: cf. FRATERNAL (sense 3) —*SYN.* SAME —**iden′·ti·cally** *adv.*

pervasive
(paragraph 8)

per·va·sive (pər vā′siv) *adj.* tending to pervade or spread throughout —**per·va′·sively** *adv.* —**per·va′·sive·ness** *n.*

phobias
(paragraph 1)

pho·bia (fō′bē ə, fō′byə) *n.* [ModL < Gr *phobos,* fear: see prec.] an irrational, excessive, and persistent fear of some particular thing or situation

Vocabulary List

Vocabulary List

psychopathology
(paragraph 5)

psycho·pa·thol·ogy (sī'kō pə thäl'ə jē) *n.* [PSYCHO- + PATHOLOGY]
1 the science dealing with the causes and development of mental
disorders **2** psychological malfunctioning, as in a mental disorder
—psy'cho·path'o·log'i·cal (-path'ə läj'i kəl) *adj.* —psy'cho·pa·
thol'o·gist *n.*

rebuttal
(paragraph 9)

re·but (ri but') *vt.* --but'·ted, --but'·ting [ME *rebuten* < Anglo-Fr
reboter < OFr *rebuter* < *re-*, back + *buter*, to thrust, push: see
BUTT[2]] **1** to contradict, refute, or oppose, esp. in a formal manner
by argument, proof, etc., as in a debate **2** [Obs.] to force back;
repel —*vi.* to provide opposing arguments —*SYN.* DISPROVE —re·
but'·table *adj.*
re·but·tal (-but''l) *n.* a rebutting, esp. in law

vocational
(paragraph 4)

vo·ca·tional (-shə nəl) *adj.* **1** of a vocation, trade, occupation, etc.
☆**2** designating or of education, training, a school, etc. intended to
prepare one for an occupation, sometimes specif. in a trade —vo·
ca'·tion·al·ism' *n.* —vo·ca'·tion·ally *adv.*

14A   VOCABULARY

Using the vocabulary words listed on pages 223–224, fill in the blanks.

1. Police statistics show that there is ___congruence___ between the
   amount of drug use and the number of burglaries in any neighborhood.

2. Specific areas of the brain control specific behaviors, and as scientists'
   knowledge of such connections improves, methods may be developed
   to repair damaged or misformed parts of the brain and cure some kinds
   of _psychopathology_ .

3. Although some people believe that fate controls their lives, polls indicate that on the average, Americans believe that they control their own
   ___destiny___ .

4. ___Genetics___ is the study of heredity in animals and plants,
   including how ___genes___ transmit various characteristics.

5. Students who plan to learn a trade choose to attend a
   ___vocational___ school.

6. People with excessive and persistent fears ought to seek professional
   counseling before ___phobias___ destroy their lives.

Name   Date

7. Expressions based on sports are ____pervasive____ in our society; even people who have never seen a basketball game may speak of being "fouled" by an unfair competitor.

8. Most people think of twins as looking absolutely alike; actually, such complete resemblance is typical only of ____identical____ ____twins____, and __fraternal twins__ often look very different from one another.

9. __The conservatism__ of candidates who call for a return to the "good old days" is appealing to voters who are uncomfortable with rapid progress.

10. The band members compiled a list of songs with social messages as a ____rebuttal____ to charges that rock music encourages irresponsible behavior.

14B   CENTRAL THEME AND MAIN IDEAS

Choose the best answer.

__c__ 1. What is the central theme of "Genes and Behavior: A Twin Legacy"?
   a. Extensive psychological tests and questionnaires have been completed by numbers of identical and fraternal twins.
   b. Carefully controlled studies show that many identical as well as fraternal twins, even when they are reared apart, tend to dress in similar fashion.
   c. Studies of twins, both identical and fraternal, provide evidence for the theory that genes have a greater influence on human behavior than is commonly thought.
   d. Thorough research about both identical and fraternal twins reveals that even if they are raised apart, they generally share the same phobias, hobbies, and gestures.

__a__ 2. What is the main idea of paragraph 2?
   a. Bouchard has studied fraternal and identical twins, some reared apart and some reared together.
   b. Bouchard has studied only identical twins, some reared apart and some together.
   c. Bouchard has studied only fraternal twins, some reared apart and some together.
   d. Bouchard has studied fraternal and identical twins, all of whom were raised apart.

___d___ 3. What is the main idea of paragraph 5?
   a. Research shows that abnormal behavior in separated, identical twins is rare.
   b. Studies reveal that female identical twins are more likely than male identical twins to develop fears and phobias.
   c. Fear of long, winding ramps seems to be genetically determined, according to the research of Dr. Bouchard.
   d. Researchers have not found enough examples of abnormal behavior in separated identical twins to be certain that a pattern exists.

14C   MAJOR DETAILS

Decide whether each detail is true (T), false (F), or not discussed (ND).

___T___ 1. Thomas J. Bouchard is the director of the Minnesota Center for Twin and Adoption Research.

___F___ 2. The behavior of separated twins is being compared with the behavior of a group of 25 pairs of twins raised together.

___T___ 3. Even though many of the separated twins have different jobs, they often share the same hobbies and interests.

___F___ 4. One pair of identical twins who burst into tears easily both cried when asked to appear on a talk show.

___ND___ 5. Twins who are afraid of water are usually also afraid of the dark and of animals.

___T___ 6. One set of separated fraternal twins both had antisocial personalities and grew up to be criminals.

___F___ 7. A woman's twin sons won mathematics competitions in Wyoming and Texas.

___ND___ 8. Social closeness is essential for happiness in humans.

___F___ 9. Environmental influences are the most important shapers of personality.

___F___ 10. Genes determine almost all personality traits.

14D   INFERENCES

Choose the best answer.

___c___ 1. *Read paragraph 1 again.* What does the author mean by "Biology may not be destiny"?

Name   Date

a. Most psychologists believe that biology controls people's destinies.

b. Most psychologists believe that biology does not control people's destinies.

c. The debate over whether biology or environment controls people's destinies has been going on for a long time.

d. The author is not sure whether biology is destiny, so she is showing that she does not support the conclusions of Bouchard's study.

___c___ 2. *Read paragraph 1 again.* Why does Bouchard say these behaviors are "things you would never think of looking at if you were going to study the genetics of behavior"?

a. These behaviors seemed too unimportant for scientists to observe.

b. These behaviors seemed too intimate to allow scientists to observe them.

c. Psychologists assumed these relatively external characteristics could not be biologically based.

d. Psychologists assumed that the causes of these behaviors were too complicated for current methods of observation.

___a___ 3. *Read paragraph 5 again.* Why does Bouchard need more information before he can make generalizations?

a. He has not yet found a strong pattern of particular kinds of abnormal behavior among separated identical twins.

b. The government says researchers must have ten examples before they can make a generalization about a psychological issue.

c. He is afraid of being sued if he makes a statement that might later be shown to be inaccurate.

d. He does not want to embarrass the people in the small group he has studied, and so he is looking for additional, anonymous twins to study.

14E CRITICAL READING: THE AUTHOR'S STRATEGIES

Choose the best answer.

___b___ 1. The main audience for "Genes and Behavior: A Twin Legacy" is

a. people who are interested in the behavior of twins.

b. people who are interested in the influence of genetics on human behavior.

c. people who are interested in similarities of identical twins.

d. people who are parents of twins.

___c___ 2. The author's purpose in writing this reading is to
a. persuade.
b. entertain.
c. inform.
d. narrate.

___b___ 3. The author's tone in this reading is
a. grim.
b. argumentative.
c. sensational.
d. sincere.

14F   READER'S PROCESS: SUMMARIZING YOUR READING

___b___ 1. What is the best summary of "Genes and Behavior: A Twin Legacy"?
a. The writer reports on a study that showed that identical and fraternal twins have similar inherited traits.
b. The writer reports on a study that showed striking similarities in the personalities, behavior, and interests of twins who were reared apart.
c. The writer reports on a study that showed that genetics is an important factor in predicting human behavior.
d. The writer reports on a study that showed that twins share many traits.

14G   READER'S RESPONSE: TO DISCUSS OR WRITE ABOUT

1. Should parents of twins encourage them to dress and act differently or alike? Using specific examples, explain your point of view.

2. Sometimes fertility drugs are used by women to increase the possibility of pregnancy. Women who use these drugs sometimes have multiple births—four or more children. How do you feel about this? Are these women violating the Law of Nature? Give specific reasons to support your point of view.

Name   Date

HOW DID YOU DO?

14 Genes and Behavior: A Twin Legacy

SKILL (number of items)	Number Correct		Points for each		Score
Vocabulary* (12)	_____	×	3	=	_____
Central Theme and Main Ideas (3)	_____	×	4	=	_____
Major Details (10)	_____	×	3	=	_____
Inferences (3)	_____	×	3	=	_____
Critical Reading: The Author's Strategies (3)	_____	×	3	=	_____
Reader's Process: Summarizing Your Reading (1)	_____	×	4	=	_____

(Possible Total: 100) *Total* _____

SPEED

Reading Time: _____ Reading Rate (page 412): _____ Words Per Minute

*Questions 4 and 8 in this exercise call for two separate answers each. In computing your score, count each separate answer toward your number correct.

Escaping the Daily Grind for Life as a House Father

Rick Greenberg

(1) "You on vacation?" my neighbor asked.

(2) My 15-month-old son and I were passing her yard on our daily hike through the neighborhood. It was a weekday afternoon and I was the only working-age male in sight.

(3) "I'm uh . . . working out of my house now," I told her.

(4) Thus was born my favorite euphemism for house fatherhood, one of those new lifestyle occupations that is never merely mentioned. Explained, yes. Defended. Even rhapsodized about. I was tongue-tied then, but no longer. People are curious and I've learned to oblige.

(5) I joined up earlier this year when I quit my job—a dead-end, ulcer-producing affair that had dragged on interminably. I left to be with my son until something better came along. And if nothing did, I'd be with him indefinitely.

(6) This was no simple transition. I had never known a house father, never met one. I'd only read about them. They were another news magazine trend. Being a traditionalist, I never dreamed I'd take the plunge.

(7) But as the job got worse, I gave it serious thought. And more thought. And in the end, I still felt ambivalent. This was a radical change that seemed to carry as many drawbacks as benefits. My dislike for work finally pushed me over the edge. That, and the fact that we had enough money to get by.

(8) Escaping the treadmill was a bold stroke. I had shattered my lethargy and stopped whining, and for that I was proud.

(9) Some friends said they were envious. Of course they weren't quitting one job without one waiting—the ultimate in middle-class taboos. That ran through my mind as I triumphantly, and without notice, tossed the letter of resignation on my boss's desk. Then I walked away wobbly-kneed.

(10) The initial trauma of quitting, however, was mitigated by my eagerness to raise our son. Mine was the classic father's lament: I felt excluded. I had become "the man who got home after dark," that other person besides Mama. It hurt when I couldn't quiet his crying.

(11) I sensed that staying home would be therapeutic. The chronic competitiveness and aggressiveness that had served me well as a daily journalist would subside. Something better would emerge, something less obnoxious. My ulcer would heal. Instead of beating deadlines, I'd be doing something important for a change. This was heresy coming from a newspaper gypsy, but it rang true.

(12) There was unease, too. I'd be adrift, stripped of the home–office–home routine that had defined my existence for more than a decade. No more earning a living. No benchmarks. Time would be seamless. Would Friday afternoons feel the same?

(13) The newness of it was scary.

(14) Until my resignation, my wife and I typified today's baby-boomer couples, the want-it-all generation. We had two salaries, a full-time nanny and guilt pangs over practicing parenthood by proxy.

(15) Now, my wife brings home the paychecks, the office problems and thanks for good work on the domestic front. With me at home, her work hours are more flexible. Nanny-less, I change diapers, prepare meals and do all the rest. And I wonder what comes next.

(16) What if I don't find another job? My field is tight. At 34, I'm not getting any more marketable and being out of work doesn't help.

(17) As my father asked incredulously: "Is this going to be what you do?"

(18) Perhaps. I don't know. I wonder myself. It's even more baffling to my father, the veteran of a long and traditional 9-to-5 career. For most of it, my mother stayed home. My father doesn't believe in trends. All he knows is that his only son—with whom he shares so many traits—has violated the natural order of men providing and women raising children. In his view, I've shown weakness and immaturity by succumbing to a bad job.

(19) But he's trying to understand, and I think he will.

(20) I'm trying to understand it myself. House fatherhood has been humbling, rewarding and unnerving.

(21) "It's different," I tell friends. "Different."

(22) Imagine never having to leave home for the office in the morning. That's how different. No dress-up, no commute. Just tumble out of bed and you're there. House fathering is not for claustrophobics.

(23) I find myself enjoying early morning shopping. My son and I arrive right after the supermarket opens. The place is almost empty. For the next hour we glide dreamily, cruising the aisles to a Muzak accompaniment. This is my idyll. My son likes it, too; he's fascinated by the spectacle.

(24) Housekeeping still doesn't seem like work, and that's by design. I've mastered the art of doing just enough chores to get by. This leaves me enough free time. Time to read and write and daydream. Time with my son. Time to think about the structure.

(25) So much time, and so little traditional structure, that the days sometimes blur together. I remember on Sunday nights literally dreading the approaching work week, the grind. Today, the close of the weekend still triggers a shiver of apprehension; I now face the prospect of a week without tangible accomplishments, a void.

(26) On our hikes to the playground, I can feel my old identity fading. All around are people with a mission, a sense of purpose. Workers. And then, there's the rest of us—the stroller and backpack contingent. The moms, the nannies, and me. I wonder if I've crossed over a line never to return.

(27) Still, the ulcer seems to be healing. I take pride in laying out a good dinner for the family and in pampering my wife after a tough day at the office. I love reading to my son. Running errands isn't even so bad. A lot of what had been drudgery or trivia is taking on new meaning; maybe I'm mellowing.

(28) Which is ironic. To be a truly committed and effective at-home parent, there must be this change—a softening, a contentment with small pleasures, the outwardly mundane. This is a time of reduced demands and lowered expectations. Progress is gradual, often agonizingly so. Patience is essential. Ambition and competitiveness are anathema. Yet eliminating these last two qualities—losing the edge—could ruin my chances of resurrecting my career. I can't have it both ways.

(29) The conflict has yet to be resolved. And it won't be unless I make a firm commitment and choose one lifestyle over the other. I'm not yet ready for that decision.

(30) In the meantime, a wonderful change is taking place in our home. Amid all the uncertainties, my son and I have gotten to know each other. He can't put a phrase together, but he confides in me. It can be nothing more than a grin or a devilish look. He tries new words on me, new shtick. We roll around a lot; we crack each other up. I'm no longer the third wheel, the man who gets home after dark. Now, I'm as much a part of his life as his mother is. I, too, can stop his crying. So far, that has made the experiment worthwhile.

(1,197 words)

Here are some of the more difficult words in "Escaping the Daily Grind for Life as a House Father."

ambivalent
(paragraph 7)

am·biva·lence (am biv′ə ləns) *n.* 〖AMBI- + VALENCE〗 simultaneous conflicting feelings toward a person or thing, as love and hate: also [Chiefly Brit.] **am·biv′a·lency** —**am·biv′a·lent** *adj.* —**am·biv′a·lently** *adv.*

anathema
(paragraph 28)

anath·ema (ə nath′ə mə) *n.*, *pl.* **-·mas** 〖LL(Ec) < Gr, thing devoted to evil; previously, anything devoted < *anatithenai*, to dedicate < *ana-*, up + *tithenai*, to place: see DO¹〗 **1** a thing or person accursed or damned **2** a thing or person greatly detested **3** *a)* a solemn ecclesiastical condemnation of a teaching judged to be gravely opposed to accepted church doctrine, or of the originators or supporters of such a teaching *b)* the excommunication often accompanying or following this condemnation —*adj.* **1** greatly detested **2** viewed as accursed or damned **3** subjected to an ecclesiastical anathema

claustrophobics
(paragraph 22)

claustro·pho·bia (klôs′trə fō′bē ə) *n.* 〖< L *claustrum* (see CLOISTER) + -PHOBIA〗 an abnormal fear of being in an enclosed or confined place —**claus′tro·pho′·bic** *adj.*

Vocabulary List

233

contingent
(paragraph 26)

con·tin·gent (kən tin′jənt) *adj.* ⟦L *contingens*, prp. of *contingere*, to touch: see CONTACT⟧ **1** [Obs.] touching; tangential **2** that may or may not happen; possible **3** happening by chance; accidental; fortuitous **4** unpredictable because dependent on chance **5** dependent (*on* or *upon* something uncertain); conditional **6** *Logic* true only under certain conditions or in certain contexts; not always or necessarily true **7** *Philos.* not subject to determinism; free —*n.* **1** [Now Rare] an accidental or chance happening **2** a share or quota, as of troops, laborers, delegates, etc. **3** a group forming part of a larger group —con·tin′·gently *adv.*

euphemism
(paragraph 4)

eu·phe·mism (yōō′fə miz′əm) *n.* ⟦Gr *euphēmismos* < *euphēmizein*, to use words of good omen < *euphēmos*, of good sound or omen < *eu-* (see EU-) + *phēmē*, voice < *phanai*, to say: see BAN[1]⟧ **1** the use of a word or phrase that is less expressive or direct but considered less distasteful, less offensive, etc. than another **2** a word or phrase so substituted (Ex.: *remains* for *corpse*) —eu′·phe·mist *n.* —eu′·phe·mis′·tic *adj.* or eu′·phe·mis′·ti·cal —eu′·phe·mis′·ti·cally *adv.*

heresy
(paragraph 11)

her·esy (her′ə sē) *n.*, *pl.* -sies ⟦ME *heresie* < OFr < L *haeresis*, school of thought, sect, in LL(Ec), heresy < Gr *hairesis*, a taking, selection, school, sect, in LGr(Ec), heresy < *hairein*, to take⟧ **1** *a*) a religious belief opposed to the orthodox doctrines of a church; esp., such a belief specifically denounced by the church *b*) the rejection of a belief that is a part of church dogma **2** any opinion (in philosophy, politics, etc.) opposed to official or established views or doctrines **3** the holding of any such belief or opinion

idyll
(paragraph 23)

idyll or idyl (īd′′l; *Brit* id′′l) *n.* ⟦L *idyllium* < Gr *eidyllion*, dim. of *eidos*, a form, figure, image: see -OID⟧ **1** a short poem or prose work describing a simple, peaceful scene of rural or pastoral life **2** a scene or incident suitable for such a work **3** a narrative poem somewhat like a short epic [Tennyson's *"Idylls* of the King"] **4** *Music* a simple, pastoral composition

lethargy
(paragraph 8)

leth·argy (leth′ər jē) *n.* ⟦ME *litarge* < OFr < LL *lethargia* < Gr *lēthargia* < *lēthargos*, forgetful < *lēthē* (see LETHE) + *argos*, idle < *a-*, not + *ergon*, WORK⟧ **1** a condition of abnormal drowsiness or torpor **2** a great lack of energy; sluggishness, dullness, apathy, etc.

mitigated
(paragraph 10)

miti·gate (mit′ə gāt′) *vt.*, *vi.* -·gat·ed, -·gat′·ing ⟦ME *mitigaten* < L *mitigatus*, pp. of *mitigare*, to make mild, soft, or tender < *mitis*, soft (see MIGNON) + *agere*, to drive: see ACT[1]⟧ **1** to make or become milder, less severe, less rigorous, or less painful; moderate **2** ⟦< confusion with MILITATE⟧ to operate or work (*against*): generally considered a loose or erroneous usage —*SYN.* RELIEVE —mit′i·gable (-i gə bəl) *adj.* —mit′i·ga′·tion *n.* —mit′i·ga′·tive *adj.* —mit′i·ga′·tor *n.* —mit′i·ga·to′ry (-gə tôr′ē) *adj.*

mundane
(paragraph 28)

mun·dane (mun′dān′, mun dān′) *adj.* ⟦LME *mondeyne* < OFr *mondain* < LL *mundanus* < L *mundus*, world (in LL(Ec), the secular world, as opposed to the church)⟧ **1** of the world; esp., worldly, as distinguished from heavenly, spiritual, etc. **2** commonplace, everyday, ordinary, etc. —*SYN.* EARTHLY —mun′·dane′ly *adv.* —mun′·dan′·ity (-dan′ə tē) *n.*, *pl.* -·ties

proxy
(paragraph 14)

proxy (präk′sē) *n.*, *pl.* prox′·ies ⟦ME *prokecie*, contr. < *procuracie*, the function of a procurator, ult. < L *procuratio*⟧ **1** the agency or function of a deputy **2** the authority to act for another **3** a document empowering a person to act for another, as in voting at a stockholders' meeting **4** a person empowered to act for another —*SYN.* AGENT

rhapsodized
(paragraph 4)

rhap·so·dize (-dīz′) *vi.* -·dized′, -·diz′·ing **1** to speak or write in an extravagantly enthusiastic manner **2** to recite or write rhapsodies —*vt.* to recite or utter as a rhapsody
rhap·sody (rap′sə dē) *n.*, *pl.* -·dies ⟦Fr *r(h)apsodie* < L *rhapsodia* < Gr *rhapsōidia* < *rhapsōidos*, one who strings songs together, reciter of epic poetry < *rhaptein*, to stitch together (< IE *werp-, *wrep-, extension of base *wer-, to turn, bend > WORM, WRAP, RAVEL) + *ōidē*, song: see ODE⟧ **1** in ancient Greece, a part of an epic poem suitable for a single recitation **2** any ecstatic or extravagantly enthusiastic utterance in speech or writing **3** great delight;

Vocabulary List

shtick
(paragraph 30)

☆**shtick** (shtik) *n.* [< E Yiddish *shtik*, pl., pranks, interpreted as sing. < *shtik*, lit., piece < MHG *stücke*] [Slang] **1** a comic scene or piece of business, as in a vaudeville act **2** an attention-getting device **3** a special trait, talent, etc. Also sp. **shtik**

taboos
(paragraph 9)

ta·boo (tə bōō′, ta-) *n., pl.* **-·boos'** [< a Polynesian language: cf. Tongan, Samoan, Maori, etc. *tapu*] **1** *a)* among some Polynesian peoples, a sacred prohibition put upon certain people, things, or acts which makes them untouchable, unmentionable, etc. *b)* the highly developed system or practice of such prohibitions **2** *a)* any social prohibition or restriction that results from convention or tradition *b) Linguis.* the substitution of one word or phrase for another because of such restriction —*adj.* **1** sacred and prohibited by taboo **2** restricted by taboo: said of people **3** prohibited or forbidden by tradition, convention, etc. —*vt.* **-booed'**, **-boo'·ing 1** to put under taboo **2** to prohibit or forbid because of tradition, convention, etc.

therapeutic
(paragraph 11)

thera·peu·tic (ther′ə pyōōt′ik) *adj.* [MqdL *therapeuticus* < Gr *therapeutikos* < *therapeutēs*, attendant, servant, one who treats medically < *therapeuein*, to nurse, treat medically] **1** *a)* serving to cure or heal; curative *b)* serving to preserve health *[therapeutic abortion]* **2** of therapeutics Also **ther′a·peu′·ti·cal** —**ther′a·peu′·ti·cally** *adv.*

15A   VOCABULARY

From the context of "Escaping the Daily Grind for Life as a House Father," explain the meaning of each of the vocabulary words shown in boldface.

1. *From paragraph 4:* Thus was born my favorite **euphemism** for house fatherhood [. . .].

   _____ less offensive expression _____

   _____

2. *From paragraph 4:* "Explained, yes. Defended. Even **rhapsodized** about."

   <u>enthusiastically spoken</u> _____

   _____

3. *From paragraph 7:* "And in the end, I still felt **ambivalent**."

   _____ conflicting feelings _____

   _____

4. *From paragraph 8:* "I had shattered my **lethargy** and stopped whining, and for that I was proud."

   _____ lack of energy _____

   _____

Name   Date   **235**

5. *From paragraph 9:* "[...] the ultimate in middle-class **taboos**."

           social restrictions

6. *From paragraph 10:* "The initial trauma of quitting, however, was **mitigated** by my eagerness to raise our son."

           made less severe

7. *From paragraph 11:* "I sensed that staying home would be **therapeutic**."

           healing

8. *From paragraph 11:* "This was **heresy** [...]."

           the rejection of a particular belief

9. *From paragraph 14:* "We had two salaries, a full-time nanny and guilt pangs over practicing parenthood by **proxy**."

           authorizing someone else to do the parenting

10. *From paragraph 22:* "House fathering is not for **claustrophobics**."

           people with an abnormal fear of being enclosed

11. *From paragraph 23:* "This is my **idyll**."

           peaceful scene of life

12. *From paragraph 26:* "[...] the stroller and backpack **contingent**."

           group

13. *From paragraph 28:* "[...] a softening, a contentment with small pleasures, the outwardly **mundane**."

           commonplace

    Name   Date

14. *From paragraph 28:* "Ambition and competitiveness are **anathema.**"

_____ detested _____

_____

15. *From paragraph 30:* "He tries new words on me, new **shtick.**"

_____ comic expression _____

_____

15B   CENTRAL THEME AND MAIN IDEAS

Choose the best answer.

__b__   1. What is the central theme of "Escaping the Daily Grind for Life as a House Father"?
   a. More fathers should quit work to take care of their children.
   b. One man finds that raising a child can be as fulfilling an occupation as a traditional career.
   c. The author discovers that he is better at being a house father than at being a journalist.
   d. House fathering is a new occupation for fathers suffering from stress and job burnout.

2. In your own words, give the main idea of paragraph 18.

   Older traditional parents view changes in traditional male

   and female roles as a violation of the natural order.

3. In your own words, give the main idea of paragraph 28.

   The change the author sees as a new effective at-home parent is a

   softenign—a release of workplace competitiveness and aggression.

__d__   4. What is the main idea of paragraph 30?
   a. The author and his son enjoy spending quality time with each other.
   b. Radical lifestyle change is often beneficial for parents experiencing child-rearing stress.
   c. Children adapt well to changes in their lifestyles.
   d. The author has succeeded in getting to know his son as well as his mother does.

15C   MAJOR DETAILS

Decide whether each detail is MAJOR or MINOR based on the context of the reading selection.

MINOR 1. Some friends were envious about the author's lifestyle change.

MINOR 2. The author was willing to be with his son until a better job came along, or indefinitely.

MINOR 3. Because of his intense dislike of his job, the author felt that staying home with his son would be therapeutic.

MINOR 4. The author usually got home from work too late to spend much time with his son.

MINOR 5. The author and his wife had a nanny.

MINOR 6. The author felt excluded from the child-raising process.

MINOR 7. The author takes his son grocery shopping.

MINOR 8. The author was a daily journalist.

MINOR 9. Now the author can stop his son's crying, too.

15D   INFERENCES

Choose the right answer.

  b 1. *Read paragraph 4 again.* The author was tongue-tied because
      a. he thought his neighbor was too nosy.
      b. he was embarrassed to admit his new lifestyle.
      c. he did not want to explain in front of his son.
      d. he thought his wife should explain the situation.

  c 2. *Read paragraph 9 again.* Why did the author walk away from his boss's desk with wobbly knees?
      a. He was worried about his boss's reaction.
      b. He was shy about quitting his job.
      c. He was nervous about quitting his job.
      d. He did not think he would be good at house fathering.

  c 3. *Read paragraph 10 again.* Why does the author describe himself as "the man who got home after dark"?
      a. The author is making a sarcastic reference to the time he returns home from work.
      b. The author prefers not to use his real name in the article.

Name   Date

c. Because of the author's work schedule, the son does not know his father nearly as well as he knows his mother.

d. The author is making a social remark about the long hours he works.

__b__ 4. *Read paragraph 15 again.* The author's remark "And I wonder what comes next" suggests that he

a. is hesitant about the change in his domestic responsibilities.

b. is eager for the challenge of new experiences.

c. resents the lowered expectations of house fathering.

d. does not feel confident about the future.

__a__ 5. *Read paragraph 22 again.* House fathering is not for claustrophobics because claustrophobics

a. would find staying at home every day too confining.

b. enjoy working in small, confined areas.

c. need to go to work every day to feel productive.

d. feel the need to work with many people in a controlled setting.

__d__ 6. *Read paragraph 26 again.* "And then there's the rest of us" implies that the author

a. is longing for his old job and sense of identity.

b. views child care as a pastime requiring few skills or expertise.

c. now identifies with a group of people who are not qualified for any other occupation.

d. sees himself as part of a group having no particular mission or sense of purpose.

15E   CRITICAL READING: FACT OR OPINION

Decide whether each statement, even if it quotes someone, contains a FACT or an OPINION.

OPINION 1. *From paragraph 7:* "This was a radical change that seemed to carry as many drawbacks as benefits."

FACT 2. *From paragraph 9:* "Some friends said they were envious."

FACT 3. *From paragraph 10:* "It hurt when I couldn't quiet his crying."

FACT 4. *From paragraph 11:* "Something better would emerge, something less obnoxious."

FACT 5. *From paragraph 15:* "With me at home, her work hours are more flexible."

15F CRITICAL READING: THE AUTHOR'S STRATEGIES

Choose the best answer.

___c___ 1. The main audience for "Escaping the Daily Grind for Life as a House Father" is
 a. anyone who wants to quit working and stay at home.
 b. anyone who thinks men should not stay home and care for their children.
 c. anyone who wants to read one man's viewpoint of the rewards of a stay-at-home parent.
 d. anyone whose job is causing them to suffer stress and illness.

___d___ 2. The author's purpose in writing this reading is to
 a. describe.
 b. persuade.
 c. entertain.
 d. explain.

___b___ 3. The author's tone in this reading is
 a. sad.
 b. thoughtful.
 c. calm.
 d. negative.

15G READER'S PROCESS: SUMMARIZING YOUR READING

___d___ 1. What is the best summary of "Escaping the Daily Grind for Life as a House Father"?
 a. A father describes a stressful job that drove him to become a house father.
 b. A father describes a typical day in the life of a house father.
 c. A father describes how people react to him now that he is a house father.
 d. A father describes his feelings about giving up his job and becoming a house father.

Name   Date

15H READER'S RESPONSE: TO DISCUSS OR WRITE ABOUT

1. If you are a male, explain how you would feel about becoming a house father, one who stays at home to raise your child(ren) while your wife works outside the home. If you are a female, explain how you would feel about working outside the home while your husband stayed at home and cared for your child(ren).

2. In order to meet their financial obligations, in many families both the husband and the wife often work outside the home and leave their child(ren) in day-care centers. What effects do you think this has on the children—emotionally, educationally, and socially? Use specific examples to support your point of view.

HOW DID YOU DO?

15 Escaping the Daily Grind for Life as a House Father

SKILL (number of items)	Number Correct		Points for each		Score
Vocabulary (15)	_____	×	2	=	_____
Central Theme and Main Ideas (4)	_____	×	4	=	_____
Major Details (9)	_____	×	2	=	_____
Inferences (6)	_____	×	3	=	_____
Critical Reading: Fact or Opinion (5)	_____	×	2	=	_____
Critical Reading: The Author's Strategies (3)	_____	×	2	=	_____
Reader's Process: Summarizing Your Reading (1)	_____	×	2	=	_____

(Possible Total: 100) *Total* _____

SPEED

Reading Time: _____ Reading Rate (page 413): _____ Words Per Minute

Forty Acres and a Holiday
Lisa Jones

(1) There are three legends told of how enslaved Africans in the Texas territory came to know of their freedom, and why the word didn't get to them until two months after the Civil War ended, which was a good two and half years after Lincoln's Emancipation Proclamation. Or, to make it plain, rather late. One legend says the messenger, a black Union soldier, was murdered. Another says he arrived, but had been delayed by mule travel. (A variation on this is that he had stopped to get married.) The third and favored is that the news was withheld by white landowners so they could bleed one last crop from slave labor. What is held as fact is that June nineteenth—the day that federal troops rode into Galveston with orders to release those kept as slaves—has been celebrated for 127 years, in Texas and beyond, as Emancipation Day, as Jubilation day, as Juneteenth. The day the last ones heard.

(2) Juneteenth, the name, is one of those fab African-Americanisms, functional, rhythmic, at once concise and not too concise. It fuses the month of June with the number nineteen, and alludes to the fact that the holiday was held in adjoining states on different days of the month as folks got the word. Early emancipation rituals were not exclusive to Texas (South Carolina and Mississippi's fall in May)—or to the South. What may have been the first emancipation ceremony was held in New York as early as 1808 to mark the legal cessation of the slave trade.

(3) No state comes close to Juneteenth in Texas, the black folks' Fourth of July, with its parades, feasting, pageants, and preachifying. Emancipation day organizations in Texas date back to the turn of the century. The most powerful image from the early days must have been former slaves themselves, who, according to tradition, marched together at the end of parade lines. By the 1950s Juneteenth Day came to be linked with, not freedom from slavery, but segregation. On Juneteenth, Texas's Jim Crow cities would allow blacks to be citizens for twelve hours a year by granting them entry into whites-only parks and zoos. With the passage of civil rights legislation in the sixties, refined black Texans abandoned Juneteenth to their country cousins and took to celebrating Independence Day in July along with their white brethren.

(4) A Juneteenth renaissance has been gathering steam since the mid eighties, spurred by the Afrocentricity crusade. Beyond being a hootenanny for black Texas (the condescending folksy portrait favored by the local press), it's become a holiday eagerly adopted nationwide by African Americans in search of cultural signposts. Not to mention one that offers, as is required these days, a dramatic tube-and-T-shirt-friendly sound bite of

© AP/World Wide Photos

Miss Juneteenth, Deneka Dove, waves to parade watchers on June 19, 2001, in Austin, Texas.

black history. The J-Day momentum is due in large part to the efforts of a man you might call Daddy Juneteenth, state representative Al Edwards from Houston. Edwards sponsored the bill that made Juneteenth an official Texas holiday thirteen years ago, a feat in a state that still closes banks for Confederate Heroes Day. Juneteenth U.S.A., Edwards's organization, tracks J-Day rites across the county and is fundraising for a national educational headquarters. To Edwards the holiday has tremendous secular and sacred promise. He sees it as an economic vehicle for African Americans, as well as a day that should be observed with almost holy remembrance: "The Jews say if they ever forget their history, may their tongues cleave to the roof of their mouth. . . . Let the same happen to us."

(5) You can find Juneteenth rituals in all regions of the country now. States like California, where Texans migrated en masse, have held Juneteenth

festivities for decades. The New York area's largest is in Buffalo, tapping into upstate's rich history of antislavery activity. Wisconsin counts at least five, including Milwaukee's, where Juneteenth has been celebrated since 1971 and is the best attended single-day cultural event in the state. Far from being family picnics, these festivals sometimes last for days, made possible by the legwork of community groups, city cooperation, and private sector donations. Juneteenth in Minneapolis, now in its seventh year, is building a rep as one of the most progressive and trend setting J-Day celebrations in the Texas diaspora. What began as a poetry reading in a church basement is now two weeks of programming, including a film festival and an Underground Railroad reenactment. At these celebrations old world often knocks against new world, when Miss Juneteenth pageants (inherited from towns like Brenham, Texas, which crowns a "Goddess of Liberty") share the stage with Afro-chic street fairs ablaze in faux kente.

(6) There are those who think Juneteenth is an embarrassment. That the holiday tells more of our ignorance and subjugation than of an inheritance that predates slavery in the Americas. Or that it's "too black" because it promotes a separate but not equal Fourth of July, or "not black enough" as it's often funded by white purses. And of course that it's far too symbolic and doesn't solve anything. What does a Juneteenth celebration mean anyway when the Freedman's Bureau never gave us our forty acres and a mule? (Not thrilled about news of the state holiday, one former Texas legislator had this to say: "Dancing up and down the streets, drinking red soda water, eating watermelons . . . I grew out of that.") But Juneteenth critics haven't put a dent in the holiday's grass-roots popularity.

(7) Folks are hungrier than ever for rituals that enshrine our identity as hyphen Americans. Kwanzaa's metamorphosis in the last few years speaks to this need. And merchandising opportunities are never far behind: Evolving in two short decades from cultural nationalist position paper to mainstream ethnic festival profiled in the *Times*'s Living Section. Kwanzaa has spawned its own designer cookbook and Santa surrogate, Father Kwanzaa. Now Juneteenth spreads like spring fever. Also gaining steam are rites of passage ceremonies for young men and women that are based on ancient African models and seek to address modern urban ills. (The National Rites of Passage Organization held its fifth annual conference this year.) And spotted last year in *Sage: A Scholarly Journal on Black Women*: plans for a Middle Passage memorial holiday that would fall near Thanksgiving.

(8) Buried in their shopping ethos, we tend to forget holidays were once holy days that once defined us in more profound ways than what Nintendo jumbo pack we got for Christmas. Michael Chaney, an arts activist in Minneapolis, believes that Juneteenth rituals could be more than acts of racial communion; they could have a role in redefining America: "We have to realize our own role as historians. We need to ascribe our treasures and offer them to the world. Juneteenth should be a day for all Americans to get in touch with the Africanism within."

(9) Juneteenth does have great possibilities as a new American holiday. Along with reuniting blood relatives, the families that emancipated slaves made embraced family beyond kin, family as community. In this tradition, modern Juneteenth doesn't circumscribe any Dick-and-Jane paean to the nuclear family. You can be a single parent, gay, from D.C. or Ann Arbor; it's a history that includes you. You can read the Emancipation Proclamation out loud or drink some red soda water if you damn please. Or just take a moment out of your day to think about all the folks that laid down nothing less than their lives so that you could see the twentieth century.

(1,235 words)

Here are some of the more difficult words in "Forty Acres and a Holiday."

Vocabulary List

cessation
(paragraph 2)

ces·sa·tion (se sā'shən) *n.* ⟦L *cessatio* < pp. of *cessare*, CEASE⟧ a ceasing, or stopping, either forever or for some time

Diaspora
(paragraph 5)

Di·as·pora (dī as'pə rə) *n.* ⟦Gr *diaspora*, a scattering < *diasperein*, to scatter < *dia-*, across + *speirein*, to sow: see SPORE⟧ **1** *a)* the dispersion of the Jews after the Babylonian Exile *b)* the Jews thus dispersed *c)* the places where they settled **2** [d-] any scattering of people with a common origin, background, beliefs, etc.

emancipation
(paragraph 1)

eman·ci·pate (ē man'sə pāt', i-) *vt.* **··pat'ed, ··pat'·ing** ⟦< L *emancipatus*, pp. of *emancipare* < *e-*, out + *mancipare*, to deliver up or make over as property < *manceps*, purchaser < *manus*, the hand (see MANUAL) + *capere*, to take (see HAVE)⟧ **1** to set free (a slave, etc.); release from bondage, servitude, or serfdom **2** to free from restraint or control, as of social convention **3** *Law* to release (a child) from parental control and supervision **—SYN.** FREE **—eman'·ci·pa'·tion** *n.* **—eman'·ci·pa'·tive** *adj.* or **eman'·ci·pa·to'ry** (-pe tôr'ē) **—eman'·ci·pa'·tor** *n.*

ethos
(paragraph 8)

ethos (ē'thäs') *n.* ⟦Gr *ēthos*, disposition, character: see ETHICAL⟧ the characteristic and distinguishing attitudes, habits, beliefs, etc. of an individual or of a group

hootenanny
(paragraph 4)

☆**hooten·anny** (hōōt''n an'ē) *n., pl.* **··nies** ⟦orig. in sense of "dingus," "thingamajig"; a fanciful coinage⟧ a meeting of folk singers, as for public entertainment

Jim Crow
(paragraph 3)

☆**Jim Crow** ⟦name of an early black minstrel song⟧ [*also* j- c-] [Informal] traditional discrimination against or segregation of blacks, esp. in the U.S. **—Jim'-Crow'** *vt., adj.* **—Jim Crow'·ism'**

246

metamorphosis
(paragraph 7)

meta·mor·pho·sis (-môr′fə sis, -môr fō′sis) *n.*, *pl.* --ses′ (-sēz′) [L < Gr *metamorphōsis* < *metamorphoun,* to transform, transfigure < *meta,* over (see META-) + *morphē,* form, shape] **1** *a)* change of form, shape, structure, or substance; transformation, as, in myths, by magic or sorcery *b)* the form resulting from such change **2** a marked or complete change of character, appearance, condition, etc. **3** *Biol.* a change in form, structure, or function as a result of development; specif., the physical transformation, more or less sudden, undergone by various animals during development after the embryonic state, as of the larva of an insect to the pupa and the pupa to the adult, or of the tadpole to the frog **4** *Med.* a pathological change of form of some tissues

paean
(paragraph 9)

paean (pē′ən) *n.* [L < Gr *paian,* hymn < *Paian,* the healing one, epithet of Apollo < *paiein,* to strike, touch < ? IE base *pēu-* > PAVE] **1** in ancient Greece, a hymn of thanksgiving to the gods, esp. to Apollo **2** a song of joy, triumph, praise, etc.

renaissance
(paragraph 4)

ren·ais·sance (ren′ə säns′, -zäns′; ren′ə säns′, -zäns′; *chiefly Brit* ri nä′səns) *n.* [Fr < *renaître,* to be born anew < OFr *renestre* < *re-* + VL **nascere,* for L *nasci,* to be born: see GENUS] **1** a new birth; rebirth; renascence **2** *a)* [R-] the style and forms of art, literature, architecture, etc. of the Renaissance *b)* [*often* R-] any revival of art, literature, or learning similar to the Renaissance —*adj.* [R-] **1** of, characteristic of, or in the style of the Renaissance **2** designating or of a style of architecture developed in Italy and western Europe between 1400 and 1600, characterized by the revival and adaptation of classical orders and design —**the Renaissance 1** the great revival of art, literature, and learning in Europe in the 14th, 15th, and 16th cent., based on classical sources: it began in Italy and spread gradually to other countries and marked the transition from the medieval world to the modern **2** the period of this revival

rituals
(paragraph 2)

ritu·al (rich′o͞o əl) *adj.* [L *ritualis*] of, having the nature of, or done as a rite or rites [*ritual* dances] —*n.* **1** a set form or system of rites, religious or otherwise **2** the observance of set forms or rites, as in public worship **3** a book containing rites or ceremonial forms **4** a practice, service, or procedure done as a rite, especially at regular intervals **5** ritual acts or procedures collectively —*SYN.* CEREMONY —rit′u·ally *adv.*

secular
(paragraph 4)

secu·lar (sek′yə lər) *adj.* [ME *seculer* < OFr < LL(Ec) *saecularis,* worldly, profane, heathen < L, of an age < *saeculum,* an age, generation < IE **seitlo-* < base **sei-,* to scatter, SOW²] **1** *a)* of or relating to worldly things as distinguished from things relating to church and religion; not sacred or religious; temporal; worldly [*secular* music, *secular* schools] *b)* of or marked by secularism; secularistic **2** ordained for a diocese **3** *a)* coming or happening only once in an age or century *b)* lasting for an age or ages; continuing for a long time or from age to age —*n.* **1** a cleric ordained for a diocese **2** a person not a cleric; layman —sec′u·larly *adv.*

subjugation
(paragraph 6)

sub·ju·gate (sub′jə gāt′) *vt.* --gat·ed, --gat·ing [ME *subiugaten* < L *subjugatus,* pp. of *subjugare,* to bring under the yoke < *sub-,* under + *jugum,* YOKE] **1** to bring under control or subjection; conquer **2** to cause to become subservient; subdue —*SYN.* CONQUER —sub′ju·ga′tion *n.* —sub′·ju·ga′·tor *n.*

16A   VOCABULARY

Choose the best answer.

  __d__ 1. The **cessation** of the slave trade meant it was
         a. discussed.
         b. celebrated.
         c. approved.
         d. stopped.

  __c__ 2. Lincoln's **Emancipation** Proclamation concerned the slaves'
         a. capture.
         b. disobedience.
         c. freedom.
         d. duties.

  __b__ 3. A **hootenanny** involves a gathering of
         a. marchers.
         b. singers.
         c. dancers.
         d. demonstrators.

  __a__ 4. **Subjugation** of a people indicates that the group has been
         a. conquered.
         b. honored.
         c. released.
         d. subdivided.

  __c__ 5. A **paean** is a song of
         a. love.
         b. hate.
         c. joy.
         d. sadness.

  __d__ 6. **Secular** refers to things that are
         a. religious.
         b. secretive.
         c. expensive.
         d. worldly.

  __b__ 7. **Diaspora** is a word used to refer to people who have
         a. rebelled.
         b. scattered.
         c. assembled.
         d. disappeared.

  __a__ 8. **Rituals** are ceremonies that involve
         a. a set form.
         b. a debate.

c. a rehearsal.

d. candlesticks.

<u>a</u>   9. **Ethos** as used in this essay means

  a. habit.

  b. purpose.

  c. bargain.

  d. celebration.

<u>c</u>   10. **Jim Crow** is a term used to refer to the policy of

  a. integration.

  b. migration.

  c. segregation.

  d. compensation.

<u>b</u>   11. **Renaissance** as used in this essay means

  a. festival.

  b. revival.

  c. holiday.

  d. revolt.

<u>d</u>   12. A **metamorphosis** occurs when something undergoes a noticeable

  a. destruction.

  b. control.

  c. restoration.

  d. change.

16B   CENTRAL THEME AND MAIN IDEAS

Choose the best answer.

<u>c</u>   1. What is the central theme of "Forty Acres and a Holiday"?

  a. Lincoln's Emancipation Proclamation freed the slaves in territories still at war with the Union.

  b. Juneteenth gets its name from a combination of June and the number nineteen.

  c. Celebrated for over one hundred years, Juneteenth has increased in popularity as an American holiday to acknowledge the freeing of the slaves.

  d. Juneteenth is the oldest known celebration of the ending of slavery.

<u>d</u>   2. What is the main idea of paragraph 1?

  a. Texas, as well as other states, has celebrated June nineteenth for over 127 years in recognition of the Emancipation Proclamation.

  b. President Abraham Lincoln issued the Emancipation Proclamation during the Civil War to free the slaves.

c. Federal troops arrived in Galveston, Texas, on June 19 to free those slaves still in bondage.

d. Three legends have been passed down to explain why Lincoln's Emancipation Proclamation failed to reach Texas until two and a half years after its issue.

___b___ 3. What is the main idea of paragraph 6?

a. The Freedmen's Bureau did not give forty acres and a mule to the freed slaves.

b. There are those who think Juneteenth is an embarrassment.

c. Juneteenth is a state holiday in Texas.

d. One of the most vocal critics of the Juneteenth holiday is a former Texas state legislator.

16C   MAJOR DETAILS

Decide whether each detail is MAJOR or MINOR based on the context of the reading selection.

MINOR   1. The black Union soldier was late bringing news of the Emancipation Proclamation to Texas because he stopped en route to marry.

MAJOR   2. Federal troops arrived in Galveston on June 19 with the news that the slaves were freed.

MINOR   3. South Carolina and Mississippi celebrate the freeing of the slaves in May.

MAJOR   4. In the 1950s, Juneteenth Day came to be linked with segregation, not slavery.

MINOR   5. One way African Americans in Texas celebrate Juneteenth is with a hootenanny.

MAJOR   6. Texas state representative Al Edwards sponsored a bill that made Juneteenth an official state holiday in 1980.

MINOR   7. A Miss Juneteenth pageant is part of the Juneteenth celebration in Texas.

16D   INFERENCES

Choose the best answer.

___c___ 1. *Read paragraph 3 again.* In the early parade, the former slaves marched at the end of parade lines because

a. they were too weak to keep the fast pace of the younger participants.

Name   Date

b. the spectators wanted to see the dancers, musicians, floats, and
honored guests first.

c. their presence served as a lasting reminder to the onlookers of
the significance of the celebration.

d. they could not afford to buy showier clothes expected to be
worn by parade participants.

<u>d</u> 2. *Read paragraph 5 again.* Why are two of the largest celebrations
now in Milwaukee and Minneapolis?
   a. These cities now have a black majority population.
   b. Attendees prefer to celebrate in the cooler climate of Wisconsin
      and Minnesota.
   c. Employers, both state and private, give employees the day off.
   d. These cities have sound financial backing and support to offer
      a wide range of activities.

<u>d</u> 3. In paragraph 5, the "faux kente" seen at the Afro-chic street fairs
is popular for all of these reasons *except*
   a. it is traditional African dress.
   b. it reminds African Americans of their ancestry.
   c. it is brightly colored material.
   d. it is inexpensive and comfortable.

<u>b</u> 4. In paragraph 7, the word *hyphen* in the phrase "hyphen Ameri-
cans" suggests any people who seek to
   a. hide their ethnic identity.
   b. emphasize their ethnic identity.
   c. recognize their ethnic language.
   d. promote their ethnic holidays.

16E CRITICAL READING: FACT OR OPINION

*Decide whether each statement, even if it quotes someone, contains a FACT or an
OPINION.*

<u>OPINION</u> 1. *From paragraph 2:* "Juneteenth, the name, is one of those fab
African-Americanisms, functional, rhythmic, at once concise and
not too concise."

<u>OPINION</u> 2. *From paragraph 3:* "No state comes close to Juneteenth in Texas,
the black folks' Fourth of July, with its parades, feasting,
pageants, and preachifying."

<u>FACT</u> 3. *From paragraph 4:* "To Edwards the holiday has tremendous sec-
ular and sacred promise."

FACT 4. *From paragraph 5:* "What began as a poetry reading in a church basement is now two weeks of programming, including a film festival and an Underground Railroad reenactment."

FACT 5. *From paragraph 6:* "Dancing up and down the streets, drinking red soda water, eating watermelons [. . .] I grew out of that."

FACT 6. *From paragraph 7:* "Kwanzaa has spawned its own designer cookbook and Santa surrogate, Father Kwanzaa."

16F CRITICAL READING: THE AUTHOR'S STRATEGIES

Choose the best answer.

__c__ 1. The main audience for "Forty Acres and a Holiday" is
   a. anyone who wants to organize or participate in a Juneteenth celebration.
   b. anyone who is interested in how African Americans feel about slavery.
   c. anyone who is interested in Juneteenth and other African-American holidays.
   d. anyone who is critical of Juneteenth or other African-American holidays.

__c__ 2. The author's purpose in writing this reading is to
   a. entertain.
   b. describe.
   c. inform.
   d. convince.

__d__ 3. The author's tone in this reading is
   a. defensive.
   b. sad.
   c. negative.
   d. reflective.

Name   Date

16G   READER'S PROCESS: SUMMARIZING YOUR READING

<u>b</u>   1. What is the best summary of "Forty Acres and a Holiday"?
   a. The writer explains the origins of the Juneteenth holiday and how it has spread from Texas to all parts of the country.
   b. The writer explains the origins of Juneteenth celebrations and why such holidays are important to African Americans.
   c. The writer explains why some African Americans wish to celebrate holidays that emphasize their own cultural traditions.
   d. The writer explains that many activities make up Juneteenth celebrations in different parts of the country.

16H   READER'S RESPONSE: TO DISCUSS OR WRITE ABOUT

1. On June 19, 1865, Major General Gordon Granger arrived in Galveston, Texas, with the news that the Civil War had ended and that the slaves were free. Describe what you think may have been the reactions to this news from the standpoint of either the former masters or the former slaves. Was it shock? Jubilation? Why did many of the free men and women leave Texas and head north? What social, educational, and/or economic challenges would they have faced?

2. Every ethnic group has certain traditions or celebrations that it recognizes and observes. Describe one that either you or your family participates in. Does it relate to a specific event in history? Is it participated in by people of other races? Does it involve special outdoor activities, food, ceremonies, contests, parades, speeches, or gifts? Be specific as to how you observe this tradition or celebration.

HOW DID YOU DO?

16 Forty Acres and a Holiday

SKILL (number of items)	Number Correct		Points for each		Score
Vocabulary (12)	_____	×	2	=	_____
Central Theme and Main Ideas (3)	_____	×	5	=	_____
Major Details (7)	_____	×	2	=	_____
Inferences (4)	_____	×	4	=	_____
Critical Reading: Fact or Opinion (6)	_____	×	3	=	_____
Critical Reading: The Author's Strategies (3)	_____	×	3	=	_____
Reader's Process: Summarizing Your Reading (1)	_____	×	4	=	_____

(Possible Total: 100) *Total* _____

SPEED

Reading Time: _____ Reading Rate (page 413): _____ Words Per Minute

Name   Date

Selection 17
My Mother's Blue Bowl

Alice Walker

(1) Visitors to my house are often served food—soup, potatoes, rice—in a large blue stoneware bowl, noticeably chipped at the rim. It is perhaps the most precious thing I own. It was given to me by my mother in her last healthy days. The days before a massive stroke laid her low and left her almost speechless. Those days when to visit her was to be drawn into a serene cocoon of memories and present-day musings and to rest there, in temporary retreat from the rest of the world, as if still an infant, nodding and secure at her breast.

(2) For much of her life my mother longed, passionately longed, for a decent house. One with a yard that did not have to be cleared with an ax. One with a roof that kept out the rain. One with a floor that you could not fall through. She longed for a beautiful house of wood or stone. Or of red brick, like the houses her many sisters and their husbands had. When I was thirteen she found such a house. Green-shuttered, white-walled. Breezy. With a lawn and a hedge and giant pecan trees. A porch swing. There her gardens flourished in spite of the shade, as did her youngest daughter, for whom she sacrificed her life doing hard labor in someone else's house, in order to afford peace and prettiness for her child, to whose grateful embrace she returned each night.

(3) But, curiously, the minute I left home, at seventeen, to attend college, she abandoned the dream house and moved into the projects. Into a small, tight apartment of few breezes, in which I was never to feel comfortable, but that she declared suited her "to a T." I took solace in the fact that it was at least hugged by spacious lawn on one side, and by forest, out the back door, and that its isolated position at the end of the street meant she would have a measure of privacy. Her move into the projects—the best housing poor black people in the South ever had, she would occasionally declare, even as my father struggled to adjust to the cramped rooms and hard, unforgiving qualities of brick—was, I now understand, a step in the direction of divestiture, lightening her load, permitting her worldly possessions to dwindle in significance and, well before she herself would turn to spirit, roll away from her.

(4) She owned little, in fact. A bed, a dresser, some chairs. A set of living-room furniture. A set of kitchen furniture. A bed and wardrobe (given to her years before, when I was a teenager, by one of her prosperous sisters). Her flowers: everywhere, inside the house and outside. Planted in anything she managed to get her green hands on, including old suitcases and abandoned

shoes. She recycled everything, effortlessly. And gradually she had only a small amount of stuff—mostly stuff her children gave her: nightgowns, perfume, a microwave—to recycle or to use.

© Liaison/Getty Images

Alice Walker, one of eight children, was born in Eatonton, Georgia, where her parents were sharecroppers. A writer since childhood, she is known today as a poet, fiction writer, essayist, biographer, and editor.

(5) Each time I visited her I marveled at the modesty of her desires. She appeared to have hardly any, beyond a thirst for a Pepsi-Cola or a hunger for a piece of fried chicken or fish. On every visit I noticed that more and more of what I remembered of her possessions seemed to be missing. One day I commented on this. Taking a deep breath, sighing and following both with a beaming big smile, which lit up her face, the room, and my heart, she said: "Yes, it's all going. I don't need it anymore. If there's anything you want, take it when you leave; it might not be here when you come back."

(6) The dishes my mother and father used daily had come from my house; I had sent them years before, when I moved from Mississippi to New York. Neither the plates nor the silver matched entirely, but it was all beautiful in her eyes. There were numerous cups, used by the scores of children from the neighborhood who continued throughout her life to come and go. But there was nothing there for me to want.

(7) One day, however, looking for a jar into which to pour leftover iced tea, I found myself probing deep into the wilderness of the overstuffed, airless pantry. Into the land of the old-fashioned, the outmoded, the outdated.

The humble and the obsolete. There was a smoothing iron, a churn. A butter press. And two large bowls. One was cream and rose with a blue stripe. The other was a deep, vivid blue. "May I have this bowl, Mama?" I asked, looking at her and at the blue bowl with delight. "You can have both of them," she said, barely acknowledging them, and continuing to put leftover food away.

(8) I held the bowls on my lap for the rest of the evening, while she watched a TV program about cops and criminals that I found too horrifying to follow. Before leaving the room I kissed her on the forehead and asked if I could get anything for her from the kitchen; then I went off to bed. The striped bowl I placed on a chair beside the door, so I could look at it from where I lay. The blue bowl I placed in the bed with me. In giving me these gifts, my mother had done a number of astonishing things, in her typically offhand way. She had taught me a lesson about letting go of possessions— easily, without emphasis or regret—and she had given me a symbol of what she herself represented in my life.

(9) For the blue bowl especially was a cauldron of memories. Of cold, harsh, wintry days, when my brothers and sister and I trudged home from school burdened down by the silence and frigidity of our long trek from the main road, down the hill to our shabby-looking house. More rundown than any of our classmates' houses. In winter my mother's riotous flowers would be absent, and the shack stood revealed for what it was. A gray, decaying, too small barrack meant to house the itinerant tenant workers on a prosperous white man's farm.

(10) Slogging through sleet and wind to the sagging front door, thankful that our house was too far from the road to be seen clearly from the school bus, I always felt a wave of embarrassment and misery. But then I would open the door. And there inside would be my mother's winter flowers: a glowing fire in the fireplace, colorful handmade quilts on all our beds, paintings and drawings of flowers and fruits and, yes, of Jesus, given to her by who knows whom—and most of all, there in the center of the rough-hewn table, which in the tiny kitchen almost touched the rusty wood-burning stove, stood the big blue bowl, full of whatever was the most tasty thing on earth.

(11) There was my mother herself. Glowing. Her teeth sparkling. Her eyes twinkling. As if she lived in a castle and her favorite princes and princesses had just dropped by to visit.

(12) The blue bowl stood there, seemingly full forever, no matter how deeply or rapaciously we dipped, as if it had no bottom. And she dipped up soup. Dipped up lima beans. Dipped up stew. Forked out potatoes. Spooned out rice and peas and corn. And in the light and warmth that was her, we dined. Thank you, Mama.

(1,259 words)

Here are some of the more difficult words in "My Mother's Blue Bowl."

barrack
(paragraph 9)

bar·rack[1] (bar′ək, ber′-) **n.** ⟦Fr *baraque* < Sp *barraca*, cabin, mud hut < *barro*, clay, mud < VL **barrum*, clay⟧ **1** [Rare] an improvised hut **2** [*pl., often with sing. v.*] *a*) a building or group of buildings for housing soldiers *b*) a large, plain, often temporary building for housing workmen, police, etc. **—vt., vi.** to house in barracks

cauldron
(paragraph 9)

cal·dron (kôl′drən) **n.** ⟦ME & Anglo-Fr *caudron* < OFr *chauderon* < L *calderia*: see CALDARIUM⟧ **1** a large kettle or boiler **2** a violently agitated condition like the boiling contents of a caldron

divestiture
(paragraph 3)

di·vest (də vest′, dī-) **vt.** ⟦altered < DEVEST⟧ **1** to strip *of* clothing, equipment, etc. **2** to deprive or dispossess *of* rank, rights, etc. **3** to disencumber or rid *of* something unwanted **4** *Law* DEVEST **—SYN.** STRIP[1]
di·vesti·ture (-ə chər) **n.** a divesting or being divested: also **di·vest′·ment** or **di·ves′·ture**

flourished
(paragraph 2)

flour·ish (flʉr′ish) **vi.** ⟦ME *florishen* < extended stem of OFr *florir*, to blossom < LL **florire* < L *florere* < *flos*, FLOWER⟧ **1** [Obs.] to blossom **2** to grow vigorously; succeed; thrive; prosper **3** to be at the peak of development, activity, influence, production, etc.; be in one's prime **4** to make showy, wavy motions, as of the arms **5** [Now Rare] *a*) to write in an ornamental style *b*) to perform a fanfare, as of trumpets **—vt. 1** to ornament with something flowery or fanciful **2** ⟦first so used by John WYCLIFFE⟧ to wave (a sword, arm, hat, etc.) in the air; brandish **—n. 1** [Rare] a thriving state; success; prosperity **2** anything done in a showy way, as a sweeping movement of the limbs or body **3** a waving in the air; brandishing **4** a decorative or curved line or lines in handwriting **5** an ornate musical passage; fanfare **6** [Obs.] a blooming or a bloom **—flour′·isher** *n.* **—flour′·ish·ing** *adj.*

frigidity
(paragraph 9)

frigid (frij′id) **adj.** ⟦ME < L *frigidus* < *frigere*, to be cold < *frigus*, coldness, frost < IE base **srīg-*, coldness > Gr *rhigos*, frost⟧ **1** extremely cold; without heat or warmth **2** without warmth of feeling or manner; stiff and formal **3** habitually failing to become sexually aroused, or abnormally repelled by sexual activity: said of a woman **—fri·gidi·ty** (fri jid′ə tē) *n.* or **frig′id·ness** **—frig′id·ly** *adv.*

itinerant
(paragraph 9)

itin·er·ant (-ənt) **adj.** ⟦LL *itinerans*, prp. of *itinerari*, to travel < L *iter* (gen. *itineris*), a walk, journey < base of *ire*, to go: see YEAR⟧ traveling from place to place or on a circuit **—n.** a person who travels from place to place **—itin′·er·antly** *adv.*

marveled
(paragraph 5)

mar·vel (mär′vəl) **n.** ⟦ME *mervaile* < OFr *merveille*, a wonder < VL *mirabilia*, wonderful things, orig. neut. pl. of L *mirabilis*, wonderful < *mirari*, to wonder at < *mirus*, wonderful: see SMILE⟧ **1** a wonderful or astonishing thing; prodigy or miracle **2** [Archaic] astonishment **—vi. ··veled** or **··velled, ··vel·ing** or **··vel·ling** to be filled with admiring surprise; be amazed; wonder **—vt.** to wonder at or about: followed by a clause

musings
(paragraph 1)

mus·ing (myo͞o′ziŋ) **adj.** that muses; meditative **—n.** meditation; reflection **—mus′·ingly** *adv.*

rapaciously
(paragraph 12)

ra·pa·cious (rə pā′shəs) *adj.* [[< L *rapax* (gen. *rapacis*) < *rapere*, to seize (see RAPE[1]) + -OUS]] **1** taking by force; plundering **2** greedy or grasping; voracious **3** living on captured prey; predatory —**ra·pa′·ciously** *adv.* —**ra·pac·ity** (rə pas′ə tē) *n.* or **ra·pa′·cious·ness**

serene
(paragraph 1)

se·rene (sə rēn′) *adj.* [[L *serenus* < IE *ksero-*, dry (> Gr *xēros*, dry, OHG *serawēn*, to dry out) < base *ksā-*, to burn]] **1** clear; bright; unclouded [a *serene* sky] **2** not disturbed or troubled; calm, peaceful, tranquil, etc. **3** [S-] exalted; high-ranking: used in certain royal titles [his *Serene* Highness] —*n.* [Old Poet.] a serene expanse, as of sky or water —*SYN.* CALM —**se·rene′·ly** *adv.* —**se·rene′·ness** *n.*

solace
(paragraph 3)

sol·ace (säl′is) *n.* [[ME < OFr *solaz* < L *solacium* < *solari*, to comfort < IE base *sel-*, favorable, in good spirits > SILLY]] **1** an easing of grief, loneliness, discomfort, etc. **2** something that eases or relieves; comfort; consolation; relief Also **sol′·ace·ment** (-mənt) —*vt.* **··aced**, **··ac·ing 1** to give solace to; comfort; console **2** to lessen or allay (grief, sorrow, etc.) —*SYN.* COMFORT —**sol′·acer** *n.*

17A VOCABULARY

Match eleven of the imaginary quotations with a vocabulary word listed on page 258–259. Write "none" for the one extra quotation.

1. "In the early 1900s, many families washed their clothes by boiling them in a kettle over an open fire."

2. "Farm laborers who move from place to place to harvest seasonal crops are not paid well."

3. "After being lost in the mountains for two days, the hungry hikers ate the beef stew greedily."

4. "As Nikita lay in front of the cozy fire, her dreamy thoughts about a summer vacation brought a smile to her face."

5. "Enid Lake was calm again after the thunderstorm had passed."

6. "In his closing arguments, attorney Lance Minor made an intense plea for his client's acquittal."

1. __cauldron__

2. __itinerant__

3. __rapaciously__

4. __musings__

5. __serene__

6. __None__

7. "The commander housed the soldiers in temporary buildings until their permanent quarters were completed."

7. ___barrack___

8. "Stephen's parents never visit him in Minnesota in the winter because of the extremely cold weather."

8. ___frigidity___

9. "The magician amazed us with his performance at the Orpheum Theater."

9. ___marveled___

10. "Getting rid of unwanted items can be done through a yard or garage sale."

10. ___divestiture___

11. "To ease the pain of his father's death, Paul ate junk food for comfort."

11. ___solace___

12. "Because of the moisture, the termites thrived in the wooden columns on my front porch.

12. ___flourished___

17B   CENTRAL THEME AND MAIN IDEAS

Choose the best answer.

__b__ 1. What is the central theme of "My Mother's Blue Bowl"?
   a. Alice Walker's mother gave away most of her possessions except several items that her children had given her.
   b. The blue bowl filled Alice Walker with fond memories of her childhood with her mother.
   c. Alice Walker often serves food in the blue bowl her mother gave her.
   d. Alice Walker was embarrassed by the poverty she grew up in and her lack of new, pretty possessions.

__d__ 2. What is the main idea of paragraph 3?
   a. Alice Walker left home at the age of seventeen.
   b. When Alice Walker went to college, her parents moved into the projects.
   c. The projects were the best housing many poor black families in the South could afford.
   d. As she aged, Alice Walker's mother wanted to own fewer and fewer possessions.

Name   Date

___a___ 3. What is the main idea of paragraph 4?
- a. Alice Walker's mother owned few worldly possessions.
- b. Alice Walker's mother liked flowers inside and outside her house.
- c. Alice Walker's mother had a wealthy sister.
- d. Alice Walker's mother believed in recycling.

17C   MAJOR DETAILS

Decide whether each detail is true (T), false (F), or not discussed (ND).

___T___ 1. Alice Walker's mother longed for a house of wood, stone, or brick.

___ND___ 2. The dream house of Alice Walker's mother was in Mississippi.

___F___ 3. Alice Walker was an only child.

___ND___ 4. Alice Walker was a college graduate.

___T___ 5. Alice Walker's mother had a fondness for Pepsi-Cola and fried chicken and fish.

___F___ 6. Alice Walker's mother had few items in her kitchen pantry.

___F___ 7. Alice Walker's mother did not own a television.

___T___ 8. Alice Walker's mother had a talent for growing flowers.

___T___ 9. Alice Walker's mother worked as a cleaning lady.

___ND___ 10. Alice Walker sometimes walked to school rather than ride the school bus.

17D   INFERENCES

Choose the best answer.

___b___ 1. *Read paragraph 6 again.* When Alice Walker left Mississippi for New York, she gave her old dishes to her mother because
- a. Alice Walker did not have enough money to buy a new set of dishes for her mother.
- b. Alice Walker knew her mother would prefer dishes that had a "history" in the family.
- c. Alice Walker feared the visiting neighborhood children would break or chip new dishes.
- d. Alice Walker did not want to pay for shipping her old dishes to her new home.

<u>b</u> 2. *Read paragraph 8 again.* Why did Alice Walker hold the bowls on her lap for the rest of the evening and then take the blue bowl to bed with her? Alice Walker
   a. was afraid her mother might change her mind.
   b. treasured the bowls and enjoyed holding them.
   c. thought her mother might break them.
   d. wanted to throw them away the first thing the next morning.

<u>d</u> 3. *Read paragraph 12 again.* What did Alice Walker imply when she wrote "And in the light and warmth that was her, we dined"?
   a. Her mother hugged them as they dined in the poorly insulated house that was cold in the winter.
   b. The family dined by candlelight because they had no electricity.
   c. Her mother entertained the family with stories that made them laugh.
   d. The children loved their mother so much that they did not notice their poor surroundings when with her.

17E CRITICAL READING: THE AUTHOR'S STRATEGIES

Choose the best answer.

<u>c</u> 1. The main audience for "My Mother's Blue Bowl" is
   a. anyone who places too much importance on material possessions.
   b. anyone who appreciates the sentimental value of worthless objects.
   c. anyone who identifies with the love and sacrifices parents make for their children.
   d. anyone who has lost a mother with whom they had a close relationship.

<u>d</u> 2. The author's purpose in writing this reading is to
   a. persuade.
   b. entertain.
   c. describe.
   d. narrate.

<u>b</u> 3. The author's tone in this reading is
   a. objective.
   b. nostalgic.
   c. emotional.
   d. scornful.

Name   Date

17F   READER'S PROCESS: SUMMARIZING YOUR READING

__c__   1. What is the best summary of "My Mother's Blue Bowl"?
   a. The writer tells about her sentimental attachment to a chipped blue bowl that belongs to her mother.
   b. The writer tells about how she received a chipped blue bowl from her mother shortly before her mother's death.
   c. The writer tells how she treasures a chipped blue bowl that reminds of her mother's way of living her life and caring for her family.
   d. The writer tells how her mother rejected material things and had very few possessions to leave to her children.

17G   READER'S RESPONSE: TO DISCUSS OR WRITE ABOUT

1. Describe a woman in your family (or one whom you have read about or studied) who succeeded despite setbacks or obstacles. Describe her fully, but focus especially on the one outstanding quality that you think helped her succeed.

2. Think of a significant possession of your parent(s) that you would like to have. What memories do you associate with this object? Is there a significant object from your childhood that you think your child(ren) would want? Why?

HOW DID YOU DO?

17   My Mother's Blue Bowl

SKILL (number of items)	Number Correct		Points for each		Score
Vocabulary (12)	_____	×	2	=	_____
Central Theme and Main Ideas (3)	_____	×	6	=	_____
Major Details (10)	_____	×	4	=	_____
Inferences (3)	_____	×	2	=	_____
Critical Reading: The Author's Strategies (3)	_____	×	3	=	_____
Reader's Process: Summarizing Your Reading (1)	_____	×	3	=	_____

(Possible Total: 100) *Total* _____

SPEED

Reading Time: _____ Reading Rate (page 413): _____ Words Per Minute

Name   Date

Selection 18
From In Search of Bernabé

Graciela Limón

(1) Luz and Arturo arrived at the Tijuana bus terminal forty hours later, exhausted and bloated from sitting in their cramped seats. As soon as they stepped out of the bus, they were approached by a woman who asked them if they wanted to cross the border that night. Without waiting for an answer, she told them she could be their guide. The price was five hundred American dollars apiece.

(2) Luz stared at the woman for a few moments, caught off guard by the suddenness of what was happening. More than her words, it was the woman's appearance that held Luz's attention. She was about thirty-five. Old enough, Luz figured, to have experience in her business. The woman was tall and slender, yet her body conveyed muscular strength that gave Luz the impression that she would be able to lead them across the border. The *coyota* returned Luz's gaze, evidently allowing time for the older woman to make up her mind. She took a step closer to Luz, who squinted as she concentrated on the woman's face. Luz regarded her dark skin and high forehead, and the deeply set eyes that steadily returned her questioning stare. With a glance, she took in the *coyota's* faded Levi's and plaid shirt under a shabby sweatshirt, and her eyes widened when she saw the woman's scratched, muddy cowboy boots. She had seen only men wear such shoes.

(3) Luz again looked into the woman's eyes. She was tough, and Luz knew that she had to drive a hard bargain. She began to cry. *"¡Señora, por favor!"* Have a heart! How can you charge so much? We're poor people who have come a long way. Where do you think we can find so many *dólares?* All we have is one hundred dollars to cover the two of us. Please! For the love of your mamacita!" The woman crossed her arms over her chest and laughed out loud as she looked into Luz's eyes. She spoke firmly. "Señora, I'm not in the habit of eating fairy tales for dinner. You've been in Mexico City for a long time. I have eyes, don't I? I can tell that you're not starving. Both of you have eaten a lot of enchiladas and tacos. Just look at those *nalgas!"* She gave Luz a quick, hard smack on her behind. Then, ignoring the older woman's look of outrage, the *coyota* continued to speak rapidly. "Look, Señora. Just to show you that I have feelings, I'll consider guiding the both of you at the reduced rate of seven hundred dollars. Half now; the rest when I get you to Los Angeles. Take it or leave it!" Luz knew that she was facing her match. She answered with one word, *"Bueno."*

(4) The *coyota* led them to a man who was standing nearby. He was wearing a long overcoat, inappropriate for the sultry weather in Tijuana. The coat had a purpose, though, for it concealed deep inner pockets which were filled with money. The *coyota* pulled Luz nearer to the man, then whispered into her ear. "This man will change your pesos into American dollars. A good rate, I guarantee." When Arturo began to move closer, the *coyota* turned on him. "You stay over there!" Arturo obeyed.

(5) Even though she felt distrust, Luz decided that she and Arturo had no alternative. However, she needed to speak with him, so she pulled him to the side. "Hijo, we're taking a big chance. We can be robbed, even killed. Remember the stories we've been hearing since we left home. But what can we do? We need someone to help us get across, so what does it matter if it's this one, or someone else? What do you say?" Arturo agreed with her. "Let's try to make it to the other side. The sooner the better. I think you made a good bargain. We have the money, don't we?" "With a little left over when we get to Los Angeles."

(6) Before they returned to where the others were waiting, she turned to a wall. She didn't want anyone to see what she was doing. Luz withdrew the amount of pesos she estimated she could exchange for a little more than seven hundred American dollars. She walked over to the money vendor, and no sooner had the man placed the green bills on her palm than she heard the *coyota*'s sharp voice. "Three hundred and fifty dollars, *por favor!*" She signaled Luz and Arturo to follow her to a waiting car. They went as far as Mesa Otay, the last stretch of land between Mexico and California. There, the *coyota* instructed them to wait until it got dark. Finally, when Luz could barely see her hand in front of her, the woman gave the signal. "*¡Vámonos!*"

(7) They walked together under the cover of darkness. As Luz and Arturo trekked behind the woman, they sensed that they were not alone, that other people were also following. Suddenly someone issued a warning, "*¡La Migra! ¡Cuidado!*" The *coyota* turned with unexpected speed, and murmured one word, "*¡Abajo!*" All three fell to the ground, clinging to it, melting into it, hoping that it would split open so that they could crawl into its safety. Unexpectedly a light flashed on. Like a giant eye, it seemed to be coming from somewhere in the sky, slowly scanning the terrain. No one moved. All that could be heard were the crickets and the dry grass rasping in the mild breeze. The light had not detected the bodies crouched behind bushes and rocks. It flashed out as suddenly as it had gone on.

(8) "*¡Vámonos!*" The *coyota* was again on her feet and moving. They continued in the dark for hours over rough, rocky terrain. The *coyota* was sure-footed but Luz and Arturo bumped into rocks and tripped over gopher holes. Luz had not rested or eaten since she had gotten off the bus. She was fatigued but she pushed herself fearing she would be left behind if she stopped. Arturo was exhausted too, but he knew that he still had reserves of energy, enough for himself and for Luz.

A sign near the United States/Mexico border warns illegal immigrants of the dangers in crossing the Yuha desert. The sign reads, "Careful! Don't risk your life to the elements. It's not worth the hardship!" Symbols represent, clockwise from left, sunstroke, mountains, rattlesnakes, canals, lack of water, and desert habitat.

© David McNew/Newsmakers/Getty Images

(9) Dawn was breaking as they ascended a hill. Upon reaching the summit, they were struck with awe at the sight that spread beneath their feet. Their heavy breathing stopped abruptly as their eyes glowed in disbelief. Below, even though diffused by dawn's advancing light, was an illuminated sea of streets and buildings. A blur of neon formed a mass of light and color, edged by a highway that was a ribbon of liquid silver. Luz and Arturo wondered if fatigue had caused their eyes to trick them because as far as they could see there was brilliance, limited only in the distance by a vast ocean. To their left, they saw the lights of San Diego unfolding beneath them, and their heart stopped when they realized that farther north, where their eyes could not see, was their destination. Without thinking, Luz and Arturo threw their arms around one another and wept.

(10) The lights of San Diego receded behind them. The *coyota* had guided Luz and Arturo over an inland trail, taking them past the U.S. Immigration station at San Onofre, and then down to connect with the highway. A man in a car was waiting for them a few yards beyond Las Pulgas Road on California Interstate 5. The driver got out of the car as they approached, extending a rough hand first to Luz, and then to Arturo. "*Me llamo Ordaz.*" Ordaz turned to the *coyota* and spoke in English. His words were casual, as if he had seen her only hours before. "You're late. I was beginning to worry."

(11) "The old bag slowed me down." The *coyota* spoke to the man in English, knowing that her clients were unable to understand her. Then, she switched to Spanish to introduce herself to Luz and Arturo. "*Me llamo Petra Traslaviña.* I was born back in San Ysidro on a dairy farm. I speak English and Spanish." There was little talk among them beyond this first encounter. The four piled into a battered Pontiac station wagon, and with Ordaz at the wheel, they headed north. The woman pulled out a pack of Mexican cigarettes, smoking one after the other, until Ordaz started to cough. He opened the window complaining, "*Por favor*, Petra, you wanna choke us to death?" "Shut up!" she retorted rapidly, slurring the English *sh*. The phrase engraved itself in Luz's memory. She liked the sound of it. She liked its effect even more, since she noticed that Ordaz was silenced by the magical phrase. Inwardly, Luz practiced her first English words, repeating them over and again under her breath.

(12) Luz and Arturo were quiet during the trip mainly because they were frightened by the speed at which Ordaz was driving. As she looked out over the *coyota*'s shoulder, Luz knew that she didn't like what she was feeling and hearing. She even disliked the smell of the air, and she felt especially threatened by the early morning fog. When the headlights of oncoming cars broke the grayness, her eyes squinted with pain. The hours seemed endless, and they were relieved when Ordaz finally steered the Pontiac off the freeway and onto the streets of Los Angeles. Like children, Luz and Arturo looked around craning their necks, curiously peering through the windows and seeing that people waited for their turn to step onto the street. Luz thought it was silly the way those people moved in groups. No one ran out onto the street, leaping, jumping, dodging cars as happened in Mexico City and back home. Right away, she missed the vendors peddling wares, and the stands with food and drink.

(13) Suddenly, Luz was struck by the thought that she didn't know where the *coyota* was taking them. As if reading Luz's mind, the woman asked, "Do you have a place you want me to take you to?" Rattled by the question, Luz responded timidly. "No. We didn't have time to think." "I thought so. It's the same with all of you."

(14) The *coyota* was quiet for a while before she whispered to Ordaz, who shook his head in response. They engaged in a heated exchange of words in English, the driver obviously disagreeing with what the *coyota* was proposing. Finally, seeming to have nothing more to say, Ordaz shrugged

his shoulders, apparently accepting defeat. The *coyota* turned to her passengers. "*Vieja*, I know of a place where you two can find a roof and a meal until you find work. But . . ." She was hesitating. "¡*Mierda!* . . . just don't tell them I brought you. They don't like me because I charge you people money."

(15) What she said next was muttered and garbled. Luz and Arturo did not understand her so they kept quiet, feeling slightly uneasy and confused. By this time Ordaz was on Cahuenga Boulevard in Hollywood. He turned up a short street, and pulled into the parking lot of Saint Turibius Church, where the battered wagon spurted, then came to a stand-still. "*Hasta aquí*. You've arrived."

(16) The *coyota* was looking directly at Luz, who thought she detected a warning sign in the woman's eyes. "It was easy this time, Señora. Remember, don't get caught by *la Migra*, because it might not be so good next time around. But if that happens, you know that you can find me at the station in Tijuana." Again, the *coyota* seemed to be fumbling for words. Then she said, "Just don't get any funny ideas hanging around these people. I mean, they love to call themselves *voluntarios*, and they'll do anything for nothing. *Yo no soy así*. I'll charge you money all over again, believe me!" The *coyota* seemed embarrassed. Stiffly, she shifted in her seat, pointing at a two-story, Spanish-style house next to the church. "See that house?" Luz nodded. "*Bueno*. Just walk up to the front door, knock, and tell them who you are, and where you're from. They'll be good to you. But, as I already told you, don't mention me."

(17) She turned to Arturo. "Take care of yourself, *muchacho*. I've known a few like you who have gotten themselves killed out there." With her chin, she pointed toward the street. When Arturo opened his mouth to speak, the *coyota* cut him off curtly. "My three hundred and fifty dollars, *por favor*." She stretched out her hand in Luz's direction without realizing that her words about other young men who resembled Arturo had had an impact on Luz. "Petra, have you by any chance met my son? His name is Bernabé and he looks like this young man."

(18) The *coyota* looked into Luz's eyes. When she spoke her voice was almost soft. "They all look like Arturo, Madre. They all have the same fever in their eyes. How could I possibly know your son from all the rest?" Luz's heart shuddered when the *coyota* called her madre. Something told her that the woman did know Bernabé. This thought filled her with new hope, and she gladly reached into her purse. She put the money into the *coyota*'s hand, saying, "*Hasta pronto*. I hope, Petra, that our paths will cross again sooner or later."

(19) Luz and Arturo were handed the small bundles they had brought with them from Mexico City. As they stepped out of the car, the engine cranked on, backfiring loudly. When it disappeared into the flow of traffic, both realized that even though only three days had passed since they had left Mexico, they had crossed over into a world unknown to them. They were aware that they were facing days and months, perhaps even years, filled with dangers neither of them could imagine.

(20) Feeling apprehensive, they were silent as they approached the large house that their guide had pointed out. They didn't know that the building had been a convent and that it was now a refuge run by priests and other volunteers. Neither realized that they were entering a sanctuary for the displaced and for those without documents or jobs. When they were shown in, Luz and Arturo were surprised at how warmly they were received. No one asked any questions. Afterwards, they were given food to eat and a place to sleep.

(2,382 words)

Here are some of the more difficult words in "In Search of Bernabé."

Vocabulary List

apprehensive
(paragraph 20)

ap·pre·hen·sive (-hen′siv) *adj.* ⟦ME < ML *apprehensivus* < pp. of L *apprehendere*, APPREHEND⟧ **1** able or quick to apprehend or understand **2** having to do with perceiving or understanding **3** anxious or fearful about the future; uneasy —**ap′·pre·hen′·sively** *adv.* —**ap′·pre·hen′·sive·ness** *n.*

clients
(paragraph 11)

cli·ent (klī′ənt) *n.* ⟦OFr < L *cliens*, follower, retainer < IE base **klei-*, to lean, as in L *clinare* (see INCLINE); basic sense, "one leaning on another (for protection)"⟧ **1** [Archaic] a person dependent on another, as for protection or patronage **2** a person or company for whom a lawyer, accountant, advertising agency, etc. is acting **3** a customer **4** a person served by a social agency **5** a nation, state, etc. dependent on another politically, economically, etc.: also **client state 6** *Comput.* a terminal or personal computer that is connected to a SERVER (sense 3) —**cli·en·tal** (klī′ən təl, klī en′təl) *adj.*

convent
(paragraph 20)

con·vent (kän′vənt, -vent′) *n.* ⟦OFr < L *conventus*, assembly (in ML(Ec), religious house, convent), orig. pp. of *convenire*, CONVENE⟧ **1** a community of nuns or, sometimes, monks, living under strict religious vows **2** the building or buildings occupied by such a community —*SYN.* CLOISTER

diffused
(paragraph 9)

dif·fuse (di fyo͞os′; *for v.*, -fyo͞oz′) *adj.* ⟦ME < L *diffusus*, pp. of *diffundere*, to pour in different directions < *dis-*, apart + *fundere*, to pour: see FOUND²⟧ **1** spread out or dispersed; not concentrated **2** using more words than are needed; long-winded; wordy —*vt., vi.* **··fused′, ··fus′·ing 1** to pour, spread out, or disperse in every direction; spread or scatter widely **2** *Physics* to mix by diffusion, as gases, liquids, etc. —*SYN.* WORDY —**dif·fuse′·ly** *adv.* —**dif·fuse′·ness** *n.*

pesos
(paragraph 4)

peso (pā′sō; *Sp* pe′sð) *n., pl.* **··sos′** (-sōz′; *Sp*, -sðs) ⟦Sp, lit., a weight < L *pensum*, something weighed < neut. pp. of *pendere*: see PENSION⟧ the basic monetary unit of: *a)* Argentina *b)* Chile *c)* Colombia *d)* Cuba *e)* the Dominican Republic *f)* Mexico *g)* the Philippines *h)* Uruguay: see the table of monetary units in the Reference Supplement

sultry
(paragraph 4)

sul·try (sul′trē) *adj.* **··trier, ··tri·est** ⟦var. of SWELTRY⟧ **1** oppressively hot and moist; close; sweltering **2** extremely hot; fiery **3** *a)* hot or inflamed, as with passion or lust *b)* suggesting or expressing smoldering passion —**sul′·trily** *adv.* —**sul′·tri·ness** *n.*

terrain
(paragraph 7)

ter·rain (tə rān′) *n.* ⟦Fr < L *terrenum* < *terrenus*, of earth, earthen < *terra*, TERRA⟧ **1** ground or a tract of ground, esp. with regard to its natural or topographical features or fitness for some use **2** *Geol.* TERRANE (sense 1)

trekked
(paragraph 7)

trek (trek) *vi.* **trekked, trek′·king** ⟦Afrik < Du *trekken*, to draw; akin to MHG *trecken*⟧ **1** [South Afr.] to travel by ox wagon **2** to travel slowly or laboriously **3** [Informal] to go, esp. on foot —*vt.* [South Afr.] to draw (a wagon): said of an ox —*n.* **1** [South Afr.] a journey made by ox wagon, or one leg of such a journey **2** any journey or leg of a journey **3** a migration **4** [Informal] a short trip, esp. on foot —**trek′·ker** *n.*

vendor
(paragraph 6)

wares
(paragraph 12)

ven·dor (ven′dər, ven dôr′) *n.* ⟦Anglo-Fr < Fr *vendre*⟧ **1** one who vends, or sells; seller **2** VENDING MACHINE

ware[1] (wer) *n.* ⟦ME < OE *waru*, merchandise, specialized use of *waru*, watchful care, in the sense "what is kept safe": for IE base see GUARD⟧ **1** any piece or kind of goods that a store, merchant, peddler, etc. has to sell; also, any skill or service that one seeks to sell: *usually used in pl.* **2** things, usually of the same general kind, that are for sale; a (specified) kind of merchandise, collectively: generally in compounds *[hardware, earthenware, glassware]* **3** dishes made of baked and glazed clay; pottery, or a specified kind or make of pottery

18A   VOCABULARY

Using the vocabulary words listed on pages 270–271, fill in this crossword puzzle.

Across

2. extremely hot
6. fearful
7. home for religious persons
8. tract of ground
10. unit of money in Latin America

Down

1. customers
3. anything for sale
4. traveled slowly
5. seller
9. spread out

Name   Date

18B   CENTRAL THEME AND MAIN IDEAS

Choose the best answer.

__d__   1. What is the central theme of "In Search of Bernabé"?
  a. Luz bargains with a *coyota* to take her and Arturo across the Mexican border to the United States.
  b. Petra Traslaviña is a *coyota* who makes her living by serving as a border guide.
  c. Luz and Arturo have over a forty-hour bus ride from their home to the Tijuana terminal.
  d. Luz and Arturo cross the United States–Mexican border illegally with the help of a *coyota* to find a missing relative.

__b__   2. What is the main idea of paragraph 2?
  a. Luz is afraid of the woman who approaches her at the Tijuana bus terminal.
  b. Luz carefully inspected the woman's appearance to determine her skill as a guide.
  c. The *coyota* was a tall, slim, and muscular woman who wore Levi's and a plaid shirt under a sweatshirt.
  d. Luz is surprised to see a woman wearing scratched, muddy cowboy boots generally worn by a male.

__a__   3. What is the main idea of paragraph 7?
  a. Luz, Arturo, and the *coyota* walked cautiously across the Mexican–United States border at night to avoid detection by the border patrol.
  b. Besides Luz and Arturo, there were others who crossed the border on foot.
  c. The immigration authorities used bright lights to search for illegal immigrants.
  d. The immigrants clung to the ground when someone issued a warning about the presence of the immigration authorities.

18C   MAJOR DETAILS

Decide whether each detail is true (T), false (F), or not discussed (ND).

__F__   1. Luz and Arturo's home was in Mexico City.

__F__   2. Luz brought the equivalent of only seven hundred American dollars to pay for a border guide.

__F__   3. The *coyota*, Luz, and Arturo trekked on foot across the border from Tijuana to Los Angeles.

__T__   4. Luz and Arturo spoke only Spanish.

Name   Date

___T___ 5. The first English words Luz practiced were *shut up*.

___T___ 6. Ordaz and Petra argued about the location where he was to take Luz and Arturo.

___F___ 7. Luz and Artuo brought a lot of clothes with them.

__ND__ 8. The *coyota* gave Ordaz half of the seven hundred dollar guide fee.

18D INFERENCES

Decide whether each statement below can be inferred (YES) or cannot be inferred (NO) from the reading selection.

__YES__ 1. *Coyota* is a word used to refer to a smuggler of illegal aliens.

__YES__ 2. A *coyota* generally expects to bargain with the illegal aliens for the guide fee.

__NO__ 3. Because the *coyota* was a United States citizen, she wanted to be paid in American dollars.

__YES__ 4. Luz and Arturo would not have been able to cross the border successfully without the *coyota*'s help.

__NO__ 5. As a border guide, the *coyota* had never been caught by immigration authorities.

__NO__ 6. The *coyota* used a fictitious name when she identified herself to Luz and Arturo.

__YES__ 7. Ordaz was a nonsmoker.

__NO__ 8. Luz and Arturo had never seen pedestrians observe traffic signals in Mexico.

__YES__ 9. Bernabé was Arturo's brother.

__NO__ 10. The *coyota* had been Bernabé's guide when he crossed the Mexican–United States border.

__NO__ 11. The *coyota* always took her clients to the convent in Los Angeles if they had no destination.

__NO__ 12. The people at the refuge center assisted illegal aliens in getting United States visas.

18E CRITICAL READING: FACT OR OPINION

Decide whether each statement, even if it quotes someone, contains a FACT or an OPINION.

FACT 1. *From paragraph 3:* From looking into the eyes of the *coyota*, Luz knew she had to drive a hard bargain.

FACT 2. *From paragraph 4:* "The coat had a purpose, though, for it concealed deep inner pockets which were filled with money."

FACT 3. *From paragraph 8:* "The *coyota* was sure-footed but Luz and Arturo bumped into rocks and tripped over gopher holes."

FACT 4. *From paragraph 9:* "Upon reaching the summit, they were struck with awe at the sight that spread beneath their feet."

OPINION 5. *From paragraph 11:* "The old bag slowed me down."

OPINION 6. *From paragraph 14:* "They don't like me because I charge you people money."

OPINION 7. *From paragraph 16:* "I mean, they love to call themselves *voluntarios*, and they'll do anything for nothing."

FACT 8. *From paragraph 17:* "I've known a few like you who have gotten themselves killed out there."

18F CRITICAL READING: THE AUTHOR'S STRATEGIES

Choose the best answer.

   b   1. The main audience for From *In Search of Bernabé* is
        a. anyone who is interested in illegal immigration.
        b. anyone who is curious about how Mexicans cross the border into California.
        c. anyone who works with immigrants who have just arrived in America.
        d. anyone who is interested in border patrol.

   c   2. The author's purpose in writing this reading is to
        a. entertain.
        b. argue.
        c. inform.
        d. describe.

   b   3. The author's tone in this reading is
        a. playful.
        b. sympathetic.
        c. pleasant.
        d. uncaring.

Name   Date

18G READER'S PROCESS: SUMMARIZING YOUR READING

__b__ 1. What is the best summary of From *In Search of Bernabé*?
   a. The author tells how Arturo and Luz sneak across the Mexican border into Los Angeles in the middle of the night.
   b. The author tells how Arturo and Luz illegally cross the Mexican border in search of Bernabé in Los Angeles.
   c. The author tells how Arturo and Luz pay a professional smuggler to help them across the Mexican border into California.
   d. The author tells how Arturo and Luz leave Mexico and go to Los Angeles to find Luz's son.

18H READER'S RESPONSE: TO DISCUSS OR WRITE ABOUT

1. Approximately 3.5 million to 4 million Mexicans live and work illegally in the United States. In California, these migrants often work at low-paying jobs: restaurants, car washes, and construction and landscape companies. Many managers say that Americans will not take these jobs. Have you ever turned down a job because of the low wage? What was the job? The duties? The pay? If you have not turned down a low-paying job, then what is your opinion of someone who needs work but declines such a job offer?

2. In recent years the Border Patrol has used personnel, equipment, technology, and tactics across the United States' most vulnerable cross points to reduce the number of illegal migrants. This has forced migrants to seek routes that are dangerous—across deserts and rivers. As a result, many migrants hire *coyotes* or *polleros,* names given the smugglers who sometimes charge as much as $1,200 for their services. In some cases, the *coyotes* have abandoned their clients in the desert without food or water when they could not keep up the pace. If you were a Mexican without the proper papers and identification to enter the United States, would you consider hiring a *coyote?* Why? Luz looked directly into the eyes of the *coyote* to determine Petra's skill as a guide. How would you go about choosing a guide? How would you prepare yourself for the trip, which can take several days across the desert? What would you take with you? Be specific.

HOW DID YOU DO?

18 In Search of Bernabé

SKILL (number of items)	Number Correct		Points for each		Score
Vocabulary (10)	_____	×	2	=	_____
Central Theme and Main Ideas (3)	_____	×	4	=	_____
Major Details (8)	_____	×	2	=	_____
Inferences (12)	_____	×	2	=	_____
Critical Reading: Fact or Opinion (8)	_____	×	2	=	_____
Critical Reading: The Author's Strategies (3)	_____	×	3	=	_____
Reader's Process: Summarizing Your Reading (1)	_____	×	3	=	_____

(Possible Total: 100) *Total* _____

SPEED

Reading Time: _____ Reading Rate (page 413): _____ Words Per Minute

Name   Date

Part 5

THINKING: GETTING STARTED

The more you read, the more able you become at applying the strategies that strengthen your abilities as an effective reader. The reading selections in Part 5 will urge you to consider and think about a variety of social issues. Keep in mind, as you read, that reading takes place at three levels: on the line, between the lines, and beyond the lines. The selections in Part 5 will particularly challenge you to move with more confidence into reading between the lines and beyond the lines. As you attend to the stated material (what is on the line) also be alert for the logical conclusions that can be drawn from the material (what is between the lines). What is not stated is often as important as what is stated.

When you read between the lines and beyond the lines, you experience most dramatically the interplay between what your eyes see and your mind thinks about. To assist you in gearing up for the readings in this section, use the visuals and accompanying questions on the next three pages to access your prior knowledge. Next, survey the related reading selections and ask questions. Then, when you read the actual selection, consider the questions you generated as you develop interpretations and conclusions about the material.

What motivates people to donate their time and energies to help to better the world? (See "Restored to the Sea.")

"Are we to understand, then, that you would have no scruples about imposing the death penalty?"

How does witnessing an execution affect some people? (See "Death Penalty Victims.")

"He likes to say we're a team, but really he's the coach and I'm the team."

Why do many married women today keep their unmarried name or hyphenate their unmarried name with their husband's last name? (See "Should a Wife Keep Her Name?")

If they think they can, they can.

How can teachers help students become more confident and "think they can"? (See "I Became Her Target.")

How do some people show their feelings toward immigrants? (See "Mute in an English-only World.")

*"I used to think it was cruel to keep a dog in the city,
but Homer's made a remarkable adjustment."*

What animals might people expect to "adjust" happily to mostly in- door living with humans? (See "Out of Their Element.")

Selection 19

Restored to the Sea

Robin Micheli

(1) In the soft orange-and-pink light of dawn, the scene at Seal Rocks on Australia's eastern coast looked like an all-night beach party. People in wet suits warmed themselves before bonfires, as families with small children carried buckets of water from shore to sand, where they worked diligently on what might have been huge sand castles.

(2) But it was rescue, not revelry, on the minds of the hardy souls who had braved the night's 43°F temperatures. An eerie black row of stranded false killer whales (so named because the creatures, though gentle, resemble real killer whales) lay helpless on the sand while beyond them, in the frigid surf, 16 others were held and rocked by shivering divers. The morning before, 49 of the whales had run ashore in New South Wales, and three had died by dusk. The survival of the pod now depended on the ministrations of the residents of the tiny hamlet of Seal Rocks, aided by hundreds of volunteers who had traveled as far as 500 miles.

(3) Why the whales ran aground is a mystery. Experts can only speculate why the creatures, which can grow up to 20' long, sometimes find themselves stranded. "Along shallow beaches, it may be that their sonar doesn't work properly," says Kerrie Haynes-Lovell, a marine-mammal trainer at Sea World in Queensland, who drove 10 hours to assist in the rescue. With no echoes bouncing back from sloping shores to guide it away, a whale may mistakenly head toward land and become disoriented. Disaster may follow. "If one whale gives out distress signals," Haynes-Lovell says, "they may all come in to help."

(4) Humans were quick to answer signals for help after the whales were discovered early on Tuesday morning, July 14, by a visitor walking on the beach. Wayne Kelly, keeper of the Sugarloaf Point Lighthouse, which sits above the rocks and sand where they foundered, says the sight of the bloodied, wailing animals was "pretty distressing. They were writhing around, obviously very uncomfortable." The 200 or so volunteers kept the whales' delicate skin moist in the sun by dousing them continuously with seawater and draping them with soaked towels. Some rescuers, like Susan Clarke, a former registered nurse from nearby Bulahdelah, "adopted" individual whales and became their protectors. "You're a really good boy," Clarke cooed, gently stroking the whale she named Hope as it took a gasping breath from its blowhole. "Hang in there. You'll be in the water soon."

(5) Rescue leaders eventually decided to transport the whales from the rough, open beach to a sheltered cove on the other side of Sugarloaf Point.

Teams of 10 to 20 volunteers began hoisting the whales, which weighed as much as 750 lbs., by hand into a trailer. During Tuesday night, 150 volunteers took turns calming the whales in the cove and making sure their blowholes stayed above water. Four people were treated for hypothermia and many others for exhaustion. Kelly Gray, 17, broke her wrist on Tuesday when a whale rolled over on it. But as soon as it was wrapped, she was back at the beach, in the water. "I couldn't leave him," she said. "How could you, when they're so reliant on you and need you so much?"

Craig Bailey / Florida Today

Volunteers try to save a beached whale until they can return it to the sea.

(6) Volunteers watched helplessly as two of the whales died on Tuesday night. The spent and emotionally drained crowd of volunteers finally had cause for rejoicing late Wednesday afternoon, when 15 of the stranded whales were led out to sea. Three of the largest, dominant bulls were towed in a wire cage a quarter mile from shore, and surfers shepherded the rest after them. Within 24 hours, they had joined another pod of whales and were spotted heading north. In the end, a total of 37 whales were saved.

(7) Their ordeal over, the whales headed east and by midday were swimming freely 12 miles from shore. Homemaker Jenny Mervyn-Jones, who was awake for 36 hours caring for one whale, watched wistfully as they prepared her whale to head out. "You almost don't want to see it go, but you'll do anything you can to save it," she said. "I really can't wait to wave goodbye to the last one and wish it the best of luck."

(697 words)

Here are some of the more difficult words in "Restored to the Sea."

blowhole
(paragraph 4)

blow·hole (-hōl′) *n.* **1** a nostril in the top of the head of whales and certain other cetaceans, through which they breathe **2** a hole through which gas or air can escape, esp. in lava **3** a hole in the ice to which seals, whales, etc. come to get air **4** a vertical opening or chimney in the roof of a sea cave through which air and water are forced by the action of the waves and the rising tides **5** a flaw in cast metal caused by an air or gas bubble

disoriented
(paragraph 3)

dis·ori·ent (dis ôr′ē ent′) *vt.* [Fr *désorienter*: see DIS- & ORIENT, *vt.*] **1** to turn away from the east: see ORIENT (*vt.* 1 & 2) **2** to cause to lose one's bearings **3** to confuse mentally, esp. with respect to time, place, and the identity of persons and objects Also **dis·o′ri·en·tate′** (-ən tāt′), **-·tat′·ed**, **-·tat′·ing** —**dis·o′ri·en·ta′·tion** *n.*

dousing
(paragraph 4)

douse[2] (dous) *vt.* **doused**, **dous′·ing** [< ? prec.] **1** to plunge or thrust suddenly into liquid **2** to drench; pour liquid over —*vi.* to get immersed or drenched —*n.* a drenching

eerie
(paragraph 2)

ee·rie or **eery** (ir′ē, ē′rē) *adj.* **-·rier**, **-·ri·est** [N Eng dial & Scot < ME *eri*, filled with dread, prob. var. of *erg*, cowardly, timid < OE *earg*, akin to Ger *arg*, bad, wicked: for IE base see ORCHESTRA] **1** [Now Rare] timid or frightened; uneasy because of superstitious fear **2** mysterious, uncanny, or weird, esp. in such a way as to frighten or disturb —*SYN.* WEIRD —**ee′·rily** *adv.* —**ee′·ri·ness** *n.*

foundered
(paragraph 4)

foun·der[1] (foun′dər) *vi.* [ME *foundren* < OFr *fondrer*, to fall in, sink < *fond*, bottom < L *fundus*, bottom: see FOUND[2]] **1** to stumble, fall, or go lame **2** to become stuck as in soft ground; bog down **3** to fill with water, as during a storm, and sink: said of a ship or boat **4** to become sick from overeating: used esp. of livestock **5** to break down; collapse; fail —*vt.* to cause to founder —*n.* [< the *vi.*, 1] LAMINITIS

hypothermia
(paragraph 5)

hypo·ther·mia (-thʉr′mē ə) *n.* [ModL < HYPO- + Gr *thermē*, heat: see WARM] a subnormal body temperature

mammal
(paragraph 3)

mam·mal (mam′əl) *n.* [< ModL *Mammalia* < LL *mammalis*, of the breasts < L *mamma*: see prec.] any of a large class (Mammalia) of warmblooded, usually hairy vertebrates whose offspring are fed with milk secreted by the female mammary glands —**mam·ma·lian** (mə mā′lē ən, ma-) *adj., n.*

ministrations
(paragraph 2)

min·is·tra·tion (min′is trā′shən) *n.* [ME *ministracion* < L *ministratio* < pp. of *ministrare*, to MINISTER] **1** MINISTRY (sense 2*a*) **2** administration, as of a sacrament **3** the act or an instance of giving help or care; service —**min′·is·tra′·tive** *adj.*

pod
(paragraph 2)

☆**pod**[2] (päd) *n.* [? special use of prec.] a small group of animals, esp. of seals or whales —*vt.* **pod′·ded**, **pod′·ding** to herd (animals) together

revelry
(paragraph 2)

rev·elry (rev′əl rē) *n., pl.* **-·ries** [ME *revelrie*] reveling; noisy merry-making; boisterous festivity

Vocabulary List

sonar
(paragraph 3)

so·nar (sō'när') *n.* ⟦*so*(*und*) *n*(*avigation*) *a*(*nd*) *r*(*anging*)⟧ an apparatus that transmits high-frequency sound waves through water and registers the vibrations reflected from an object, used in finding submarines, depths, etc.

speculate
(paragraph 3)

specu·late (spek'yə lāt') *vi.* **-·lat'ed, -·lat'·ing** ⟦< L *speculatus,* pp. of *speculari,* to view < *specula,* watchtower < *specere,* to see: see SPY⟧ **1** to think about the various aspects of a given subject; meditate; ponder; esp., to conjecture **2** to buy or sell stocks, commodities, land, etc., usually in the face of higher than ordinary risk, hoping to take advantage of an expected rise or fall in price; also, to take part in any risky venture on the chance of making huge profits — *SYN.* THINK[1] —**spec'u·la'·tor** *n.*

writhing
(paragraph 4)

writhe (rīth) *vt.* **writhed, writh'·ing** ⟦ME *writhen* < OE *writhan,* to twist, wind about, akin to ON *rītha* < IE base **wer-,* to bend, twist > WREATH, WRY⟧ to cause to twist or turn; contort —*vi.* **1** to make twisting or turning movements; contort the body, as in agony; squirm **2** to suffer great emotional distress, as from embarrassment or revulsion —*n.* a writhing movement; contortion —**writh'er** *n.*

19A   VOCABULARY

Choose the best answer.

___c___ 1. **Dousing** as used in "Restored to the Sea" means to
  a. drown out.
  b. keep moist.
  c. pour water over.
  d. splash playfully.

___d___ 2. An **eerie** feeling would best be described as
  a. extremely funny.
  b. heart warming.
  c. suspicious.
  d. frightening or disturbing.

___b___ 3. If the whale **foundered,** it
  a. sank in deep waters.
  b. became stuck or grounded.
  c. traveled in small groups.
  d. rolled all the way over.

___c___ 4. A person suffering from **hypothermia** has
  a. a serious lung disease.
  b. a high fever.
  c. extremely low body temperature.
  d. a cold or allergy.

Name   Date

c   5. The whale's **blowhole** can best be described as
    a. its dorsal fin.
    b. an opening for taking in water.
    c. a nostril through which it breathes.
    d. an organ used for swimming and balancing.

b   6. A **disoriented** person is likely to be
    a. unaccustomed to confusion.
    b. mentally confused.
    c. helplessly nervous.
    d. unfamiliar with directions.

d   7. If the editorial writer **speculated** on the senator's problem, she
    a. engaged in a risky business venture with him.
    b. turned all of her information over to the press.
    c. disregarded the likely outcome.
    d. reflected on its various aspects.

c   8. **Revelry** at a funeral could best be described as
    a. a violation of the law.
    b. showing respect.
    c. inappropriate.
    d. suspicious behavior.

d   9. A **pod** of whales is usually considered to
    a. have identical features.
    b. swim only with their mates.
    c. be dangerous to outsiders.
    d. be a small group.

a   10. A **mammal** is a(n)
    a. warmblooded vertebrate.
    b. animal with fins.
    c. ocean-faring fish.
    d. member of the whale family.

c   11. A person who is **writhing** in pain
    a. should go to a hospital.
    b. has tremendous willpower.
    c. is suffering great distress.
    d. needs to lie down.

c   12. **Ministrations,** as used in "Restored to the Sea," means to
    a. conduct religious services.
    b. give directions or verbal assistance.

        c. administer help or give care.

        d. cure one's illness.

__d__ 13. **Sonar** would most probably be used to

        a. count the number of whales in a pod.

        b. track submarines through the ocean.

        c. calculate ocean depths.

        d. all of the above.

19B   CENTRAL THEME AND MAIN IDEAS

Follow the directions for each item that follows.

__b__ 1. The story is mainly about

        a. volunteers who have traveled from all over Australia to help.

        b. the rescue of stranded whales by concerned citizens.

        c. the hardships many volunteers endured.

        d. a malfunction in the whales' sonar.

__c__ 2. The underlying central theme of "Restored to the Sea" is that

        a. rescuing stranded false killer whales is dangerous work.

        b. volunteers became attached to the whales and even named them.

        c. caring for creatures in distress can be a rewarding experience.

        d. most of the whales were eventually saved by the volunteers.

3. In your own words, give the main idea of paragraph 3.
The whales' sonar may have malfunctioned, causing the whales to become disoriented.

_____

__c__ 4. What is the main idea of paragraph 5?

        a. The whales were moved from the open beach to a sheltered cove.

        b. Whales weigh as much as 750 lbs. each and were difficult for the volunteers to move.

        c. The volunteers battled exhaustion and cold but were devoted.

        d. Faithful volunteers who were injured returned to the rescue again.

Name   Date

19C   MAJOR DETAILS

Decide whether each detail is true (T), false (F), or not discussed (ND).

__F__ 1. Stranded false killer whales are known to attack humans.

__F__ 2. Volunteers from Seal Rocks rescued 37 of the whales.

__ND__ 3. One whale was the cause of the stranding of 49 others.

__T__ 4. Some volunteers traveled great distances to help.

__T__ 5. The whales' malfunctioning sonar may have led them astray.

__ND__ 6. Humans are quick to answer calls to help any animal in distress.

__ND__ 7. The volunteers' previous training prepared them for the rescue attempt.

__ND__ 8. Whales are by nature nervous creatures.

19D   INFERENCES

Decide whether each statement that follows can be inferred (YES) or cannot be inferred (NO) from the reading selection.

__NO__ 1. In paragraph 1 the volunteers were celebrating with a beach party because the work had not yet begun.

__NO__ 2. Scientific studies proved why the whales became stranded.

__YES__ 3. Like humans, whales can become excited and distressed.

__NO__ 4. If a whale's blowhole remains under water indefinitely, the animal will drown.

__YES__ 5. Watching helpless whales die was an event the volunteers were prepared for when they began the mission.

__NO__ 6. It is common for whales to become stranded.

__YES__ 7. The size of the whales hampered the volunteers' attempts to rescue them.

__NO__ 8. False killer whales become stranded more often than gray whales.

<u>YES</u>   9. The volunteers felt a sense of accomplishment after saving 37 of the whales.

<u>YES</u> 10. Kerrie Haynes-Lovell had worked with whales before.

19E   CRITICAL READING: THE AUTHOR'S STRATEGIES

Choose the best answer.

<u>c</u>   1. The main audience for "Restored to the Sea" is
 a. people who became attached to the whales they tended.
 b. people who use the beach on Australia's eastern coast.
 c. people who show concern for animals in distress.
 d. people who helped get the whales back out to sea.

<u>a</u>   2. The author's purpose in writing this reading is to
 a. persuade.
 b. warn.
 c. describe.
 d. entertain.

<u>d</u>   3. The author's tone in this reading is
 a. confused.
 b. amazed.
 c. questioning.
 d. admiring.

19F   READER'S PROCESS: SUMMARIZING YOUR READING

<u>a</u>   1. What is the best summary of "Restored to the Sea"?
 a. The author tells how 200 volunteers in Australia made extraordinary efforts to save the lives of a large group of beached whales.
 b. The author tells how a group of beached whales might have lost their sense of direction and ended up on a beach in Australia.
 c. The author tells how buckets of water and wet towels applied to beached whales can help save their lives.
 d. The author tells how a large group of beached whales in Australia were saved by 200 volunteers.

    Name   Date

19G READER'S RESPONSE: TO DISCUSS OR WRITE ABOUT

1. Often you read in the newspaper about people who participate in efforts to rescue an animal, such as a cat in a tree or a duckling in a sewer drain. Why do you think people willingly give of their time and effort to rescue stranded animals?

2. Have you ever worked as a volunteer after a natural disaster, such as a flood or tornado? Why did you do this? What were the benefits? Would you do it again? Give specific reasons.

HOW DID YOU DO?
19 Restored to the Sea

SKILL (number of items)	Number Correct		Points for each		Score
Vocabulary (13)	_____	×	2	=	_____
Central Theme and Main Ideas (4)	_____	×	5	=	_____
Major Details (8)	_____	×	3	=	_____
Inferences (10)	_____	×	2	=	_____
Critical Reading: The Author's Strategies (3)	_____	×	2	=	_____
Reader's Process: Summarizing Your Reading (1)	_____	×	4	=	_____

(Possible Total: 100) *Total* _____

SPEED

Reading Time: _____ Reading Rate (page 413): _____ Words Per Minute

Selection 20
Death Penalty Victims

Bob Herbert

(1) Leighanne Gideon was twenty-six when she witnessed an execution for the first time. Ms. Gideon is a reporter for *The Huntsville Item* in Texas, and part of her job has been to cover executions. Nowhere in the Western world is the death penalty applied as frequently as in Texas. Ms. Gideon has watched as fifty-two prisoners were put to death.

(2) In a documentary to be broadcast today on National Public Radio's *All Things Considered,* Ms. Gideon says: "I've walked out of the death chamber numb and my legs feeling like rubber sometimes, my head not really feeling like it's attached to my shoulders. I've been told it's perfectly normal—everyone feels it—and after awhile that numb feeling goes away. And indeed it does." But other things linger. "You will never hear another sound," Ms. Gideon says, "like a mother wailing whenever she is watching her son be executed. There's no other sound like it. It is just this horrendous wail and you can't get away from it. . . . That wail surrounds the room. It's definitely something you won't ever forget."

(3) Not much attention has been given to the emotional price paid by the men and women who participate in—or witness—the fearful business of executing their fellow beings. The documentary, titled "Witness to an Execution," is narrated by Jim Willett, the warden at the unit that houses the execution chamber in Huntsville, where all of the Texas executions take place. "Sometimes I wonder," Mr. Willett says, "whether people really understand what goes on down here, and the effect it has on us."

(4) Fred Allen was a guard whose job was to help strap prisoners on the gurneys on which they would be killed. He participated in 130 executions and then had a breakdown, which he describes in the documentary. I called him at his home in Texas. He is still shaken. "There were so many," he said, his voice halting and at times trembling. "A lot of this stuff I just want to try to forget. But my main concern is the individuals who are still in the process. I want people to understand what they're going through. Because I don't want what happened to me to happen to them."

(5) Everyone understands that the condemned prisoners have been convicted of murder. No one wants to free them. But this relentless bombardment of state-sanctioned homicide is another matter entirely. It is almost impossible for staff members and others in the death chamber to ignore the reality of the prisoners as physically healthy human beings—men and (infrequently) women who walk, talk, laugh, cry and sometimes pray. Killing them is not easy. "It's kind of hard to explain what you actually feel when you talk to a man, and you kind of get to know that person," says Kenneth

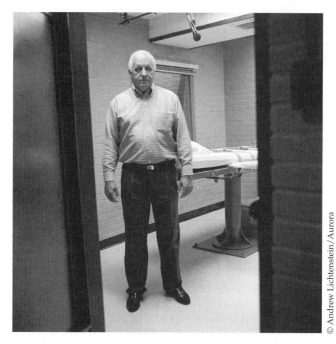

Warden Jim Willett stands in the death chamber at the Huntsville prison in Texas.

© Andrew Lichtenstein/Aurora

Dean, a major in the Huntsville corrections unit. "And then you walk him out of a cell and you take him in there to the chamber and tie him down and then a few minutes later he's gone." Jim Brazzil, a chaplain in the unit, recalls a prisoner who began to sing as his final moment approached: "He made his final statement and then after the warden gave the signal, he started singing `Silent Night.' And he got to the point, `Round yon virgin, mother and child,' and just as he got `child' out, was the last word."

(6) David Isay, who co-produced the documentary with Stacy Abramson, said: "It is certainly chilling to hear the process of what goes on, the ritual of the execution. The folks who do these executions are just regular, sensitive people who are doing it because it's their job. And it has an enormous impact on some of them." The Rev. Carroll Pickett, a chaplain who was present for ninety-five executions in Huntsville before he retired in 1995, told me in a telephone conversation that symptoms of some kind of distress were common among those who participated in the executions. "Sure," he said. "It affects you. It affects anybody." I asked how it had affected him. "Well," he said, "I think it was a contributing factor to a triple bypass I had about eighteen months later. Just all of the stress, you know? I have to say that when I retired I probably had had as much as I could take." I asked Fred Allen, who suffered the breakdown, if his view on the death penalty had changed. "Yes," he said. Then after a long pause, he said, "There's nothing wrong with an individual spending the rest of his life in prison."

(763 words)

Here are some of the more difficult words in "Death Penalty Victims."

Vocabulary List

bombardment
(paragraph 5)

bom·bard (bäm bärd'; *for n.* bäm'bärd') *vt.* ⟦Fr *bombarder* < *bombarde*, mortar < *bombe*, BOMB⟧ **1** to attack with or as with artillery or bombs **2** to keep attacking or pressing with questions, suggestions, etc. **3** to direct a stream of particles at (atomic nuclei) to produce nuclear transmutations —*n.* the earliest type of cannon, originally for hurling stones —*SYN.* ATTACK —**bom·bard'·ment** *n.*

chaplain
(paragraph 5)

chap·lain (chap'lən) *n.* ⟦ME *chapelain* < OFr < ML *capellanus*, orig., custodian of St. Martin's cloak: see CHAPEL⟧ **1** a clergyman attached to a chapel, as of a royal court **2** a minister, priest, or rabbi serving in a religious capacity with the armed forces, or in a prison, hospital, etc. **3** a clergyman, or sometimes a layman, appointed to perform religious functions in a public institution, club, etc. —**chap'·laincy** *n., pl.* **··cies** —**chap'·lain·ship'** *n.*

condemned
(paragraph 5)

con·demn (kən dem') *vt.* ⟦ME *condempnen* < OFr *condemner* < L *condemnare* < *com-*, intens. + *damnare*, to harm, condemn: see DAMN⟧ **1** to pass an adverse judgment on; disapprove of strongly; censure **2** *a*) to declare to be guilty of wrongdoing; convict *b*) to pass judicial sentence on; inflict a penalty upon *c*) to doom ☆**3** to take (private property) for public use by the power of eminent domain; expropriate **4** to declare unfit for use or service [to con-demn a slum tenement] —*SYN.* CRITICIZE —**con·dem'·nable** (-dem'nə bəl, -ə bəl) *adj.* —**con·demn'er** *n.*

documentary
(paragraph 2)

docu·men·tary (däk'yoo ment'ə rē, -yə-) *adj.* **1** consisting of, sup-ported by, contained in, or serving as a document or documents **2** designating or of a film, TV program, etc. that dramatically shows or analyzes news events, social conditions, etc., with little or no fictionalization —*n., pl.* **··ries** a documentary film, TV show, etc.

execution
(paragraph 1)

ex·ecu·tion (ek'si kyoo'shən) *n.* ⟦ME *execucion* < Anglo-Fr < OFr *execution* < L *executio, exsecutio*: see EXECUTOR⟧ **1** the act of executing; specif., *a*) a carrying out, doing, producing, etc. *b*) a putting to death as in accordance with a legally imposed sentence **2** the manner of doing or producing something, as of performing a piece of music or a role in a play **3** [Archaic] effective action, esp. of a destructive nature **4** *Law a*) a writ or order, issued by a court, giving authority to put a judgment into effect *b*) the legal method afforded for the enforcement of a judgment of a court *c*) the act of carrying out the provisions of such a writ or order *d*) the making valid of a legal instrument, as by signing, sealing, and delivering

gurneys
(paragraph 4)

gur·ney (gʉr'nē) *n., pl.* **··neys** ⟦< ?⟧ a stretcher or cot on wheels, used in hospitals to move patients

homicide
(paragraph 5)

homi·cide (häm'ə sīd', hō'mə-) *n.* **1** ⟦ME < OFr < LL *homicidium*, manslaughter, murder < L *homicida*, murderer < *homo*, a man (see HOMO¹) + *caedere*, to cut, kill: see -CIDE⟧ any killing of one human being by another: cf. MURDER, MANSLAUGHTER **2** ⟦ME < OFr < L *homicida*⟧ a person who kills another

horrendous
(paragraph 2)

hor·ren·dous (hô ren'dəs, hə-) *adj.* ⟦L *horrendus* < prp. of *horrere*: see HORRID⟧ horrible; frightful —**hor·ren'·dously** *adv.*

relentless
(paragraph 5)

re·lent·less (-lis) *adj.* **1** not relenting; harsh; pitiless **2** persistent; unremitting —**re·lent'·lessly** *adv.* —**re·lent'·less·ness** *n.*

sanctioned
(paragraph 5)

sanc·tion (saŋk'shən) *n.* ⟦< Fr or L: Fr < L *sanctio* < *sanctus*: see SAINT⟧ **1** the act of a recognized authority confirming or ratifying an action; authorized approval or permission **2** support; encour-agement; approval **3** something that gives binding force to a law, or secures obedience to it, as the penalty for breaking it, or a reward for carrying it out **4** something, as a moral principle or influence, that makes a rule of conduct, a law, etc. binding **5** *a*) a coercive measure, as a blockade of shipping, usually taken by sev-eral nations together, for forcing a nation considered to have vio-lated international law to end the violation *b*) a coercive measure, as a boycott, taken by a group to enforce demands: *often used in pl.* **6** [Obs.] a formal decree; law —*vt.* to give sanction to; specif., *a*) to ratify or confirm *b*) to authorize or permit; countenance —*SYN.* APPROVE —**sanc'·tion·able** *adj.*

20A VOCABULARY

Using the vocabulary words listed on page 293, fill in this crossword puzzle.

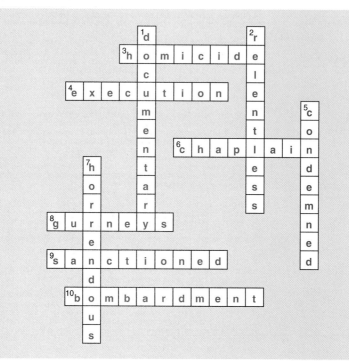

Across

3. murder
4. put to death
6. minister
8. stretchers
9. approved
10. attack

Down

1. program
2. persistent
5. declared guilty
7. horrible

Name   Date

20B CENTRAL THEME AND MAIN IDEAS

Choose the best answer.

__d__ 1. What is the central theme of "Death Penalty Victims"?
a. Huntsville is the "prison city" of Texas.
b. Prison chaplains play a vital role in death row executions.
c. Media reporters are permitted to witness death row executions.
d. Death row executions affect both participants and observers.

__b__ 2. What is the main idea of paragraph 5?
a. Death row inmates have been convicted of murder.
b. Executing death row inmates is not easy.
c. Death row inmates are physically healthy human beings.
d. Executing a death row inmate takes only a few minutes.

20C MAJOR DETAILS

Decide whether each detail is true (T), false (F), or not discussed (ND).

__F__ 1. Ms. Gideon is a television reporter.

__T__ 2. All of Texas's executions take place in Huntsville, Texas.

__ND__ 3. Death row inmates are permitted to order any food they want for their final meal.

__ND__ 4. Executions of death row inmates occur at 12 midnight.

__T__ 5. The warden signals when the lethal injection is to start.

__T__ 6. Family members of death row inmates are permitted to view the execution.

__T__ 7. More men than women are on Texas's death row.

__ND__ 8. Texas began using the lethal injection for executions in 1982.

20D INFERENCES

Decide whether each of the following statements can be inferred (YES) or cannot be inferred (NO) from the reading selection.

__YES__ 1. The death row inmate is strapped to the gurney so he will not jump up or move during the execution procedure.

__NO__ 2. Fred Allen misses his job as a guard at the Huntsville prison.

__NO__ 3. A lethal injection is more humane than execution by electrocution, gas, hanging, or firing squad.

__YES__ 4. Part of the responsibility of a chaplain is to be in the death chamber at the time of execution.

__NO__ 5. Major Kenneth Dean is the head of the tie-down team at the Huntsville prison.

__NO__ 6. Witnessing executions affects the guards more than it does the warden.

20E   CRITICAL READING: FACT OR OPINION

Decide whether each statement, even if it quotes someone, contains a FACT or an OPINION.

__FACT__ 1. *From paragraph 1:* "Nowhere in the Western world is the death penalty applied as frequently as in Texas."

__OPINION__ 2. *From paragraph 2:* "You will never hear another sound," Ms. Gideon says, "like a mother wailing whenever she is watching her son be executed."

__OPINION__ 3. *From paragraph 5:* "No one wants to free them [death row inmates]."

__FACT__ 4. *From paragraph 6:* "The Rev. Carroll Pickett [. . .] told me in a telephone conversation that symptoms of some kind of distress were common among those who participated in the executions."

__OPINION__ 5. *From paragraph 6:* "There's nothing wrong with an individual spending the rest of his life in prison."

20F   CRITICAL READING: THE AUTHOR'S STRATEGIES

Choose the best answer.

__a__ 1. The main audience for "Death Penalty Victims" is
   a. People who are interested in the execution process and its effects on the participants and observers.
   b. people whose job it is to carry out executions.
   c. people who are opposed to the death penalty.
   d. people who are in favor of the death penalty.

Name   Date

___a___ 2. The author's purpose in writing this reading is to
   a. expose.
   b. narrate.
   c. entertain.
   d. describe.

___b___ 3. The author's tone in this reading is
   a. angry.
   b. solemn.
   c. forgiving.
   d. critical.

20G   READER'S PROCESS: SUMMARIZING YOUR READING

___b___ 1. What is the best summary of "Death Penalty Victims"?
   a. The author discusses the job of wardens on death row and the feelings they have after carrying out executions.
   b. The author discusses a documentary on the emotional and long-term effects of witnessing and carrying out executions on death row in Texas.
   c. The author discusses the reaction of a journalist and a warden who have witnessed and carried out a number of executions in Texas.
   d. The author discusses the human side of putting prisoners to death and the toll it takes on workers who are just doing their jobs.

20H   READER'S RESPONSE: TO DISCUSS OR WRITE ABOUT

1. In 1976 the Supreme Court reinstated capital punishment. Today, more than 3,500 inmates sit on Death Row. At least one state, Illinois, has passed a moratorium, a legal delay, on carrying out the death penalty. Are you in favor of such a moratorium for the state where you live? Is your viewpoint based on a moral, ethical, or religious viewpoint? If so, explain in detail. If you are not in favor of a moratorium, why?

2. On the day of execution in Texas, a death row inmate is allowed five witnesses plus a spiritual advisor. The victims are allowed five witnesses. Under what conditions would you attend an execution as a witness for either the inmate or the victim? How do you think viewing an execution would affect you physically, mentally, and emotionally?

HOW DID YOU DO?

20 Death Penalty Victims

SKILL (number of items)	Number Correct		Points for each		Score
Vocabulary (10)	_____	×	2	=	_____
Central Theme and Main Ideas (2)	_____	×	7	=	_____
Major Details (8)	_____	×	3	=	_____
Inferences (6)	_____	×	3	=	_____
Critical Reading: Fact or Opinion (5)	_____	×	3	=	_____
Critical Reading: The Author's Strategies (3)	_____	×	2	=	_____
Reader's Process: Summarizing Your Reading (1)	_____	×	3	=	_____

(Possible Total: 100) *Total* _____

SPEED

Reading Time: _____ Reading Rate (page 413): _____ Words Per Minute

Name   Date

Selection 21
Should a Wife Keep Her Name?

Norman Lobsenz

(1) Encouraged by feminism to maintain their separate identities, many brides have chosen to keep their maiden name* or to combine it somehow with their husband's name. Yet the emotional and technical problems that arise from this decision have made some women think twice.

(2) "I felt an obligation to carry on the family name and heritage," says Catherine Bergstrom-Katz, an actress. "But I also believed that combining our names was the fair thing to do; if I was going to take my husband's name, the least he could do was take mine." Her husband's legal name now is also Bergstrom-Katz. Though he does not use it at work, it is on all the couple's legal documents—mortgage, house deed, insurance and credit cards. Mail comes addressed to both spouses under their own names, their hyphenated name and, says Catherine, "sometimes to 'Allan Bergstrom.'" The couple's first child was named Sasha Bergstrom-Katz.

(3) Not all wives are so adamant. Some use their maiden name in business and their husband's name socially. And a growing number of women who once insisted on hyphenating maiden and married names have dropped the hyphen and are using the maiden name as a middle name.

(4) Despite the popular use of linked, merged or shared names, "there is still a surprising amount of opposition to the idea," says Terri Tepper, who for many years ran an information center in Barrington, Illinois, advising women who wished to retain their maiden names. Family counselors point out that it triggers highly emotional reactions, not only between the couple but also among parents and in-laws. "What about your silver and linens?" one woman asked her daughter. "How can I have them monogrammed if you and Bill have different names?"

(5) While such concerns may seem relatively trivial, there are others that raise significant issues.

- *Control and commitment.* "Names have always been symbols of power," says Constance Ahrons, a therapist at the University of Southern California. "To a modern woman, keeping her name is a symbol of her independence. But a man may feel that implies a lack of commitment to him and to the marriage." Thus when a San Diego woman

---

*Alternate terms for "maiden name" are often preferred because they are considered less demeaning to women; such terms include "given name," "family name," and "premarriage name," although these alternatives are only beginning to come into widespread use.

told her fiancé she had decided to keep her name, he was hurt. "Aren't you proud to be my wife?" he asked. Most men are more understanding. When Maureen Poon, a publicist, married Russell Fear, her English-Irish husband sympathized with his wife's desire to preserve her Chinese-Japanese heritage, especially since she was an only child. "We began married life as Poon-Fear," says Maureen. "I've since dropped the hyphen—it just confuses too many people—but Russell continues to use it when we're out together. He feels that we are 'Poon-Fear,' that we are one."

- *Cultural differences.* "Men raised in a macho society find it hard to accept a wife who goes by her own name," says Dr. Judith Davenport, a clinical social worker. For example, New York–born Jennifer Selvy, now a riding instructor in Denver, says her Western-rancher fiancé was horrified that she wanted to keep her name. "What will my friends say?" he protested. "Nobody will believe we're married!" His distress was so real that Selvy reluctantly yielded.

- *What to name the children.* When couples began hyphenating surnames, it was amusing to consider the tongue-twisters that might plague the next generation. But psychologists point out that youngsters with complex names are often teased by classmates or embarrassed if their parents have different names. And how does one explain to grandparents that their grandchild, apple of their eye, will not be carrying on the family name?

- *Technical troubles.* While there are no legal barriers in any state to a woman's keeping her maiden name—or resuming it in midmarriage—technology can cause complications. Hyphenated names are often too long for computers to handle; others are likely to be filed incorrectly. One reason Maureen Poon-Fear dropped the hyphen in her name was "it created a problem in consistency." She explains: "The Department of Motor Vehicles lists me as POONFEAR. Some of my charge accounts are listed under 'P' and others under 'F,' and I was concerned about the effect on my credit rating if my payments were not properly credited."

(6) Given the difficulties of keeping one's maiden name in a society that has not yet fully adjusted to the idea, should a woman make the effort to do so?

(7) "Clearly, yes, if the name has value to her in terms of personal, family or professional identity," says Alan Loy McGinnis, co-director of the Valley Counseling Center in Glendale, California. "But if keeping one's maiden name makes either spouse feel less secure about the relationship, perhaps the couple needs to find another way to symbolize mutual commitment. After all, marriage today needs all the reinforcement it can get."

(792 words)

Here are some of the more difficult words in "Should a Wife Keep Her Name?"

Vocabulary List

adamant
(paragraph 3)

ada·mant (ad′ə mənt, -mant′) *n.* ⟦ME & OFr < L *adamas* (gen. *adamantis*), the hardest metal < Gr *adamas* (gen. *adamantos*) < *a-*, not + *daman*, to subdue: see TAME⟧ **1** in ancient times, a hard stone or substance that was supposedly unbreakable **2** [Old Poet.] unbreakable hardness —*adj.* **1** too hard to be broken **2** not giving in or relenting; unyielding —*SYN.* INFLEXIBLE —**ad′a·mantly** *adv.*

commitment
(paragraph 5)

com·mit (kə mit′) *vt.* ··**mit′·ted**, ··**mit′·ting** ⟦ME *committen* < L *committere*, to bring together, commit < *com-*, together + *mittere*, to send: see MISSION⟧ **1** to give in charge or trust; deliver for safe-keeping; entrust; consign [we *commit* his fame to posterity] **2** to put officially in custody or confinement [*committed* to prison] **3** to hand over or set apart to be disposed of or put to some purpose [to *commit* something to the trash heap] **4** to do or perpetrate (an offense or crime) **5** to bind as by a promise; pledge; engage [*committed* to the struggle] **6** to make known the opinions or views of [to *commit* oneself on an issue] **7** to refer (a bill, etc.) to a commit-tee to be considered —*vi.* [Informal] to make a pledge or promise: often with *to* —**commit to memory** to learn by heart; memorize —**commit to paper** (or **writing**) to write down; record —**com·mit′·table** *adj.*
SYN.—**commit**, the basic term here, implies the delivery of a person or thing into the charge or keeping of another; **entrust** implies committal based on trust and confidence; **confide** stresses the private nature of information entrusted to another and usually connotes intimacy of relationship; **consign** suggests formal action in transferring something to another's possession or control; **relegate** implies a consigning to a specific class, sphere, place, etc., esp. one of inferiority, and usually suggests the literal or figurative removal of something undesirable

com·mit·ment (-mənt) *n.* **1** a committing or being committed **2** official consignment by court order of a person as to prison or a mental hospital **3** a pledge or promise to do something **4** dedica-tion to a long-term course of action; engagement; involvement **5** a financial liability undertaken, as an agreement to buy or sell secu-rities **6** the act of sending proposed legislation to a committee

feminism
(paragraph 1)

femi·nism (fem′ə niz′əm) *n.* ⟦< L *femina*, woman + -ISM⟧ **1** [Rare] feminine qualities **2** *a*) the principle that woman should have political, economic, and social rights equal to those of men *b*) the movement to win such rights for women —**fem′i·nist** *n.*, *adj.* —**fem′i·nis′·tic** *adj.*

heritage
(paragraph 5)

her·it·age (her′ə tij) *n.* ⟦ME < OFr < *heriter* < LL(Ec) *hereditare*, to inherit < L *hereditas*: see HEREDITY⟧ **1** property that is or can be inherited **2** *a*) something handed down from one's ancestors or the past, as a characteristic, a culture, tradition, etc. *b*) the rights, burdens, or status resulting from being born in a certain time or place; birthright
SYN.—**heritage**, the most general of these words, applies either to property passed on to an heir, or to a tradition, culture, etc. passed on to a later generation [our *heritage* of freedom]; **inherit-ance** applies to property, a characteristic, etc. passed on to an heir; **patrimony** strictly refers to an estate inherited from one's father, but it is also used of anything passed on from an ances-tor; **birthright**, in its stricter sense, applies to the property rights of a first-born son

macho
(paragraph 5)

ma·cho (mä′chō) *n.*, *pl.* ··**chos** (-chōz, -chōs) ⟦Sp < Port, ult. < L *masculus*, MASCULINE⟧ **1** an overly assertive, virile, and domineer-ing man **2** MACHISMO —*adj.* exhibiting or characterized by machismo; overly aggressive, virile, domineering, etc.

mutual
(paragraph 7)

mu·tual (myōō′chōō əl) *adj.* ⟦LME *mutuall* < MFr *mutuel* < L *mutuus*, mutual, reciprocal < *mutare*, to change, exchange: see MISS¹⟧ **1** *a)* done, felt, etc. by each of two or more for or toward the other or others; reciprocal *[mutual* admiration*] b)* of, or having the same relationship toward, each other or one another *[mutual* enemies*]* **2** shared in common; joint *[our mutual* friend*]* **3** designating or of a type of insurance in which the policyholders elect the directors, share in the profits, and agree to indemnify one another against loss —**mu′·tu·al′·ity** (-al′ə tē) *n.*, *pl.* **-ties** —**mu′·tu·ally** *adv.*

SYN.—**mutual** may be used for an interchange of feeling between two persons *[John and Joe are mutual* enemies*]* or may imply a sharing jointly with others *[the mutual* efforts of a group*]*; **reciprocal** implies a return in kind or degree by each of two sides of what is given or demonstrated by the other *[a reciprocal* trade agreement*]*, or it may refer to any inversely corresponding relationship *[the reciprocal* functions of two machine parts*]*; **common** simply implies a being shared by others or by all the members of a group *[our common* interests*]*

plague
(paragraph 5)

plague (plāg) *n.* ⟦ME *plage* < MFr < L *plaga*, a blow, misfortune, in LL(Ec), plague < Gr *plēgē, plaga* < IE *plaga*, a blow < base *plag-*, to strike > FLAW²⟧ **1** anything that afflicts or troubles; calamity; scourge **2** any contagious epidemic disease that is deadly; esp., bubonic plague **3** [Informal] a nuisance; annoyance **4** *Bible* any of various calamities sent down as divine punishment: Ex. 9:14, Num. 16:46 —*vt.* **plagued, plagu′·ing 1** to afflict with a plague **2** to vex; harass; trouble; torment —*SYN.* ANNOY —**plagu′er** *n.*

resuming
(paragraph 5)

re·sume (ri zōōm′, -zyōōm′) *vt.* **··sumed′, ··sum′·ing** ⟦ME *resumen*, to assume < MFr *resumer* < L *resumere* < *re-*, again + *sumere*, to take: see CONSUME⟧ **1** *a)* to take, get, or occupy again *[to resume* one's seat*] b)* to take back or take on again *[to resume* a former name*]* **2** to begin again or go on with again after interruption *[to resume* a conversation*]* **3** to summarize or make a résumé of —*vi.* to begin again or go on again after interruption —**re·sum′·able** *adj.*

surnames
(paragraph 5)

sur·name (sʉr′nām′) *n.* ⟦ME < *sur-* (see SUR-¹) + *name*, infl. by earlier *surnoun* < OFr *surnom* < *sur-* + *nom* < L *nomen*, NAME⟧ **1** the family name, or last name, as distinguished from a given name **2** a name or epithet added to a person's given name (Ex.: Ivan *the Terrible*) —*vt.* **··named′, ··nam′·ing** to give a surname to

symbolize
(paragraph 7)

sym·bol (sim′bəl) *n.* ⟦< Fr & L: Fr *symbole* < L *symbolus*, *symbolum* < Gr *symbolon*, token, pledge, sign by which one infers a thing < *symballein*, to throw together, compare < *syn-*, together + *ballein*, to throw: see BALL²⟧ **1** something that stands for, represents, or suggests another thing; esp., an object used to represent something abstract; emblem *[the dove is a symbol* of peace*]* **2** a written or printed mark, letter, abbreviation, etc. standing for an object, quality, process, quantity, etc., as in music, mathematics, or chemistry **3** *Psychoanalysis* an act or object representing an unconscious desire that has been repressed —*vt.* **··boled** or **··bol·led, ··bol·ing** or **··bol·ling** SYMBOLIZE

sym·bol·ize (-līz′) *vt.* **··ized′, ··iz′·ing** ⟦Fr *symboliser* < ML *symbolizare*⟧ **1** to be a symbol of; typify; stand for **2** to represent by a symbol or symbols —*vi.* to use symbols —**sym′·boli·za′·tion** *n.* —**sym′·bol·iz′er** *n.*

21A VOCABULARY

Using the vocabulary words listed on pages 301–302, fill in the blanks.

1. Adopting a child demands a tremendous emotional
   __commitment__ .

2. To succeed in getting into better physical shape, amateur athletes must
   be __adamant__ about exercising regularly, no matter how
   tempted they may be to skip a workout.

3. In successful marriages, the partners realize that they share
   __mutual__ rights as well as responsibilities.

4. The new owners of the house did not know that mosquitoes would
   __plague__ them each summer.

5. After working as a clown in a circus for six months, my neighbor
   recently returned home and is now __resuming__ his career as a
   stockbroker.

6. Many forms, including employment applications, require people to
   give their __surnames__ before their first names.

7. Instead of the groom's giving the bride a ring, many couples now prefer double-ring ceremonies because they want the exchange of rings to
   __symbolize__ their equality of partnership.

8. In recent years many people are choosing to study a foreign language,
   and many select the language of their grandparents as a way of preserving their __heritage__ .

9. Little boys raised in a __macho__ culture may grow up to feel
   they are superior to women, but such an attitude is resented by many
   women today.

10. Over the last quarter century, the principles of __feminism__
    have encouraged many women to pursue careers that their mothers
    often did not have the chance to consider.

21B CENTRAL THEME AND MAIN IDEAS

Choose the best answer.

__c__ 1. What is the central theme of "Should a Wife Keep Her Name?"
   a. The use of hyphenated surnames causes confusion because the wife may seem not to be committed to the marriage, the children face ridicule, and computer errors are likely to occur.
   b. Some men are horrified by their fiancées' wish to keep their maiden names, in part because these men feel their friends will not believe a couple is married unless the woman adopts the man's name.
   c. Technical and emotional problems that sometimes arise when a woman does not take her husband's name are causing some women to think through the issues before they make a decision about their married surnames.
   d. Feminism is seen as the force behind the modern phenomenon of women keeping their maiden names after they get married.

__d__ 2. What is the main idea of paragraph 5?
   a. Many concerns about women's married surnames often seem relatively trivial.
   b. The important issues about women's surnames after marriage are control and commitment, cultural differences, and what to name the children.
   c. Most men are understanding about their wives' desire to keep their maiden names or to hyphenate their maiden and married names.
   d. Some concerns about women's married surnames have raised a number of significant issues.

3. In your own words, give the main idea of paragraph 4?
   There is still a surprising amount of opposition to the idea of
   linked, merged, or shared names.

21C MAJOR DETAILS

Decide whether each detail is MAJOR or MINOR based on the context of the reading selection.

MAJOR   1. Many brides have chosen to keep their maiden names.

Name   Date

MINOR 2. Catherine Bergstrom-Katz is an actress.

MAJOR 3. Even though her husband does not use their hyphenated name at work, Bergstrom-Katz appears on all the family's legal documents.

MAJOR 4. Some women have decided to use their maiden names as middle names.

MAJOR 5. The issue of linked names can trigger highly emotional reactions.

MINOR 6. One woman is worried about what monograms to put on silver and linens that she wants to give her daughter who is keeping her maiden name.

MINOR 7. Maureen Poon-Fear's husband is of English-Irish descent.

MAJOR 8. Russell Poon-Fear feels he and his wife are one, so he continues to use their hyphenated surnames.

MINOR 9. Jennifer Selvy is now a riding instructor in Denver.

MAJOR 10. Psychologists point out that youngsters with complex names are often teased by classmates.

MAJOR 11. Jennifer Selvy's fiancé worried about what his friends would think if his wife kept her name.

MAJOR 12. Hyphenated surnames sometimes create problems in keeping official government and financial records consistent.

21D INFERENCES

Choose the best answer.

_a_ 1. Read paragraph 5 again. Why have names always been symbols of power?
   a. Traditionally, when a woman married and took her husband's name, he gained complete legal and financial control of her life.
   b. Many primitive tribes used to name people after animals, hoping the animals' powers would transfer to their namesakes.
   c. Traditionally, when a husband's surname is associated with great political and financial power, the man feels he is sharing that power with his wife by giving her his name.
   d. Knowing someone's name can enable anyone to look up that person's records and thereby pry into his or her life.

_b_ 2. Read paragraph 5 again. What does Russell Poon-Fear think of his marriage?

a. Because of his own background, he is glad that he has married someone of mixed heritage.
b. He considers that through marriage his wife has become his partner in all aspects of life.
c. He feels protective of his wife because she has no other family.
d. He feels that without his wife he had no identity.

___c___ 3. Read paragraph 7 again. Alan Loy McGinnis says "marriage today needs all the reinforcement it can get." He is implying that
a. people often marry for the wrong reasons, so many marriages are very fragile.
b. divorce has become too easy, so a couple has to avoid all causes for disagreements if they want their marriage to last.
c. modern marriages face many pressures from within and from outside sources.
d. married couples have to resist the influence of people who want to encourage the couple to get divorced.

21E CRITICAL READING: THE AUTHOR'S STRATEGIES

Choose the best answer.

___b___ 1. The main audience for "Should a Wife Keep Her Name?" is
a. husbands of women who have kept their maiden names.
b. women who are undecided about keeping their maiden names.
c. readers who favor the idea of women keeping their maiden names.
d. women who prefer to keep their marriage a secret.

___c___ 2. The author's purpose in writing this reading is to
a. persuade.
b. narrate.
c. inform.
d. describe.

___c___ 3. The author's tone in this reading is
a. positive.
b. negative.
c. objective.
d. noncommittal.

21F READER'S PROCESS: SUMMARIZING YOUR READING

___c___ 1. What is the best summary of "Should a Wife Keep Her Name?"?

Name   Date

a. The author discusses why using a hyphenated name after marriage can create confusion.

b. The author discusses how some women who wanted to keep their maiden names changed their minds.

c. The author discusses the issues women face as they make the decision to use a hyphenated name or to keep their maiden name after marriage.

d. The author discusses the reactions of friends and family members when women don't take their husband's name after marriage.

21G READER'S RESPONSE: TO DISCUSS OR WRITE ABOUT

1. Do you think that husbands of women who hyphenate their names should also hyphenate their names, as Maureen Poon-Fear's husband did? Why or why not?

2. What is the difference between being called equal and being treated as equal? Using a specific example, describe the difference.

HOW DID YOU DO?
21 Should a Wife Keep Her Name

SKILL (number of items)	Number Correct		Points for each		Score
Vocabulary (10)	_____	×	4	=	_____
Central Theme and Main Ideas (3)	_____	×	8	=	_____
Major Details (12)	_____	×	2	=	_____
Inferences (3)	_____	×	1	=	_____
Critical Reading: The Author's Strategies (3)	_____	×	2	=	_____
Reader's Process: Summarizing Your Reading (1)	_____	×	3	=	_____
	(Possible Total: 100) *Total*				_____

SPEED

Reading Time: _____ Reading Rate (page 413): _____ Words Per Minute

Selection 22

I Became Her Target

Roger Wilkins

(1) My favorite teacher's name was "Deadeye" Bean. Her real name was Dorothy. She taught American history to eighth graders in the junior high section of Creston, the high school that served the north end of Grand Rapids, Michigan. It was the fall of 1944. Franklin D. Roosevelt was president; American troops were battling their way across France; Joe DiMaggio was still in the service; the Montgomery bus boycott was more than a decade away, and I was a 12-year-old black newcomer in a school that was otherwise all white.

(2) My mother, who had been a widow in New York, had married my stepfather, a Grand Rapids physician, the year before, and he had bought the best house he could afford for his new family. The problem for our new neighbors was that their neighborhood had previously been pristine (in their terms) and they were ignorant about black people. The prevailing wisdom in the neighborhood was that we were spoiling it and that we ought to go back where we belonged (or alternatively, ought not intrude where we were not wanted). There was a lot of angry talk among the adults, but nothing much came of it.

© 1998 Arizona State University

Roger Wilkins, distinguished lawyer, award-winning journalist, educator, and civil rights activist, is currently the Clarence J. Robinson Professor of History and American Culture at George Mason University and a commentator for National Public Radio.

(3) But some of the kids, those first few weeks, were quite nasty. They threw stones at me, chased me home when I was on foot and spat on my bike seat when I was in class. For a time, I was a pretty lonely, friendless and sometimes frightened kid. I was just transplanted from Harlem, and here in Grand Rapids, the dominant culture was speaking to me insistently. I can see now that those youngsters were bullying and culturally disadvantaged. I knew then that they were bigoted, but the culture spoke to me more powerfully than my mind and I felt ashamed for being different—a nonstandard person.

(4) I now know that Dorothy Bean understood most of that and deplored it. So things began to change when I walked into her classroom. She was a pleasant-looking single woman, who looked old and wrinkled to me at the time, but who was probably about 40. Whereas my other teachers approached the problem of easing in their new black pupil by ignoring him for the first few weeks, Miss Bean went right at me. On the morning after having read our first assignment, she asked me the first question. I later came to know that in Grand Rapids, she was viewed as a very liberal person who believed, among other things, that Negroes were equal.

(5) I gulped and answered her question and the follow-up. They weren't brilliant answers, but they did establish the facts that I had read the assignment and that I could speak English. Later in the hour, when one of my classmates had bungled an answer, Miss Bean came back to me with a question that required me to clean up the girl's mess and established me as a smart person.

(6) Thus, the teacher began to give me human dimensions, though not perfect ones for an eighth grader. It was somewhat better to be an incipient teacher's pet than merely a dark presence in the back of the room onto whose silent form my classmates could fit all the stereotypes they carried in their heads.

(7) A few days later, Miss Bean became the first teacher ever to require me to think. She asked my opinion about something Jefferson had done. In those days, all my opinions were derivative. I was for Roosevelt because my parents were and I was for the Yankees because my older buddy from Harlem was a Yankee fan. Besides, we didn't have opinions about historical figures like Jefferson. Like our high school building or old Mayor Welch, he just was.

(8) After I had stared at her for a few seconds, she said: "Well, should he have bought Louisiana or not?"

(9) "I guess so," I replied tentatively.

(10) "Why?" she shot back.

(11) Why! What kind of question was that, I groused silently. But I ventured an answer. Day after day, she kept doing that to me, and my answers became stronger and more confident. She was the first teacher to give me the sense that thinking was part of education and that I could form opinions that had some value.

(12) Her final service to me came on a day when my mind was wandering and I was idly digging my pencil into the writing surface on the arm of my chair. Miss Bean impulsively threw a hunk of gum eraser at me. By amazing chance, it hit my hand and sent the pencil flying. She gasped,

and I crept mortified after my pencil as the class roared. That was the ice breaker. Afterward, kids came up to me to laugh about "Old Deadeye Bean." The incident became a legend, and I, a part of that story, became a person to talk to. So that's how I became just another kid in school and Dorothy Bean became "Old Deadeye."

(800 words)

Here are some of the more difficult words in "I Became Her Target."

Vocabulary List

bigoted
(paragraph 3)

bigot (big′ət) *n.* ⟦Fr < OFr, a term of insult used of Normans, apparently a Norman oath < ? ME *bi god*, by God⟧ **1** a person who holds blindly and intolerantly to a particular creed, opinion, etc. **2** a narrow-minded, prejudiced person —*SYN.* ZEALOT —**big′·oted** *adj.* —**big′·ot·edly** *adv.*

boycott
(paragraph 1)

boy·cott (boi′kät′) *vt.* ⟦after Capt. C. C. *Boycott*, land agent ostracized by his neighbors during the Land League agitation in Ireland in 1880⟧ **1** to join together in refusing to deal with, so as to punish, coerce, etc. **2** to refuse to buy, sell, or use /to *boycott* a newspaper/ —☆*n.* an act or instance of boycotting

Deadeye
(paragraph 1)

dead·eye (-ī′) *n.* **1** a round, flat block of wood with three holes in it for a lanyard, used in pairs on a sailing ship to hold the shrouds and stays taut **2** [Slang] an accurate marksman

derivative
(paragraph 7)

de·riva·tive (də riv′ə tiv) *adj.* ⟦ME *derivatif* < LL *derivativus* < L *derivatus*, pp. of *derivare*: see fol.⟧ **1** derived **2** using or taken from other sources; not original **3** of derivation —*n.* **1** something derived **2** *Chem.* a substance derived from, or of such composition and properties that it may be considered as derived from, another substance by chemical change, esp. by the substitution of one or more elements or radicals **3** *Finance* a contract, as an option or futures contract, whose value depends on the value of the securities, commodities, etc. that form the basis of the contract **4** *Linguis.* a word formed from another or others by derivation **5** *Math.* the limiting value of a rate of change of a function with respect to a variable; the instantaneous rate of change, or slope, of a function (Ex.: the derivative of *y* with respect to *x*, often written dy/dx, is 3 when y = 3x) —**de·riv′a·tively** *adv.*

de·rive (di rīv′) *vt.* ··**rived′**, ··**riv′·ing** ⟦ME *deriven* < OFr *deriver* < L *derivare*, to divert, orig., to turn a stream from its channel < *de-*, from + *rivus*, a stream: see RIVAL⟧ **1** to get or receive (something) *from* a source **2** to get by reasoning; deduce or infer **3** to trace from or to a source; show the derivation of **4** *Chem.* to obtain or produce (a compound) from another compound by replacing one element with one or more other elements —*vi.* to come (*from*); be derived; originate —*SYN.* RISE —**de·riv′·able** *adj.* —**de·riv′er** *n.*

dominant
(paragraph 3)

domi·nant (däm′ə nənt) *adj.* ⟦L *dominans*, prp. of *dominari*: see fol.⟧ **1** exercising authority or influence; dominating; ruling; prevailing **2** *Genetics* designating or relating to that one of any pair of allelic hereditary factors which, when both are present in the germ plasm, dominates over the other and appears in the organism: opposed to RECESSIVE: see MENDEL'S LAWS **3** *Music* based upon the fifth tone of a diatonic scale —*n.* **1** *Ecol.* that species of plant or animal most numerous in a community or exercising control over the other organisms by its influence upon the environment **2** *Genetics* a dominant character or factor **3** *Music* the fifth note of a diatonic scale —**dom′i·nantly** *adv.*

SYN.—**dominant** refers to that which dominates or controls, or has the greatest effect /*dominant* characteristics in genetics/; **predominant** refers to that which is at the moment uppermost in importance or influence /the *predominant* reason for his refusal/; **paramount** is applied to that which ranks first in importance, authority, etc. /of *paramount* interest to me/; **preeminent** implies prominence because of surpassing excellence /the *preeminent* writer of his time/; **preponderant** implies superiority in amount, weight, power, importance, etc. /the *preponderant* religion of a country/

groused
(paragraph 11)

grouse[2] (grous) [Informal] *vi.* **groused, grous'·ing** ⟦orig. Brit army slang < ?⟧ to complain; grumble —*n.* a complaint —**grous'er** *n.*

incipient
(paragraph 6)

in·cip·i·ent (in sip'ē ənt) *adj.* ⟦L *incipiens*, prp. of *incipere*, to begin, lit., take up < *in-*, in, on + *capere*, to take: see HAVE⟧ in the first stage of existence; just beginning to exist or to come to notice /an *incipient* illness/ —**in·cip'i·ence** *n.* or **in·cip'i·ency** —**in·cip'i·ently** *adv.*

insistently
(paragraph 3)

in·sist (in sist') *vi.* ⟦MFr *insister* < L *insistere*, to stand on, pursue diligently, persist < *in-*, in, on + *sistere*, to stand, redupl. of *stare*, STAND⟧ to take and maintain a stand or make a firm demand: often with *on* or *upon* —*vt.* **1** to demand strongly **2** to declare firmly or persistently —**in·sist'er** *n.* —**in·sist'ingly** *adv.*

in·sist·ent (-tənt) *adj.* ⟦L *insistens*⟧ **1** insisting or demanding; persistent in demands or assertions **2** compelling the attention /an *insistent* rhythm/ —**in·sist'·ently** *adv.*

mortified
(paragraph 12)

mor·ti·fy (môrt'ə fī') *vt.* **-·fied', -·fy·ing** ⟦ME *mortifien* < OFr *mortifier* < LL(Ec) *mortificare*, to kill, destroy < L *mors*, death (see MORTAL) + *facere*, to make, DO¹⟧ **1** to punish (one's body) or control (one's physical desires and passions) by self-denial, fasting, etc., as a means of religious or ascetic discipline **2** to cause to feel shame, humiliation, chagrin, etc.; injure the pride or self-respect of **3** [Now Rare] to cause (body tissue) to decay or become gangrenous **4** to destroy the vitality or vigor of —*vi,* **1** to practice MORTIFICA-TION (sense 1*a*) **2** [Now Rare] to decay or become gangrenous —**SYN.** ASHAMED —**mor'·ti·fi·er** *n.*

pristine
(paragraph 2)

pris·tine (pris'tēn', -tin; pris tēn'; *chiefly Brit* pris'tīn') *adj.* ⟦L *pristinus*, former < OL *pri*, before: see PRIME⟧ **1** characteristic of the earliest, or an earlier, period or condition; original ☆**2** still pure; uncorrupted; unspoiled /*pristine* beauty/ —**pris'·tine·ly** *adv.*

ventured
(paragraph 11)

ven·ture (ven'chər) *n.* ⟦ME, aphetic for *aventure*: see ADVENTURE⟧ **1** a risky or dangerous undertaking; esp., a business enterprise in which there is danger of loss as well as chance for profit **2** something on which a risk is taken, as the merchandise in a commercial enterprise or a stake in gambling **3** chance; fortune: now only in **at a venture**, by mere chance; at random —*vt.* **-·tured, -·tur·ing** **1** to expose to danger or risk /to *venture* one's life/ **2** to expose (money, merchandise, etc.) to chance of loss **3** to undertake the risk of; brave /to *venture* a storm/ **4** to express at the risk of criticism, objection, denial, etc. /to *venture* an opinion/ —*vi.* to do or go at some risk —**ven'·turer** *n.*

22A VOCABULARY

From the context of "I Became Her Target," explain the meaning of each of the vocabulary words shown in boldface.

1. *From paragraph 1:* My favorite teacher's name was **"Deadeye"** Bean.

someone who shoots well

Name   Date

2. *From paragraph 1:* The Montgomery bus **boycott** was more than a decade away, and I was a 12-year-old black newcomer in a school that was otherwise all white.

   refusal to use
   _____

   _____

3. *From paragraph 2:* The problem for our new neighbors was that their neighborhood had previously been **pristine.**

   unspoiled
   _____

   _____

4. *From paragraph 3:* I was just transplanted from Harlem, and here in Grand Rapids, the **dominant** culture was speaking to me **insistently.**

   prevailing . . . demandingly
   _____

   _____

   _____

   _____

5. *From paragraph 3:* I knew then that they were **bigoted.**

   narrow-minded
   _____

   _____

6. *From paragraph 6:* It was somewhat better to be an **incipient** teacher's pet than merely a dark presence in the back of the room.

   just coming into existence
   _____

   _____

7. *From paragraph 7:* In those days, all my opinions were **derivative.**

   not original
   _____

   _____

8. *From paragraph 11:* What kind of question was that, I **groused** silently. But I **ventured** an answer.

complained . . . risked

9. *From paragraph 12:* I crept **mortified** after my pencil as the class roared.

ashamed

22B   CENTRAL THEME AND MAIN IDEAS

Choose the best answer.

_c_ 1. What is the central theme of "I Became Her Target"?
   a. Roger Wilkins's teacher did not like him and asked him trick questions because he was black and she was a racist.
   b. Roger Wilkins's classmates had been raised by their parents to be racists, and until they were forced to be nice to Wilkins, they had no idea what black people were really like.
   c. Roger Wilkins's teacher helped him realize his worth and get the respect of the other students by challenging him to show his intelligence and answer hard questions.
   d. Roger Wilkins's classmates became his friends once they realized that he and they shared a dislike of their American history teacher.

_d_ 2. What is the main idea of paragraph 7?
   a. Roger Wilkins did not like being called on to answer hard questions.
   b. Roger Wilkins did not know anything about President Jefferson.
   c. All of Roger Wilkins's opinions were derived from his parents or friends.
   d. Roger Wilkins was not used to being asked to think and form his own opinions.

_a_ 3. What is the main idea of paragraph 12?
   a. Miss Bean helped Roger Wilkins gain his classmates' acceptance by throwing an eraser at him when his attention wandered.

b. Miss Bean always looked for opportunities to embarrass her students by throwing erasers at them.

c. Miss Bean had only pretended to be interested in Roger Wilkins's education, but she was a racist underneath.

d. Roger Wilkins was accepted by his classmates only after he mortified Miss Bean in front of them.

22C   MAJOR DETAILS

Decide whether each detail is true (T), or false (F), or not discussed (ND).

__T__   1. Roger Wilkins's favorite teacher was Dorothy Bean.

__T__   2. He was in her eighth-grade American history class in 1944.

__ND__ 3. Before Wilkins, no black student had ever attended Creston High School in Grand Rapids, Michigan.

__ND__ 4. Wilkins's mother met his stepfather in New York.

__F__   5. The adults in Wilkins's new neighborhood threw stones at his house because they wanted his family to move away.

__T__   6. Miss Bean asked Roger Wilkins the very first question on the very first assignment.

__T__   7. Dorothy Bean was viewed as a very liberal person, who believed, among other things, that blacks were equal to whites.

__F__   8. Roger Wilkins had never been to Harlem.

__T__   9. Miss Bean kept asking Roger Wilkins questions day after day until his answers became increasingly confident.

__ND__ 10. It was the tradition at Creston High School to give teachers nicknames.

22D   INFERENCES

Choose the best answer.

__b__   1. *Read paragraphs 1, 2, and 4 again.* Why does the author change from using the word "black" in these paragraphs to using the word "Negroes" in the last sentence of paragraph 4?
   a. By using the word "Negroes," the author shows that he is prejudiced against his own black people.
   b. The preferred, formal term for blacks was "Negroes" in 1944, and the author wants to recreate that time for the reader.

c. The author assumes that the words "Negroes" and "blacks" are interchangeable, although today the preferred term is "blacks."

d. The author prefers the word "Negroes," even though in 1987, when he wrote this essay, the preferred word was "blacks."

___d___ 2. *Read paragraph 3 again.* What is the author implying when he calls the white students "culturally disadvantaged," a term that is usually applied to undereducated minority people?

a. The author is not aware of how the term is usually used.

b. The author is implying that the students at Creston High School had not gotten a good education and had not developed good study habits.

c. The author is trying to be polite by using a nice word for "stupid."

d. The author is being mildly sarcastic, applying a term to these students that they or their parents might have applied to him.

___a___ 3. *Read paragraph 6 again.* Why did Roger Wilkins feel "it was somewhat better to be an incipient teacher's pet than merely a dark presence in the back of the room"?

a. He preferred being liked by the teacher to being liked by no one at all.

b. He felt that being teacher's pet might result in his getting special privileges or a higher grade.

c. He did not like the other students and did not care what they thought of him.

d. He did not like sitting in the back of the room, and he hoped that Miss Bean would change his seat.

22E   CRITICAL READING: THE AUTHOR'S STRATEGIES

Choose the best answer.

___b___ 1. The main audience for "I Became Her Target" is

a. any reader who enjoys a good story.

b. any reader who has had a bad experience in school.

c. any reader who has fond memories of a teacher.

d. any reader who has experienced being the "new kid."

___d___ 2. The author's purpose in writing this reading is to

a. inform.

b. illustrate.

c. warn.

d. narrate.

Name   Date

__a__ 3. The author's tone in this reading is
        a. heartfelt.
        b. serious.
        c. upset.
        d. disappointed.

21F   READER'S PROCESS: SUMMARIZING YOUR READING

__d__ 1. What is the best summary of "I Became Her Target"?
        a. The author tells a story about a time in his childhood when he felt alone and unwanted in school.
        b. The author tells the story of an incident with a teacher that involved a flying eraser and a nickname that stuck.
        c. The author tells a story that illustrates what it's like to be the only black child in an all-white school.
        d. The author tells a story that illustrates how a teacher can influence the life of a child through the craft of teaching.

21G   READER'S RESPONSE: TO DISCUSS OR WRITE ABOUT

1. Suppose the "best house" you could "afford" (paragraph 2) were in a neighborhood where people of your race, religion, or ethnic background are not wanted. Would you move into that neighborhood? Explain your point of view fully.

2. Discuss a teacher or other adult who had a big impact on you when you were growing up. Using specific details and examples, describe the way in which he or she affected you.

HOW DID YOU DO?

22　I Became Her Target

SKILL (number of items)	Number Correct		Points for Each		Score
Vocabulary (11)	_____	×	3	=	_____
Central Theme and Main Ideas (3)	_____	×	4	=	_____
Major Details (10)	_____	×	4	=	_____
Inferences (3)	_____	×	1	=	_____
Critical Reading: The Author's Strategies (3)	_____	×	3	=	_____
Reader's Process: Summarizing Your Reading (1)	_____	×	3	=	_____
		(Possible Total: 100) *Total*			_____

SPEED

Reading Time: _____ Reading Rate (page 414): _____ Words Per Minute

Selection 23

Mute in an English-Only World

Chang-rae Lee

(1) When I read of the trouble in Palisades Park, New Jersey, over the proliferation of Korean-language signs along its main commercial strip, I unexpectedly sympathized with the frustrations, resentments, and fears of the longtime residents. They clearly felt alienated and even unwelcome in a vital part of their community. The town, like seven others in New Jersey, has passed laws requiring that half of any commercial sign in a foreign language be in English. Now I certainly would never tolerate any exclusionary ideas about who could rightfully settle and belong in the town. But having been raised in a Korean immigrant family, I saw every day the exacting price and power of language, especially with my mother, who was an outsider in an English-only world.

(2) In the first years we lived in America, my mother could speak only the most basic English, and she often encountered great difficulty whenever she went out. We lived in New Rochelle, New York, in the early 1970's, and most of the local businesses were run by the descendants of immigrants who, generations ago, had come to the suburbs from New York City. Proudly dotting Main Street and North Avenue were Italian pastry and cheese shops, Jewish tailors and cleaners, and Polish and German butchers and bakers. If my mother's marketing couldn't wait until the weekend, when my father had free time, she would often hold off until I came home from school to buy the groceries. Though I was only six or seven years old, she insisted that I go out shopping with her and my younger sister. I mostly loathed the task, partly because it meant I couldn't spend the afternoon playing catch with my friends but also because I knew our errands would inevitably lead to an awkward scene, and that I would have to speak up to help my mother.

(3) I was just learning the language myself, but I was a quick study, as children are with new tongues. I had spent kindergarten in almost complete silence, hearing only the high nasality of my teacher and comprehending little but the cranky wails and cries of my classmates. But soon, seemingly mere months later, I had already become a terrible ham and mimic, and I would crack up my father with impressions of teachers, his friends, and even himself. My mother scolded me for aping his speech, and the one time I attempted to make light of hers I rated a roundhouse smack on my bottom.

Eight towns in New Jersey have passed laws that half of any commercial sign in a foreign language be in English, unlike these Korean-only signs in Los Angeles, California.

© J. Nordell/The Image Works

(4) For her, the English language was not very funny. It usually meant trouble and a good dose of shame, and sometimes real hurt. Although she had a good reading knowledge of the language from university classes in South Korea, she had never practiced actual conversation. So, in America she used English flashcards and phrase books and watched television with us kids. And she faithfully carried a pocket workbook illustrated with stick-figure people and compound sentences to be filled in. But none of it seemed to do her much good. Staying mostly at home to care for us, she didn't have many chances to try out sundry words and phrases. When she did, say, at the window of the post office, her readied speech would stall, freeze, sometimes altogether collapse.

(5) One day was unusually harrowing. We ventured downtown in the new Ford Country Squire my father had bought her, an enormous station wagon that seemed as long—and deft—as an ocean liner. We were shopping for a special meal for guests visiting that weekend, and my mother had heard that a particular butcher carried fresh oxtails, which she needed for a traditional soup. We'd never been inside the shop, but my mother would pause before its window, which was always lined with whole hams, crown roasts, and ropes of plump handmade sausages. She greatly esteemed the bounty with her eyes, and my sister and I did also, but despite our desirous cries she'd turn us away and instead buy the

packaged links at the Finast supermarket, where she felt comfortable looking them over and could easily spot the price. And, of course, not have to talk. But that day she was resolved. The butcher store was crowded, and as we stepped inside the door jingled a welcome. No one seemed to notice. We waited for some time, and people who entered after us were now being served. Finally, an old woman nudged my mother and waved a little ticket, which we hadn't taken. We patiently waited again, until one of the beefy men behind the glass display hollered our number. My mother pulled us forward and began searching the cases, but oxtails were nowhere to be found. The man, his big arms crossed, sharply said, "Come on, lady, whaddya want?" The butcher looked as if my mother had put something sour in his mouth, and he glanced back at the lighted board and called the next number.

(6) Before I knew it, she had rushed us outside and back in the wagon, which she had double-parked because of the crowd. She was furious, almost vibrating with fear and grief, and I could see she was about to cry. She wanted to go back inside but now the driver of the car we were blocking wanted to pull out. She was shooing us away. My mother, who had just earned her driver's license, started furiously working the pedals. But in her haste she must have flooded the engine, for it wouldn't turn over. The driver started honking and then another car began honking as well, and soon it seemed the entire street was shrieking at us.

(7) In the following years, my mother grew steadily more comfortable with English. In Korean, she could be fiery, stern, deeply funny and ironic; in English just slightly less so. If she was never quite fluent, she gained enough confidence to make herself clearly known to anyone, and particularly to me.

(8) Five years ago, she died of cancer, and some months after we buried her I found myself in the driveway of my father's house, washing her sedan. I liked taking care of her things; it made me feel close to her. While I was cleaning out the glove compartment, I found her pocket English workbook, the one with the silly illustrations. I had not seen it in nearly twenty years. The yellowed pages were brittle and dog-eared. She had fashioned a plain-paper wrapping for it, and I wondered whether she meant to protect the book or hide it.

(9) I doubt that she would have appreciated doing the family shopping on the new Broad Avenue of Palisades Park. But I like to think, too, that she would have understood those who now complain about the Korean-only signs. I wonder what these same people would have done if they had seen my mother studying her English workbook—or lost in a store. Would they have nodded gently at her? Would they have lent a kind word?

(1,775 words)

Here are some of the more difficult words in "Mute in an English-Only World."

alienated
(paragraph 1)

alien·ate (āl′yən āt′, āl′ē ən-) *vt.* -·at′ed, -·at′ing ⟦< L *alienatus*, pp. of *alienare* < *alius*, other: see ELSE⟧ **1** to transfer the ownership of (property) to another **2** to make unfriendly; estrange *[his behavior alienated his friends]* **3** to cause to be withdrawn or detached, as from one's society **4** to cause a transference of (affection) — **al′iena′·tor** *n.*

aping
(paragraph 3)

ape (āp) *n.* ⟦ME < OE *apa*; akin to Ger *affe* < Gmc *apan*, prob. < OSlav *opica*⟧ **1** any gibbon or great ape **2** loosely, any Old or New World monkey **3** a person who imitates; mimic **4** a person who is uncouth, gross, clumsy, etc. —*vt.* aped, ap′·ing to imitate or mimic —*SYN.* IMITATE —**go ape** [Slang] to become mad; also, to become wildly enthusiastic —**ape′·like′** *adj.* —**ap′er** *n.*

bounty
(paragraph 5)

bounty (-tē) *n., pl.* -ties ⟦ME *bounte* < OFr *bonte* < L *bonitas*, goodness < *bonus*, good: see BONUS⟧ **1** generosity in giving **2** something given freely; generous gift **3** a reward, premium, or allowance, esp. one given by a government for killing certain harmful animals, raising certain crops, etc. —*SYN.* BONUS

deft
(paragraph 5)

deft (deft) *adj.* ⟦ME *defte, dafte*: see DAFT⟧ skillful in a quick, sure, and easy way; dexterous —*SYN.* DEXTEROUS —**deft′ly** *adv.* —**deft′·ness** *n.*

descendants
(paragraph 2)

de·scend·ant (dē sen′dənt, di-) *adj.* ⟦ME *descendaunt* < OFr *descendant* < L *descendens*, prp. of *descendere*: see prec.⟧ descending: also **de·scend′·ent** —*n.* **1** a person who is an offspring, however remote, of a certain ancestor, family, group, etc. **2** something that derives from an earlier form

exacting
(paragraph 1)

ex·act·ing (eg zak′tiŋ, ig-) *adj.* **1** making severe or excessive demands; not easily satisfied; strict *[an exacting teacher]* **2** demanding great care, patience, effort, etc.; arduous *[an exacting job]* —*SYN.* ONEROUS —**ex·act′·ingly** *adv.*

harrowing
(paragraph 5)

har·row[1] (har′ō) *n.* ⟦ME *harwe* < ? OE *hearwa*: akin to ON *harfr* < IE *(s)kerp-*: see HARVEST⟧ a frame with spikes or sharp-edged disks, drawn by a horse or tractor and used for breaking up and leveling plowed ground, covering seeds, rooting up weeds, etc. —*vt.* **1** to draw a harrow over (land) **2** to cause mental distress to; torment; vex —*vi.* to take harrowing *[ground that harrows well]* —**har′·rower** *n.* —**har′·row·ing** *adj.* —**har′·row·ingly** *adv.*

DISK HARROW

loathed
(paragraph 2)

loathe (lōth) *vt.* loathed, loath′·ing ⟦ME *lothen* < OE *lathian*, to be hateful < base of *lath*: see prec.⟧ to feel intense dislike, disgust, or hatred for; abhor; detest —*SYN.* HATE —**loath′er** *n.*

proliferation
(paragraph 1)

pro·lif·er·ate (prō lif′ə rāt′, prə-) *vt.* -·at′ed, -·at′ing ⟦back-form. < *proliferation* < Fr *prolifération* < *proliféré*, PROLIFEROUS + -ATION⟧ **1** to reproduce (new parts) in quick succession **2** to produce or create in profusion —*vi.* **1** to grow by multiplying new parts, as by budding, in quick succession **2** to multiply rapidly; increase profusely —**pro·lif′·era′·tion** *n.*

resolved
(paragraph 5)

re·solved (ri zälvd', -zôlvd') *adj.* firm and fixed in purpose; determined; resolute —**re·solv'·edly** (-zäl'vid lē, -zôl'-) *adv.*

sundry
(paragraph 4)

sun·dry (sun'drē) *adj.* ⟦ME *sundri* < OE *syndrig,* separate < *sundor,* apart: see SUNDER & -Y²⟧ various; miscellaneous; divers *[sundry* items of clothing*]* —**pron.** [*with pl. v.*] sundry persons or things: used mainly in the phrase **all and sundry,** everybody; one and all

wails
(paragraph 3)

wail (wāl) *vi.* ⟦ME *wailen* < ON *væla,* to lament < *væ,* WOE⟧ **1** to express grief or pain by long, loud cries **2** to make a plaintive, sad, crying sound *[the wind wailing* in the trees*]* **3** [Slang] *Jazz* to play in an intense or inspired manner —**vt.** [Archaic] **1** to lament; mourn *[to wail* someone's death*]* **2** to cry out in mourning or lamentation —**n.** **1** a long, pitiful cry of grief and pain **2** a sound like this **3** the act of wailing —**SYN.** CRY —**wail'er** *n.*

Vocabulary List

23A   VOCABULARY

Choose the best answer.

__c__ 1. An **alienated** person feels
    a. friendly.
    b. happy.
    c. withdrawn.
    d. confident.

__d__ 2. **Aping** someone else's actions means
    a. accepting.
    b. ridiculing.
    c. changing.
    d. imitating.

__a__ 3. A **bounty** is
    a. generous.
    b. small.
    c. level.
    d. inappropriate.

__a__ 4. A surgeon needs **deft** hands, hands that are
    a. skillful.
    b. germ free.
    c. smooth.
    d. small.

b 5. A **descendant** is a person who is a(n) _____ of a certain ancestor, family, or group.
   a. conspirator
   b. offspring
   c. deadbeat
   d. advocate

a 6. The word **exacting** is closest in meaning to
   a. demanding.
   b. examining.
   c. offending.
   d. increasing.

b 7. A **harrowing** experience is one that causes
   a. mischief.
   b. distress.
   c. happiness
   d. inconvenience.

d 8. To be **loathed** is to be
   a. lost.
   b. liked.
   c. envied.
   d. hated.

c 9. A **proliferation** of signs suggests a(n)
   a. decrease.
   b. absence.
   c. increase.
   d. assortment.

a 10. Someone who is **resolved** to enter a store is
   a. determined.
   b. ready
   c. prepared.
   d. reluctant.

c 11. **Sundry** as used in this essay means
   a. superb.
   b. selective.
   c. various.
   d. specific.

d 12. The **wail** of a grief-stricken person is best described as (a)
   a. soothing sound.
   b. whisper.

Name   Date

c. lively chatter.

d. high-pitched cry.

23B   CENTRAL THEME AND MAIN IDEAS

Choose the best answer.

__b__ 1. Another title for this selection could be
 a. Shopping in Palisades, New Jersey
 b. A Mother's Difficulty with English
 c. Preserving English as a National Language
 d. Role Reversal in Immigrant Families

__c__ 2. The main idea of paragraph 2 is
 a. As a child, Chang-rae Lee lived in New Rochelle, New York.
 b. A wide variety of shops dotted Main Street and North Avenue.
 c. Chang-rae Lee's mother had difficulty speaking English when she shopped.
 d. Chang-rae Lee and his sister sometimes accompanied their mother on shopping trips.

__d__ 3. The main idea of paragraph 5 is
 a. Chang-rae Lee's mother drove downtown in the family's new Ford station wagon to shop.
 b. Chang-rae Lee's mother shopped at Finast supermarket because she could buy packaged meat.
 c. One butcher shop carried a wide selection of meat, including hams, roasts, and sausages.
 d. Shopping for oxtails in a butcher shop resulted in an upsetting experience for Chang-rae Lee's mother.

23C   MAJOR DETAILS

Decide whether each detail is true (T), false (F), or not discussed (ND).

__T__ 1. Eight towns in New Jersey passed laws requiring that half of any commercial sign in a foreign language be in English.

__F__ 2. Chang-rae Lee's family was from Japan.

__T__ 3. Chang-rae Lee did not like shopping with his mother.

__F__ 4. Chang-rae Lee had difficulty learning English when he started school.

__T__ 5. Most businesses in New Rochelle were run by descendants of Asian immigrants.

_F_ 6. Chang-rae Lee's mother disapproved of Lee's making fun of his father's English.

_ND_ 7. Chang-rae Lee's mother had taken only basic English courses at the university in South Korea.

_T_ 8. Chang-rae Lee's mother had a better command of reading English than speaking it.

23D   INFERENCES

Decide whether each statement below can be inferred (YES) or cannot be inferred (NO) from the reading selection.

_NO_ 1. In the early 1970s, Chang-rae Lee's family was the only Korean family in New Rochelle.

_NO_ 2. Chang-rae Lee's father resented having to give up his free time to shop with his wife.

YES 3. Chang-rae Lee's mother watched children's cartoons on television to help her learn English.

_NO_ 4. Chang-rae Lee's mother had a job outside the home.

YES 5. The butcher could not speak Korean.

_NO_ 6. Chang-rae Lee's mother knew it was illegal to double-park outside the butcher shop.

23E   CRITICAL READING: FACT OR OPINION

Decide whether each statement, even if it quotes someone, contains a FACT or an OPINION.

FACT 1. From paragraph 1: "But having been raised in a Korean immigrant family, I saw everyday the exacting price and power of language [. . .]"

FACT 2. From paragraph 4: "For her, the English language was not very funny."

OPINION 3. From paragraph 6: "But in her haste she must have flooded the engine, for it wouldn't turn over."

Name   Date

FACT 4. From paragraph 8: "I liked taking care of her things; it made me feel close to her."

OPINION 5. From paragraph 9: "I doubt that she would have appreciated doing the family shopping on the new Broad Avenue of Palisades Park."

23F   CRITICAL READING: THE AUTHOR'S STRATEGIES

Choose the best answer.

__c__ 1. The main audience for "Mute in an English-Only World" is
a. anyone who has lived in a bilingual community.
b. anyone who has English as a second language.
c. anyone who doesn't appreciate the hardships of immigrants.
d. anyone who has ever studied a foreign language in high school.

__c__ 2. The author's purpose in writing this reading is to
a. describe.
b. entertain.
c. convince.
d. argue.

__b__ 3. The author's tone in this reading is
a. angry.
b. reflective.
c. calm.
d. humorous.

23G   READER'S PROCESS: SUMMARIZING YOUR READING

__a__ 1. What is the best summary of "Mute in an English-Only World"?
a. The author tells a story that shows how people feel when faced with a language barrier in their own community.
b. The author tells a story about the frustration of a Korean woman who cannot speak English.
c. The author tells a story about a community in New Jersey that became populated by Korean businesses with signs in their own language.
d. The author tells a story that illustrates how difficult it can be to learn to speak a foreign language even after you study it in school.

23H   READER'S RESPONSE: TO DISCUSS OR WRITE ABOUT

1. The United States is a country of immigrants. Europeans began to arrive in the United States in the seventeenth century. Immigrants are still coming to the United States. Why do so many people resent the recent influx of immigrants to the United States? Be specific with your reasons.

2. Lee mentions that many of the businesses in his neighborhood were run by descendants of immigrants, many of whom had parents and grandparents who had struggled with English. Why do you think the butcher was so hateful and irritated with Lee's mother when she did not answer his question? Did Lee's mother have any other choice but to run from the store? Have you ever been treated rudely by a salesperson? If so, explain how you reacted.

HOW DID YOU DO?

23   Mute in an English-Only World

SKILL (number of items)	Number Correct		Points for each		Score
Vocabulary (12)	_____	×	2	=	_____
Central Theme and Main Ideas (3)	_____	×	3	=	_____
Major Details (8)	_____	×	2	=	_____
Inferences (6)	_____	×	4	=	_____
Critical Reading: Fact or Opinion (5)	_____	×	3	=	_____
Critical Reading: The Author's Strategies (3)	_____	×	3	=	_____
Reader's Process: Summarizing Your Reading (1)	_____	×	3	=	_____

(Possible Total: 100) *Total* _____

SPEED

Reading Time: _____ Reading Rate (page 414): _____ Words Per Minute

Name   Date

Selection 24
Out of Their Element

Bob Akin

(1) The oil field was the world, and Houston in the late '70s was just the place for a new college graduate. After finding work downtown, I searched for housing that was close and cheap. Just south of Richmond on Mandell, I stood before a somewhat disjointed, three-story red-brick house hiding behind two enormous sycamores. A three-story house was an oddity in the neighborhood, or anywhere in Houston, and it had a loosely hung-together look as though the architect could not quite make the pieces fit. I walked down the driveway on the right to the back, where two buildings of garage apartments filled the lot.

(2) Annie was a compact, gray-haired woman whose carriage belied a strength acquired from many years of work. She mounted the hall stairs and opened a door to the left to show me a small, modest one-bedroom apartment. "I clean on Tuesdays and Fridays. Just leave the trash outside in the hall," she said. I liked the soft resonance in her voice. She took my check and gave me the key.

(3) Downtown Houston was a panorama of sleek banks, stores and oil companies. Everywhere, the glossy opulence of new steel and glass testified to the city's wealth. I chatted with the clerks at Foley's and the counterman at James' Coney Island, but I was aware that they were really too busy to visit. Surrounded by people, I knew virtually no one. When sunset turned the streets into great purple canyons, I felt an acute pang for my old small-town university neighborhood. There, we swapped news on front porches in the evenings, knew everybody who lived around us and dropped by to visit without calling, except on Sunday mornings. Familiarity so long taken for granted was now a precious commodity that I lacked. I reminded myself that meeting new people and making friends took time, but the feelings of isolation and aloneness would sometimes nag at me like bad children. My head understood that new characters in the common story were out there, but my voice had not yet found a kindred spirit to talk to.

(4) Mellow fall turned to frosty winter that year. I came home one damp, fog-glazed night to find a badly rumpled *People* magazine outside my door. After dinner, I thumbed through it absently while Fleetwood Mac kept me company. The articles were dull until I came across one about an older couple who kept a pet gorilla in their house. They had acquired him in South Africa, having spent some 30 years there as missionaries. The great ape was orphaned while still an infant. They adopted him and, unable to

part with their surrogate child, brought him back to the United States. A gorilla in the house was an exotic and ridiculous idea that intrigued me. Like a lightning bolt, the faces in the picture on the page leapt out at me. Annie and her husband, Charlie, glowed with their proud adoptee, Hugo. Surely there was some mistake. Yet the article clearly identified the couple, the neighborhood and the city. A 500-pound, fully grown male jungle gorilla was living not 30 feet from my doorstep. I was delirious with amazement.

This gorilla is what Hugo looked like.

Bruce Coleman, Inc.

(5) I raced down the stairs but slowed to a creep at the back door to the house. No lights reflected from the windows. Circling the house like a thief, I peered for a clue to its primordial resident. Visions from *Murders in the Rue Morgue* danced on the porch roofs and gables. With a seminaked beauty slung over his shoulder, Hugo arced the rooftops like the champion in a silent movie. My straining ears heard only the muted night, wet rubber on asphalt. Daylight would come before my curiosity could be satisfied.

(6) Annie's smile was practiced and indulgent. The acrobats in my stomach were doing somersaults as the anticipation of a new first experience made me giddy. Bright February sun made the house's interiors seem old, dark and faded. Where does one keep a gorilla in the house?

(7) Annie led me through two short hall-ways into their living room. "He's quite intelligent, really. About the same as a 4- to 5-year-old child. When he first sees you, he'll make an awful rumpus, but you mustn't let

on that you're afraid. If you do, he'll never stop. Just stand quietly, and in a few minutes he'll come to the window to get a good look at you." My heart felt like the congas that Hugo must have heard when he was growing up. We crossed the room to a window set in the far end of a wall facing the rear of the house. Through the window I saw a large, wide room made of concrete with steel bars to the left. Severed tree trunks, a few boulders and hanging ropes filled the space. A tire swing on a hemp-style cable hung from the ceiling. At the far end, Hugo sat playing with a small object that I could not see. When Annie spoke to him, his great head swung around sharply, and for a moment he froze, cutting his eyes straight at me. He rose slowly and then charged toward the window at full speed, slamming into it with a thunderous sound. He bellowed with rage, pounded his chest and threw himself around the caged room, smashing into everything in his path. He attacked the window again to roar and beat the bars. I was fairly shocked in place and too riveted to move or speak. He leapt on the steel bars to the left and rocketed himself back and forth, screaming his displeasure. He jumped to the ledges on the right wall, up and down, over and over, beating the walls and floor with his fists, his arms, his whole body. Hugo rammed the window again, those fierce explosive eyes piercing through me. Then he stopped.

(8) Hugo backed away from the window to the center of the room, where he circled slowly and dropped to all fours, his roadwide back a perfect horizontal to the ground. He crept to the window and, swaying his head ever so slightly, examined me with cool interest. Those enormous shining black eyes regarded me with what seemed like amusement, as though I was the object of curiosity. As we stared at each other, I could see reflected in his eyes some fixtures in the room, the old chair and standing brass lamp next to me, and finally, an outline image of myself. Hugo became so still that it was almost like looking into an ebony mirror. What did he see? What pictures and sounds coursed through his childlike consciousness? For an undefined moment, the bars, the window, the room and all around me were swept away, and I was the entity out of place in the gray-green twilight of his rain forest, a world without mechanism or man. Hugo's delicate breathing and primal scent were thick on my skin. His quixotic smile held me transfixed.

(9) Annie's returning voice made me realize that she had not been there for some time. "His favorite foods are spaghetti, ice cream and potato chips. He's particularly fond of bright, shiny things that move or make noise. I think he likes you," Annie said, busying herself around the room while I slowly came back to my senses. "We used to go inside the cage to play with him but not anymore. The last time Charlie went in, it took a whole day for him to get out. Hugo didn't want to let him go. Lonely, you know. We finally distracted him with Charlie's watch. He still has it in there." Hugo and I wondered at each other a bit longer, and then I left; it was Hugo's dinnertime.

(10) Hugo visited my consciousness often in the following days and weeks; he would peer out at me from the low branches of ancient magnolias, look over my shoulder at the coffee machine in the office or widen his eyes from behind the banana display at Weingarten's. Annie invited me into the hall that ran parallel to Hugo's room. "You mustn't get close enough for him to touch you. He's liable to take your arm and not want to let go." "How old is he?" I asked. "About 17, middle-aged for a gorilla."

(11) In Hugo's room I saw items I had not noticed before: pillows, quilts, blankets, and a storehouse of toys and stuffed animals. The pallet where he slept looked thick and comfortable. Candy bar wrappers and a potato chip bag peeked out from under a large grinning Snoopy Dog. "Do you think you will ever get another ape for Hugo, a friend, or maybe a mate?" "Heavens no. He costs a fortune to feed as it is. Besides, there really isn't room." "Will Hugo ever return to the wild? I mean, do you ever plan to go back to Africa?" Annie's voice was gentle and patient. "Hugo couldn't survive in the wild. We have always taken care of him. Our other children here come and go, but Hugo stays. He's happy here."

(12) An odd assortment of people, as seemingly disjointed as the house itself, lived in Annie's and Charlie's rooms. A neighbor had told me that they were mostly foster children or transients who were fighting addiction, criminal records or mental illness. It came as no surprise. Annie and Charlie were childless. Being their child had doomed Hugo to a lifetime of imprisonment.

(13) Hugo crept to the bars like a timid child. Less than five feet from me, he arched his head up and sniffed the air. He gently curled his mammoth hands around the bars and eyed me while rocking his head. He cocked that massive skull to one side as coyly as a debutante. I smiled. The sense of his presence awed one, like the roar of Niagara Falls or a star-riddled summer night. His movement was small and precise, a ballet dancer possessed of delicately cathartic destruction. He settled on the floor to groom his fur with patient fingers, an invitation for me to come closer. The pull to touch that luminous giant was fearsome and magnetic. Finished with her chores, Annie called me to follow her back into the living room.

(14) A rainy Tuesday afternoon found me sitting outside Hugo's room watching him watch me. A great, fine figure of his species, in the wild he would have possessed a harem of females. But there would be no offspring, no son of Hugo to reflect his image back to him. My sense of isolation dwindled in the shadow of his life.

(15) I would visit Hugo several times, but as weeks turned into months, my new city life demanded more and more attention. Dates, business dinners and Astros games with new buddies took the place of long evening walks and time with Hugo.

(16) My solitary walls had melted, but he was still alone. He did not seem unhappy, yet I wondered if Annie and Charlie felt that the price he had paid was worth it to them. For a while, Hugo gave me something above an awareness of the value of freedom—a sublime sense of choice.

(17) Heavy rains came with spring, and one wet day I met Annie sweeping damp leaves from the driveway. Hugo had come down with pneumonia during the last torrential flooding. An elderly veterinarian had shot Hugo with a pellet of antibiotics from outside the bars of his room. Much sicker than even Annie and Charlie had realized, Hugo had gone to sleep, never to wake up.

(18) Enough years have passed that every picture or mention of monkeys, apes, orangutans or gorillas does not conjure up Hugo's ghost. Yet sometimes he comes at odd moments, like an old friend who just dropped by to look into my face and see how I am doing. I remember Hugo's scent, his size, his gentle childlike movement and some intangible conundrum. What fascinated me most even then were Hugo's eyes. They still do.

(2,008 words)

Here are some of the more difficult words in "Out of Their Element."

carriage
(paragraph 2)

car·riage (kar′ij; *for 2, usually* kar′ē ij′) *n.* 〖ME *cariage*, baggage, transport < Anglo-Fr, cart, carriage < *carier*, CARRY〗 **1** the act of carrying; transportation **2** the cost of carrying; transportation charge **3** [Archaic] *a)* management or handling *b)* conduct; behavior **4** manner of carrying the head and body; posture; bearing **5** *a)* a four-wheeled passenger vehicle, usually horse-drawn and often private *b) short for* BABY CARRIAGE **6** [Brit.] a railroad passenger car **7** a wheeled frame or support for something heavy [a gun *carriage*] **8** a moving part (of a machine) for supporting and shifting something [the *carriage* of a typewriter] —*SYN.* BEARING

commodity
(paragraph 3)

com·mod·ity (kə mäd′ə tē) *n., pl.* -**ties** 〖ME & OFr *commodite*, benefit, profit < L *commoditas*, fitness, adaptation < *commodus*: see COMMODE〗 **1** any useful thing **2** anything bought and sold; any article of commerce **3** [*pl.*] basic items or staple products, as of agriculture or mining **4** [Archaic] personal advantage

conundrum
(paragraph 18)

co·nun·drum (kə nun′drəm) *n.* 〖16th-c. Oxford University L slang for pedant, whim, etc.; early sp. *quonundrum*〗 **1** a riddle whose answer contains a pun (Ex.: "What's the difference between a jeweler and a jailer?" "One sells watches and the other watches cells.") **2** any puzzling question or problem —*SYN.* MYSTERY[1]

doomed
(paragraph 12)

doom[1] (do͞om) *n.* 〖ME & OE *dom*, lit., what is laid down, decree, akin to Goth *doms*, judgment < IE base *dhē-*: see DO[1]〗 **1** [Historical] a statute; decree **2** a judgment; esp., a sentence of condemnation **3** destiny; fate **4** tragic fate; ruin or death **5** Judgment Day —*vt.* **1** to pronounce judgment on; condemn; sentence **2** to destine to a tragic fate **3** to ordain as a penalty —*SYN.* FATE

entity
(paragraph 8)

en·tity (en′tə tē) *n., pl.* --**ties** 〖< Fr *entité* or ML *entitas* < L *ens* (gen. *entis*), prp. of *esse*, to be: see IS[1]〗 **1** being; existence **2** a thing which has definite, individual existence outside or within the mind; anything real in itself

luminous
(paragraph 13)

lu·mi·nous (lo͞o′mə nəs) *adj.* 〖ME < L *luminosus* < *lumen*, LIGHT[1]〗 **1** giving off light; shining; bright **2** filled with light; illuminated **3** glowing in the dark, as paint with a phosphor in it **4** clear; readily understood **5** intellectually brilliant —*SYN.* BRIGHT —**lu′·mi·nously** *adv.* —**lu′·mi·nous·ness** *n.*

missionaries
(paragraph 4)

mis·sion·ary (-er′ē) *adj.* 〖ModL (Ec) *missionarius*〗 of or characteristic of missions or missionaries, esp. religious ones —*n., pl.* --**ar′·ies** a person sent on a mission, esp. on a religious mission: also **mis′·sioner** (-ər)

Vocabulary List

opulence
(paragraph 3)

opu·lent (äp′yo͞o lənt, -yə-) *adj.* ⟦L *opulentus* or *opulens* < *ops:* see OPUS⟧ **1** very wealthy or rich **2** characterized by abundance or profusion; luxuriant —*SYN.* RICH —**op′u·lence** *n.* or **op′u·lency** —**op′u·lently** *adv.*

pang
(paragraph 3)

pang (paŋ) *n.* ⟦< ? LME *pronge:* see PRONG⟧ a sudden, sharp, and brief pain, physical or emotional; spasm of distress

panorama
(paragraph 3)

pano·rama (pan′ə ram′ə, -rä′mə) *n.* ⟦coined (c. 1789) by Robert Barker (1739-1806), Scot artist < PAN- + Gr *horama*, a view < *horan*, to see < IE base *wer-*, to heed > WARD, GUARD⟧ **1** *a*) a picture or series of pictures of a landscape, historical event, etc., presented on a continuous surface encircling the spectator; cyclorama *b*) a picture unrolled before the spectator in such a way as to give the impression of a continuous view **2** an unlimited view in all directions **3** a comprehensive survey of a subject **4** a continuous series of scenes or events; constantly changing scene —**pan′o·ram′ic** *adj.* —**pan′o·ram′i·cally** *adv.*

primordial
(paragraph 5)

pri·mor·dial (prī môr′dē əl) *adj.* ⟦ME < LL *primordialis* < L *primordium*, the beginning < *primus*, first (see PRIME) + *ordiri*, to begin (see ORDER)⟧ **1** first in time; existing at or from the beginning; primitive; primeval **2** not derivative; fundamental; original **3** *Biol.* earliest formed in the development of an organism, organ, structure, etc.; primitive —**pri·mor′·di·ally** *adv.*

quixotic
(paragraph 8)

quix·otic (kwik sät′ik) *adj.* **1** [*often* Q-] of or like Don Quixote **2** extravagantly chivalrous or foolishly idealistic; visionary; impractical or impracticable: also **quix·ot′i·cal** —**quix·ot′i·cally** *adv.*

rumpus
(paragraph 7)

rum·pus (rum′pəs) *n.* ⟦< ?⟧ [Informal] an uproar or commotion

sublime
(paragraph 16)

sub·lime (sə blīm′) *adj.* ⟦L *sublimus* < *sub-*, up to + *limen*, lintel (hence, orig. up to the lintel): see LIMEN⟧ **1** noble; exalted; majestic **2** inspiring awe or admiration through grandeur, beauty, etc. **3** [Informal] outstandingly or supremely such [*a* man of *sublime* taste] **4** [Archaic] *a*) elated; joyful *b*) proud; lofty; haughty *c*) upraised; aloft —*vt.* **·limed′**, **··lim′·ing** ⟦ME *sublimen* < MFr *sublimer* < ML *sublimare* < L, to lift high < the adj.⟧ **1** to make sublime **2** SUBLIMATE (*vt.* 1) —*vi.* SUBLIMATE —**the sublime** sublime quality; sublimity —**sub·lime′ly** *adv.* —**sub·lime′·ness** *n.*

surrogate
(paragraph 4)

sur·ro·gate (sur′ə git, -gāt′; *for v.*, -gāt′) *n.* ⟦L *surrogatus*, pp. of *surrogare*, to elect in place of another, substitute < *sub-* (see SUB-) + *rogare*, to ask: see ROGATION⟧ **1** a deputy or substitute **2** in some states, probate court, or a judge of this court **3** *Psychiatry* a substitute figure, esp. a person of some authority, who replaces a father or mother in one's feelings **4** a woman who, by prior agreement, becomes pregnant and bears a child for another woman, who will raise the child as its mother —*adj.* of or acting as a surrogate —*vt.* **··gat′ed**, **··gat′·ing** to put in another's place as a substitute or deputy

24A   VOCABULARY

Using the dictionary entries on pages 333–334, fill in the blanks.

1. As he walked down the hospital corridor, his _____carriage_____ was that of a man in his eighties, not his sixties.

Name   Date

2. From the 110th floor of the Sears Tower in Chicago, people can see a ___panorama___ of stores, hotels, restaurants, and office buildings.

3. As I drove through Chickasaw Gardens and saw the expensive cars in the driveways, I became aware of the neighborhood's ___opulence___ .

4. The first time eight-year-old Meg slept over at a friend's home, she felt a ___pang___ of homesickness.

5. When the electricity went off at night, the one ___commodity___ I did not have was a flashlight.

6. The first Sunday of each month, the minister asks every church member to contribute two dollars to help support ___missionaries___ in foreign countries.

7. After we bought the puppy, we put a stuffed sock to serve as a ___surrogate___ mother in her cardboard box.

8. H. G. Wells wrote, "___Primordial___ man could have had little or no tradition before the development of speech."

9. My parents told my friends and me to play in the basement, so they would not hear the ___rumpus___ we made.

10. In her grief, she had come to question her ___entity___ .

11. In some New York restaurants, waiters exhibit ___quixotic___ behavior by giving two menus: one with prices to the males and another without prices to their female companions.

12. Passengers aboard the *Titanic* were ___doomed___ to a watery grave after the ship hit an iceberg.

13. As they drove along the beautiful Blue Ridge Parkway in Virginia, they found the view of the mountains ___sublime___ .

14. Many stars are more ___luminous___ than our sun.

15. A ___conundrum___ is a riddle whose answer involves a play on words, as in "When is a door, not a door? When it is 'ajar.'"

24B   CENTRAL THEME AND MAIN IDEAS

Choose the best answer.

  b   1. What is the central theme of "Out of Their Element"?
         a. Annie and Charlie adopted a gorilla that had been orphaned in Africa.
         b. Hugo was intended to reside in the animal world, not the human world.
         c. Annie and Charlie's home was open to anyone without a place to live—even a gorilla.
         d. A gorilla makes a fascinating pet.

  b   2. What is the main idea of paragraph 3?
         a. Downtown Houston was a modern city with banks, stores, and oil companies.
         b. Raised in a small town, the author felt a sense of loneliness in a large city like Houston.
         c. Living in a small town is better than living in a large city.
         d. After moving to Houston, the author had difficulty making friends at first.

24C   MAJOR DETAILS

Decide whether each detail is MAJOR or MINOR based on the context of the reading selection.

MINOR   1. Bob Akin was a recent college graduate.

MINOR   2. Annie cleaned the apartment on Tuesdays and Fridays.

MAJOR   3. Annie and Charlie were missionaries in Africa.

MAJOR   4. Bob Akin read in *People* magazine about a couple who kept a gorilla in their house.

MAJOR   5. Hugo's cage contained severed tree trunks, some boulders, hang zing ropes, and a tire on a cable.

MAJOR   6. Upon seeing Bob Akin the first time, the gorilla bellowed with rage, pounded his chest, and leapt from one side of the cage to the other.

MINOR   7. Hugo's favorite foods were spaghetti, ice cream, and potato chips.

MAJOR   8. Hugo was seventeen years old.

MAJOR   9. Hugo would never have another gorilla for a friend or a mate.

Name   Date

MAJOR 10. Annie and Charlie were childless.

MAJOR 11. Hugo came down with pneumonia a few months after Bob Akin had met him.

MINOR 12. A veterinarian used a gun to shoot antibiotics into Hugo.

24D   INFERENCES

Decide whether each statement below can be inferred (YES) or cannot be inferred (NO) from the reading selection.

NO   1. Bob Akin searched for housing near his work downtown because he did not own a car.

NO   2. In the early evenings, Bob Akin felt especially alone and longed to return to being a college student.

YES   3. Foley's, James' Coney Island, and Weingarten's were stores in Houston.

NO   4. Fleetwood Mac rented an apartment next door to Bob Akin.

YES   5. The window through which Bob Akin viewed Hugo had no glass.

YES   6. Although Hugo was powerful and strong, his movements and behavior at times appeared innocent and gentle to Bob Akin.

NO   7. If Bob Akin had gotten close enough for Hugo to touch him, Hugo would have bitten Akin's arm.

YES   8. Bob Akin believed Annie and Charlie should not have brought Hugo back from Africa and caged him in a private home.

NO   9. Torrential rains caused Hugo to develop pneumonia.

YES   10. Annie and Charlie treated Hugo as if he might have been their child.

24E   CRITICAL READING: FACT OR OPINION

Decide whether each statement, even if it quotes someone, contains a FACT or an OPINION.

OPINION   1. *From paragraph 1:* Houston in the late 1970s was an ideal location for a recent college graduate.

FACT   2. *From paragraph 4:* The magazine article identified the couple, the neighborhood, and the city where the 500-pound gorilla lived.

OPINION 3. *From paragraph 7:* "He's quite intelligent, really. About the same as a 4- to 5-year-old child."

FACT 4. *From paragraph 8:* Bob Akin could see reflected in Hugo's eyes some fixtures in the room, the old chair, and an outline image of himself.

OPINION 5. *From paragraph 9:* "I think he likes you, [. . .]."

FACT 6. *From paragraph 11:* Feeding Hugo was expensive for Annie.

OPINION 7. *From paragraph 11:* "Hugo couldn't survive in the wild. [. . .] He's happy here."

FACT 8. *From paragraph 15:* Bob Akin's dates, business matters, and Astros games with new friends took the place of long evening walks and time with Hugo.

24F CRITICAL READING: THE AUTHOR'S STRATEGIES

Choose the best answer.

 b 1. The main audience for "Out of Their Element" is
   a. anyone who has been alone in a strange city.
   b. anyone who has ever experienced isolation, aloneness, and confinement.
   c. anyone who feels sorry for animals kept in captivity.
   d. anyone who has experienced the loss of a pet.

 a 2. The author's purpose in writing this reading is to
   a. expose.
   b. narrate.
   c. entertain.
   d. persuade.

 a 3. The author's tone in this reading is
   a. thoughtful.
   b. unforgiving.
   c. critical.
   d. forgiving.

24G READER'S PROCESS: SUMMARIZING YOUR READING

 c 1. What is the best summary of "Out of Their Element"?
   a. A man tells how the "parents" of a gorilla try to make their captive "child" happy.

Name   Date

b. A man tells how he moves to Houston and meets a captive gorilla that is far lonelier than he is.

c. A man tells how a caged gorilla helped him appreciate the choices he was able to make during a lonely period of his life.

d. A man tells how a couple cared for their pet gorilla in their home until it died of pneumonia.

24H   READER'S RESPONSE: TO DISCUSS OR WRITE ABOUT

1. Do you think Annie and Charlie were cruel to keep Hugo imprisoned in their house? If so, how do you justify people's keeping pets in their homes— a cat, dog, or bird? Are domesticated animals better off set free or kept as pets? Defend your position with specific reasons.

2. A zoo is viewed by many people as a prison for animals, birds, and reptiles. Although the animals are placed in roomy pens, cages, or tanks, their freedom is still limited. Assume you are the voice for an animal in the zoo. Plead your argument for or against being set free.

HOW DID YOU DO?
24 Out of Their Element

SKILL (number of items)	Number Correct		Points for each		Score
Vocabulary (15)	_____	×	2	=	_____
Central Theme and Main Ideas (2)	_____	×	5	=	_____
Major Details (12)	_____	×	2	=	_____
Inferences (10)	_____	×	2	=	_____
Critical Reading: Fact or Opinion (8)	_____	×	1	=	_____
Critical Reading: The Author's Strategies (3)	_____	×	2	=	_____
Reader's Process: Summarizing Your Reading (1)	_____	×	2	=	_____

(Possible Total: 100) *Total*   _____

SPEED

Reading Time: _____ Reading Rate (page 414): _____ Words Per Minute

Name	Date	**339**

Part 6

THINKING: GETTING STARTED

In Part 6 you will encounter a wider variety of types of reading than before in this book. Try to use these selections to the fullest: They are challenging so that you can stretch your mind. You may find that your comprehension, your exercise scores, your reading rate, or other areas slip back somewhat at first. Do not be discouraged. Some kinds of reading are supposed to be slower than other kinds. Also, mistaken answers give you a chance to learn and to catch on to the more subtle aspects of reading. If you have worked through most of Parts 2–5 in this book, you are ready to dig into material that will help you grow stronger as a reader.

The final four reading selections in this section are especially distinct from those you've read thus far. Selections 27 and 28, taken from textbooks used in college courses, offer you opportunities to practice and reinforce your knowledge of the SQ3R technique, as discussed in the Chapter 3 of this book. Selection 29 is a short story that has many unspoken subtexts only hinted at by the story, so it allows you, the reader, one of the special joys of reading: the chance to compose a world in the privacy of your mind. The last selection presents you with the opportunity to read pictures, illustrations, charts, and graphs and assess your ability to understand and interpret the image or visual information. As preparation for this challenging set of readings, jump-start your thinking by looking over the images in the next three pages and answering the questions that accompany them.

What important and increasingly visible role do bomb-sniffing dogs play in an effort to keep the public safe at airports? (See "They Sniff Out Trouble.")

How important is a young person's determination in making a dream come true? (See "She Made Her Dream Come True.")

In what ways do you work to strengthen and improve your ability to remember what you learn in school and what you need to do in daily life? (See "Long-Term Memory.") What techniques do you know about for reducing stress in your life? Which of them do you use regularly? (See "A Personal Stress Survival Guide.")

Now that medicines are available today to treat physical and emotional problems, do you think we need medicines to make people fall permanently into love with one person? (See "The Chaser.")

Selection 25

They Sniff Out Trouble

Gail Buchalter

(1) Sgt. Mark McMurray slides his hands quickly across the cars in the parking lot, instructing his partner, Brandy, a Labrador mix, to sniff "high" or "low" for possible explosives. Inhaling voraciously, Brandy follows McMurray's orders. Suddenly, she stops and sits down—her signal that she has found a bomb. But no bomb squad was called in on this day. Mark McMurray and Brandy were one of the 94 regional championship teams from police departments, the Central Intelligence Agency, airports, and military facilities competing at the sixth annual National Detector Dog Trials, last April in Huntsville, Alabama. The "bomb" Brandy found was actually a nonworking explosive.

(2) Today, there are close to 15,000 patrol dogs in the US, 80% of which are crossed-trained in work that includes detecting narcotics, cadavers, and bombs. The annual Dog Trials—sponsored by the US Police Canine Association, one of several certifying organizations—helps establish a national standard for detector dogs. More important, it gives teams a chance to test skills that someday could save lives. "Protecting the public is what we are all about," says McMurray, 41, the K-9 Unit supervisor in Huntsville, which earned top honors in the bomb-detection category at the trials.

(3) As national security has tightened, bomb-sniffing dogs have become increasingly visible. "Since Sept. 11, our calls have at least doubled," says McMurray. "Whenever there's a breach of security at Huntsville International Airport, Brandy and I are called to rescreen the airplanes, luggage and people." McMurray has noticed a change in the public's attitude toward these dogs. "People used to feel that their rights were being violated when we searched them," he says. "Now they enjoy seeing our dogs and feel more secure."

(4) How are bomb dogs trained? To teach Brandy to recognize the six basic odors of explosives, McMurray says, he used a method called "odor imprintation." He placed 20 different odor combinations in Brandy's toys and played fetch. Eventually, he hid the bomb odors in small cans. As methods of concealing explosives evolve—including using shoes, as Richard Reid is accused of doing on a flight last December—so does the training. "We began putting small cans with odors in volunteers' socks," says McMurray. "Now I say 'shoe,' and Brandy searches low."

(5) Detector dogs—which typically include German shepherds, retrievers and Belgian Malinois—also rely on their highly developed prey drive, the instinctual need to hunt to survive. Brandy's drive was so strong that, as

a puppy, all she wanted to do was chase balls. She was so unaffectionate that her owners decided to donate her to the Huntsville Police. (Most police departments buy their dogs from breeders.) McMurray gave her a reason to hunt and, in return, got a partner and a pet. "Brandy's a member of our family," says McMurray, who takes her home at the end of their workday, as do most handlers. Then it's back to work for these top bomb-detectors. "We've never found a real bomb," says Murray. "I'll be happy if we never do."

(497 words)

Here are some of the more difficult words in "They Sniff Out Trouble."

Vocabulary List

cadavers
(paragraph 2)

ca·daver (kə dav′ər) *n.* [L, prob. < *cadere*, to fall: see CASE[1]] a dead body, esp. of a person; corpse, as for dissection —*SYN.* BODY —**ca·dav′·eric** *adj.*

canine
(paragraph 2)

ca·nine (kā′nīn′) *adj.* [L *caninus* < *canis*, dog: see HOUND[1]] **1** of or like a dog **2** of the family (Canidae) of carnivores that includes dogs, wolves, jackals, and foxes —*n.* **1** a dog or other canine animal **2** a sharp-pointed tooth on either side of the upper jaw and lower jaw, between the incisors and the bicuspids, having a long single root; a cuspid or (in the upper jaw) eyetooth: see TEETH, illus.: in full **canine tooth**

detector
(paragraph 1)

de·tec·tor (dē tek′tər, di-; *also, esp. for 2 & 3,* dē′tek′-) *n.* **1** a person or thing that detects **2** an apparatus or device for indicating the presence of something, as electric waves **3** DEMODULATOR

evolve
(paragraph 4)

evolve (ē välv′, -vôlv′; i-) *vt.* **evolved′, evolv′ing** [L *evolvere*, to roll out or forth < *e-*, out + *volvere*, to roll: see WALK] **1** to develop by gradual changes; unfold **2** to set free or give off (gas, heat, etc.) **3** to produce or change by evolution —*vi.* **1** to develop gradually by a process of growth and change ☆**2** to become disclosed; unfold —

inhaling
(paragraph 1)

in·hale (in hāl′, in′hāl′) *vt.* **··haled′, ··hal′ing** [L *inhalare* < *in-*, in + *halare*, to breathe: see EXHALE] **1** to draw (air, vapor, etc.) into the lungs; breathe in **2** [Informal] to consume rapidly or voraciously [to *inhale* one's dinner] —*vi.* **1** to draw air, vapor, etc. into the lungs **2** to draw tobacco smoke into the lungs when smoking

patrol
(paragraph 2)

pa·trol (pə trōl′) *vt., vi.* **··trolled′, ··trol′·ling** [Fr *patrouiller*, altered < OFr *patouiller*, to paddle, puddle, patrol < *pate*, paw: see PATOIS] to make a regular and repeated circuit of (an area, town, camp, etc.) in guarding or inspecting —*n.* [Fr *patrouille* < the *v.*] **1** the act of patrolling **2** a person or persons patrolling **3** *a*) a small group of soldiers sent on a mission, as for reconnaissance *b*) a group of ships, airplanes, etc. used in guarding **4** a subdivision of a troop of Boy Scouts or Girl Scouts —**pa·trol′·ler** *n.*

prey
(paragraph 5)

prey (prā) *n.* [ME *preye* < OFr *preie* < L *praeda* < base of *prehendere*, to seize: see PREHENSILE] **1** [Archaic] plunder; booty **2** an animal hunted or killed for food by another animal **3** a person or thing that falls victim to someone or something **4** the mode of living by preying on other animals [a bird of *prey*] —*vi.* **1** to plunder; rob **2** to hunt or kill other animals for food **3** to make profit from a victim as by swindling **4** to have a wearing or harmful influence; weigh heavily Generally used with *on* or *upon* —**prey′er** *n.*

voraciously
(paragraph 1)

vo·ra·cious (vô rā′shəs, və-) *adj.* [L *vorax* (gen. *voracis*), greedy to devour < *vorare*, to devour < IE base *gwer-*, to devour, GORGE > Gr *bora*, food (of carnivorous beasts), L *gurges*, gorge] **1** greedy in eating; devouring or eager to devour large quantities of food; ravenous; gluttonous **2** very greedy or eager in some desire or pursuit; insatiable [a *voracious* reader] —**vo·ra′·ciously** *adv.* —**vo·rac′·ity** (-ras′ə tē) *n.* or **vo·ra′·cious·ness**

25A   VOCABULARY

Using the dictionary entries on page 346, fill in the blanks.

1. _____Inhaling_____ the strong fumes, Erika began to cough.

2. Policemen use bicycles, not _____patrol_____ cars, at the pedestrian mall.

3. The hungry lion _____devoured_____ the food.

4. Buds _____evolve_____ into flowers.

5. Birds and mice are the _____prey_____ of cats.

6. The medical examiner is often asked to perform an autopsy on _____cadavers_____ .

7. A smoke _____detector_____ can prevent loss of life.

8. A _____canine_____ belongs to a group of meat-eating animals, including wolves and foxes.

25B   CENTRAL THEME AND MAIN IDEAS

Choose the best answer.

__c__ 1. What is the central theme of "They Sniff Out Trouble"?
 a. U.S. Police Canine Association sponsors annual Dog Trials.
 b. Alabama policeman trains bomb-sniffing dogs.
 c. Police use detector dogs to protect people from bombs.
 d. Trainer uses hand signals to instruct bomb-sniffing dog.

__b__ 2. What is the main idea of paragraph 4?
 a. Richard Reid is accused of hiding a bomb in his shoes.
 b. Trainers use "odor imprintation" to train dogs.
 c. Brandy can detect as many as twenty odors.
 d. Brandy searches "low" when she hears the word shoe.

25C   MAJOR DETAILS

Fill in the word or words that correctly complete each statement.

1. Sgt. Mark McMurray sometimes uses __hand__ signals for Brandy to sniff for possible explosives.

2. To signal she has found a bomb, Brandy _stops_ and _sits_ down.

3. Today there are nearly 15,000 _patrol_ dogs in the United States.

4. The annual Dog Trials help establish a _national_ _standard_ for detector dogs.

5. Since _September 11_, the request for bomb-sniffing dogs has at least _doubled_.

6. In hunting for explosives, detector dogs also rely on the highly developed _prey_ _drive_.

7. Brandy's drive was so strong as a _puppy_, all she wanted to do was chase _balls_.

8. Sgt. McMurray gave her a _reason_ to _hunt_ and, in return, got a _partner_ and a _pet_.

25D   INFERENCES

Decide whether each statement below can be inferred (YES) or cannot be inferred (NO) from the reading selection.

_NO_ 1. A Labrador is the best breed of dog to train for detecting explosives.

_NO_ 2. Before Brandy became a part of the K-9 Unit, she underwent militaristic obedience training.

YES 3. In case of a violation in security at an airport, most travelers would understand the need to delay a flight for rescreening.

_NO_ 4. Brandy's owners considered having her put down before they donated her to the Huntsville Police Department.

YES 5. Brandy is happy working as a bomb-detector dog.

25E   CRITICAL READING: THE AUTHOR'S STRATEGIES

Choose the best answer.

_a_ 1. Gail Buchalter's main audience for "They Sniff Out Trouble" is people who
   a. want to know how patrol dogs are trained.
   b. are afraid of all dogs, including patrol dogs.
   c. want to learn how to trick sniffing patrol dogs.
   d. want to raise and train patrol dogs.

Name   Date

___c___ 2. The author's primary purpose in this reading is to
   a. argue.
   b. describe.
   c. inform.
   d. persuade.

___d___ 3. The author's tone in this reading is
   a. sincere.
   b. sensational.
   c. sympathetic.
   d. straightforward.

25F   READER'S PROCESS: SUMMARIZING A READING

___a___ 1. What is the best summary of "They Sniff Out Trouble"?
   a. Patrol dogs, sometimes called bomb dogs or detector dogs, are trained to recognize the scent of six different kinds of explosives. Brandy, trained by Sgt. Mark McMurray, is a regional champion in official Dog Trials, and she excels on the job at airports.
   b. Brandy, a dog trained by Sgt. McMurray to recognize the scent of six different explosives, won a regional championship and is now entered in the U.S. Police Canine Association's annual National Detector Dog Trials.
   c. About fifteen thousand dogs have been trained in the United States to recognize the scent of explosives. Sgt. McMurray trained bomb-dog Brandy, who was donated to the police department and is now his pet.
   d. The sixth-annual National Detector Dog Trials has attracted competing teams of trainers and dogs from police departments, the Central Intelligence Agency (CIA), and the military. Brandy, a bomb dog trained by Sgt. McMurray, has won a championship.

25G   READER'S RESPONSE: TO DISCUSS OR WRITE ABOUT

1. Because of the increase in international terrorism, the security measures at airports have increased significantly. Do you think the changes, such as those involving baggage, personal identification and screening, have made flying safer than before? If you have flown recently, what was your experience with the new security measures?

2. Bomb-sniffing dogs are chosen because of their hunting skills as well as their sense of smell. A dog's smell is fifty times more sensitive than a human's. With this gift, dogs are employed to track missing persons, locate illegal drugs, detect firearms or explosives, and find the point of origin when arson has been committed. If you were involved in a situation where a dog was used to assist, would you trust the findings of the dog? Do you think animals should be given so much responsibility? Explain your response.

HOW DID YOU DO?

25 They Sniff Out Trouble

SKILL (number of items)	Number Correct		Points for Each		Score
Vocabulary (8)	_____	×	2	=	_____
Central Theme and Main Ideas (2)	_____	×	9	=	_____
Major Details* (14)	_____	×	2	=	_____
Inferences (5)	_____	×	4	=	_____
Critical Reading: The Author's Strategies (3)	_____	×	5	=	_____
Reader's Process: Summarizing Your Reading (1)	_____	×	5	=	_____

(Possible Total: 100) *Total* _____

SPEED

Reading Time: _____ Reading Rate (page 414): _____ Words Per Minute

*Questions 2 and 8 in this exercise call for separate answers. In computing your score, count each separate answer toward your number correct.

Name   Date

Selection 26

She Made Her Dream Come True

Michael Ryan

(1) To appreciate where Maria Vega is today, you have to understand where she was 22 years ago. "My family and I traveled up the East Coast throughout the growing season," this daughter of migrant workers recalled. "I went to five or six schools a year, from Florida to Pennsylvania."

(2) Maria Vega's view of life was formed in transient shacks with communal baths. In most schools she attended, Maria was placed in remedial classes, falling further behind in her studies. Homework, if any was assigned, was difficult to finish. "There was a lot of noise at night from the men who got drunk after work to forget about their troubles," she said. But every few months visitors from a different kind of world arrived. "Toward the end of the season in each state, the doctors and nurses would come," she said. These public health workers brought young Maria comfort—and relief from the frequent infections that have left a welter of scar tissue in her ear canals. They also brought her an idea: "I started to have this dream that I would become a doctor," she recalled. "But I never thought it was possible."

(3) Although Maria's two brothers, two sisters and parents formed a close-knit, supportive family, they had nothing in the way of financial resources. "During the holidays, my mom would sit us down and give us the same speech every year: 'There are no gifts under the tree—there is no tree,' " Maria said. What her family did give her was its support for her dream. "They told me to do what I wanted," she said, "and if it didn't work out, I could always come home to them."

(4) When Maria was in the 10th grade, her mother decided to stay in one place for a season, finding farm work around Homestead, Fla., so that Maria and her older sister could spend the year in one school. "Until that year, I had never taken a final exam," Maria told me. She worked so hard in high school that she earned a scholarship to Miami-Dade Community College. But even the basic, introductory chemistry course at Miami-Dade was difficult for her. "I had to take it twice," she said. "But I learned how to ask for help." As she recounted her story, Maria frequently talked about the people who helped her. "I know I didn't get here on my own," she said. Her junior college teachers provided extra assistance. They helped her get into the University of Miami, where she entered the pre-med program, supporting herself by working as a waitress and an aerobics instructor. School administrators, impressed by her

effort, helped arrange scholarships and loans. Some professors even lent Maria textbooks. She graduated from Miami on time, with a Bachelor of Science in psychology.

(5) But her bachelor's degree was not an automatic ticket to medical school. Her scores on the Medical College Admissions Test, the standard medical school admissions test, were mediocre. "I guess I panicked when I took it the first time," she said. "Or maybe I didn't know enough." Maria applied to 20 medical schools, but she was rejected everywhere. "I didn't give up," Maria said. "I thought I'd try again next year." She took a job as a receptionist, then applied to a program at Boston University that helps prepare bright but disadvantaged students for medical school. "Her enthusiasm, and her determination to achieve her goal, showed that she is a remarkable young woman," said Dr. Kenneth Edelin, the dean who administers the program.

(6) Finally, Maria was admitted to Boston University's medical school. She is now a second-year student. "It's hard," Maria said, "but I'll do what it takes to get through." Maria isn't sure yet about her eventual medical specialty, but she already knows what her approach to doctoring is going to be. "I think I can relate to patients who don't live in middle-class conditions," she said. "If somebody comes in and says they don't have the money to get medicine, I've been there. Victims of violence or alcohol or drug abuse—I grew up surrounded by that."

(7) Every September, Maria Vega's parents come to the end of their circuit—picking tomatoes in Pennsylvania before going back to Florida to begin the process again. Someday, Maria hopes to be able to help them to a better life. But for now, when her parents come north, she takes a bus to see them. "When I get there, my mom says, 'Here grab a bucket,' so I do," Maria said. For a few days, Maria Vega, medical student, is once again Maria Vega, migrant worker, holding on to her history and her values. As Maria's anatomy professor, Linda Wright, told me: "She's going to be a fantastic doctor."

(803 words)

Here are some of the more difficult words in "She Made Her Dream Come True."

anatomy
(paragraph 7)

anato·my (ə nat'ə mē) *n., pl.* --**mies** ⟦ME & OFr *anatomie* < LL *anatomia* < Gr *anatomia, anatomē,* a cutting up < *anatemnein* < *ana-,* up + *temnein,* to cut: see -TOMY⟧ **1** the dissecting of an animal or plant in order to determine the position, structure, etc. of its parts **2** the science of the morphology or structure of animals or plants **3** the structure of an organism or body **4** a detailed analysis **5** [Archaic] a skeleton

circuit
(paragraph 7)

cir·cuit (sur'kit) *n.* ⟦ME < OFr < L *circuitus,* a going around, circuit < *circumire* < *circum* (see CIRCUM-) + *ire,* to go: see YEAR⟧ **1** the line or the length of the line forming the boundaries of an area **2** the area bounded **3** the act of going around something; course or journey around /the moon's *circuit* of the earth/ **4** *a)* the regular journey of a person performing certain duties, as of an itinerant preacher or a judge holding court at designated places *b)* the district periodically traveled through in the performance of such duties *c)* the route traveled ☆**5** the judicial district of a U.S. Court of Appeals **6** *a)* a number of associated theaters at which plays, movies, etc. are shown in turn *b)* a group of nightclubs, resorts, etc. at which entertainers appear in turn ☆*c)* a sequence of contests or matches held at various places, in which a particular group of athletes compete; also, an association or league of athletic teams /the professional bowlers' *circuit*/ **7** *Elec. a)* a complete or partial path over which current may flow *b)* any hookup, wiring, etc. that is connected into this path, as for radio, television, or sound reproduction —*vi.* to go in a circuit —*vt.* to make a circuit about —*SYN.* CIRCUMFERENCE —**cir'·cuital** *adj.*

communal
(paragraph 2)

com·mu·nal (kə myōōn'əl, käm'yə nəl) *adj.* ⟦ME & OFr < LL *communalis*⟧ **1** of a commune or communes **2** of or belonging to the community; shared, or participated in, by all; public **3** designating or of social or economic organization in which there is common ownership of property —**com·mu·nal·i·ty** (käm'yōō nal'ə tē) *n.* —**com'·mu·nally** *adv.*

mediocre
(paragraph 5)

me·dio·cre (mē'dē ō'kər, mē'dē ō'kər) *adj.* ⟦Fr *médiocre* < L *mediocris* < *medius,* middle (see MID¹) + *ocris,* a peak < IE base *ak-,* sharp > L *acer*⟧ **1** neither very good nor very bad; ordinary; average **2** not good enough; inferior

migrant
(paragraph 1)

mi·grant (mī'grənt) *adj.* ⟦L *migrans,* prp. of *migrare*⟧ migrating; migratory —*n.* **1** a person, bird, or animal that migrates ☆**2** a farm laborer who moves from place to place to harvest seasonal crops

specialty
(paragraph 6)

spe·cialty (spesh'əl tē) *n., pl.* --**ties** ⟦ME *specialte* < OFr *especialté*⟧ **1** a special quality, feature, point, characteristic, etc. **2** a thing specialized in; special interest, field of study or professional work, etc. **3** the state of being special **4** an article or class of article characterized by special features, superior quality, novelty, etc. /a bakery whose *specialty* is pie/ **5** *Law* a special contract, obligation, agreement, etc. under seal, or a contract by deed —*adj.* **1** designating or of a store or stores that specialize in selling certain types of goods or to certain types of customers **2** of such goods or customers

transient
(paragraph 2)

tran·sient (tran'shənt, -sē ənt; -zhənt, -zē ənt) *adj.* ⟦L *transiens,* prp. of *transire:* see TRANSIT⟧ **1** *a)* passing away with time; not permanent; temporary; transitory *b)* passing quickly or soon; fleeting; ephemeral ☆**2** staying only for a short time /the *transient* population at resorts/ —*n.* ☆**1** a transient person or thing /transients at a hotel/ **2** *Elec.* a temporary component of a current, resulting from a voltage surge, a change from one steady-state condition to another, etc. —**tran'·sience** *n.* or **tran'·sien·cy** —**tran'·sient·ly** *adv.*

welter
(paragraph 2)

wel·ter (wel'tər) *vi.* ⟦ME *weltren* < MDu *welteren,* freq. formation akin to OE *wealtan,* to roll, boil up: for IE base see WELL¹⟧ **1** *a)* to roll about or wallow, as a pig does in mud *b)* to be deeply or completely involved /to *welter* in work/ **2** to be soaked, stained, or bathed /to *welter* in blood/ **3** to tumble and toss about: said as of the sea —*n.* **1** a tossing and tumbling, as of waves **2** a confusion; turmoil

Vocabulary List

26A VOCABULARY

From the context of "She Made Her Dream Come True," explain the meaning of each vocabulary word shown in boldface.

1. *From paragraph 1:* "My family and I traveled up the East Coast throughout the growing season," this daughter of **migrant** workers recalled.

   farm laborer who moves
   _____

2. *From paragraph 2:* Maria Vega's view of life was formed in **transient** shacks with **communal** baths.

   temporary . . . public
   _____
   _____
   _____

3. *From paragraph 2:* . . . frequent infections that left a **welter** of scar tissue in her ear canals.

   a roll
   _____

4. *From paragraph 5:* Her scores on the MCAT . . . were **mediocre.**

   average
   _____

5. *From paragraph 6:* Maria isn't sure yet about her eventual medical **specialty.** . . .

   field of study
   _____

6. *From paragraph 7:* Every September, Maria Vega's parents come to the end of their **circuit.** . . .

   regular journey
   _____

Name   Date

7. *From paragraph 7:* As Maria's **anatomy** professor, Linda Wright, told me: "She's going to be a fantastic doctor."

an animal's structure _____

_____

26B   CENTRAL THEME AND MAIN IDEAS

Choose the best answer.

__c__ 1. What is the central theme of "She Made Her Dream Come True"?
   a. Given financial support and encouragement, migrant workers can succeed in medical school.
   b. Maria Vega's overcoming problems related to finance, health, and education will help her be a sympathetic doctor.
   c. Through determination Maria Vega overcame poverty and educational disadvantages to qualify for medical school.
   d. Maria Vega plans to provide her family a better lifestyle when she becomes a doctor.

2. In your own words, give the main idea of paragraph 4.
   Teachers and college administrators were impressed with Maria Vega's hard work, so they provided her moral support and finances to realize her goal of graduating from college as a pre-medical major.

__d__ 3. What is the main idea of paragraph 5?
   a. Maria Vega's Bachelor of Science degree did not ensure her admission to a medical school.
   b. Twenty medical schools rejected Maria Vega's application to enroll.
   c. Maria Vega's enrolling in a Boston University program for disadvantaged students helped prepare her for medical school.
   d. Maria Vega's determination and enthusiasm helped her to achieve her goal to enroll in medical school.

26C   MAJOR DETAILS

Decide whether each detail is MAJOR or MINOR based on the context of the reading selection.

MAJOR 1. Public health workers influenced Maria Vega's dream to become a doctor.

MINOR 2. Maria Vega's family consisted of her parents, two brothers, and two sisters.

MAJOR 3. Maria Vega learned to ask for help when she had difficulties with her studies.

MINOR 4. Maria Vega's college major was psychology.

MINOR 5. After graduating from the University of Miami, Maria Vega worked as a receptionist.

MINOR 6. Maria Vega borrowed textbooks from college professors.

MAJOR 7. Maria Vega's parents are migrant workers.

MAJOR 8. Maria Vega took her college chemistry course twice before she passed it.

MINOR 9. Maria takes a bus when she goes to visit her parents.

MAJOR 10. Maria Vega was placed in remedial classes at most schools she attended.

26D INFERENCES

Decide whether each of the following statements can be inferred (YES) or cannot be inferred (NO) from the reading selection.

NO 1. Maria Vega was twenty-two years old when this was written.

NO 2. Maria Vega thought her ear infections would prevent her from becoming a doctor.

YES 3. Frequent moves to different states negatively affected Maria Vega's academic performance in school.

NO 4. Maria Vega resented her parents' not giving her presents at Christmas.

NO 5. Because of Maria Vega's health problems, her mother decided to stay in one location when Maria was a sophomore.

NO 6. Maria Vega's staying in one school for an entire year allowed her to make lifelong friends.

NO 7. Maria Vega's employment as a waitress and aerobics instructor was good preparation for her becoming a doctor.

Name   Date

YES 8. Maria Vega's willingness to help her family harvest crops when she visits them indicates she upholds her family's history and values.

YES 9. Maria Vega will most likely not become wealthy when she becomes a doctor.

26E CRITICAL READING: FACT OR OPINION

Decide whether each statement, even if it quotes someone, contains a FACT or an OPINION.

FACT 1. *From paragraph 2:* During their visits, the health workers brought relief and comfort to Maria Vega.

OPINION 2. *From paragraph 5:* "Her enthusiasm, and her determination to achieve her goal, showed that she is a remarkable woman [. . .]."

FACT 3. *From paragraph 7:* Maria Vega's family harvested crops from Florida to Pennsylvania.

OPINION 4. *From paragraph 7:* "She's going to be a fantastic doctor."

26F CRITICAL READING: THE AUTHOR'S STRATEGIES

Choose the best answer.

c 1. The main audience for "She Made Her Dream Come True" is
   a. readers who are migrant workers.
   b. readers who are trying to get into medical school.
   c. readers who are inspired by stories about people who overcome hardships.
   d. readers who don't understand the lives of migrant workers.

b 2. The author's purpose in writing this reading is to
   a. persuade.
   b. inform.
   c. describe.
   d. entertain.

d 3. The author's tone in this reading is
   a. negative.
   b. concerned.
   c. sad.
   d. inspired.

26G   READER'S PROCESS: SUMMARIZING YOUR READING

__a__ 1. What is the best summary of "She Made Her Dream Come True"?
   a. The writer tells how the daughter of migrant workers achieved her goal to study medicine.
   b. The writer tells how a young woman studied hard but still had trouble getting into medical school.
   c. The writer tells how a young medical student joins her family of migrant workers in the fields each year.
   d. The writer tells how a young woman learned to ask for the help she needed to go to college and apply for medical school.

26H   READER'S RESPONSE: TO DISCUSS OR WRITE ABOUT

1. Some children have to change schools one or more times between kindergarten and the twelfth grade. If this happened to you, what effect did such moving have on you? If this did not happen to you, what do you imagine the effect on you would have been?

2. Many college students are required or strongly urged to take one or more "remedial" courses (such as Developmental Reading, Basic Writing, Basic Math). If this has happened to you, what do you think are the advantages and disadvantages, both academic and social, of taking such courses? If this did not happen to you, what do you imagine would have been the academic and social advantages and disadvantages for you?

Name   Date

HOW DID YOU DO?

26 She Made Her Dream Come True

SKILL (number of items)	Number Correct		Points for each		Score
Vocabulary (8)	_____	×	2	=	_____
Central Theme and Main Ideas (3)	_____	×	5	=	_____
Major Details (10)	_____	×	3	=	_____
Inferences (9)	_____	×	3	=	_____
Critical Reading: Fact or Opinion (4)	_____	×	1	=	_____
Critical Reading: The Author's Strategies (3)	_____	×	2	=	_____
Reader's Process: Summarizing Your Reading (1)	_____	×	2	=	_____

(Possible Total: 100) *Total*   _____

SPEED

Reading Time: _____ Reading Rate (page 414): _____ Words Per Minute

Selection 27

Long-Term Memory *in* *Fundamentals of Psychology*

Joseph Calkin and Richard S. Perrotto

(1) Everything you know—every word, name, fact, date, experience, definition, and skill—is contained in your long-term memory (LTM), where information is stored unconsciously for an extended period of time. How long do your memories last in LTM? No precise answer can be given. LTM duration can be as brief as a few minutes and as long as a lifetime. Many people believe that LTM is permanent, but the evidence is not conclusive. The duration of LTM depends on several factors, including the strength of the memory, its meanings, and how much it is used.

(2) How much do you know? If you started to remember everything in your LTM right now, you would probably spend the rest of your life and not finish. If short-term memory (STM) is a memory workbench where information is stored for a short period of time and in limited space, your LTM is a vast warehouse of information with no apparent limit. Surely there are millions of items stored in your LTM, but researchers have no way of estimating the maximum capacity of LTM. Although its upper limit is unknown, your everyday experience tells you that LTM holds an astounding amount of information.

THE ORGANIZATION OF LONG-TERM MEMORY

(3) The enormous LTM warehouse contains many types of knowledge, and its contents are highly organized in terms of several qualities of those memories. Four aspects of LTM have been identified and named: **semantic, episodic, procedural,** and **implicit** memory. These aspects of LTM organization are summarized in Table 1.

(4) Language is an essential part of your memory. Factual knowledge based on words, phrases, sentences, and other verbal information is contained in your **semantic memory.** Like a dictionary, semantic memory is based on **semantic codes,** representations of information in terms of the meaning of words. To appreciate the scope of semantic memory, just consider the many definitions, names, formulas, and other facts that you have learned since elementary school. Your semantic memory does not exist as thousands of independent bits of knowledge, but is organized by complex **association networks,** or groups of memories linked together on the basis of meaning.

Semantic Memory
Memory for factual knowledge based on verbal information

361

Table 1 Organization of Long-Term Memory

Semantic memory	Impersonal facts based on semantic, or verbal, codes
Episodic memory	Personal, autobiographical facts; flashbulb memories
Procedural memory	Skills, habits, stimulus-response associations
Implicit memory	Memories learned and retrieved without conscious effort

(5) As a demonstration, start with a familiar word, *dog* and call to mind every word association you can, for example, *pet, companion, mammal,* and so on. Then, do the same for each of those associations, and for all the associations linked to them, and so on. Before long, you will realize that the web of your word associations is almost endless. These complex semantic associations control your ability to understand and remember language-based facts. Your semantic memory is impersonal, lacking any obvious connection with specific life experiences. For instance, when you remember 2 + 2 = 4 you probably do not connect it with the situation in which you first learned it.

(6) By contrast, your **episodic memory** contains very personal, autobiographical facts—facts that are tied to episodes in your life and often ones that contain significant emotional meaning. Think of the birth of your young siblings, a great party you attended, a family tragedy, and other events from your personal past—these recollections reveal your episodic memory.

Episodic (epp-ee-sod-ik) Memory
Memory for personal, autobiographical facts

(7) A special type of episodic memory is a **flashbulb memory,** a vivid recollection of an emotionally powerful event. Your flashbulb memories seem like moments frozen in time, and their emotional associations are thought to be responsible for their vividness. For example, some people report flashbulb memories for January 28, 1986, the day the space shuttle *Challenger* exploded, killing the crew, while broadcast nationwide on television. Many flashbulb memories are more personal, such as the death of a close friend or the day you won the lottery. Although they seem very clear, flashbulb memories are not necessarily accurate, and people often recall with confidence false details of those events.

(8) Your memory for learned responses and action patterns is **procedural memory.** Learned skills and behaviors, as well as stimulus-response associations, are contained in your procedural memory. Countless everyday activities depend on procedural memory, as when you drive a car, play the piano, use a tool, or carry on a

Procedural Memory
Memory for learned responses and action patterns

conversation. Such behavior may be acquired through conditioning and cognitive learning. In addition, procedural memory controls your automatic conditioned responses to stimuli. The next time you experience fear upon entering your dentist's office, you can thank your procedural memory for the reminder.

(9) Semantic and episodic memories taken together are sometimes called **declarative memory,** which requires conscious effort to learn and retrieve. For example, you must exert conscious effort to memorize a new formula in math (semantic memory).

(10) Many memories, however, are acquired and remembered automatically with little or no conscious involvement. These make up your **implicit memory.** In fact, a lot of procedural memory is implicit, such as conditioned fears and other emotional responses. You do not consciously control their acquisition or activation by stimuli.

> **Implicit (im-pliss-it) Memory**
> Memories learned and retrieved without conscious effort

(11) Research on the **priming effect** illustrates that implicit memory controls your unconscious retrieval of stored information. In a typical study, subjects are "primed" by exposure to some stimuli, and later their memory is tested without asking them to consciously remember the stimuli. Priming improves their memory despite the subjects' lack of awareness of learning or remembering the stimuli. Imagine that you are in such a study: You are shown some words (the priming list), which you must identify as nouns or verbs (Refer to Table 2). Later, another series of words (the test list) is presented very rapidly, and you are asked simply to indicate which words you perceive. You are most likely to perceive the test list words that were on the priming list even though you did not try to memorize or retrieve them.

(12) Although implicit and declarative (semantic and episodic) memory have distinctive features, they are not completely independent. Rather, these aspects of LTM interact to provide you with richly integrated memories. Do you remember how to ride a bicycle? If you can describe this skill in words (semantic memory), recall yourself doing it in a specific situation (episodic memory), and show it in action (procedural memory), you are illustrating the integrated facets of your LTM. Recent studies suggest that declarative and implicit memory work together to create complex abilities and knowledge, such as learning the rules of language usage and classifying your experiences into organized concepts.

Table 2   Priming Effect Study of Implicit Memory

Priming List	Test List	Primed Implicit Memory
rabbit	bird	rabbit
swim	rabbit	write
car	write	
write	house	

LONG-TERM MEMORY PROCESSES

(13) As you have learned, LTM contains many types of stored information. The complex organization of knowledge in LTM depends on a number of factors. The **depth-of-processing** model explains the strength and durability of LTM as the result of encoding processes. In this view, a "deep" memory is acquired by semantic codes that represent facts through language. Without semantic codes, memory is "shallow" and quite easily forgotten. A deep memory is more lasting and meaningful than a shallow one, and it is easier to recollect. This model suggests that memories based on several codes are deeper than those based on a single code.

Depth-of-Processing Model
View that memory strength depends on encoding processes

(14) Research on combined semantic codes and imagery supports this notion. This effect may be illustrated by a **paired-associates recall task,** in which you are given word pairs to remember (for example, house-pencil, fish-tree), and later you must recall one of the words when the other is presented. For instance, when shown *tree* you must say *fish.* If you use visual images along with the words to encode the paired associates, your recall is improved, especially for concrete words like those in Figure 27.1.

Figure 27.1   Imagery in a Paired-Associates Recall Task

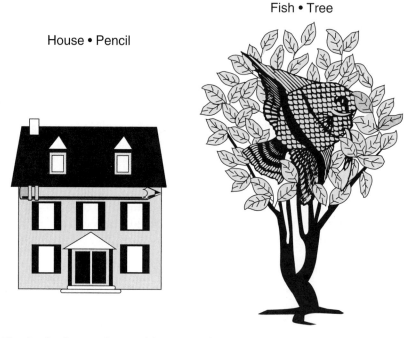

Fish • Tree

House • Pencil

The depth-of-processing model suggests that a combination of semantic and image codes will produce a deeper memory than will a single code. When subjects use visual images and word pairs to encode the information, their memory for the word association improves.

(15) In 1932, British psychologist Frederick Bartlett proposed that memories are reconstructions of events based partly on fact and partly on schemas, or personal beliefs about reality. In his classic study, he read a Native American folktale to his English subjects and later asked them to remember it. Their memories of the story showed changes that reflected their culture-based schemas. For instance, instead of recalling that the Indians hunted for seals in canoes, some subjects remember that they were fishing in boats.

(16) In the tradition of Bartlett, many psychologists today consider **reconstructive memory** to be an act of remembering in which facts, personal beliefs, and inferences are all woven together. In reconstructing a past event, you often fill in the gaps with "facts" that you believe, on the basis of your personal schemas, might have occurred. In addition, you rely on familiar patterns

Reconstructive Memory
Remembering affected by schemas, personal beliefs, and inferences

of events stored as **memory scripts** that give you a framework for remembering. Try to remember what you did at 4:00 P.M. exactly six months ago. If it was a Wednesday during the school year, you might find yourself using your "typical-Wednesday-afternoon-at-school" script to reconstruct what you probably did. Have you ever noticed that each time you tell a story it is a little different than the last time because you add new elements or drop old details with each telling? Facts learned after a memory is formed can change it, and even the act of remembering sometimes alters the memory being recalled. Reconstructive memory is also open to the power of suggestion, as shown in a study by psychologists Elizabeth Loftus and John Palmer in which subjects saw a filmed car accident and were later asked how fast the cars were going. The questions were phrased either in terms of when the cars "hit" or when they "crashed." Subjects who were asked the "crashed" version recalled much higher speeds because the wording suggests that the cars were moving faster.

(17) Your ability to retrieve a memory often depends on having the proper cues at the time you try to remember. When your retrieval is influenced by stimulus cues, you show evidence of **cue-dependent memory.** Two forms of cue-dependent memory are **context-dependent memory** and **state-dependent memory.** If you try to recall some

Cue-Dependent Memory
Memory influenced by cues in the situation or emotional state

information in a situation that is similar to the one in which you learned that information, you tend to perform better than when you try in a situation that differs from the learning one. This phenomenon, called **context-dependent memory,** is the result of associations formed between situation cues and the information at the time it is learned. An example of context-dependent memory is a study of scuba divers who learned some words under water and later recalled them better when under water than on land. You can examine **context-dependent memory** in yourself by studying some material while listening to music and later testing yourself on half of the material with the same music playing and on the other half without any music. You should find that your memory is better when the music is playing.

(18) The power of situational cues may explain a curious phenomenon called déjà vu (French for "already seen") in which you feel that you recognize someone or some place with no basis for the memory in your experience. For example, on entering a house for the first time, it may seem familiar, as if you had been there before. Déjà vu is a false recognition due to subtle cues in the situation. Perhaps something about the house, such as an odor or room design, triggers partial memory of another place in which similar cues were present, thus giving you the feeling of familiarity.

(19) Have you ever noticed that when you are happy you remember many experiences with a similar happy feeling, or that when depressed you recall other depressing events? Such observations point to **state-dependent memory;** your state of mind influences you to retrieve memories that were formed in a similar state. Studies of state-dependent memory show that emotional states prime your retrieval of experiences with similar emotional features.

(1,949 words)

Vocabulary List

Here are some of the more difficult words in "Long-Term Memory."

cognitive
(paragraph 8)

cog·ni·tion (käg nish′ən) *n.* ⟦ME *cognicioun* < L *cognitio*, knowledge < *cognitus*, pp. of *cognoscere*, to know < *co-*, together + *gnoscere*, KNOW⟧ **1** the process of knowing in the broadest sense, including perception, memory, and judgment **2** the result of such a process; perception, conception, etc. —**cog·ni′·tional** *adj.* —**cog′·ni·tive** (-nə tiv) *adj.*

conclusive
(paragraph 1)

con·clu·sive (-siv) *adj.* ⟦LL *conclusivus* < pp. of L *concludere*, CONCLUDE⟧ that settles a question; final; decisive —**con·clu′·sively** *adv.* —**con·clu′·sive·ness** *n.*

duration
(paragraph 1)

du·ra·tion (doo rā′shən, dyoo-) *n.* ⟦ME *duracioun* < ML *duratio* < pp. of L *durare*: see DURABLE⟧ **1** continuance in time **2** the time that a thing continues or lasts

encoding
(paragraph 13)

en·code (en kōd′, in-) *vt.* **··cod′ed, ··cod′·ing** **1** to convert (a message, information, etc.) into code **2** to convert (data) by applying an electronic code —**en·cod′er** *n.*

imagery
(paragraph 14)

im·agery (im′ij rē, -ər ē) *n., pl.* **··ries** ⟦ME *imagerie* < OFr⟧ **1** [Now Rare] images generally; esp., statues **2** mental images, as produced by memory or imagination **3** descriptions and figures of speech

perceive
(paragraph 11)

per·ceive (pər sēv′) *vt., vi.* **··ceived′, ··ceiv′·ing** ⟦ME *perceyven* < OFr *perceivre* < L *percipere*, to take hold of, feel, comprehend < *per*, through + *capere*, to take: see HAVE⟧ **1** to grasp mentally; take note (of); observe **2** to become aware (of) through one of the senses, esp. through sight —*SYN.* DISCERN —**per·ceiv′·able** *adj.* —**per·ceiv′·ably** *adv.* —**per·ceiv′er** *n.*

retrieve
(paragraph 9)

re·trieve (ri trēv′) *vt.* **··trieved′, ··triev′·ing** ⟦ME *retreven* < inflected stem of OFr *retrouver* < *re-*, again + *trouver*, to find: see TROVER⟧ **1** to get back; recover **2** to restore; revive *[to retrieve one's spirits]* **3** to rescue or save **4** to set right or repair (a loss, error, etc.); make good **5** to recall to mind ☆**6** *Comput.* to gain access to (data) that is on a floppy disk, hard drive, etc. **7** *Hunting* to find and bring back (killed or wounded small game): said of dogs **8** *Racket Sports* to return (a ball that is hard to reach) —*vi.* *Hunting* to retrieve game —*n.* **1** any retrieval ☆**2** a retrieving of the ball in tennis, etc. —*SYN.* RECOVER —**re·triev′·able** *adj.*

schemas
(paragraph 15)

schema (skē′mə) *n., pl.* **-mata** (-mə tə) 〚Gr *schēma*: see SCHEME〛 **1** an outline, diagram, plan, or preliminary draft **2** *Psychol.* a mental image produced in response to a stimulus, that becomes a framework or basis for analyzing or responding to other related stimuli

siblings
(paragraph 6)

sib·ling (sib′liŋ) *n.* 〚20th-c. revival of OE, a relative: see SIB & -LING¹〛 one of two or more persons born of the same parents or, sometimes, having one parent in common; brother or sister

stimulus-response
(paragraph 8)

stimu·lus (-ləs) *n., pl.* **-u·li′** (-lī′) 〚L, a goad, sting, torment, pang, spur, incentive: see STYLE〛 **1·**something that rouses or incites to action or increased action; incentive **2** *Physiol., Psychol.* any action or agent that causes or changes an activity in an organism, organ, or part, as something that excites an end organ, starts a nerve impulse, activates a muscle, etc.

subtle
(paragraph 18)

sub·tle (sut′'l) *adj.* **sub′·tler** (-lər, -′l ər), **sub′·tlest** 〚ME *sotil* < OFr *soutil* < L *subtilis*, fine, thin, precise, orig., closely woven < *sub-* (see SUB-) + *tela*, web < *texla* < *texere*, to weave: see TECHNIC〛 **1** thin; rare; tenuous; not dense or heavy *[a subtle gas]* **2** *a)* capable of making or noticing fine distinctions in meaning, etc. *[a subtle thinker]* *b)* marked by or requiring mental keenness *[subtle reasoning]* **3** delicately skillful or clever; deft or ingenious *[a subtle filigree]* **4** not open or direct; crafty; sly **5** delicately suggestive; not grossly obvious *[a subtle hint]* **6** working insidiously; not easily detected *[a subtle poison]* —**sub′·tle·ness** *n.* —**sub′·tly** *adv.*

27A   VOCABULARY

From the context of "Long-Term Memory," explain the meaning of each of the vocabulary words shown in boldface.

1. *From paragraph 1:* **LTM duration** can be as brief as a few minutes and as long as a lifetime.
   continuance in time

2. *From paragraph 1:* Many people believe that LTM is permanent, but the evidence is not **conclusive.**
   final

3. *From paragraph 6:* Think of the birth of your young **siblings,** a great party you attended, a family tragedy . . .
   brothers or sisters

Name   Date   **367**

4. *From paragraph 8:* Learned skills and behaviors, as well as **stimulus-response** associations, are contained in your procedural memory.

something that causes an action

5. *From paragraph 8:* Such behavior may be acquired through conditioning and **cognitive** learning.

knowing process

6. *From paragraph 9:* Semantic and episodic memories taken together are called declarative memory, which requires conscious effort to learn and **retrieve.**

recover

7. *From paragraph 11:* You are most likely to **perceive** the test list words that were on the priming list even though you did not try to memorize or retrieve them.

grasp mentally

8. *From paragraph 13:* The depth-of-processing model explains the strength and durability of LTM as the result of **encoding** processes.

converting information

9. *From paragraph 14:* Research on combined semantic codes and **imagery** supports this notion.

mental images

Name   Date

10. *From paragraph 15:* Their memories of the story showed changes that reflected their culture-based **schemas.**

    plans _____

    _____

11. *From paragraph 18:* Catherine devised a **subtle** scheme to get some money.

    not easily detected _____

    _____

27A2   SPECIAL TEXTBOOK VOCABULARY

Key terms in this textbook selection are explained as they are discussed. Referring to "Long-Term Memory," fill in the blanks.

1. ____Semantic____ memory contains factual knowledge based on words, phrases, sentences, and other verbal information.

2. The memory for very personal, autobiographical facts is ____episodic____.

3. A ____flashbulb____ memory is a vivid recollection of a more personal, emotionally powerful event.

4. Your memory for learned responses and action patterns is ____procedural____ memory.

5. ____Declarative____ memory requires a conscious effort to learn and retrieve.

6. ____Implicit____ memory is learned and retrieved without conscious effort.

7. The view that memory strength depends on encoding processes is the ____depth-in-processing____ model.

8. Remembering affected by schemas, personal beliefs, and inferences is ____reconstructive____ memory.

9. __Cue-dependent__ memory is influenced by cues in the situation or emotional state.

10. __Context-dependent__ memory results from associations formed between cues and the information learned at the time.

11. Your mind's ability to retrieve memories that were formed in a similar state is __state-dependent__ memory.

27B   CENTRAL THEME AND MAIN IDEAS

Choose the best answer.

__c__ 1. The textbook selection "Long-Term Memory" covers a topic that could be part of a course in
   a. physics.
   b. mathematics.
   c. study skills.
   d. writing.

__b__ 2. The main purpose of paragraphs 3 through 11 is to
   a. show the differences between long-term memory and short-term memory.
   b. name and explain how the four types of long-term memory are organized in humans.
   c. discuss the importance of language in stimulating the memory process in humans.
   d. list methods to help people retain information in long-term memory.

__a__ 3. The main idea of paragraph 13 is the view that
   a. memories based on several semantic codes are deeper than those based on a single code.
   b. long-term memory contains many types of information stored in the human brain.
   c. short-term memory is "shallow" and is easy to remember.
   d. the organization of knowledge in long-term memory is complex so it is usually forgotten.

Name   Date

27C   MAJOR DETAILS

Decide whether each detail is true (T), false (F), or not discussed (ND).

 ND 1. Information stored in short-term memory is stored for twenty-four hours and then forgotten.

  F   2. Semantic memory exists as thousands of independent bits of knowledge.

  T   3. Flashbulb memories are not necessarily accurate.

 ND 4. Eyewitness memories are just as prone to error as other memories are.

  T   5. According to Figure 1, a deeper memory is possible through combining semantic and visual codes.

 ND 6. Memories grow weaker over time.

  F   7. Flashbulb memories do not involve emotions.

 ND 8. Memories are stored in both the left side and the right side of the brain.

27D   CRITICAL READING: FACT OR OPINION

Decide whether each statement contains a FACT or an OPINION.

OPINION 1. *From paragraph 1:* "Many people believe that long-term memory is permanent [. . .]."

FACT 2. *From paragraph 5:* "Your semantic memory is impersonal [. . .]."

FACT 3. *From paragraph 8:* Everyday activities, such as driving a car or playing the piano, depend on your procedural memory.

FACT 4. *From paragraph 11:* "Research on the priming effect illustrates that implicit memory controls your unconscious retrieval of stored information."

OPINION 5. *From paragraph 17:* "You should find that your memory is better when the music is playing."

27E   CRITICAL READING: THE AUTHOR'S STRATEGIES

Choose the best answer.

__a__ 1. The main audience for "Long-Term Memory" in *Fundamentals of Psychology* is
   a. students studying psychology.
   b. students trying to improve their memory.
   c. students studying different types of memory.
   e. students studying long-term memory.

__d__ 2. The author's purpose in writing this reading is to
   a. describe.
   b. convince.
   c. illustrate.
   d. inform.

__b__ 3. The author's tone in this reading is
   a. critical.
   b. straightforward.
   c. gentle.
   d. positive.

27F   READER'S PROCESS: SUMMARIZING YOUR READING

__d__ 1. What is the best summary of "Long-Term Memory in Fundamentals of Psychology"?
   a. The author explains the difference between long-term and short-term memory.
   b. The author explains how the mind organizes long-term memories.
   c. The author explains how the mind processes long-term memory.
   d. The author defines long-term memory and explains how it works.

27G   READER'S RESPONSE: TO DISCUSS OR WRITE ABOUT

1. Memory experts believe people can increase their ability to remember with memory aids, such as a mnemonic device. Mnemonic devices include rhymes, clues, mental pictures, and other methods. For example, many people remember the number of days in a month by using a verse that begins, "Thirty days hath September . . ." What are some mnemonic devices you use or know of to recall information?

2. If there were a drug available that claimed to improve memory, would you take it? If not, why? Should it be available to everyone? Would you support its use for victims of assault, sexual abuse, natural disaster, or terrible accidents? Why or why not?

HOW DID YOU DO?
27 Long-Term Memory

SKILL (number of items)	Number Correct		Points for each		Score
Vocabulary (11)	_____	×	2	=	_____
Special Textbook Vocabulary (11)	_____	×	2	=	_____
Central Theme and Main Ideas (3)	_____	×	6	=	_____
Major Details (8)	_____	×	2	=	_____
Critical Reading: Fact or Opinion (5)	_____	×	2	=	_____
Critical Reading: The Author's Strategies (3)	_____	×	3	=	_____
Reader's Process: Summarizing Your Reading (1)	_____	×	3	=	_____

(Possible Total: 100) *Total*   _____

SPEED

Reading Time: _____ Reading Rate (page 414): _____ Words Per Minute

Name   Date   **373**

A Personal Stress Survival Guide
in An Invitation to Health

Dianne Hales

(1) Although stress is a very real threat to emotional and physical well-being, its impact depends not just on what happens to you, but on how you handle it. If you tried to predict who would become ill based simply on life-change units or other stressors, you'd be correct only about 15% of the time. The inability to feel in control of stress, rather than stress itself, is often the most harmful.

(2) In studying individuals who manage stress so well that they seem "stress-resistant," researchers have observed that these individuals share many of the following traits:

- They respond actively to challenges. If a problem comes up, they look for resources, do some reading or research, and try to find a solution rather than giving up and feeling helpless. Because they've faced numerous challenges, they have confidence in their abilities to cope.

- They have personal goals, such as getting a college degree or becoming a better parent.

- They rely on a combination of planning, goal setting, problem solving, and risk taking to control stress.

- They use a minimum of substances such as nicotine, caffeine, alcohol, or drugs.

- They regularly engage in some form of relaxation, from meditation to exercise to knitting, at least fifteen minutes a day.

- They tend to seek out other people and become involved with them.

(3) In order to achieve greater control over the stress in your life, start with some self-analysis: If you're feeling overwhelmed, ask yourself: Are you taking an extra course that's draining your last ounce of energy? Are you staying up late studying every night and missing morning classes? Are you living on black coffee and jelly doughnuts? While you may think that you don't have time to reduce the stress in your life, some simple changes can often ease the pressure you're under and help you achieve your long-term goals. One of the simplest, yet most effective, ways to

work through stress is by putting your feelings into words that only you will read. The more honest and open you are as you write, the better. In studies at Southern Methodist University, psychologist James Pennebaker, Ph.D., found that college students who wrote in their journals about traumatic events felt much better afterward than those who wrote about superficial topics. Recording your experiences and feelings on paper or audiotape may help decrease stress and enhance well-being. Since the small ups and downs of daily life have an enormous impact on psychological and physical well-being, getting a handle on daily hassles will reduce your stress load.

Chart 1: How to Cope with Stress

A. Recognize your stress signals. Is your back bothering you more? Do you find yourself speeding or misplacing things? Force yourself to stop whenever you see these early warnings and say, "I'm under stress; I need to do something about it."

B. Keep a stress journal. Focus on intense emotional experiences and "autopsy" them away to try to understand why they affected you the way they did. Rereading and thinking about your notes may help you discern the underlying reasons for your response and garner insights that can help you cope better in the future.

C. Try "stress-inoculation." Rehearse everyday situations that you find stressful, such as speaking in class. Think of how you might handle the situation, perhaps by breathing deeply before you talk, or visualizing yourself speaking with confidence.

D. Put things in proper perspective. When you're feeling hassled, stop and breathe deeply and slowly five times. Ask yourself: Will I remember what's made me so upset a month from now? If you had to rank this problem on a scale of 1 to 10, with worldwide catastrophe as 10, where would it rate? If this were the worst thing to happen to you this year, would you feel lucky?

E. Think of one simple thing that could make your life easier. What if you put up a hook to hold your keys so that you didn't spend five minutes searching for them every morning? Doing something, however small, will boost your sense of control.

POSITIVE COPING MECHANISMS

(4) After a perfectly miserable, aggravating day, a teacher comes home and yells at her children for making too much noise. Another individual, after an equally stressful day, jokes about what went wrong during the all-time most miserable moment of the month. Both of these people are using **defense mechanisms**—actions or behaviors that help protect their sense of self-worth. The first is displacing anger onto someone else; the second uses humor to vent frustration.

(5) Under great stress, we all may turn to negative defense mechanisms to alleviate anxiety and eliminate conflict. These can lead to maladaptive behavior, such as rationalizing overeating by explaining to yourself that you need the extra calories to cope with the extra stress in your life. **Coping mechanisms** are healthier, more mature and adaptive ways of dealing with stressful situations. While they also ward off unpleasant emotions, they usually are helpful rather than harmful. The most common are:

(6) ■ **Sublimation,** the redirection of any drives considered unacceptable into socially acceptable channels. For example, someone who is furious with a friend or relative may go for a long run to sublimate anger.

(7) ■ **Religiosity,** in which one comes to terms with a painful experience, such as a child's death, by experiencing it as being in accord with God's will.

(8) ■ **Humor,** which counters stress by focusing on comic aspects. Medical students, for instance, often make jokes in anatomy lab as a way of dealing with their anxieties about working with cadavers.

(9) ■ **Altruism,** which takes a negative experience and turns it into a positive one. For example, an HIV-positive individual may talk to teenagers about AIDS (Acquired Immune Deficiency Syndrome) prevention.

MANAGING TIME

(10) Every day you make dozens of decisions, and the choices you make about how to use your time directly affect your stress level. If you have a big test on Monday and a term paper due Tuesday, you may plan to study all weekend. Then, when you're invited to a party Saturday night, you go. Although you set the alarm for 7:00 A.M. on Sunday, you don't pull yourself out of bed until noon. By the time you start studying, it's 4:00 P.M., and anxiety is building inside you. How can you tell if you've lost control of your time? The following are telltale symptoms of poor time management:

■ Rushing.

■ Chronic inability to make choices or decisions.

- Fatigue or listlessness.

- Constantly missed deadlines.

- Not enough time for rest or personal relationships.

- A sense of being overwhelmed by demands and details and having to do what you don't want to do most of the time.

One of the hard lessons of being on your own is that your choices and your actions have consequences. Stress is just one of them. But by thinking ahead, being realistic about your workload, and sticking to your plans, you can gain better control over your time and your stress levels.

OVERCOMING PROCRASTINATION

(11) Putting off until tomorrow what should be done today is a habit that creates a great deal of stress for many students. The three most common types of procrastination are: putting off unpleasant things, putting off difficult tasks, and putting off tough decisions. Procrastinators are most likely to delay by wishing they didn't have to do what they must or by telling themselves they "just can't get started," which means they never do.

(12) People procrastinate, not because they're lazy, but to protect their self-esteem and make a favorable impression. "Procrastinators often perceive their worth as based solely on task ability, and their ability is determined only by how well they perform on completed tasks," notes psychologist Joseph Ferrari, Ph.D. "By never completing the tasks, they are never judged on their ability, thus allowing them to maintain an illusion of competence."

Chart 2 Breaking Out of the Procastination Trap

A. Keep track of the tasks you're most likely to put off, and try to figure why you don't want to tackle them. Think of alternative ways to get tasks done. If you put off library readings, figure out if the problem is getting to the library or the reading itself. If it's the trip to the library, arrange to walk over with a friend whose company you enjoy.

B. Keep a daily "To Do" list. Rank items according to priorities: A, B, C. Evaluate the items. Should any B's be A's? Schedule your days so the A's get accomplished.

→

Chart 2 Breaking Out of the Procastination Trap, continued

C. Try not to fixate on half-completed projects. Divide large tasks, such as a term paper, into smaller ones, and reward yourself when you complete a part.

D. Do what you like least first. Once you have it out of the way, you can concentrate on the tasks you do enjoy.

E. Build time into your schedule for interruptions, unforeseen problems, unexpected events, and so on, so you aren't constantly racing around.

F. Beware of overcommitment. Establish ground rules for meeting your own needs (including getting enough sleep and making time for friends) before saying yes to any activity.

G. Learn to live according to a three-word motto: Just do it!

GOING WITH THE FLOW

(13) Americans enjoy less free time than people in many other societies—and we often don't know how to make the most of the free time we do have. According to the Americans' Use of Time Project, when we don't have to do anything else, most Americans mainly watch television: an average of 15.1 hours every week—compared with 4.9 hours visiting friends, 4.3 talking, 3.1 traveling, 2.8 reading, and 2.2 for either sports or hobbies. Yet when asked what they like to do, men and women rank playing with children, active sports, socializing and talking with family members much higher than watching TV. Three quarters of Americans believe the amount of stress in their lives is within their control. How do they prefer to handle stress? Exercise, 42%; Slowing down, 17%; Taking time off, 11%; Watching television, 7%; and Meditating, 3%.

(14) So why do we end up in front of the tube? Often it's simply because, while we carefully schedule our weekdays, we let our weekends and other free time drift. "Everybody who works looks forward to time off to do something they really enjoy, but very few do," observes psychologist Mihaly Czikszentmihalyi, Ph.D., author of *Flow: The Psychology of Optimal Experience.* "When you get home, you feel listless, so you fall into the passive leisure trap of watching television—even though it isn't a really satisfying form of relaxation."

(15) There is an alternative, but it requires two things: prior planning and organization. "It's difficult to enjoy leisure time unless you prepare for it," says Czikszentmihalyi. "Left to themselves, things turn into a muddle; they deteriorate. To get any real psychological benefit from your free time, you have to invest some energy into it. Quality relaxation takes what I call spontaneous coordination." The first step is making leisure a priority. Too often, in our work-obsessed culture, we feel bad about simply feeling good. "We greatly undervalue relaxation," observes David Sobel, M.D., a specialist in behavioral medicine and coauthor of *Healthy Pleasures.* "It requires a certain amount of self-esteem to believe that you deserve to do something just because you enjoy it."

(16) But don't assume that the best leisure activities are expensive or elaborate. Often they're not. What they offer is flow, which Czikszentmihalyi defines as a state of altered consciousness that occurs when we are so focused, so immersed in what we're doing that we lose sense of time or anything else. The moment becomes everything. People find this sort of transcendental experience in different ways: playing chess, dancing, listening to music. Very often flow involves being outdoors—gardening, hiking, biking, sitting under a shady tree, looking for falling stars on a summer night, crunching through newly fallen snow. "Nature has a measurable restorative effect with respect to stress," says environmental psychologist Robert Ulrich, Ph.D., of Texas A&M University. Follow your own inclinations, whether or not they lead outdoors, to find your personal sources of flow.

RELAXATION TECHNIQUES

(17) Relaxation is the physical and mental state opposite that of stress. Rather than gearing up for fight or flight, our bodies and minds grow calmer and work more smoothly. We're less likely to become frazzled and more capable of staying in control. The most effective relaxation techniques include progressive relaxation, visualization, meditation, mindfulness, and biofeedback.

(18) **Progressive relaxation** works by intentionally increasing and then decreasing tension in the muscles. While sitting or lying down in a quiet, comfortable setting, you tense and release various muscles, beginning with those of the hand, for instance, and then proceeding to the arms, shoulders, neck, face, scalp, chest, stomach, buttocks, genitals, and so on, down each leg to the toes. Relaxing the muscles can quiet the mind and restore internal balance.

(19) **Visualization** or guided memory involves creating mental pictures that calm you down and focus your mind. Some people use this technique to promote healing when they are ill. The Glaser study showed that elderly residents of retirement homes in Ohio who learned progressive relaxation

and guided imagery enhanced their immune function and reported better health than did the other residents. Visualization skills require practice and, in some cases, instruction by qualified health professionals.

(20) **Meditation** has been practiced in many forms over the ages, from the yogic techniques of the Far East to the Quaker silence of more modern times. Meditation helps a person reach a state of relaxation, but with the goal of achieving inner peace and harmony. There is no one right way to meditate, and many people have discovered how to meditate on their own, without even knowing what it is they are doing. Among college students, meditation has proven especially effective in increasing relaxation. Most forms of meditation have common elements: sitting quietly for fifteen to twenty minutes once or twice a day, concentrating on a word or image, and breathing slowly and rhythmically. If you wish to try meditation, it often helps to have someone guide you through your first sessions. Or try tape recording your own voice (with or without favorite music in the background) and playing it back to yourself, freeing yourself to concentrate on the goal of turning the attention within.

(21) **Mindfulness** is a modern-day form of an ancient Asian technique that involves maintaining awareness in the present moment. You tune in to each part of your body, scanning from head to toe, noting the slightest sensation. You allow whatever you experience—an itch, an ache, a feeling of warmth—to enter your awareness. Then you open yourself to focus on all the thoughts, sensations, sounds, and feelings that enter your awareness. Mindfulness keeps you in the here-and-now, thinking about what is rather than about "what if" or "if only."

(22) **Biofeedback** is a method of obtaining feedback, or information, about some physiological activity occurring in the body. An electronic monitoring device attached to a person's body detects a change in an internal function and communicates it back to the person through a tone, light, or meter. By paying attention to this feedback, most people can gain some control over functions previously thought to be beyond conscious control, such as body temperature, heart rate, muscle tension, and brain waves. Biofeedback training consists of three stages:

A. Developing increased awareness of a body state or function.

B. Gaining control over it.

C. Transferring this control to everyday living without use of the electronic instrument.

(23) The goal of biofeedback for stress reduction is a state of tranquility, usually associated with the brain's production of alpha waves (which are slower and more regular than normal waking waves). After several training sessions, most people can produce alpha waves more or less at will.

(2,646 words)

Here are some of the more difficult words in "A Personal Stress Survival Guide."

alleviate
(paragraph 5)

al·le·vi·ate (ə lē′vē āt′) *vt.* **··at′ed, ··at′·ing** ⟦ME *alleviaten* < LL *alleviatus*, pp. of *alleviare*, for L *allevare* < *ad-*, to + *levis*, LIGHT²⟧ **1** to make less hard to bear; lighten or relieve (pain, suffering, etc.) **2** to reduce or decrease [to *alleviate* poverty] —*SYN.* RELIEVE —al·le′·via·tor *n.* —al·le′·via·tive *adj.* or al·le′·via·to′ry (-ə tôr′ē)

discern
(Chart 1, Item B)

dis·cern (di sʉrn′, -zʉrn′) *vt.* ⟦ME *discernen* < OFr *discerner* < L *discernere* < *dis-*, apart + *cernere*, to separate: see HARVEST⟧ **1** to separate (a thing) mentally from another or others; recognize as separate or different **2** to perceive or recognize; make out clearly —*vi.* to perceive or recognize the difference —dis·cern′·ible *adj.* —dis·cern′·ibly *adv.*

garner
(Chart 1, Item B)

gar·ner (gär′nər) *n.* ⟦ME *gerner* < OFr *grenier* < L *granarium*, granary < *granum*, GRAIN⟧ a place for storing grain; granary —*vt.* **1** to gather up and store in or as in a granary **2** to get or earn **3** to collect or gather

immersed
(paragraph 16)

im·merse (i mʉrs′) *vt.* **··mersed′, ··mers′·ing** ⟦< L *immersus*, pp. of *immergere*, to dip, plunge into: see IN-¹ & MERGE⟧ **1** to plunge, drop, or dip into or as if into a liquid, esp. so as to cover completely **2** to baptize by submerging in water **3** to absorb deeply; engross [*immersed* in study]

maladaptive
(paragraph 5)

mal·ad·ap·ta·tion (mal′ad əp tā′shən) *n.* inadequate or faulty adaptation —mal′·adap′·tive (-ə dap′tiv) *adj.*

ad·ap·ta·tion (ad′əp tā′shən) *n.* ⟦Fr < ML *adaptatio*: see ADAPT⟧ **1** an adapting or being adapted **2** a thing resulting from adapting [this play is an *adaptation* of a novel] **3** a change in structure, function, or form that improves the chance of survival for an animal or plant within a given environment **4** the natural reactions of a sense organ to variations in the degree of stimulation **5** *Sociology* a gradual change in behavior to conform to the prevailing cultural patterns —ad′·ap·ta′·tional *adj.*

physiological
(paragraph 22)

physi·ol·ogy (fiz′ē äl′ə jē) *n.* ⟦Fr *physiologie* < L *physiologia* < Gr: see PHYSIO- & -LOGY⟧ **1** the branch of biology dealing with the functions and vital processes of living organisms or their parts and organs **2** the functions and vital processes, collectively (of an organism, or of an organ or system of organs) —phys′i·ol′o·gist *n.*

procrastination
(paragraph 11)

pro·cras·ti·nate (prō kras′tə nāt′, prə-) *vi., vt.* **··nat′ed, ··nat′·ing** ⟦< L *procrastinatus*, pp. of *procrastinare* < *pro-*, forward (see PRO-²) + *crastinus*, belonging to the morrow < *cras*, tomorrow⟧ to put off doing (something unpleasant or burdensome) until a future time; esp., to postpone (such actions) habitually —pro·cras′·ti·na′·tion *n.* —pro·cras′·ti·na′·tor *n.*

psychological
(paragraph 3)

psycho·logi·cal (sī′kə läj′i kəl) *adj.* **1** of psychology **2** of the mind; mental **3** affecting or intended to affect the mind Also **psy′cho·log′ic** —psy′cho·log′i·cally *adv.*

superficial
(paragraph 3)

su·per·fi·cial (soo͞′pər fish′əl) *adj.* ⟦ME *superficyall* < L *superficialis* < *superficies*: see fol.⟧ **1** *a*) of or being on the surface [a *superficial* burn] *b*) of or limited to surface area; plane [*superficial* measurements] **2** concerned with and understanding only the easily apparent and obvious; not profound; shallow **3** quick and cursory [a *superficial* reading] **4** seeming such only at first glance; merely apparent [a *superficial* resemblance] —su′·per·fi′·ci·al′·ity (-ē al′ə tē) *n., pl.* **-ties** —su′·per·fi′·cially *adv.* —su′·per·fi′·cial·ness *n.*

SYN.—**superficial** implies concern with the obvious or surface aspects of a thing [*superficial* characteristics] and, in a derogatory sense, lack of thoroughness, profoundness, significance, etc. [*superficial* judgments]; **shallow**, in this connection always derogatory, implies a lack of depth of character, intellect, meaning, etc. [*shallow* writing]; **cursory**, which may or may not be derogatory, suggests a hasty consideration of something without pausing to note details [a *cursory* inspection] —*ANT.* deep, profound

tranquility
(paragraph 22)

tran·quil·lity or **tran·quil·ity** (traŋ kwil′ə tē, tran-) *n.* the quality or state of being tranquil; calmness; serenity

transcendental
(paragraph 16)

tran·scen·den·tal (tran′sen dent′′l) *adj.* ⟦ML *transcendentalis*⟧ **1** *a*) TRANSCENDENT (sense 1) *b*) SUPERNATURAL **2** abstract; metaphysical **3** of or having to do with transcendentalism **4** in Kantian philosophy, based on those elements of experience which derive not from sense data but from the inherent organizing function of the mind, and which are the necessary conditions of human knowledge; transcending sense experience but not knowledge **5** *Math. a*) not capable of being a root of any algebraic equation with rational coefficients *b*) of, pertaining to, or being a function, as a logarithm, trigonometric function, exponential, etc., that is not expressible algebraically in terms of the variables and constants (opposed to ALGEBRAIC, sense 2)) —**tran′·scen·den′·tally** *adv.*

vent
(paragraph 4)
[*vt.* form]

vent[1] (vent) *n.* ⟦ME *venten* < OFr *venter,* to blow (or aphetic < OFr *esventer,* to expose to the air, let out < *es-,* out + *venter*) < VL **ventare* < L *ventus,* WIND[2]⟧ **1** [Rare] the action of escaping or passing out, or the means or opportunity to do this; issue; outlet **2** expression; release *[giving* vent *to emotion]* **3** *a*) a small hole or opening to permit passage or escape, as of a gas ☆*b*) a small triangular window or, now esp., an opening on or beneath the dashboard, for letting air into the passenger compartment of a motor vehicle **4** in early guns, the small hole at the breech through which a spark passes to set off the charge **5** the opening in a volcano from which gas and molten rock erupt **6** *Zool.* the excretory opening in animals; esp., the external opening of the cloaca in birds, reptiles, amphibians, and fishes —*vt.* **1** to make a vent in or provide a vent for **2** to allow (steam, gas, etc.) to escape through an opening **3** to give release or expression to **4** to relieve or unburden by giving vent to feelings *[to* vent *oneself in curses]*

28A1   VOCABULARY

From the context of "A Personal Stress Survival Guide," explain each of the vocabulary words shown in boldface.

1. *From paragraph 3:* . . . college students who wrote in their journals about traumatic events felt much better afterward than those who wrote about **superficial** topics.

   shallow
   _____

   _____

2. *From paragraph 3:* Since the small ups and downs of daily life have an enormous impact on **psychological** and physical well-being, getting a handle on daily hassles will reduce your stress load.

mental

3. *From Chart 1, Item B:* Rereading and thinking about your notes may help you **discern** the underlying reasons for your response and **garner** insights that can help you cope better in the future.
recognize . . . gather

4. *From paragraph 4:* The second [person] uses humor to **vent** frustration.
release

5. *From paragraph 5:* Under great stress, we all may turn to negative defense mechanisms to **alleviate** anxiety and eliminate conflict.
relieve

6. *From paragraph 5:* These can lead to **maladaptive** behavior, such as overeating. . . .
unsuitable

7. *From paragraph 11:* The three most common types of **procrastination** are putting off unpleasant things, putting off difficult tasks, and putting off tough decisions.
postponing actions

8. *From paragraph 16:* What they offer is flow, which Czikszentmihalyi defines as a state of altered consciousness that occurs when we are so focused, so **immersed** in what we're doing that we lose sense of time or anything else.

Name   Date

absorbed _____

_____

9. *From paragraph 16:* People find this sort of **transcendental** experience in different ways.

supernatural _____

_____

10. *From paragraph 22:* Biofeedback is a method of obtaining feedback, or information, about some **physiological** activity occurring in the body.

organic _____

_____

11. *From paragraph 23:* The goal of biofeedback for stress reduction is a state of **tranquility.**

calmness _____

_____

28A2   SPECIAL TEXTBOOK VOCABULARY

Key terms in this textbook selection are explained as they are discussed. Referring to "A Personal Stress Survival Guide," fill in the blanks.

1. __Defense mechanisms__ are actions or behaviors that people use to protect their sense of self-worth.

2. Redirecting an unacceptable drive into a socially acceptable channel is __sublimation__ .

3. __Religiosity__ is the practice of one's trying to accept a painful experience as being in agreement with God's will.

4. Medical students use jokes, or _____humor_____ , to counteract stress they encounter during anatomy lab.

5. Turning a negative experience into a positive one is _____altruism_____ .

6. <u>Progressive relaxation</u>   occurs when a person intentionally increases and then decreases tension in various muscles according to a set sequence.

7. One's creating and using mental pictures to calm oneself and focus the mind is <u>visualization</u> .

8. <u>Meditation</u>   can involve sitting quietly, concentrating, or breathing slowly and rhythmically to achieve a state of relaxation.

28B   CENTRAL THEME AND MAIN IDEAS

Choose the best answer.

<u>b</u> 1. The central theme of "A Personal Stress Survival Guide" is
   a. how unbalanced stress distribution on metal parts can cause failure of machinery resulting in serious accidents.
   b. how important is the maintenance of good mental health through all stages of life, from childhood through old age.
   c. how people can learn to handle stress: first, by learning the types of stress and, second, by using ways to minimize their effects.
   d. how to handle the trauma that can follow having almost died in a major disaster, such as a tornado, flood, or hurricane.

<u>b</u> 2. The main purpose of paragraph 2 is to
   a. describe and discuss the possible signals of stress overload.
   b. identify the common traits found in those who control stress.
   c. describe and discuss the behaviors that lead to stress.
   d. recommend involvement with other people to avoid stress.

<u>d</u> 3. The main idea of paragraph 4 is that
   a. teachers may take out their stress from work by yelling at their own children.
   b. joking about a stressful day at work can relieve stress.
   c. protecting one's sense of self-worth is necessary during stressful times.
   d. people use defense mechanisms to protect against stress.

Name   Date

28C   MAJOR DETAILS

Fill in the word or words that correctly complete each statement.

1. The impact of stress depends not just on what ___happened___ to you, but on how you ___handle___ it.

2. An effective way to deal with stress is writing about your ___feelings___ in ___words___ that only you will read.

3. Some strategies to help you cope with stress include ___recognizing___ your stress signals, ___keeping___ a stress journal, ___trying___ "stress-inoculation," ___putting___ things in proper perspective, and ___thinking___ of one thing to simplify your life.

4. Symptoms of __poor time management__ include rushing, the inability to make choices, fatigue, missed deadlines, and not enough time for rest.

5. The Americans' Use of Time Project showed that Americans spend the greater amount of their free time __watching television__ .

6. To make effective use of free time requires __prior planning__ and ___organization___ .

7. In our work-obsessed culture, David Sobel observes "we greatly undervalue ___relaxation___ ."

28D   INFERENCES

Decide whether each statement can be inferred (YES) or cannot be inferred (NO) from the reading selection.

__YES__ 1. Stress management includes striving for a personal goal because it provides reasons for choices made.

YES 2. Stress management includes using a minimum of substances, such as nicotine and caffeine, because these stimulants can affect a person's thought processes.

NO 3. Procrastinators have high self-esteem.

NO 4. Stress counseling is available through many resources.

28E CRITICAL READING: FACT OR OPINION

Decide whether each statement contains a FACT or an OPINION.

OPINION 1. *From paragraph 1:* "The inability to feel in control of stress, rather than stress itself, is often the most harmful."

FACT 2. *From paragraph 11:* "Putting off until tomorrow what should be done today is a habit that creates a great deal of stress for many students."

OPINION 3. *From paragraph 12:* "People procrastinate, not because they're lazy, but to protect their self-esteem and make a favorable impression."

FACT 4. *From paragraph 13:* "Three-quarters of Americans believe the amount of stress in their lives is within their control."

FACT 5. *From paragraph 14:* "Everybody who works looks forward to time off to do something they really enjoy [. . .]."

FACT 6. *From paragraph 19:* "The Glaser study of elderly residents of retirement homes in Ohio showed that residents who practiced progressive relaxation and guided imagery enhanced their immune function and reported better health than the other residents."

OPINION 8. *From paragraph 20:* "Among college students meditation has proven especially effective in increasing relaxation."

28F CRITICAL READING: THE AUTHOR'S STRATEGIES

Choose the best answer.

d 1. The main audience for "A Personal Stress Survival Guide" in *An Invitation to Health* is
   a. students studying health.
   b. students that procrastinate.

Name   Date

      c. students who don't know how to relax.

      d. students who need advice on handling stress.

__d__ 2. The author's purpose in writing this reading is to

      a. persuade.

      b. expose.

      c. entertain.

      d. inform.

__d__ 3. The author's tone in this reading is

      a. judgmental.

      b. critical.

      c. encouraging.

      d. objective.

28G   READER'S PROCESS: SUMMARIZING YOUR READING

__b__ 1. What is the best summary of "A Personal Stress Survival Guide" in *An Invitation to Health*?

      a. The author discusses why Americans watch too much television.

      b. The author discusses methods that can reduce stress in everyday life.

      c. The author discusses how students can avoid procrastinating.

      d. The author discusses how keeping a journal can help reduce stress.

28H   READER'S RESPONSE: TO DISCUSS OR WRITE ABOUT

1. Stress can either help or hurt a person. Good stress provides a challenge. Bad stress is harmful physically and/or psychologically. Discuss several situations that illustrate either good or bad stress in your life or in a friend's life.

2. Give an example of a stressful situation involving you and a family member, coworker, friend, or classmate. Were you able to change the situation? If so, explain what you did. If not, explain the coping techniques you used to handle the situation.

Name   Date

HOW DID YOU DO?

28 A Personal Stress Survival Guide

SKILL *(number of items)*	*Number Correct*		*Points for each*		*Score*
Vocabulary* (12)	_____	×	2	=	_____
Special Textbook vocabulary(8)	_____	×	2	=	_____
Central Theme and Main Ideas (3)	_____	×	4	=	_____
Major Details** (14)	_____	×	2	=	_____
Inferences (4)	_____	×	1	=	_____
Critical Reading: Fact or Opinion (7)	_____	×	1	=	_____
Critical Reading: The Author's Strategies (3)	_____	×	2	=	_____
Reader's Process: Summarizing Your Reading (1)	_____	×	3	=	_____

(Possible Total: 100) *Total*   _____

SPEED

Reading Time: _____ Reading Rate (page 415): _____ Words Per Minute

*Question 3 in this exercise calls for two separate answers. In computing your score, count each separate answer toward your number correct.

**Questions 1, 2, and 6 in this exercise call for two separate answers. Question 3 calls for five separate answers. In computing your score, count each separate answer toward your number correct.

Name   Date

Selection 29
The Chaser

John Collier

(1) Alan Austen, as nervous as a kitten, went up certain dark and creaky stairs in the neighborhood of Pell Street, and peered about for a long time on the dim landing before he found the name he wanted written obscurely on one of the doors.

(2) He pushed open this door, as he had been told to do, and found himself in a tiny room, which contained no furniture but a plain kitchen table, a rocking-chair, and an ordinary chair. On one of the dirty buff-colored walls were a couple of shelves, containing in all perhaps a dozen bottles and jars.

(3) An old man sat in the rocking-chair, reading a newspaper. Alan, without a word, handed him the card he had been given. "Sit down, Mr. Austen," said the man very politely. "I am glad to make your acquaintance."

(4) "Is it true," asked Alan, "that you have a certain mixture that has—er—quite extraordinary effects?"

(5) "My dear sir," replied the old man, "my stock in trade is not very large—I don't deal in laxatives and teething mixtures—but such as it is, it is varied. I think nothing I sell has effects which could be precisely described as ordinary."

(6) "Well, the fact is—" began Alan.

(7) "Here, for example," interrupted the old man, reaching for a bottle from the shelf. "Here is a liquid as colorless as water, almost tasteless, quite imperceptible in coffee, milk, wine, or any other beverage. It is also quite imperceptible to any known method of autopsy."

(8) "Do you mean it is a poison?" cried Alan, very much horrified.

(9) "Call it a glove-cleaner if you like," said the old man indifferently. "Maybe it will clean gloves. I have never tried. One might call it a life-cleaner. Lives need cleaning sometimes."

(10) "I want nothing of that sort," said Alan.

(11) "Probably it is just as well," said the old man. "Do you know the price of this? For one teaspoonful, which is sufficient, I ask five thousand dollars. Never less. Not a penny less."

(12) "I hope all your mixtures are not as expensive," said Alan apprehensively.

(13) "Oh dear, no," said the old man. "It would be no good charging that sort of price for a love potion, for example. Young people who need a love potion very seldom have five thousand dollars. Otherwise they would not need a love potion."

(14) "I am glad to hear that," said Alan.

(15) "I look at it like this," said the old man. "Please a customer with one article, and he will come back when he needs another. Even if it is more costly. He will save up for it, if necessary."

(16) "So," said Alan, "you really do sell love potions?"

(17) "If I did not sell love potions," said the old man, reaching for another bottle, "I should not have mentioned the other matter to you. It is only when one is in a position to oblige that one can afford to be so confidential."

(18) "And these potions," said Alan. "They are not just—just—er—"

(19) "Oh, no," said the old man. "Their effects are permanent, and extend far beyond casual impulse. But they include it. Bountifully, insistently. Everlastingly."

(20) "Dear me!" said Alan, attempting a look of scientific detachment. "How very interesting!"

(21) "But consider the spiritual side," said the old man.

(22) "I do, indeed," said Alan.

(23) "For indifference," said the old man, "they substitute devotion. For scorn, adoration. Give one tiny measure of this to the young lady—its flavor is imperceptible in orange juice, soup, or cocktails—and however gay and giddy she is, she will change altogether. She will want nothing but solitude, and you."

(24) "I can hardly believe it," said Alan. "She is so fond of parties."

(25) "She will not like them any more," said the old man. "She will be afraid of the pretty girls you may meet."

(26) "She will actually be jealous?" cried Alan in rapture. "Of me?"

(27) "Yes, she will want to be everything to you."

(28) "She is, already. Only she doesn't care about it."

(29) "She will, when she has taken this. She will care intensely. You will be her sole interest in life."

(30) "Wonderful!" cried Alan.

(31) "She will want to know all you do," said the old man. "All that has happened to you during the day. Every word of it. She will want to know what you are thinking about, why you smile suddenly, why you are looking sad."

(32) "That is love!" cried Alan.

(33) "Yes," said the old man. "How carefully she will look after you! She will never allow you to be tired, to sit in a draught, to neglect your food. If you are an hour late, she will be terrified. She will think you are killed, or that some siren has caught you."

(34) "I can hardly imagine Diana like that!" cried Alan, overwhelmed with joy.

(35) "You will not have to use your imagination," said the old man. "And, by the way, since there are always sirens, if by any chance you should, later on, slip a little, you need not worry. She will forgive you, in the end. She will be terribly hurt, of course, but she will forgive you—in the end."

(36) "That will not happen," said Alan fervently.

(37) "Of course not," said the old man. "But, if it did, you need not worry. She would never divorce you. Oh, no! And, of course, she herself will never give you the least, the very least, grounds for—uneasiness."

(38) "And how much," said Alan, "is this wonderful mixture?"

(39) "It is not as dear," said the old man, "as the glove-cleaner, or life-cleaner, as I sometimes call it. No. That is five thousand dollars, never a penny less. One has to be older than you are, to indulge in that sort of thing. One has to save up for it."

(40) "But the love potion?" said Alan.

(41) "Oh, that," said the old man, opening the drawer in the kitchen table, and taking out a tiny, rather dirty-looking phial. "That is just a dollar."

(42) "I can't tell you how grateful I am," said Alan, watching him fill it.

(43) "I like to oblige," said the old man. "Then customers come back, later in life, when they are rather better off, and want more expensive things. Here you are. You will find it very effective."

(44) "Thank you again," said Alan. "Good-by."

(45) "Au revoir," said the old man.

(1,075 words)

Here are some of the more difficult words in "The Chaser."

au revoir
(paragraph 45)

au re·voir (ō'rə vwär') [[Fr < *au*, to the + *revoir*, seeing again < L *revidere*, see again < *re*-, again + *videre*, see: see VISION]] until we meet again; goodbye: implies temporary parting

autopsy
(paragraph 7)

au·top·sy (ô'täp'sē, ôt'əp sē) *n., pl.* **-sies** [[ML & Gr *autopsia*, a seeing with one's own eyes < Gr *autos*, self + *opsis*, a sight < *ōps*, EYE]] **1** an examination and dissection of a dead body to discover the cause of death, damage done by disease, etc.; postmortem **2** a detailed critical analysis of a book, play, etc., or of some event —*vt.* **-sied**, **-sy·ing** to examine (a body) in this manner

bountifully
(paragraph 19)

boun·ti·ful (-tə fəl) *adj.* **1** giving freely and graciously; generous **2** provided in abundance; plentiful —**boun'·ti·fully** *adv.* —**boun'·ti·ful·ness** *n.*

chaser
(title)

chaser[1] (chā'sər) *n.* [[CHASE[1] + -ER]] **1** a person or thing that chases or hunts; pursuer **2** a gun formerly placed on the stern (**stern chaser**) or bow (**bow chaser**) of a ship, used during pursuit by or of another ship ☆**3** a mild drink, as water, ginger ale, or beer, taken after or with whiskey, rum, etc.

confidential
(paragraph 17)

con·fi·den·tial (kän'fə den'shəl) *adj.* **1** told in confidence; imparted in secret **2** of or showing trust in another; confiding **3** entrusted with private or secret matters *[a confidential agent]* — *SYN.* FAMILIAR —**con'·fi·den'·ti·al'·ity** (-shē al'ə tē) *n.* or **con'·fi·den'·tial·ness** —**con'·fi·den'·tially** *adv.*

Vocabulary List

draught
(paragraph 33)

draught (draft, dräft) *n.*, *vt.*, *adj. now chiefly Brit. sp.* of DRAFT

draft (draft, dräft) *n.* ⟦ME *draught*, a drawing, pulling, stroke < base of OE *dragan*, DRAW⟧ **1** *a*) a drawing or pulling, as of a vehicle or load *b*) the thing, quantity, or load pulled **2** *a*) a drawing in of a fish net *b*) the amount of fish caught in one draw **3** *a*) a taking of liquid into the mouth; drinking *b*) the amount taken at one drink **4** *a*) a portion of liquid for drinking; specif., a dose of medicine *b*) [Informal] a portion of beer, ale, etc. drawn from a cask **5** *a*) a drawing into the lungs, as of air or tobacco smoke *b*) the amount of air, smoke, etc., drawn in **6** a rough or preliminary sketch of a piece of writing **7** a plan or drawing of a work to be done **8** a current of air, as in a room, heating system, etc. **9** a device for regulating the current of air in a heating system **10** a written order issued by one person, bank, firm, etc., directing the payment of money to another; check **11** a demand or drain made on something

imperceptible
(paragraph 7)

im·per·cep·ti·ble (im′pər sep′tə bəl) *adj.* ⟦Fr < ML *imperceptibilis*: see IN-² & PERCEPTIBLE⟧ not plain or distinct to the senses or the mind; esp., so slight, gradual, subtle, etc. as not to be easily perceived —**im′·per·cep′·ti·bil′·i·ty** *n.* —**im′·per·cep′·ti·bly** *adv.*

obscurely
(paragraph 1)

ob·scure (əb skyoor′, äb-) *adj.* ⟦OFr *obscur* < L *obscurus*, lit., covered over < *ob-* (see OB-) + IE **skuro-* < base **(s)keu-*, to cover, conceal > HIDE¹, SKY⟧ **1** lacking light; dim; dark; murky [the *obscure* night] **2** not easily perceived; specif., *a*) not clear or distinct; faint or undefined [an *obscure* figure or sound] *b*) not easily understood; vague; cryptic; ambiguous [an *obscure* explanation] *c*) in an inconspicuous position; hidden [an *obscure* village] **3** not well-known; not famous [an *obscure* scientist] **4** *Phonet.* pronounced as (ə) or (i) because it is not stressed; reduced; neutral: said of a vowel —*vt.* **··scured′, ··scur′·ing** ⟦L *obscurare* < the adj.⟧ **1** to make obscure; specif., *a*) to darken; make dim *b*) to conceal from view; hide *c*) to make less conspicuous; overshadow [a success that *obscured* earlier failures] *d*) to make less intelligible; confuse [testimony that *obscures* the issue] **2** *Phonet.* to make (a vowel) obscure —*n.* [Rare] OBSCURITY —**ob·scure′·ly** *adv.* —**ob·scure′·ness** *n.*

SYN.—**obscure** applies to that which is perceived with difficulty either because it is concealed or veiled or because of obtuseness in the perceiver [their reasons remain *obscure*]; **vague** implies such a lack of precision or exactness as to be indistinct or unclear [a *vague* idea]; **enigmatic** and **cryptic** are used of that which baffles or perplexes, the latter word implying deliberate intention to puzzle [*enigmatic* behavior, a *cryptic* warning]; **ambiguous** applies to that which puzzles because it allows of more than one interpretation [an *ambiguous* title]; **equivocal** is used of something ambiguous that is deliberately used to mislead or confuse [an *equivocal* answer] —*ANT.* **clear, distinct, obvious**

phial
(paragraph 41)

phial (fī′əl) *n.* ⟦ME *fiole* < OFr < Prov *fiola* < ML < L *phiala* < Gr *phialē*, broad, shallow drinking vessel⟧ a small glass bottle; vial

rapture
(paragraph 26)

rap·ture (rap′chər) *n.* ⟦ML *raptura*: see RAPT & -URE⟧ **1** the state of being carried away with joy, love, etc.; ecstasy **2** an expression of great joy, pleasure, etc. **3** a carrying away or being carried away in body or spirit: now rare except in theological usage —*vt.* **··tured′, ··tur·ing** [Now Rare] to enrapture; fill with ecstasy —*SYN.* ECSTASY —**the rapture** [*often* **the R-**] in some Christian theologies, the bodily ascent into heaven just before Armageddon of those who are saved (see SAVE¹, *vt.* 8) —**rap′·tur·ous** *adj.* —**rap′·tur·ous·ly** *adv.*

siren
(paragraph 33)

si·ren (sī′rən) *n.* ⟦ME *syrene* < OFr < LL *Sirena*, for L *Siren* < Gr *Seirēn* < ? *seira*, cord, rope (hence, orig. ? one who snares, entangles) < IE base **twer-*, to grasp⟧ **1** *Gr. & Rom. Myth.* any of several sea nymphs, represented as part bird and part woman, who lure sailors to their death on rocky coasts by seductive singing **2** a woman who uses her sexual attractiveness to entice or allure men; a woman who is considered seductive **3** *a*) an acoustical device in which steam or air is driven against a rotating, perforated disk so as to produce sound; specif., such a device producing a loud, often wailing sound, used esp. as a warning signal *b*) an electronic device that produces a similar sound **4** any of a family (Sirenidae) of slender, eel-shaped salamanders without hind legs; esp., the mud eel

29A   VOCABULARY

Using the vocabulary words listed on pages 393–394, fill in this crossword puzzle.

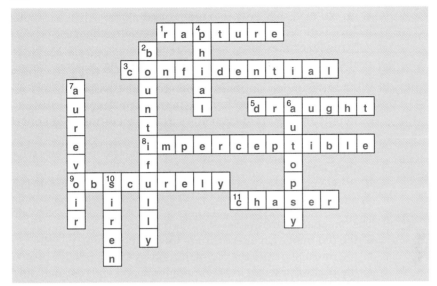

Across

1. an expression of great happiness and delight
3. told or divulged in secret
5. air current
8. insignificant or not easily perceived
9. not distinctly or clearly
11. The _____ following his beer was simply a glass of water.

Down

2. given freely or graciously; abundantly
4. a small glass container
6. An _____ determined the cause of death.
7. the French expression for "farewell"
10. an enchantress or seductive woman

Name   Date

29B   CENTRAL THEME AND MAIN IDEAS

Choose the best answer.

__c__   1. The central theme of "The Chaser" is that
   a. an old man sells only two types of potions.
   b. love potions may cause distinct personality changes.
   c. "true love" may also have a dark side.
   d. there are inherent dangers involved in using potions.

__b__   2. What is the underlying assumption of "The Chaser"?
   a. The effects of love potions are permanent and irreversible.
   b. People will resort to even more drastic measures to get out of a love relationship than to get into one.
   c. Young people have less money than older people to buy what they want.
   d. A love potion may cause unfounded jealousy and unsolicited adoration.

__a__   3. The unexpected main idea of paragraph 9 is
   a. the old man's cavalier attitude toward poisoning people.
   b. the unusual names the old man chooses to disguise his poison.
   c. the philosophy that lives sometimes need to be "cleaned out."
   d. that of the two potions the old man sells, one is poison.

__c__   4. The main idea of paragraph 43 is that
   a. the old man is pleased that his customers are happy with his potions.
   b. the old man is aware that he has a tremendous service to offer his customers.
   c. the old man is willing to give his customers what they think they want now, knowing that they'll be back later for a more expensive deadly potion.
   d. the old man is anxious for his customers to return so that he can sell them more of the same potion at a higher price.

Name   Date

29C MAJOR DETAILS

Decide whether each detail is MAJOR or MINOR based on the context of the reading selection.

MINOR 1. The potion seller's tiny room was at the top of the dark and creaky stairs.

MAJOR 2. There was a tremendous difference in price between the two potions.

MAJOR 3. The old man refers to his poison as a "life-cleaner."

MAJOR 4. The effects of the love potion are permanent.

MAJOR 5. Diana will forgive Alan's indiscretions, "in the end."

MINOR 6. The potion seller is an old man.

MAJOR 7. The old man sells only two potions.

MINOR 8. The potion seller's room contained only the barest of furniture and shelves hung on dirty buff-colored walls.

MAJOR 9. The poison is imperceptible in any autopsy.

MAJOR 10. Of his two potions, the old man tells Alan about his "life-cleaner" first.

MINOR 11. Diana is very fond of parties.

MAJOR 12. The old man hints that all customers who purchase the first potion return later in life for the second.

29D INFERENCES

Choose the best answer.

b 1. The word "chaser" in the title refers to
   a. the orange juice, soup, or cocktail mixed with the love potion.
   b. the poisonous potion taken to counter the effects of the love potion.
   c. a mild drink taken following a stronger alcoholic drink.
   d. the love potion purchased from the old man by young customers.

___c___ 2. *Read paragraph 13 again.* The author implies that
   a. young people seldom have a need for love potions.
   b. young people in love are generally poor but are mostly indifferent to their poverty.
   c. anyone with $5000 will have no need for a love potion because his money will make him desirable.
   d. expensive love potions would be wasted on young people, who rarely have much money anyway.

___c___ 3. *Read paragraph 17 again.* The old man is implying that
   a. his potions can be very expensive and are a well-kept secret.
   b. if he did not sell love potions, Alan would not have come to see him in the first place.
   c. if he did not sell love potions, he would have no need to sell another potion to "cure" the effects of love potions.
   d. admitting to the need for a love potion is a very confidential matter.

___a___ 4. *Read paragraphs 31–33 again.* Alan's exclamation of "That is love!" is answered with a flat "Yes." The old man's lack of enthusiasm is likely the result of
   a. his awareness that this love will eventually become clinging, possessive, and destructive.
   b. his belief that true love does not truly exist.
   c. his own experience with a past tragic love.
   d. his lack of interest in Alan's reaction to the potion's effects.

___c___ 5. *Read paragraph 35 again.* The author uses the expression "in the end" twice, each time following the statement "She will forgive you." He does this because
   a. Alan must be persistent in asking Diana for forgiveness.
   b. Alan should be careful of these sirens and try to avoid them.
   c. Diana is likely to play the martyr first and inflict some guilt before granting forgiveness.
   d. Diana will be slow to forgive because of her confusion over Alan's unfaithfulness.

Name   Date

  _a_   6. *Read paragraph 39 again.* The author implies that
        a. the poison is more expensive because people want it more badly than the love potion.
        b. young people have not lived long enough to have the problems associated with needing a "life-cleaner."
        c. older people can expect to need "life-cleaners" and are more willing to use poisons.
        d. the poison is a precious commodity because of its inherently expensive ingredients.

  _d_   7. *Read paragraphs 44–45 again.* While Alan bids the old man "goodby," the old man responds with "au revoir," implying that
        a. he is more sophisticated than Alan.
        b. he has not been in the United States long enough yet to converse easily in English.
        c. Alan is also fluent in French and understands the exchange.
        d. the parting is not permanent, and Alan will be coming back.

29E   CRITICAL READING: THE AUTHOR'S STRATEGIES

Choose the best answer.

  _d_   1. The main audience for "The Chaser" is
        a. anyone who wants to attract a loved one.
        b. anyone who believes in love potions.
        c. anyone who has dreamed of poisoning a lover.
        d. anyone who enjoys a love story with an ironic twist.

  _a_   2. The author's purpose in writing this reading is to
        a. entertain.
        b. warn.
        c. narrate.
        d. convince.

  _a_   3. The author's tone in this reading is
        a. ironic.
        b. dramatic.
        c. conversational.
        d. serious.

29F   READER'S PROCESS: SUMMARIZING YOUR READING

__c__   1. What is the best summary of "The Chaser"?
   a. A young man goes to buy a love potion from an old man who sells him one for a dollar.
   b. A young man goes to buy a love potion from an old man who also sells poison.
   c. A young man goes to buy a love potion from an old man who counts on love turning to hate.
   d. A young man goes to buy a love potion and learns how it will win his lover's devotion.

29G   READER'S RESPONSE: TO DISCUSS OR WRITE ABOUT

1. Do you believe in the manufacture and distribution of a medication, such as a love potion, to affect a person's feelings for someone else? This medication might be prescribed in a situation of unrequited love. What are the advantages of such a medication? Are there any dangers? To whom would this be prescribed? Give specific support to convince your audience to consider your point of view.

2. Assume a friend came to you for advice about marriage. Would you encourage the person to marry for love, money, or some other factor? Explain fully.

HOW DID YOU DO?

29 The Chaser

SKILL (number of items)	Number Correct		Points for each		Score
Vocabulary (11)	_____	×	2	=	_____
Central Theme and Main Ideas (4)	_____	×	4	=	_____
Major Details (12)	_____	×	2	=	_____
Inferences (7)	_____	×	4	=	_____
Critical Reading: The Author's Strategies (3)	_____	×	2	=	_____
Reader's Process: Summarizing Your Reading (1)	_____	×	4	=	_____

(Possible Total: 100) *Total* _____

SPEED

Reading Time: _____ Reading Rate (page 415): _____ Words Per Minute

Reading Charts, Graphs, Illustrations, and Pictures

Chapter 9 of this textbook presents a discussion of how to read visuals. Visuals, like images, charts, and graphs, are alternate texts used by authors to communicate their message to the reader. Visuals can be read using the same strategies used to read written texts. However, you do need to adapt those strategies to the particular characteristics of visuals. For example, with graphs and charts, you will not only read the data in the graph/chart, but also read the title and key, which will support you in understanding what is being presented. With visuals like pictures and illustrations, it is necessary to first identify the main images and visual clues. The main images are those elements of the picture or illustration that are most pronounced. The visual clues may be the less-pronounced elements in the visual or the way the various elements are presented in relation to each other. After identifying main images and visual clues, you can then make inferences about what they communicate and, ultimately, determine the intended message of the visual. Initially, adapting the reading strategies you have learned to visuals may be challenging, but with practice you can gain ease and effectiveness.

College students live in an increasingly visual world—video games, Internet sites, and print advertising, for example—and must adjust to this shift by becoming proficient readers of alternate texts. The skills and strategies you practice in this selection are designed to support you in reading the more common types of alternate texts you will encounter in your personal and academic experiences. Use the reading strategies you've been developing throughout your use of this textbook as you read the following visuals and answer the questions that accompany them.

30A   READING GRAPHS/CHARTS

Review Figures 30.1, 30.2, and 30.3 and answer the following questions.

1. According to Figure 30.1, what do the percentages represent? The proportion of new employees who have the writing skills desired

2. According to Figure 30.2, in what industries is writing considered in promotions at least 40% of the time? Mining, Manufacturing, Transportation/Utilities, Fire, and Services

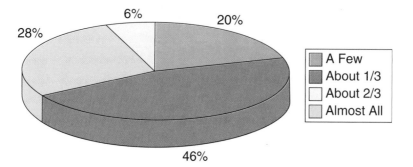

Figure 30.1 Business Leaders Say What Proportion of New Employees Have the Writing Skills Desired

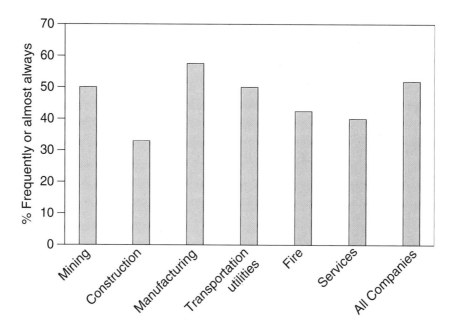

Figure 30.2 Writing Often a Consideration in Professional Promotion

Name   Date

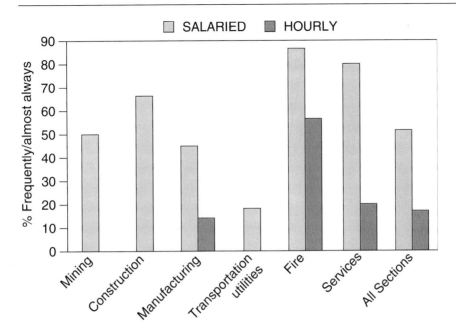

Figure 30.3 Many Companies Consider Writing in Hiring

3. According to Figure 30.3, in which two sectors are hourly workers less likely to get hired if they have poor writing skills? Fire and Services

30B READING IMAGES

Review the image in Figure 30.4 and answer the following questions.

1. What are the main images in the illustration? The people going in the building and coming out and falling off the edge, and the buildings in the background.

2. What type of building are the figures walking into? What visual clue(s) let(s) you know this? A schoolhouse. The people have books in their hands and walk out wearing graduation caps.

Name   Date

Figure 30.4

3. What is the primary message of the illustration? What visual clue(s) support(s) your response? <u>Answers may vary. The primary message is that graduates are falling into the gap between what their education has given them and what the business world needs. The clues are the gap, the conveyer belt sending them over the edge, and the high-rise buildings across the gap.</u>

30C READING IMAGES

Review the image in Figure 30.5 and answer the following questions.

1. What are the main images in the illustration? <u>The cellular phone, the floating envelopes, the antennae in the background, and the snakes.</u>

2. What do the envelopes represent? What visual clue(s) let(s) you know this? <u>E-mail or text messages sent through the phone. The envelopes are coming from the phone and appear to be being transmitted by the antennae through space.</u>

Name   Date

Figure 30.5

3. What is the primary message of the illustration? What visual clue(s) support(s) your response? Answers may vary. The primary message is that sometimes dangerous or harmful communications are being sent through e-mail or text messages. The visual clue is the group of snakes traveling with the envelopes that are coming from the phone.

30D   READING IMAGES

Review the image in Figure 30.6 and answer the following questions.

1. What are the main images in the illustration? The billboard featuring a credit card with a jaw trap drawn around it.

2. What do the words on the billboard add to the visual image? The words "Total Security Protection makes our cards safer" indicates that

Name   Date

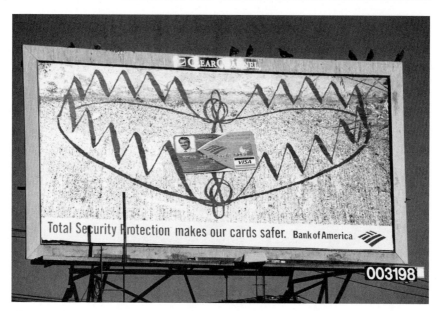

Figure 30.6

the jaw trap is provided by the credit card company to protect the credit card owner.

3. **What is the primary message of the illustration? What visual clue(s) supports your response?** Answers may vary. The primary message is that the owner of the credit card being featured can feel safe knowing his/her card is protected.

Name   Date

Appendix 1

Progress Chart and Reading Rate Table

PROGRESS CHARTS

Total Score on Skill-Building Exercises Graph*

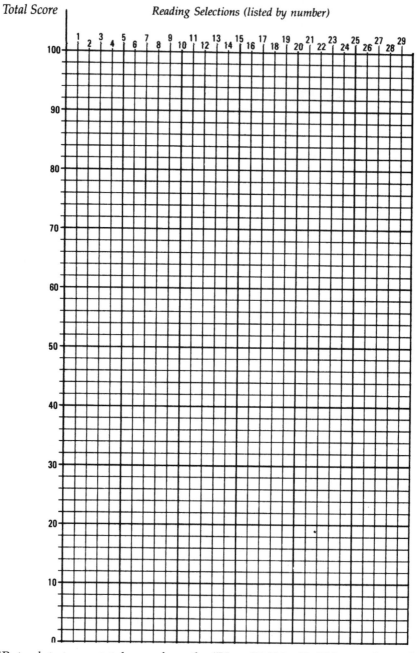

*Put a dot at your total score from the "How Did You Do?" box at the end of each reading selection. Connect the dots with a line to see your progress.

Reading Rate Table

Here's how to figure your reading rate. Time your reading to the nearest half-minute. Next, locate your time in the left column of this table. Then, stay on the line that lists your time and move to the right to locate the column for

Time in half-minute intervals	Reading Selections (listed by number)						
	PART 2						PART 3
	1	2	3	4	5	6	7
1.	498	563	722	775	986	1956	215
1.5	332	375	481	517	657	1304	143
2	249	282	361	388	493	978	108
2.5	199	225	289	310	394	782	86
3	166	188	241	258	329	652	72
3.5	142	161	206	221	282	559	61
4	125	141	181	194	247	489	54
4.5	111	125	160	172	219	435	48
5	97	113	144	155	197	391	
5.5	91	102	131	141	179	356	
6	83	94	120	129	164	326	
6.5	77	87	111	111	152	301	
7	71	80	103	103	141	279	
7.5	66	75	96	97	131	261	
8		70	90	91	123	245	
8.5		66	85	86	116	230	
9			80	82	110	217	
9.5			76	78	104	206	
10			72	74	99	196	
10.5			69	70	94	186	
11			66	67	90	178	
11.5				65	86	170	
12					82	163	
12.5					79	156	
13					76	150	
13.5					73	145	
14					70	140	
14.5					68	135	
15					66	130	
15.5						126	
16						122	
16.5						119	
17						115	
17.5						112	
18						109	
18.5						106	
19						103	
19.5						100	
20						98	

the particular reading selection you have just completed. The number you meet is the number of words per minute you read in that reading selection. **This number of words per minute is your reading rate.** (If you would like to chart your reading rate, you can use the graph on page 416).

Time in half-minute intervals	Reading Selections (listed by number)					PART 4	
	8	9	10	11	12	13	14
1	415	850	1004	1396	1808	520	694
1.5	277	567	669	931	1205	346	463
2	208	425	502	698	904	260	342
2.5	166	340	402	558	723	208	278
3	138	283	335	465	603	173	231
3.5	119	243	287	399	516	149	198
4	104	213	251	349	452	130	174
4.5	92	189	223	310	402	116	154
5	83	170	201	279	362	104	139
5.5	75	155	183	254	329	95	126
6	69	141	167	233	301	87	116
6.5	64	131	155	215	278	80	107
7		121	143	199	258	74	99
7.5		113	134	186	241	69	93
8		106	126	175	226	65	87
8.5		100	118	164	213	61	82
9		94	112	155	201		77
9.5		89	106	147	190		73
10		85	100	140	181		69
10.5		81	96	133	172		66
11		77	91	127	164		63
11.5		74	87	121	157		
12		71	84	116	151		
12.5		68	80	112	145		
13		65	77	107	139		
13.5			74	103	134		
14			72	98	129		
14.5			69	96	125		
15			67	93	121		
15.5			65	90	117		
16				87	113		
16.5				85	110		
17				82	106		
17.5				80	103		
18				78	100		
18.5				75	98		
19				73	95		
19.5				72	93		
20				69	90		

Time in half-minute intervals	Reading Selections (listed by number)						
					PART 5		
	15	16	17	18	19	20	21
1	1197	1235	1259	2382	697	763	792
1.5	798	823	839	1588	465	509	528
2	599	618	630	1191	349	381	396
2.5	479	494	504	953	279	305	317
3	399	412	420	794	232	254	264
3.5	342	353	360	681	199	218	226
4	299	309	315	596	174	191	198
4.5	266	274	280	529	155	170	176
5	239	247	252	476	139	153	158
5.5	218	224	230	433	127	139	144
6	200	206	210	397	116	127	132
6.5	184	190	194	366	107	117	122
7	171	176	180	340	100	109	113
7.5	168	165	168	318	93	102	106
8	150	154	157	298	87	95	99
8.5	141	145	148	280	82	90	93
9	133	137	140	265	77	85	88
9.5	126	130	133	251	73	80	83
10	120	124	126	238	70	76	79
10.5	114	118	120	227	66	73	75
11	109	112	114	217	63	69	72
11.5	104	107	109	207	61	66	69
12	100	103	105	199		64	
12.5	96	99	101	191			
13	92	95	97	183			
13.5	89	91	93	176			
14	86	88	90	170			
14.5	83	85	87	164			
15	80	82	84	159			
15.5	77	80	81	154			
16	75	77	79	149			
16.5	73	75	76	144			
17	70	73	74	140			
17.5	68	71	72	136			
18	67	69	70	132			
18.5		68		128			
19		65		125			
19.5		63		122			
20		62		119			

413

Time in half-minute intervals	Reading Selections (listed by number)					
				PART 6		
	22	23	24	25	26	27
1	800	1775	2008	497	803	1949
1.5	533	1183	1339	331	535	1299
2	400	888	1004	249	402	975
2.5	320	710	803	199	321	780
3	267	592	669	166	268	650
3.5	229	507	574	142	229	557
4	200	444	502	124	201	487
4.5	178	394	446	110	178	433
5	160	355	402	99	161	390
5.5	145	323	365	90	146	354
6	133	296	335	83	134	325
6.5	123	273	309	76	124	300
7	114	253	287	71	115	278
7.5	107	237	267	66	107	260
8	100	222	251		100	244
8.5	94	209	236		94	229
9	89	197	223		89	217
9.5	84	187	211		85	205
10	80	176	200		80	195
10.5	76	169	191		76	186
11	73	161	183		73	177
11.5	70	154	175		70	169
12	67	148	167		67	162
12.5		142	161		64	156
13		137	154			150
13.5		131	149			144
14		127	143			139
14.5		122	138			134
15		118	134			130
15.5		115	130			126
16		111	125			122
16.5		108	122			118
17		104	118			115
17.5		101	115			111
18		99	112			108
18.5		96	109			105
19		93	106			103
19.5		91	103			100
20		89	100			97
20.5			98			95
21			96			93
21.5			93			91
22			91			89
22.5			89			87
23			87			85
23.5			85			83
24			84			81
24.5			82			80
25			80			78

Time in half-minute intervals	Reading Selections (listed by number)				
	28	*29*	*continued*	*28*	*29*
1	2646	1075	**16**	165	67
1.5	1764	717	**16.5**	160	65
2	1323	538	**17**	156	63
2.5	1058	430	**17.5**	151	61
3	882	358	**18**	147	60
3.5	756	307	**18.5**	143	
4	662	269	**19**	139	
4.5	588	239	**19.5**	136	
5	529	215	**20**	132	
5.5	481	196	**20.5**	129	
6	441	179	**21**	126	
6.5	407	165	**21.5**	123	
7	378	154	**22**	120	
7.5	353	143	**22.5**	118	
8	331	134	**23**	115	
8.5	311	127	**23.5**	113	
9	294	119	**24**	110	
9.5	279	113	**24.5**	108	
10	265	108	**25**	106	
10.5	252	102	**25.5**	103	
11	241	98	**26**	102	
11.5	230	94	**26.5**	100	
12	221	90	**27**	98	
12.5	212	86	**27.5**	96	
13	204	83	**28**	95	
13.5	196	80			
14	189	77	**28.5**	93	
14.5	182	74	**29**	91	
15	176	72	**29.5**	90	
15.5	171	69	**30**	88	

(continued at upper right)

Reading Rate Graph*

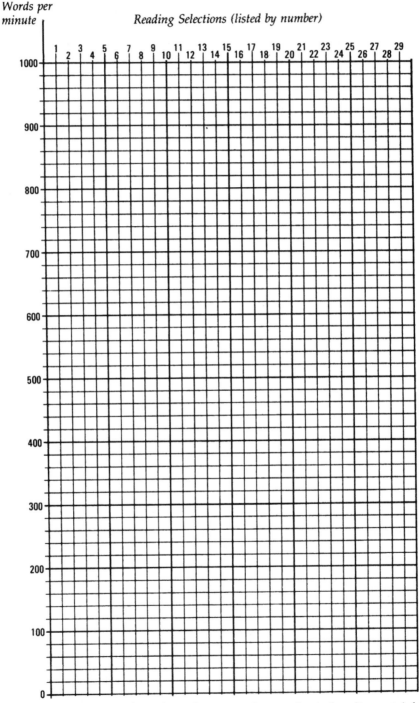

Words per minute

Reading Selections (listed by number)

*Put a dot at the number of words you read per minute (reading rate) for
each reading selection. Use pages 411–415 to compute your rate. Connect
the dots with a line to see your progress.

Appendix 2

Guide to Dictionary Use*

With a good dictionary you can do much more than check the meanings or spellings of words. The Fourth Edition of *Webster's New World College Dictionary,* the dictionary featured in *Structured Reading,* is an example of a very good dictionary. The entries are clearly written, and they offer many resources of particular interest to students. This Guide to Dictionary Use can help you understand the basic features of the entries so that you can use them fully. For more details, consult the explanatory material in the front and back sections of the dictionary itself.

Main Entry Word

The technical term for each word included in the dictionary is **main entry word.** When you look up a word, the list of main entry words is what you consult. Listed alphabetically, they stand out because they are set in dark print (called *boldface*). If more than one spelling is given for a main entry word, the first spelling shown is the one more widely used. **Dictionary entry** is the technical term for the paragraph of information given for a main entry word. This textbook contains **294** entries from the Fourth Edition of *Webster's New World College Dictionary.*

Definitions

If a word has more than one meaning, its various **definitions** are listed in numerical order. The original meaning of the word (which is sometimes—but not always—outdated) comes first. The most recent meaning of the word appears last. Sometimes added information is given at the end of the entry, after the most recent meaning. You can tell this is happening because labels precede such information. The labels are explained here in the sections "Parts of Speech Labels," "Usage Labels," and "Field of Study Labels." For example, in the entry for *siren* (used with Selection 29 in this textbook) definition 3 gives the most recent general meaning. The first definition gives a special meaning, as the label *Gr.&Rom.Myth.* indicates.

*Based on "Guide to the Use of the Dictionary," *Webster's New World College Dictionary*, Fourth Edition.

si·ren (sī′rən) *n.* ⟦ME *syrene* < OFr < LL *Sirena*, for L *Siren* < Gr *Seirēn* < ? *seira*, cord, rope (hence, orig. ? one who snares, entangles) < IE base **twer-*, to grasp⟧ **1** *Gr. & Rom. Myth.* any of several sea nymphs, represented as part bird and part woman, who lure sailors to their death on rocky coasts by seductive singing **2** a woman who uses her sexual attractiveness to entice or allure men; a woman who is considered seductive **3** *a*) an acoustical device in which steam or air is driven against a rotating, perforated disk so as to produce sound; specif., such a device producing a loud, often wailing sound, used esp. as a warning signal *b*) an electronic device that produces a similar sound **4** any of a family (Sirenidae) of slender, eel-shaped salamanders without hind legs; esp., the mud eel

To decide which meaning of a word fits your situation, review the context in which the word is being used. The context can tell you whether an older or recent meaning of a word applies. Ways to figure out a word's meaning from its context are discussed in this textbook on pages 18–24.

Americanisms

An open star (☆) in front of a word tells you that the word is an **Americanism.** This means that the word has its origins in the United States.

☆**avo·cado** (av′ə kä′dō, ä′və-) *n., pl.* **--dos** ⟦altered (infl. by earlier Sp *avocado*, now *abogado*, advocate) < MexSp *aguacate* < Nahuatl *a:wakaλ*, avocado, lit., testicle; so named from its shape⟧ **1** a widespread, thick-skinned, pear-shaped tropical fruit, yellowish green to purplish black, with a single large seed and yellow, buttery flesh, used in salads; alligator pear **2** the tree (*Persea americana*) of the laurel family on which it grows **3** a yellowish-green color

AVOCADO

Syllabification

For pronunciation and writing purposes, words can be divided into syllables, unless a word has a single vowel sound, such as *kiss.* Each syllable represents a single vowel sound and usually its adjacent consonants. **Syllabification,** also called **word division,** becomes important for writers when space runs out at the end of a line and a word has to be carried over onto the next line. Words can be divided only at breaks for syllables.

In *Webster's New World College Dictionary,* the parts of boldface entry words are separated by a heavy centered period [•]. The heavy centered period indicates one or more places where a word can be acceptably divided at the end of a line. The entry for *proliferate* (used with Selection 23 in this book) illustrates the heavily centered period for word division.

pro·lif·er·ate (prō lif′ə rāt′, prə-) *vt.* **--at′ed, --at′·ing** ⟦back-form. < *proliferation* < Fr *prolifération* < *prolifère*, PROLIFEROUS + -ATION⟧ **1** to reproduce (new parts) in quick succession **2** to produce or create in profusion —*vi.* **1** to grow by multiplying new parts, as by budding, in quick succession **2** to multiply rapidly; increase profusely —**pro·lif′·era′·tion** *n.*

Pronunciation

The symbols in parentheses immediately following the main entry word show **pronunciation.** You can figure out the sound indicated by each symbol by consulting a dictionary's key to pronunciation. A "Key to Pronunciation" from *Webster's New World College Dictionary* is shown here. A more complete "Guide to Pronunciation" appears on pp. xxii–xxiv of this dictionary. To get used to the key, practice first with entries for words familiar to you. Then once you are comfortable with the key, practice with entries for words that are new to you. You can practice with the sample entries in this guide and with the entries with each selection in this textbook.

PRONUNCIATION KEY

Symbol	Key Words	Symbol	Key Words
a	asp, fat, parrot	b	bed, fable, dub, ebb
ā	ape, date, play, break, fail	d	dip, beadle, had, dodder
ä	ah, car, father, cot	f	fall, after, off, phone
		g	get, haggle, dog
e	elf, ten, berry	h	he, ahead, hotel
ē	even, meet, money, flea, grieve	j	joy, agile, badge
		k	kill, tackle, bake, coat, quick
i	is, hit, mirror	l	let, yellow, ball
ī	ice, bite, high, sky	m	met, camel, trim, summer
		n	not, flannel, ton
ō	open, tone, go, boat	p	put, apple, tap
ô	all, horn, law, oar	r	red, port, dear, purr
ᴏᴏ	look, pull, moor, wolf	s	sell, castle, pass, nice
o͞o	ooze, tool, crew, rule	t	top, cattle, hat
yo͞o	use, cute, few	v	vat, hovel, have
yᴏᴏ	cure, globule	w	will, always, swear, quick
oi	oil, point, toy	y	yet, onion, yard
ou	out, crowd, plow	z	zebra, dazzle, haze, rise
u	up, cut, color, flood	ch	chin, catcher, arch, nature
ʉr	urn, fur, deter, irk	sh	she, cushion, dash, machine
		th	thin, nothing, truth
ə	a in ago	*th*	then, father, lathe
	e in agent	zh	azure, leisure, beige
	i in sanity	ŋ	ring, anger, drink
	o in comply	ʼ	[indicates that a following l
	u in focus		or n is a syllabic consonant,
ər	perhaps, murder		as in *cattle* (kat″l), *Latin*
			(lat″n); see full explanation
			on p. xiii]

Parts of Speech Labels

The first **part of speech** of a word is given after the pronunciation information in an entry. Parts of speech are abbreviated in the dictionary. They are shown in dark italic print. Here are major abbreviations and their meanings.

n.	noun
n. pl.	plural noun
vt.	transitive verb

419

vi.	intransitive verb
v. aux.	auxiliary verb
adj.	adjective
adv.	adverb
prep.	preposition
conj.	conjunction
pron.	pronoun
interj.	interjection

Some words are used as more than one part of speech. If you are unsure which part of speech applies to the word in the context you are dealing with, look at all the definitions in an entry to see what works for your context. To help you work with context, use the information about using context to figure out a word's meaning, discussed in this textbook on pages 18–24.

The entry for *surfaced* (used with Selection 9 in this textbook) illustrates that one word can have multiple meanings. The meanings differ as to the part of speech (noun, verb) and within a part of speech.

> **sur·face** (sur′fis) *n.* ⟦Fr < *sur-* (see SUR-¹) + *face*, FACE, based on L *superficies*⟧ **1** *a)* the outer face, or exterior, of an object *b)* any of the faces of a solid *c)* the area or extent of such a face **2** superficial features, as of a personality; outward appearance **3** AIRFOIL **4** *Geom.* an extent or magnitude having length and breadth, but no thickness —*adj.* **1** of, on, or at the surface **2** intended to function or be carried on land or sea, rather than in the air or under water [*surface* forces, *surface* mail] **3** merely apparent; external; superficial —*vt.* **··faced, ··fac·ing 1** to treat the surface of, esp. so as to make smooth or level **2** to give a surface to, as in paving **3** to bring to the surface; esp., to bring (a submarine) to the surface of the water —*vi.* **1** to work at or near the surface, as in mining **2** to rise to the surface of the water **3** to become known, esp. after being concealed —**sur′·facer** *n.*

Inflected Forms

The form of a word when it becomes plural or a participle or when it changes its tense is called its **inflected form.** Information about inflected forms comes after the part of speech label. Inflected forms are shown in small dark print. Information for *heresy* (used with Selection 15 in this textbook) illustrates the plural noun form of the word; information for *dispel* (used with Selection 11 in this textbook) illustrates letter doubling when -*ed* is added and when -*ing* is added.

> **her·esy** (her′ə sē) *n., pl.* **-sies** ⟦ME *heresie* < OFr < L *haeresis*, school of thought, sect, in LL(Ec), heresy < Gr *hairesis*, a taking, selection, school, sect, in LGr(Ec), heresy < *hairein*, to take⟧ **1** *a)* a religious belief opposed to the orthodox doctrines of a church; esp., such a belief specifically denounced by the church *b)* the rejection of a belief that is a part of church dogma **2** any opinion (in philosophy, politics, etc.) opposed to official or established views or doctrines **3** the holding of any such belief or opinion

> **dis·pel** (di spel′) *vt.* **··pelled′, ··pel′·ling** ⟦ME *dispellen* < L *dispellere* < *dis-*, apart + *pellere*, to drive: see FELT⟧ to scatter and drive away; cause to vanish; disperse —*SYN.* SCATTER

Word History

For most main entry words, the **word history,** known as **etymology,** is given in brackets after the main entry word, its pronunciation, and any inflected forms. Abbreviations and symbols present information and origins, and words from languages other than English appear in italics. Etymology often suggests a word's flavor. The sample dictionary entries in this guide use these frequently used symbols and abbreviations.

<	derived from
+	plus
Fr	French (MFr = Middle French; OFr = Old French)
Gr	classical Greek
IE	Indo-European
ME	Middle English
L	Latin (LL = Late Latin; VL = Vulgar Latin)
OE	Old English

Usage Labels

The customary way words are used—their **usage**—depends on many factors. The two major influences are the formality of occasion on which the word is used and the location where the word is used. Whenever a word or sense may not be appropriate for formal writing, the dictionary entry gives usage information. Usage labels are shown in brackets following a main entry word or one of its numbered definitions. Here are the most frequently seen usage labels and their meanings.

[Brit.]	*British:* commonly accepted meaning in British English
[Informal]	*informal:* used in conversation and informal writing
[Dial.]	*dialect:* used in certain geographical areas of the United States
[Obs.]	*obsolete:* no longer in use
[Old Poet.]	*poetic:* used chiefly in earlier poetry or for poetic meaning
[Slang]	*slang:* highly informal and generally considered not standard; acceptable when used for effect or mood to convey a highly informal context

The entry for *rumpus* (used with Selection 24 in this textbook) indicates that it has an informal sense. The entry for *deadeye* (used with Selection 22 in this textbook) says that one of its meanings (definition 2) is slang.

rum·pus (rum′pəs) *n.* ⟦< ?⟧ [Informal] an uproar or commotion

dead·eye (-ī′) *n.* **1** a round, flat block of wood with three holes in it for a lanyard, used in pairs on a sailing ship to hold the shrouds and stays taut **2** [Slang] an accurate marksman

Field of Study Labels

Many words have special meanings when used in the context of various **fields of study.** For example, the entry for *derivative* (used in Selection 22 of this textbook) starts with its usual meanings as an adjective and then as a noun. Then come abbreviated labels that indicate special meanings from various fields of study: chemistry, linguistics, and math.

de·riva·tive (də riv′ə tiv) *adj.* ⟦ME *derivatif* < LL *derivativus* < L *derivatus*, pp. of *derivare*: see fol.⟧ **1** derived **2** using or taken from other sources; not original **3** of derivation —*n.* **1** something derived **2** *Chem.* a substance derived from, or of such composition and properties that it may be considered as derived from, another substance by chemical change, esp. by the substitution of one or more elements or radicals **3** *Finance* a contract, as an option or futures contract, whose value depends on the value of the securities, commodities, etc. that form the basis of the contract **4** *Linguis.* a word formed from another or others by derivation **5** *Math.* the limiting value of a rate of change of a function with respect to a variable; the instantaneous rate of change, or slope, of a function (Ex.: the derivative of y with respect to x, often written dy/dx, is 3 when $y = 3x$) —**de·riv′a·tively** *adv.*

Synonyms

When a word has **synonyms** whose meanings may or may not be interchanged with it, the dictionary entry ends with the symbol **SYN.** followed by a word in small capital letters. When you look up that word, you will find at the end of its entry a **synonymy**—a list of synonyms with definitions that explain slight differences in meaning, among the words listed. The synonymy is signaled by the symbol *SYN.-*. To decide which synonym fits your situation, review the context in which the word appears and match it to the definitions in the synonymy. The entry for *intrude* (used with Selection 10 in this textbook) offers a synonymy of three words.

in·trude (in trōōd′) *vt.* **-·trud′ed, -·trud′·ing** ⟦L *intrudere* < *in-*, in + *trudere*, to thrust, push: see THREAT⟧ **1** to push or force (something in or upon) **2** to force (oneself or one's thoughts) upon others without being asked or welcomed **3** *Geol.* to force (liquid magma, etc.) into or between solid rocks —*vi.* to intrude oneself —**in·trud′er** *n.*

The following three pages show a sample dictionary page, with labels for your reference.

Cerritos / cevitamic acid   230

Cer·ri·tos (se rē′tōs) [Sp, little hills] city in SW Calif.: suburb of Los Angeles: pop. 53,000 — American place name with etymology

Cerro de Pasco (ser′ō dä päs′kō) mining town in the mountains of WC Peru: alt. *c.* 14,000 ft. (4,250 m): pop. 72,000

cert 1 certificate **2** certified

cer·tain (surt″n) *adj.* [ME & OFr < VL *certanus < L certus, determined, fixed, orig. pp. of cernere, to distinguish, decide, orig., to sift, separate: see HARVEST] **1** fixed, settled, or determined **2** sure (to happen, etc.); inevitable **3** not to be doubted; unquestionable [certain evidence] **4** not failing; reliable; dependable [a certain cure] **5** controlled; unerring [his certain aim] **6** without any doubt; assured; sure; positive [certain of his innocence] **7** not named or described, though definite and perhaps known [a certain person] **8** some, but not very much; appreciable [to a certain extent] —*pron.* [with pl. v.] a certain indefinite number; certain ones (of) —*SYN.* SURE —**for certain** as a certainty; without doubt — Idiomatic phrase

cer·tain·ly (-lē) *adv.* beyond a doubt; surely

cer·tain·ty (-tē) *n.* [ME certeinte < OFr certaineté] **1** the quality, state, or fact of being certain **2** pl. **-ties** anything certain; definite act —**of a certainty** [Archaic] without a doubt; certainly

SYN.—**certainty** suggests a firm, settled belief or positiveness in the truth of something; **certitude** is sometimes distinguished from the preceding as implying an absence of objective proof, hence suggesting unassailable blind faith; **assurance** suggests confidence, but not necessarily positiveness, usually in something that is yet to happen [I have assurance of his continuing support/; **conviction** suggests a being convinced because of satisfactory reasons or proof and sometimes implies earlier doubt —*ANT.* doubt, skepticism — Synonymy

cer·tes (sur′tēz′) *adv.* [ME & OFr < VL *certas, for L certo, surely < certus: see CERTAIN] [Archaic] certainly; verily

cer·ti·fi·a·ble (surt′ə fī′ə bəl) *adj.* that can be certified —**cer′ti·fi′a·bly** (-blē) *adv.*

cer·tifi·cate (sər tif′i kit; *for v.,* -kāt′) *n.* [ME & OFr certificat < ML certificatum < LL certificatus, pp. of certificare, CERTIFY] a written or printed statement by which a fact is formally or officially certified or attested; specif., *a*) a document certifying that one has met specified requirements, as for teaching *b*) a document certifying ownership, a promise to pay, etc. —*vt.* **-cat·ed, -cat·ing** to attest or authorize by a certificate; issue a certificate to —**cer·tif′i·ca·tor** *n.* — Derived entries —**cer·tif′i·ca·to·ry** (-kə tôr′ē) *adj.* — Part-of-speech labels

certificate of deposit a certificate issued by a bank or a savings and loan association acknowledging the receipt of a specified sum of money in a special kind of time deposit drawing interest and requiring written notice for withdrawal

certificate of incorporation a legal document stating the name and purpose of a proposed corporation, the names of its incorporators, its stock structure, etc.

certificate of origin a certificate submitted by an exporter to those countries requiring it, listing goods to be imported and stating their place of origin

cer·ti·fi·ca·tion (surt′ə fi kā′shən) *n.* [Fr] **1** a certifying or being certified **2** a certified statement

cer·ti·fied (surt′ə fīd′) *adj.* **1** vouched for; guaranteed **2** having, or attested to by, a certificate — Americanism

☆certified check a check for which a bank has guaranteed payment, certifying there is enough money on deposit to cover the check

☆certified mail 1 a postal service for recording the mailing and delivery of a piece of first-class mail **2** mail recorded by this service: it is not insurable

☆certified public accountant a public accountant certified by a State examining board as having met the requirements of State law

Inflected forms —

cer·ti·fy (surt'ə fī') *vt.* **-fied', -fy'ing** [ME *certifien* < OFr *certifier* < LL *certificare* < L *certus*, CERTAIN + -FY] **1** to declare (a thing) true, accurate, certain, etc. by formal statement, often in writing; verify; attest **2** to declare officially insane and committable to a mental institution ☆**3** to guarantee the quality or worth of (a check, document, etc.); vouch for **4** to issue a certificate or license to **5** [Archaic] to assure; make certain —*vi.* to testify (*to*) —*SYN.* APPROVE —**cer'ti·fi'er** *n.*

Usage label —

cer·ti·o·ra·ri (sur'shē ə rer'ē) *n.* [ME < LL, lit., to be made more certain: a word in the writ] *Law* a discretionary writ from a higher court to a lower one, or to a board or official with some judicial power, requesting the record of a case for review

Field label —

cer·ti·tude (sur'tə tōōd', -tyōōd') *n.* [OFr < LL(Ec) *certitudo* < L *certus*, CERTAIN] **1** a feeling of absolute sureness or conviction **2** sureness; inevitability —*SYN.* CERTAINTY

ce·ru·le·an (sə rōō'lē ən) *adj.* [L *caeruleus*; prob. < *caelulum*, dim. of *caelum*, heaven: for IE base see CESIUM] sky-blue; azure

ce·ru·men (sə rōō'mən) *n.* [< L *cera*, wax; sp. infl. by ALBUMEN] EARWAX —**ce·ru'mi·nous** (-mə nəs) *adj.*

ce·ruse (sir'ōōs', sə rōōs') *n.* [OFr < L *cerussa* < ? Gr *kēroessa*, waxlike < *kēros*, wax] **1** WHITE LEAD **2** a former cosmetic containing white lead

ce·rus·site (sir'ə sīt', sə rus'īt') *n.* [< L *cerussa* (see prec.) + -ITE¹] native lead carbonate, PbCO₃, widely distributed in crystalline or massive form

Biographical entry —

Cer·van·tes (Sa·a·ve·dra) (ther vän'tes sä'ä ved'rä; *E* sər van'tēz'), **Mi·guel de** (mē gel' *the*) 1547-1616; Sp. novelist, poet, & playwright; author of *Don Quixote*

cer·ve·lat (ser və lä', -lät') *n.* [Fr] a dry, smoked sausage of beef and pork Also sp. **cer·ve·las'** (-lä')

cer·vi·cal (sur'vi kəl) *adj.* [< L *cervix* (gen. *cervicis*), the neck + -AL] *Anat.* of the neck or cervix

cer·vi·ces (sər vī'sēz', sur'və-) *n.* alt. pl. of CERVIX

cer·vi·ci·tis (sur'və sīt'is) *n.* [see -ITIS] inflammation of the cervix of the uterus

cer·vi·co- (sur'vi kō', -kə) [< L *cervix*, neck] *combining form* cervical [*cervicitis*] Also, before a vowel, **cer'vic-**

cer·vid (sur'vid') *adj.* [< ModL *Cervidae*, name of the family (< L *cervus*, stag, deer < IE *kerewos*, horned, a horned animal < base *ker-*, HORN) + -ID] of the deer family

Cer·vin (môn ser van'), **Mont** Fr. name of the MATTERHORN

Main entry word —

cer·vine (sur'vīn', -vin) *adj.* [L *cervinus* < *cervus*: see CERVID] of or like a deer

cer·vix (sur'viks) *n., pl.* **cer·vi·ces** (sər vī'sēz', sur'və-) or **-vix·es** [L, the neck] **1** the neck, esp. the back of the neck **2** a necklike part, as of the uterus or urinary bladder

Ce·sar·e·an or **Ce·sar·i·an** (sə zer'ē ən) *adj., n.* CAESAREAN

Etymology —

ce·si·um (sē'zē əm) *n.* [ModL, orig. neut. of L *caesius*, bluish-gray (< IE base *(s)kai-*, bright > -HOOD): so named (1860) by Robert Wilhelm BUNSEN because of the blue line seen in the spectroscope] a soft, silver-white, ductile, metallic chemical element, the most electropositive of all the elements: it ignites in air, reacts vigorously with water, and is used in photoelectric cells: symbol, Cs; at. wt., 132.905; at. no., 55; sp. gr., 1.892; melt. pt., 28.64°C; boil. pt., 670°C: a radioactive isotope (**cesium-137**) with a half-life of 30.17 years is a fission product and is used in cancer research, radiation therapy, etc.

Čes·ké Bu·de·jo·vi·ce (ches'ke bōō'de yô'vit sə) city in SW Czechoslovakia, on the Vltava River: pop. 93,000

Čes·ko·slo·ven·sko (ches'kô slô ven'skô) *Czech name of* CZECHOSLOVAKIA

ces·pi·tose (ses'pə tōs') *adj.* [ModL < L *caespes*, turf, grassy field + -OSE²] growing in dense, matlike clumps without creeping stems, as moss, grass, etc.

cess (ses) *n.* [prob. < ASSESS] in Ireland, an assessment; tax: now used only in **bad cess to** bad luck to

ces·sa·tion (se sā'shən) *n.* [L *cessatio* < pp. of *cessare*, CEASE] a ceasing. or stopping, either forever or for some time —— Pronunciation

ces·sion (sesh'ən) *n.* [OFr < L *cessio* < *cessus*, pp. of *cedere*, to yield: see CEDE] a ceding or giving up (of rights, property, territory, etc.) to another

ces·sion·ar·y (sesh'ə ner'ē) *n., pl.* **-ar·ies** *Law* ASSIGNEE

cess·pit (ses'pit') *n.* [< fol. + PIT²] a pit for garbage, excrement, etc.

cess·pool (-pōōl') *n.* [< ? It *cesso*, privy < L *secessus*, place of retirement (in LL, privy, drain): see SECEDE] **1** a deep hole or pit in the ground, usually covered, to receive drainage or sewage from the sinks, toilets, etc. of a house **2** a center of moral filth and corruption —— Definitions

ces·ta (ses'tə) *n.* [Sp, basket < L *cista*: see CHEST] in jai alai, the narrow, curved, basketlike racket strapped to the forearm, in which the ball is caught and hurled against a wall

c'est la vie (se lä vē') [Fr] that's life; such is life

ces·tode (ses'tōd') *n.* [CEST(US)¹ + -ODE²] any of a class (Cestoda) of parasitic flatworms, with a ribbonlike body and no intestinal canal; tapeworm —*adj.* of such a worm —— Scientific name

ces·toid (-toid') *adj.* ribbonlike, as a tapeworm

ces·tus¹ (-təs) *n.* [L < Gr *kestos*, a girdle; akin to *kentein*, to stitch: see CENTER] in ancient times, a woman's belt or girdle

ces·tus² (-təs) *n.* [L *caestus* < *caedere*, to strike, cut down: see -CIDE] a contrivance of leather straps, often weighted with metal, worn on the hand by boxers in ancient Rome

ce·su·ra (si zyoor'ə, -zhoor'ə) *n., pl.* **-ras** or **-rae** (-ē) CAESURA

CETA Comprehensive Employment and Training Act

ce·ta·cean (sə tā'shən) *n.* [< ModL < L *cetus*, large sea animal, whale < Gr *kētos* + -ACE(A) + -AN] in some systems of classification, any of an order (Cetacea) of nearly hairless, fishlike water mammals, lacking external hind limbs, but having paddlelike forelimbs, including whales, porpoises, and dolphins —*adj.* of the cetaceans Also **ce·ta'ceous** (-shəs)

ce·tane (sē'tān') *n.* [< L *cetus* (see prec.) + -ANE] a colorless, liquid alkane, $C_{16}H_{34}$, found in petroleum and, sometimes, in vegetable matter, and used to test fuel oils

cetane number a number that increases with higher quality, representing the ignition properties of diesel engine fuel oils: it is determined by the percentage of cetane that must be mixed with a standard liquid to match the fuel oil's performance in a standard test engine: see OCTANE NUMBER —— Foreign phrase

ce·te·ris pa·ri·bus (set'ər is par'ə bəs) [L, other things being equal] all else remaining the same

ce·tol·o·gy (sə täl'ə jē) *n.* [< L *cetus*, whale (see CETACEAN) + -OLOGY] the branch of zoology that deals with whales —**ce·to·log·i·cal** (sēt'ə läj'i kəl) *adj.* —**ce·tol'o·gist** *n.*

Ce·tus (sēt'əs) [L, whale] an equatorial constellation near Pisces

Ceu·ta (syoot'ə; *Sp* thā'ōō tä') Spanish seaport in NW Africa, opposite Gibraltar: an enclave in Morocco: pop. 71,000

Cé·vennes (sā ven') mountain range in S France, west of the Rhone: highest peak, 5,755 ft. (1,754 m) —— Cross-reference

ce·vi·che (sə vē'chä', -chē') *n.* [Sp SEVICHE]

ce·vi·tam·ic acid (sē'vī tam'ik, -vi-) [< C + VITAM(IN) + -IC] ASCORBIC ACID

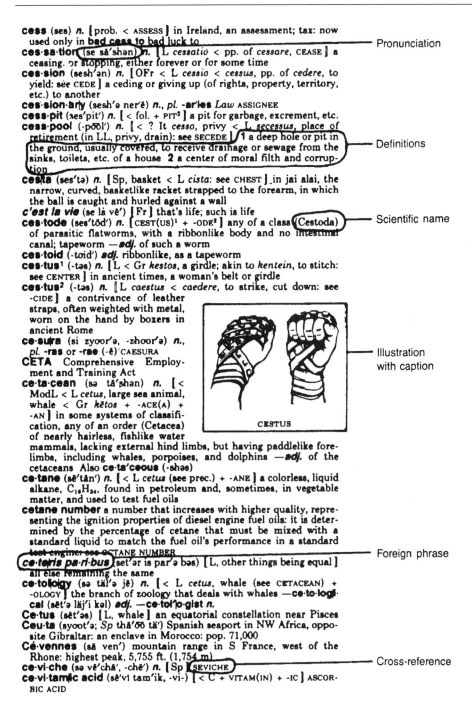

CESTUS —— Illustration with caption

Credits

Vocabulary Index

General Index

Instructor's Guide

The major features of this Instructor's Guide include the following:

- "Readability" offers a discussion of what a readability index is and the limitations that operate with all readability indexes. Also, the cloze procedure is described as an alternative way for teachers to assess the suitability of reading material. Finally, a complete list of readability statistics and related profile data is presented for each of the twenty-nine reading selections in the text.
- "Reading Selections Listed by Types and Themes" helps instructors match readings to student interest and also serves as an aid to help students experience different readings of the same type: narration, exposition, argumentation, and textbook extracts.
- "How to Use *Structured Reading* in a Variety of Instructional Settings" suggests the effective use of the text in the classroom, in labs, and for self-instruction.
- "Teaching Strategies for *Structured Reading*" discusses specific instructional techniques for using the text. These expand the ideas presented to the student in the text's opening chapters, Part One, Skills for Reading. Included are teaching approaches for reading speed; vocabulary study; predicting; the comprehension skills of reading on, between, and beyond the lines; and helping students make informed opinions about what they read.

We have continued to find that research in the teaching of reading to adults demonstrates that the reading skills treated in depth in *Structured Reading* are precisely those that are most effective in helping students improve their reading skills. Studies indicate, among other findings, that

- Grade point averages rise when students are in reading courses that emphasize finding main ideas, recognizing and interpreting inferences, and differentiating fact from opinion.
- Students improve in reading when they assess their own difficulties and chart their progress.
- Students improve when reading skills are applied to material in content areas.

Structured Reading and the material in this Instructor's Guide incorporate the findings of these studies in its teaching strategies and reading content.

Capable and confident readers are one of our nation's best resources. *Structured Reading* is intended to help prepare students to become effective, literate participants in our nation's future. This Instructor's Guide strives to help teachers use the text as effectively and easily as possible. We hope the added resources for this Seventh Edition prove useful and stimulating.

READABILITY

To help instructors predict students' ability to read the selections in this text, we provide readability indexes later in this section. The indexes are based on the fact that certain features of any reading selection can be counted. These features include the average number of words per sentence, syllables per word, and sentences per a given block of words. These counts can be combined in a variety of ways to yield a readability index. Many readability indexes are available, and although there is some correlation among the indexes, their findings vary.

In addition to variations among indexes, all readability indexes have important limitations. Many aspects of a reading selection cannot be quantified. Content load, complexity of thought, humor, and irony cannot be reduced to numbers. Thus, for example, although the selection "The Chaser," with its frequent one and two syllable words, has a Fry readability index equivalent to a 5.0, its irony and dialogue make the material much too difficult for a student finishing fifth grade.

A further limitation of readability indexes derives from their necessary overemphasis on product rather than process. Reading is the result of a powerful interaction between the written page, the eye, and the brain. Thus, reading ability is affected by the prior knowledge that a reader brings to a given reading selection, as well as other factors. The classic source for teachers wanting to learn more about this psycholinguistic analysis of the reading process is Frank Smith's *Understanding Reading* (third edition, 1982: Holt, Rinehart and Winston), available in many libraries.

THE CLOZE PROCEDURE

An alternative way for teachers to assess the suitability of reading material—this time for individual students—is the cloze procedure. The cloze procedure is based on the theory that human beings dislike fragmentation and tend to bring unity and wholeness to anything that seems fragmented. In the reading process, this same idea operates. When words are omitted from a sentence, readers try to supply them to make sense out of the passage. This ability to logically complete the author's idea is an indication of a student's reading ability.

To prepare cloze materials, the teacher types a section of a reading as follows: (1) type the first and last sentence; (2) beginning with the second sentence, delete every fifth word and indicate the deletion with a blank line, which should be a standard length no matter how long the word that is being deleted;

(3) do not stop until you have at least fifty blanks—which means a passage of about 250 words. Then the student reads the passage aloud and supplies the missing words or writes them in the blanks. For testing purposes, cloze procedures demand that the exact word be supplied. For teaching purposes, however, a suitable synonym is acceptable. If a student can supply words for 65 percent of the blanks, that student can work independently with the material. If the student can give words for 41 percent to 64 percent of the blanks, the material is at a suitable instructional level. If the student can provide words for only 40 percent or less of the blanks, that student will find the material frustrating.

THE STATISTICS

With this perspective about readability indexes and with the knowledge that there are alternative individualized methods of determining suitability of materials, instructors can use the data that follow as *one* measure of the difficulty level of the reading selections in *Structured Reading*. The readabilities for the Dale Index were calculated using a computer program, *Readability Calculations,* by Michael Schuyler. The readability for the Flesch Reading Ease Index was calculated by using Microsoft Word. From the computer-generated sentence/syllable information, the Fry Index was determined using the *Fry Readability Scale* (Extended).

DEFINITIONS OF THE FRY, DALE, AND FLESCH INDEXES

Each test is a sampling of running words, which is analyzed according to frequency, complexity, and sentence length. The Fry Index is more efficient to use at the primary level, whereas the Dale and Flesch indexes rank higher readability levels because of their complexity. Independently, these reading indexes measure readability through distinct methods and formulas. In total, these three reading indexes depend on the 100-word count procedure for readability, yet their formulas are quite distinct. In essence, each relies on two factors: word difficulty and sentence length and complexity.

HOW TO USE THE FRY INDEX

Select three 100-word passages from the beginning, middle, and end of a book. Skip proper nouns. Now count the total number of sentences in each word passage (estimating to the nearest tenth of a sentence). Average these three numbers by adding them and dividing by three. Next, count the total number of syllables in each 100 word sample. There is a syllable for each vowel sound and word endings such as T, ED, EL, or LE. For convenience, count every syllable over one in each word and add 100. Average the total number of syllables for the three samples. Plot on the Fry Readability Estimate the average number of sentences and the average number of syllables per 100 words. Perpendicular lines mark off approximate grade-level areas.

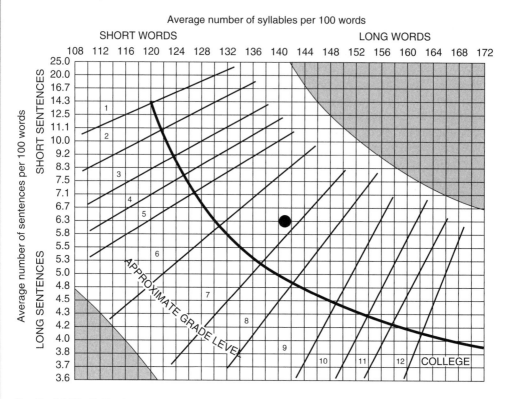

Average number of syllables per 100 words

Fry Readability Estimate
by Edward Fry, Rutgers University Reading Center, New Brunswick, NJ 08904

HOW TO USE THE DALE-CHALL FORMULA (FOR GRADES 4–16)

Dale-Chall involves mathematical computations partly validated by teachers' and librarians' judgments of material difficulty, which is arbitrary. This index calls for 100-word counts, sentence complexity, and vocabulary. The vocabulary portion relies on a set list of 3,000 words and words not on the list that are declared unfamiliar; it is this percentage of "unfamiliar" words that determines the difficulty level of the passage. Dale-Chall uses sentence length as the simplest measure of grammatical complexity. Grammatical studies of difficulty level (counting prepositional phrases, adverbial clauses, and other various grammatical matters) rank higher because of their complexity.

HOW TO USE FLESCH

There are two formulas for calculating Flesch: Formula A and Formula B. For our purposes, we will discuss only Formula A. Formula A assesses R.E.: "reading ease." Take 3–5 samples from a book; these may be taken from every third paragraph or every other page. Count 100 words. Count contractions and hyphenated words as one and count as words numbers or letters separated by a space. Compute the number of syllables per 100 words and then figure the average sentence length within this sample. Now divide the number of words in the sentences by the number of sentences.

The "reading ease" score puts your sample on a scale between 0 (which means practically unreadable) to 100 (which is supposedly easy for any literate person).

Readability Statistics

	Average Sentence Length	*Average Syllables per Word*	*Flesch Reading Ease Index*	*Dale Index*	*Fry Index (Hand Calculated)*
PART 2					
1. A Real Loss	22.2	1.2	81.3	7.22	7
2. Tyranny of Weakness	N/A	1.3	64.4	6.6	7
3. *Don't Sell Your Ambitions Short	N/A	N/A	82	5.7	6
4. Darkness at Noon	N/A	1.4	74.8	7.76	8
5. *To Catch a Thief	N/A	N/A	68	6.6	8
6. *Seoul Searching	N/A	N/A	92	6.8	2
AVERAGES					6.3
PART 3					
7. Summer	16.6	1.5	74.6	8.07	7
8. *Brains the Ultimate Sex Appeal	N/A	N/A	61	7.9	10
9. The Girl with the Large Eyes	20.8	1.2	81.4	7.05	7
10. Flour Children	N/A	1.5	85.1	7.1	7
11. The Magic Words Are "Will You Help Me?"	N/A	N/A	81.1	7.2	7
12. *Family and Friends Share Pain and Questions	N/A	N/A	87	6.1	5
AVERAGES					7.2
PART 4					
13. How to Stay Alive	12.0	1.5	64	7.73	7
14. Genes and Behavior: A Twin Legacy	17.5	1.5	48.4	8.13	9
15. Escaping the Daily Grind for Life as a House Father	N/A	1.3	68.0	6.3	8
16. Forty Acres and a Holiday	N/A	N/A	62.6	8	9
17. My Mother's Blue Bowl	N/A	N/A	70.8	6.6	6
18. From *In Search of Bernabé*	N/A	N/A	68.77	6.1	6.6
AVERAGES					7.6

Readability Statistics (continued)

	Average Sentence Length	Average Syllables per Word	Flesch Reading Ease Index	Dale Index	Fry Index (Hand Calculated)
PART 5					
19. Restored to the Sea	N/A	1.4	57.1	8.0	8
20. Death Penalty Victims	N/A	N/A	60.91	7.4	10
21. Should a Wife Keep Her Name?	15.0	1.5	69.6	8.22	8
22. I Became Her Target	15.1	1.4	73.4	7.78	9
23. Mute in an English-Only World	N/A	N/A	62.99	6.4	8.3
24. Out of Their Element	N/A	N/A	57.5	6.7	8
AVERAGES					8.5
PART 6					
25. * They Sniff Out Trouble	N/A	N/A	59	9.2	10
26. She Made Her Dream Come True	N/A	N/A	71.6	6.6	9
27. Long-Term Memory	N/A	N/A	32.2	9.7	13
28. A Personal Stress Survival Guide	N/A	N/A	47.8	8.3	9
29. The Chaser	N/A	1.3	73.9	6.7	5
AVERAGES					9.2

READING LEVELS: ACTIVITY PASSAGES, CHS. 7–13, PART ONE

Chapter 7: What Are "Central Theme" and "Main Ideas"?

- *Activity K:* "Dealing with Unhappy and Difficult Customers" from *Investing for Dummies:* 9.0
- *Activity L:* From *Direct from Dell,* by Michael Dell with Catherine Friedman: 9.8
- *Activity M:* From *Catfish and Mandala,* by Andrew X. Pham: 4
- *Activity N:* From *Fish for All Seasons,* by Kitty Crider: 7.9

Chapter 8: What Are "Major Details"?

- *Activity O:* From *Learn Horseback Riding in a Weekend* by Mark Gordon Watson: 6.9
- *Activity P:* From *Manchester Mammoth Book of Fascinating Information,* by Richard B. Manchester: 8.7
- *Activity Q:* From *The Cake Mix Doctor,* by Anne Byrn: 9.6
- *Activity R:* From *Careers and Occupations,* by Catherine Dubiec Holm: 10.4

Chapter 9: How Can Maps, Outlines, and Visuals Help with Reading?

- *Activity S:* Elephants 9.4
- *Activity T:* From "You Are How You Eat" by Enid Nemy 8.4

Chapter 10: What Are "Inferences"?

- *Activity V:* From *Travels with Lizbeth,* by Lars Eighner: 7.4
- *Activity W:* From *Let's Get Well,* by Adelle Davis: 8.6
- *Activity X:* From the *New Yorker,* "Saint Valentine's Day." 1949; reprinted in Josephine Ohayan, ed. *All For Love:* 8.8
- *Activity Y:* From *Computers,* 7th edition, by Larry Long and Nancy Long: 8.9

Chapter 11: What Is "Critical Reading"?

- *Activity Z:* From *Warriors Don't Cry,* by Melba Pattillo Beals: 8.2
- *Activity AA:* From *Words Still Count with Me,* by Herbert Mitgang: 8.2
- *Activity BB:* From *Hispanics,* "Top Ten Cities for Hispanics," by Diana A. Terry-Azios: 11.3
- *Activity CC:* From *Total Television,* 4th edition, by Alex McNeil: 11.3

Chapter 12: Critical Reading: What Are "The Author's Strategies"?

- *Activity DD:* From "You Are How You Eat," by Enid Nemy: 6.5
- *Activity EE:* From "Home" in *Steps in Composition,* by Lynn Quitman Troyka and Jerrold Nudelman 8.0
- *Activity FF:* From "American Schools Should Take a Lesson from Japan" in *Steps in Composition,* by Lynn Quitman Troyka and Jerrold Nudelman 10.5
- *Activity GG:* From *Baseball Anecdotes,* by Daniel Okrent and Steve Wulff 14.6

Chapter 13: Critical Reading: What Is a "Summary"?

- *Activity HH:* From "Houses to Save the Earth, " by Seth Shulman 14.6
- *Activity II:* From "In Praise of the F Word, " by Mary Sherry 11.4
- *Activity JJ:* From "A Lady's Life in the Rocky Mountains, " by Isabella L. Bird 6.8
- *Activity KK:* From "Every Kid Needs Some Manual Arts, " by William Raspberry 9.1

READING SELECTIONS LISTED BY TYPES AND THEMES

In *Structured Reading,* Seventh Edition, the reading selections are grouped into five parts, each of increasing difficulty according to their readability statistics and teacher judgments. Within each section, the selections are presented according to their length, from shortest to longest. This is done so that students can systematically develop their reading skills.

At times, however, teachers want to capture and expand on their students' interests by assigning reading selections according to their types or their related themes. This list will help such an approach. Because most of the reading selections fit into many different categories, most of the selections are listed here more than once.

Types

Narration

7 "Summer," p. 155
8 "Brains the Ultimate Sex Appeal," p. 161
9 "The Girl with the Large Eyes," p. 169
10 "Flour Children," p. 177
11 "The Magic Words Are 'Will You Help Me?'" p. 187
12 "Family and Friends Share Pain and Questions," p. 197
13 "How to Stay Alive" (satire), p. 213
15 "Escaping the Daily Grind for Life as a House Father," p. 231
17 "My Mother's Blue Bowl," p. 255
22 "I Became Her Target," p. 309
24 "Out of Their Element," p. 329
29 "The Chaser," p. 391

Exposition

1 "A Real Loss," p. 95
10 "Flour Children," p. 177
14 "Genes and Behavior: A Twin Legacy," p. 221
16 "Forty Acres and a Holiday," p. 243
19 "Restored to the Sea," p. 281
20 "Death Penalty Victims," p. 291
26 "She Made Her Dream Come True," p. 351

Argumentation

4 "Darkness at Noon," p. 121
6 "Seoul Searching," p. 141
13 "How to Stay Alive," p. 213
20 "Death Penalty Victims," p. 291
21 "Should a Wife Keep Her Name?," p. 299

Textbook Extracts

27 "Long-Term Memory" (psychology), p. 366
28 "A Personal Stress Survival Guide" (psychology), p. 375

Themes

Multicultural

6 "Seoul Searching," p. 141
9 "The Girl with the Large Eyes," p. 169
16 "Forty Acres and a Holiday," p. 243
17 "My Mother's Blue Bowl," p. 255
18 From *In Search of Bernabé*, p. 265

HOW TO USE *STRUCTURED READING* IN A VARIETY OF INSTRUCTIONAL SETTINGS

Structured Reading offers a systematized program for the development of reading skills. The book is designed to engage students through hands-on practice of skills using the strategies presented in Part One and by working with the exercises that follow each reading selection. The logical sequence of exercises that consistently follows each selection is constructed to lead students to discover insights into the reading process and into the critical thinking processes involved in reading.

Because *Structured Reading* is basically an anthology-style book, it could be misused as a workbook in which students simply read selections and complete exercises. This is not the intention of the book. *Structured Reading* is designed to engage students' thinking processes as they improve their comprehension skills by cumulative exposure to questions that delve beneath the surface.

Structured Reading can be used effectively in various types of reading programs, including those based in the classroom or lab. The following suggestions are intended to provide you with ideas for using the text in those settings.

THE CLASSROOM

Reading selections at various levels of readability and of different types and themes help make *Structured Reading* a useful resource for both large- and small-group classroom instruction. Here are some ideas for using the text in a classroom setting:

1. **Introduction of instructional strategies.** Introduce systematically each of the strategies discussed in Part One, beginning on page 1 in the text: reading speed, vocabulary, predicting, and the comprehension skills of reading on, between, and beyond the lines. Incorporate a vocabulary card system as a strand throughout the entire text. Use the "Thinking: Getting Started" ideas at the beginning of each section in the text as organizers for the skills you can present to the entire class in discussion. Encourage thorough discussion of the questions following each reading selection. Help develop evaluative skills and divergent thinking by insisting that students explain why wrong options are not correct.

2. **Teaching strategies.** Use the teaching ideas in the next section of this guide as you work with *Structured Reading*.

3. **Writing.** Incorporate writing into your reading class. Writing helps students learn by putting material into their own language. *Structured Reading* makes connections between reading and writing in two concrete ways. First, an exercise on "Critical Reading: The Author's Strategies" is included in the set of exercises that follows each of the text's reading selections. Here the focus is on the approaches that the author uses to relate information to the reader. The elements that you will focus on are audience, purpose, and tone.

Second, the "Reader's Response" exercise that follows each of the reading selections suggests topics for writing or discussion based on the subjects in the reading selection.

Reading teachers who integrate writing into their courses find that students' overall language abilities are strengthened. Students discover the relationships between the composing process and the reading process, so their skills improve more quickly. A rich compendium of practical ideas for incorporating writing into the curriculum can be found in *How to Handle the Paper Load*, published by the National Council of Teachers of English in 1979. Some basic suggestions include

a. Writing is best taught as a process. The stages of prewriting, drafting, and revising are similar to these reading steps: prereading, reading for the general content, and reviewing for clarification.

b. Reading teachers can use the process model of writing. Teachers can ask students for a prewriting think sheet instead of a finished assignment. This shows students how important prewriting is. Also, such a think sheet assignment requires the teacher only to read it, jot any added ideas to help, and return it. Correcting is not the point here.

Teachers can ask students to hand in a draft of an assignment. Because a draft is only the first written version, teachers can read the assignments and make suggestions about how the writer might further develop the content. Correcting is not the point here either. Correcting is one of the points for teachers when revised, final versions are asked for. This must be done from time to time, but not for every assignment.

c. Classroom peers can help in the revision process. Groups of three to five students can be formed for the purpose of reviewing each other's work based on a teacher-prepared guide sheet for listening and responding.

d. Grading can be focused. Focused grading means that only certain features are selected for attention. The focus can be on quality of ideas (basic premise and support given for it), or on variety of language (strong verbs, nongeneral adjectives, good metaphors), or on grammar, and so on. Instructors who feel hesitant to return a paper unless every error has been corrected can rest assured that error correction does not guarantee that students will not repeat the same mistakes. If each returned assignment contains a photocopied sheet explaining that the grading focused on a particular aspect of the writing, students will be clear about the requirements.

TEN-STEP PROCEDURE FOR CLASSROOM INSTRUCTION

1. **Preview vocabulary.** Begin the assignment with instructor-led pronunciation of vocabulary.

   Being able to pronounce words correctly is a first step in building self-confidence in the reading process. It decreases oral reading reluctance among students when called on to read. After pronunciations, students may work with definitions individually or in small groups to complete vocabulary cards and to practice word usage.

2. **Complete a five to ten-minute prereading activity.** Make predictions and/or conduct a brainstorming activity (freewriting, asking questions, or making a list) related to the selection title or to an instructor query related to the subject contents.

   Such an activity activates the mind for further discovery and reading. It serves as an advanced organizer, and more importantly, it allows students to make connections and to construct relationships. Thus, students become actively involved in the reading process by (1) establishing a purpose for reading and (2) bringing background knowledge to the forefront for better comprehension. For Selection 9, "The Girl with the Large Eyes," students are asked to brainstorm everything they can think of related to African culture.

3. **Make the assignment to read the selection and to answer the comprehension questions.** Because student reading rates vary, this works more effectively as an out-of-class assignment. Such an approach allows for reading rate flexibility among students and more quality time in the classroom.

4. **Begin class with instructor-led pronunciation of vocabulary.** Have students repeat word pronunciations several times.

   Students who experience difficulty with reading often become too preoccupied with pronunciations to the extent of losing out on the more important aspect—comprehension. By taking care of this problem on the front end, the student is freed to focus on the issue at hand.

5. **Survey the selection.** Call on volunteer(s) to conduct the survey: read (1) the title, (2) the entire first and last paragraphs, and (3) the first sentences of paragraphs in between—all as they appear in the selection.

   This is of special importance if the selection is read as a homework assignment. Surveying whets the appetite and refreshes the memory.

6. **Conduct a vocabulary review.** Answer vocabulary questions and spend time with usage.

7. **Discuss answers to follow-up questions.** Call on volunteers or "round robin" to answer follow-up questions from the selection and to give support for answers. (See suggestions in the strategies section of this guide.)

   Students should read questions and possible answers and discuss reasons for choosing and/or not choosing an answer.

8. **Complete "Comprehension Boosters."** Depending on the selection, students should complete these short information-processing exercises in the *Instructor's Resource Manual* either *before* or *after* responses are given to the follow-up questions to each selection. Boosters vary in function as follows:

   a. To assist students in comprehension of some of the more difficult follow-up questions (see "The Girl with the Large Eyes" and "Genes and Behavior: A Twin Legacy")

   b. To highlight a reading concept not focused on in the text (see "A Real Loss," "My Mother's Blue Bowl," "They Sniff Out Trouble," and "Out of Their Element")

   c. To assess overall understanding and effectiveness of instruction (see "Flour Children," "A Personal Stress Survival Guide," and "The Magic Words Are 'Will You Help Me?'")

   d. To develop proficiency in identifying language concepts (see "A Real Loss," "Escaping the Daily Grind for Life as a House Father," "Brains the Ultimate Sex Appeal," "Tyranny of Weakness," and "My Mother's Blue Bowl")

   e. To serve as a culminating activity testing mental alertness (see "Genes and Behavior: A Twin Legacy," "How to Stay Alive," and "Long-Term Memory")

   f. To fill a void (see "Restored to the Sea," "To Catch a Thief," and "The Chaser")

   g. To vary the classroom routine (see "The Chaser," "Restored to the Sea," and "A Personal Stress Survival Guide")

9. **Complete supplementary vocabulary and/or writing activities.** Additional vocabulary exercises in the *Instructor's Resource Manual* may be completed and checked on an ongoing basis or held over as a review prior to tests. The writing activities are quite useful in that they assist in the debriefing process that aids in storage of knowledge for future use.

10. **Chart progress.** Encourage students to keep a record of their performance on the graphs in the back section of the text.

For variety, try one or all of the following:

I. **Student-led class discussions**

After completing at least Part 2 of the *Structured Reading* text, students may either choose or be assigned a reading selection of interest. The student assumes responsibility for this selection when it is scheduled for review in class. The student completes the assignment early and confers with the instructor on pronunciations, definitions, comprehension, and instructional strategies to be employed prior to the date of presentation. This individualized instructional conference gives the instructor a valid assessment of the student's current status and overall concept development in the course.

On the day of the presentation, the student takes charge: sits up front with the instructor (who will assist as needed with the selection), leads vocabulary, summarizes the selection, distributes extra activities, calls on respondents to answer questions, and awards bonus points for special activities or difficult questions. The student receives bonus points for participation.

II. **Detonator (most difficult question = bonus points)**

Students may work individually or in groups to answer the most difficult question (as identified by the instructor) in some selections. One by one or group by group, students take answer(s) to the instructor for a "quick check." For a correct response, students may earn bonus points to be added to their reading comprehension test score and either be dismissed or paired with a student who finds the activity academically challenging. If incorrect, students must remain in class for more in-depth study and/or assistance. This type of activity not only rewards the more advanced student but also provides extra attention to the academically challenged student in areas of need. Moreover, this personal contact with the instructor or a mentor can prove invaluable to the student's progress.

III. **Collaboration**

Collaborative learning is based on the idea that learning is a natural, social act. Thus, by talking and discussing among themselves, students can share ideas that may assist them in solving problems, answering comprehension questions, and in some instances, even creating new knowledge. Involving peer critiquing, this exchange of ideas during group discussions is motivational to students and quite appropriate to the reading selections in the *Structured Reading* text. For this reason, a procedure for ease of implementation follows.

Objective: Students of varying abilities will work together in small groups to discuss comprehension questions and to generate consensus answers.

A. *Preparation*
   1. **Materials**—In addition to the *Structured Reading* text, a routing chart is essential to determine where each student is at all times. (See Tables 1 and 2 and the following explanation.)
   2. **Initial Grouping Activity**—Group students so that each group of four or five represents a microcosm of the class (age, race, gender, ability). Plan for groups to participate in an initial group activity **to get acquainted, to identify roles** (recorder, leader, timer, etc.), and **to practice consensus building.** The members of this group make up the primary group.

B. *Implementation*
   1. **Assignment**—Each student is responsible for reading the selection and answering follow-up questions.
   2. **Primary Group**—This is the principal group to which each student belongs. Given about twenty minutes per selection, students discuss questions, verify answers, reach consensus, and record consensus answers to be turned in to the instructor.
   3. **Expert Group (Optional)**—At least one member from each primary group makes up the expert group membership. This group meets for about ten minutes to verify primary group consensus answers related to only one skill category: (1) Main Idea and Central Theme, (2) Details, (3) Inferences, or (4) Critical Reading. Each representative records expert group consensus answers and returns to the primary group to present findings.
   4. **Primary Group Revisited**—Back in the primary group, members listen to reasons given for different responses. They either accept or reject the representative's findings before submitting final consensus responses to the instructor.
   5. **Wrap-up**—The instructor checks and returns responses to each group, awards bonus points, and leads class discussion as needed. Problem areas are clarified, and any questions are answered, either by the instructor or selected group members.

C. *Evaluation*
   1. **Formative**—Some type of monitoring is the key to effective collaborative groups, checking for total team involvement and appropriate social interactions. Therefore, following each collaborative activity, students should evaluate individual and group effectiveness and determine avenues for improvement.
   2. **Summative**—Individual students should complete the reading comprehension test and turn it in. Before receiving a test grade,

group members work together to produce consensus answers for that same test. Students' final grade is an average of the two scores.

Table 1: Principle Routing Chart (4-Member Groups)

	Primary Groups				
Expert Groups	1	2	3	4	5
A	1	2	3	4	5
B	6	7	8	9	10
C	11	12	13	14	15
D	16	17	18	19	20

EXPLANATION OF TABLE 1

Table 1 shows a class of twenty students—each given a number and divided into five, four-member primary groups, shown vertically. For example, Primary Group 1 consists of students numbered 1, 6, 11, and 16; Group 2, 2, 7, 12, and 17; Group 3, 3, 8, 13, and 18; Group 4, 4, 9, 14, and 19; and Group 5, 5, 10, 15, and 20. These same students in the four, five-member horizontal groups (A–D) represent the expert groups, showing at least one representative from each primary group.

Table 2: Expert Group Weekly Rotations

	Week Number			
Concept Skills	1	2	3	4
Central Theme & Main Idea	A	B	C	D
Details	B	C	D	A
Inferences	C	D	A	B
Critical Reading	D	A	B	C

EXPLANATION OF TABLE 2

Table 2 shows that same class of twenty students from the Primary Groups being rotated in Expert Groups over a four-week period so that all students are given an opportunity to be exposed to focused group work on a particular concept skill (Central Theme and Main Ideas, Details, Inferences, and Critical Reading) during the four-week cycle. For example, during Week 1, students in Expert Group A (numbers 1–5) from Table 1 will focus on central theme and main ideas during their ten-minute stay in the expert group. During this same time, Expert Group B (students 6–10) will focus on details, and so on. However, during Week 2, the concept skill for each expert group changes. Expert Group B students will work on central theme and main ideas, and Expert Group C will focus on details.

THE LAB AND SELF-INSTRUCTION

Structured Reading can be used in reading labs or for self-instruction in individualized programs when students have controlled access to the Answer Key in the *Instructor's Edition*. Here are some suggestions for effectively using the text in this setting:

1. **Access to the Answer Key.** Instruct students to finish the reading and exercises before they check the answers. Some of the readings and exercises might be reserved for assessment purposes; thus part of the key should be under the supervisor's control.
2. **Written answers.** Ask students occasionally to write out why they chose a particular answer. Instruct students to support their answer with specific references to the reading selection and to share their reasoning for eliminating the alternative answers in multiple-choice items. This works well because much of the emphasis in the text is on reasoning and evaluation.
3. **Group discussion.** Integrate small-group discussion with lab-based and individualized programs. Base the discussions on reading selections in the text. Encourage students to share their answers, discuss their disagreements, and offer informed opinions about what they read. A teacher-prepared guide sheet can help students organize the discussion session.
4. **Poll sheets.** If student groups are not feasible, post "poll sheets" in the lab asking students to enter their opinions about issues raised in the reading selections. This helps motivate students who have not read particular selections to investigate them, and it also provides readers with a forum to express their opinions.

TEACHING STRATEGIES FOR *STRUCTURED READING*

Part One of *Structured Reading* introduces several instructional strategies to the student (pages 1–90). That section is a central component of the text. The purpose is to explain to students the process of reading and then to provide students with practical techniques to apply to the readings and to the practice exercises in the text.

This section of the *Instructor's Guide* offers teachers objectives for the student related to each of the strategies. This section also provides additional teaching ideas to implement classroom instruction of the strategies.

READING SPEED

Objective for the student: To understand the key factors that affect reading rate and to learn practical techniques to achieve increases in speed and improvement in comprehension.

Structured Reading emphasizes that reading is a meaning-making process. Researchers in reading speed have demonstrated that the mind does about 90 to 95 percent of the work in reading while the eyes contribute only about 5 to 10 percent. Rather than focusing on training eye movement, instruction in reading speed is therefore most effective when it helps students discover how best to extract meaning from print. The text's section on reading speed, pages 12–17, gives the student information about the many factors that affect reading speed: background knowledge of the subject being read about, purposes for reading a particular selection, the difficulty of the material, and ways people actually read. Here are some ways instructors can help students come to understand some of these concepts and, in the process, establish new habits to increase reading rate:

1. **Inventory of interests.** Take an informal inventory of interests in the class. Consult the "Themes" list in the "Reading Selections Listed by Types and Themes" in this guide. Find out which students, for example, have an interest or background in human behavior, health, or multicultural topics. First, assign readings in the student's area of interest. Next, have the students read in an area they know little about. Compare the influence of background knowledge (and interest) on reading rates and comprehension scores. Discuss problems with concentration and comprehension of unfamiliar material. Suggest ways to solve the problems (for example, finding easier-to-read material on a subject to increase prior knowledge before reading the less-accessible material).

2. **Types.** Assign readings of the same type as listed in "Reading Selections Listed by Types and Themes" in this guide. Using the statistics in the "Readability" section choose selections at differing levels of readability. For example, assign the two narratives "My Mother's Blue Bowl" (readability: 6) and "I Became Her Target" (readability: 9). Discuss how length of the article, vocabulary level, sentence length, and other factors affect the difficulty of the material and therefore influence speed and comprehension. The goal here is not to imply that students stay with only easy material; the goal is to urge students to take risks and not get discouraged. When students know why they are running into difficulty, they can mobilize to overcome it.

3. **Cloze exercises.** Develop cloze exercises as explained in "Readability" in this guide. Develop cloze paragraphs from readings with differing readability levels. Show students that the ability to complete an author's idea logically indicates whether or not the material is too hard or too easy for each reader.

4. **Vocabulary exercises.** Identify readings of the same type at differing levels as described in item 2. Administer the vocabulary exercises that

follow each reading selection and group of dictionary entries. The "Additional Vocabulary Exercises" in the *Instructor's Resource Manual* are an alternate source. Use the vocabulary exercise as a pretest prior to the reading of the selection. Discuss how the results of this pretest can help a student predict the ability to comprehend the article. Explain that one useful technique to help reading comprehension is to preview the vocabulary before reading the selection, and if many words are difficult, to scan their definitions before reading. Additionally, show students that a preview provides a way to help them understand ideas prior to the reading of a selection.

5. **Purpose.** Assign three readings of various types (consult "Reading Selections Listed by Types and Themes" in this guide). One might be a narrative like "My Mother's Blue Bowl," another an argumentative essay like "How to Stay Alive," and another a textbook extract like "Long-Term Memory." Referring to the chart in the text on page 13 have students decide their purposes for reading. Discuss the concept of **reading flexibility;** that is, efficient readers learn to develop various reading rates depending on their **purpose** for reading particular material. Skillful readers also learn to slow down or speed up within a particular reading as they meet unfamiliar or familiar material.

6. **Rate-building techniques.** Integrate the teaching of rate-building techniques with each new reading in the text. These techniques are eliminating "white space," reading by clustering ideas, and pacing through print. Approximately one-third of a page of print—the part in the margin—is blank. Efficient readers automatically indent their eyes about four or five spaces in from each margin on a page of print so that their field of vision eliminates the surrounding white space. By eliminating white space, the readers save time and can, therefore, increase their speed.

   To demonstrate these techniques, write the first two paragraphs of "I Became Her Target," p. 309 on the chalkboard. Then, incorporate the following procedure into your introduction of each of the new reading selections: Have the students "prepare the print" prior to the reading of each selection (if you prefer, this procedure can come after a vocabulary preview). Now instruct the students to

   - Draw margin lines about five letter spaces in from each margin throughout the entire reading
   - Cluster ideas using slash marks throughout the first few paragraphs of each selection
   - Pace through the print as a preread by taking one or two minutes using a hand to move through the entire reading to develop the mechanics of the technique

   The key to helping students eliminate poor habits is to teach them how to establish new good ones. The preceding procedure will help students establish a productive reading routine.

As the students apply the procedure, discuss the importance of developing a "soft focus" when working with margin lines as slash marks. Rather than "stare" at the boundary lines as they read, students need to be aware that they are searching for ideas that connect. The artificial marks and the hand will seem less of a distraction if instructors focus students' attention back on the fact that they are trying to get meaning from the print.

7. **Seeing more than one word.** Respond to those students who may insist that it is necessary to focus on every word when they read, and that their peripheral vision simply cannot see more than one word at a time. Develop an easy cloze paragraph at the independent reading level of students in the class (see "Readability" in this guide for instructions on developing a cloze exercise). Use the results of this exercise to demonstrate that the mind can "fill in the blanks," even when some of the words are missing. Also, ask the students to infer the point of the material before they fill in the words.

Use another method to demonstrate the mind's ability to take in more than one word at a time by putting the following on the board:

educational   (takes up 11 letter spaces)
in the past   (takes up 11 letter spaces including breaks between words)

Explain to students that if they focus in the middle of the word "educational" they can "see" it all at once. Most students will acknowledge they read it as one word, not syllable by syllable (ed/u/ca/tion/al). Next, point out that the idea cluster "in the past" also takes up eleven letter spaces. Have students "soft focus" on the phrase so that they will "see" it. Then, most importantly, show that they read it in one cluster as well: educational; in the past.

8. **Rate goals.** Help students set reasonable goals for improving their reading rates: 25 to 50 words per minute faster each session for reading material of the same type and level of difficulty. Clarify that speed without comprehension is meaningless, and explain that increases in reading speed usually go hand in hand with better comprehension. Researchers find that with slow reading, the mind has time to wander and take "mental vacations." It is important, then, that students strive to keep their minds working to full potential.

Discuss the fact that students who balk at taking risks by speeding up generally have concentration difficulties, and often they regress and subvocalize to aid their comprehension. These are major crutches that work against efficient reading. Subvocalization is appropriate about 50 percent of the time—when a reader encounters a new word, unfamiliar idea, or key concept. Regression is appropriate only when it is conscious—when the reader chooses to reread a particularly difficult passage, for example. Help students break the habits of subvocalizing every word and rereading sentences by encouraging them to do the following:

- Use a blank 3×5 card as a pacer. The card should move **down** the print, not follow under the lines of print. The card should move at a consistent pace, not moving back to allow rereading of a missed sentence. This helps focus the reader's attention on the task. It also helps readers become aware of "mental vacations" while reading. For students who seem frustrated with the technique, have them use the card only on the first few paragraphs of a reading to set the pace.
- Have students avoid focusing on the problem of subvocalization. Instead encourage them to push themselves to read slightly faster than the rate at which they "hear" all the words. The rate should be slightly uncomfortable, but comprehension adequate. Subvocalization lessens when rates go above about 250 wpm, or the fastest rate at which a person can comprehend individual words being said.

VOCABULARY

Objective for the student: To learn how to use context clues, word parts, the dictionary, and a personal vocabulary card system to effect an increase in word knowledge.

In *Structured Reading*, new vocabulary words are presented in context, and a complete dictionary entry is provided for each new word. The concept is that because words are handles for ideas, an understanding of key vocabulary is crucial for good comprehension and reading rate. For each reading selection the vocabulary list might often be presented prior to reading. The words should be discussed as part of the preview. The "Additional Vocabulary Exercises" in the *Instructor's Resource Manual* provide practice and reinforcement for the vocabulary list for each reading.

But only adding new words to students' vocabulary is not enough. Students need to learn strategies that they can use when they encounter words they do not know whether in the reading selections in this text or in any other material. Here are some strategies students can use:

CONTEXT CLUES

The text's section on vocabulary, pages 17–23 provides students with four types of context clues: a restatement clue, a contrast clue, an example clue, and a definition context clue.

Students will need **practice** with context, however, to master the concept fully. Weak readers rarely realize that awareness of context plays a pivotal role in the reading process. For example, when a reader sees the words "once upon a," that reader always knows from the context that there is a 99 percent chance that the next word will be "time." This ability to predict what words will come next becomes easier as a reader becomes more experienced. This ability to use context to predict is indispensable for efficient comprehension and good reading speeds.

Some students need help discovering the concept of context, and most need practice in using clues to help predict the meaning of words. Here are some ideas for implementing the teaching of context clues:

1. **Concept of context.** Demonstrate the concept of context by designing short cloze passages (see "Readability" in this guide). Instruct students to fill in the blanks according to the meaning of the surrounding words. You can simplify this task for the student by using the maze technique. Delete every fifth word, but instead of leaving only a blank for the deletion, provide three alternative responses.

2. **Importance of context.** Try to convince students of the importance of learning a word in context. Demonstrate the importance of knowing the context by asking students to define some simple words: for example, **fox, good, island.** Then give students sentences, each using the word in a different context. Ask students how the definitions change depending on the context:

   > Define **fox:**
   > Define **fox** in "Senator White is certainly a political **fox.**"
   > Define **fox** in "I saw a dead **fox** on the side of the road this morning."
   > Define **good:**
   > Define **good** in "**Good** children never stay out past 2:00 a.m."
   > Define **good** in "Now is the time for all **good** men to come to the aid of their country."
   > Define **good** in "All I need to be happy is **good** food, **good** drink, and **good** company."
   > Define **island:**
   > Define **island** in "No man is an **island** unto himself."
   > Define **island** in "I saw a blind woman stranded on the pedestrian **island.**"

3. **Sophisticated language and context.** Help students become aware that sophisticated language demands a careful look at the context. Subtle differences in definitions may not always reveal whether a word is used incorrectly or not. For example, the dictionary lists the definition of **sift** as **examine** for the sentence, "The Senate investigators had to **sift** through many presidential papers to find the evidence they needed." Yet it would be incorrect to use the word **sift** as a synonym for **examine** in this sentence: "I took my dog to the vet so he could **sift** his eye."

   Many words in *Structured Reading* can have various meanings depending on the context. Encourage students to develop sentences using the following words in various contexts to examine the differences in meaning:

> antennae, p. 96; carriage, p. 333; circuit, p. 353; consensus, p.179; craned, p. 96; draught, p. 394; harrow, p. 322; siren, p. 394.

4. **Context clue exercises.** Develop context clue exercises based on the vocabulary words from the reading selections in the text. Give students practice with the four types of clues.

   Emphasize the importance of students' determining the correct meaning of the word, rather than only identifying the types of clues.

5. **Context clues and other strategies.** Make students aware that the meaning of all words cannot always be figured out from the context. Weak readers are often discouraged when they discover that examining the context will not always yield meaning. Help such students learn that professional writers try to be as clear and accessible to their readers as possible, but many concepts need sophisticated words that do not have simple substitutes. Explain that students can use other resources to help them out, particularly analysis of the word parts and dictionary entries.

DICTIONARY

Dictionary entries are provided for each of the vocabulary words identified for study from the reading selections in *Structured Reading*. Using the dictionary entries with the students, instructors can read through each entry to help students discover which meaning of the word fits the context of the sentence. Vocabulary entries in *Webster's New World College Dictionary*, Fourth Edition, use dots for syllabification. The dots indicate where a word can be acceptably divided at the end of a line.

The Seventh Edition of *Structured Reading* provides an updated "Guide to the Dictionary" written in language understandable to the developmental reader. It appears in the Appendix to the text. To help instructors give students practice in its principles, this Guide offers exercises in using the pronunciation guide, understanding syllabication, finding synonyms, determining the correct forms of inflected nouns and verbs, as well as prefix and suffix practice in the "Dictionary Skills Exercises" in the *Instructor's Resource Manual*. Dictionary skills are taught most effectively when they relate to a real task of discovering meaning, but these exercises can provide preliminary practice.

"Transparency Masters: Dictionary Entries," in the *Instructor's Resource Manual*, are provided to help instructors lead discussions on the various elements of a dictionary entry.

The entries for **crane** and for **missionaries** (with **mission**) demonstrate that many words have multiple meanings and that students must consider context when they use a dictionary entry. The entry for **contingent** shows that one word can occur as many different parts of speech. The entries for **derivative** (with **derive**) and for **dominant** illustrate the varying fields of study that call on a single word in different ways. The entry for **exclude** offers synonyms that list and explain subtle differences among synonyms. The presentation of these entries follows the order of explanation offered in *Structured Reading*'s "Guide to Dictionary Use" that appears in the Appendix to the text. Also, the entries **crane** and **derivative** (with **derive**) are illustrations of information presented in the "Guide to Dictionary Use." The pronunciation key shown on one of the transparency masters in the *Instructor's Resource Manual* also appears in the text's "Guide to Dictionary Use." It is offered to help instructors lead students to the correct pronunciation of the entries from *Webster's New World College Dictionary*, Fourth Edition, reproduced in *Structured Reading*.

As students learn to use context clues, word parts, and the dictionary as useful resources while working with the vocabulary in *Structured Reading*, they will need a personal system of regular vocabulary study to help them learn new words. One method of developing and practicing with vocabulary cards is described for the student on pages 28–31 of the text. A sample vocabulary card also appears on page 28 and is reproduced in the "Transparency Masters: Vocabulary Study" section of the *Instructor's Resource Manual*. Here are ways to incorporate a vocabulary card practice system into classroom instruction:

INTRODUCTION OF THE TECHNIQUE

Introduce the format of the vocabulary cards and point out all the elements that make up the study of a word. When planning a lecture and discussion involving your students, choose one word to examine with the class, such as the word **aggressive** (which appears on page 106 in the text). Make up numbered envelopes and in each write on a piece of paper one element of the vocabulary cards. Do not identify on the envelope which element is contained inside.

In envelope 1 put the word to be studied, **aggressive.**

In envelope 2 put the pronunciation of the word as listed in the dictionary.

In envelope 3 put the context in which the word appeared.

In envelope 4 put all the definitions of the word.

In envelope 5 put the word broken down into its word parts.

In envelope 6 put the word used in a student-designed sentence.

Hand out the six envelopes randomly to the class without explanation. Draw a large vocabulary card on the board. Use the sample card on page 28 in the text as a model. Then ask for the student with envelope 1 to read what is inside. Enter the word on the card drawn on the board. Then ask the student with envelope 2 to do the same, but because it is the pronunciation, you will have to spell it out. Ask the class if anyone recognizes what it is, and what the symbols mean. You can lead this discussion by referring students to the pronunciation key in the text's Appendix "Guide to Dictionary Use" (also a transparency master in the *Instructor's Resource Manual*). Proceed with all the other envelopes in the same manner, taking time to discuss each element of vocabulary study as you enter the information on the board. For example, when the students have revealed all the definitions, have the class examine which one best fits the context. Eliminate all the other definitions so that students learn that the definition of a word in context should not be encumbered with several definitions to learn at one time. When the word parts are revealed, discuss the basics of word part analysis and show how when combined with context, the word parts contribute to help determine the meaning of a word.

At the end of the discussion, you will have a very complete vocabulary card on the board. Turn the students' attention to page 28 in the text, which summarizes how to make a vocabulary card (you can add or delete some of the elements as you see fit).

Structured Reading recommends that students choose ten words each week found in their readings. In addition to the method for study explained in the text, a regular practice routine in the classroom can help students as paired teams. Develop a checklist by expanding the sample of the one that follows. Have students orally "practice test" each other. Instruct them to read the word and context clue from their partner's cards, asking the partner for definitions. Have the students keep track of their own results so that they can learn which words are particularly difficult to master. Once or twice during the semester, use this list and the cards to test students individually on their personal vocabulary list.

PERSONAL VOCABULARY WORD LIST

		Team Practice Dates		
Date entered	Word to learn	Results of practices		
1.				
2.				
3.				

Key: "✓" = correct, "-" = incorrect; definition correct 3 times in a row indicates mastery.

Predicting

Objective for the student: To learn the preparation step for reading—predicting—for greater concentration and comprehension.

Predicting is presented in *Structured Reading* on pages 8–9 as a pre-reading step crucial to active reading and good comprehension. One approach that emphasizes the use of predictions in reading comprehension, the Directed Thinking and Reading Activity, was developed by Russell D. Stauffer. The approach is explained in his book, *Directing the Reading-Thinking Process* (Harper and Row, 1975). This approach calls for a predict-read-prove cycle. The student consciously predicts what a selection will be about after reading the title or other introductory material. Then the student guesses what will come next based on reading the first few paragraphs. These predictions are hypotheses that are confirmed or rejected as the reading continues.

The DTRA derives from two research-based findings about the reading process. First, that reading requires the active participation of the reader—making predictions, checking them out for accuracy, refining them, and moving along. Second, the approach allows for trial and error and risk taking. When students share their predictions, they see that several answers are possible. This encourages divergent thinking. It allows a student to think, "Well, I made a decent guess but I guessed wrong; now that I know something about the selection, maybe my next guess will be more on target." The atmosphere of right or wrong shifts to an atmosphere of open investigation.

In reading fiction, predicting involves thinking about what will happen next. In reading nonfiction, predicting additionally involves summoning up whatever prior knowledge the students have about the subject at hand and predicting from the title what the main idea of the piece will be. Here are some suggestions for encouraging students to practice predicting:

1. **Introduction of predicting.** Introduce the technique to the class by asking students how they usually begin a textbook assignment. Most will answer that they simply pick it up and start to read it. Then ask the athletes in the class how they start out their activity for the day. The joggers and dancers might say they stretch, the football players might say they run short sprints, and so on. Conduct a discussion of what happens if athletes do not warm up in these ways. Injuries and poor performance are among the possible answers. Make the point that in reading, to start out "cold" without a warm-up—previewing the title, predicting the main point, reading the first few paragraphs, and making further predictions about the content—will result in lack of concentration and focus. Also, emphasize that one of the advantages of the predicting step is to refocus attention from a previous activity to the one at hand. When making predictions after reading the title and first few paragraphs, the reader can know that his or her mind is on the reading and not on a prior telephone conversation, math paper, or stack of unpaid bills.

2. **Prediction examples.** Get students thinking concretely about predictions by bringing to class four different types of empty picture frames in different sizes, for example a modern chrome frame, an old-looking etched wood frame, a highly-decorative gilt frame, and a plain white

plastic frame. Ask students what they can predict about the picture that might be placed in each frame. Students might mention size, style, age, and color. Compare the predictions they made to the "frame" they will get when they read the title and first few paragraphs of a reading—the "complete picture," the main ideas and details, will fit into that frame when they do the thorough reading.

3. **Visuals.** Use the "Thinking: Getting Started" sections of visuals and questions that precede each of the five parts in the text to help students think about the prior knowledge they have on the subjects they will read about. Each poster, ad, or cartoon refers to one or more of the reading selections that follow in that part. For each selection, there is a question to lead students into making a connection between the visual and the reading selection.

4. **Reading selections.** To demonstrate how reading the title and first few paragraphs can help with accurate predictions of some of the main points, several readings in this text can be used for this purpose. Some of these include

> Forty Acres and a Holiday, p. 243; "Escaping the Daily Grind for Life as a House Father," p. 231; "Darkness at Noon," p. 121; "Genes and Behavior: A Twin Legacy," p. 221; "Restored to the Sea," p. 281; and "Long-Term Memory," p. 366.

Other reading selections do not reveal the main points in such an obvious way, but will engage interest when the students find that what they thought to be true may not be true at all. Some examples are

> "A Real Loss," p. 95 The beginning of this essay describes a pleasant scene between a man and a girl. What is "the real loss?" Will it be the loss of life of the girl? A loss of innocence? Will the man cause the loss?

> "The Girl with the Large Eyes," p. 169 This symbolic tale does not have its true meaning revealed until the unusual characters and events are analyzed.

> "Summer," p. 155 What seems to begin as a description of a boyhood summer turns into a tragedy that makes an unforgettable impression on the author.

> "How to Stay Alive," p. 213 It is often difficult to predict the main point of a satiric piece. The phrase "Once upon a time. . ." may clue the reader that there is more to this essay than is exactly stated.

ON, BETWEEN, AND BEYOND THE LINES

Objective for the student: To learn how to determine central theme, main ideas, and images; identify key details; draw correct inferences; distinguish fact from opinion; understand how the author's strategies influence the reader; and make judgments about what has been read.

Chapter 6, Part One, page 32 in *Structured Reading*, discusses the three major comprehension levels students will encounter: literal, critical, and analytical. Each reading selection contains follow-up questions that deal with those levels. Here are some ways to help students learn to apply them.

1. **Literal.** Encourage students not to skip illustrations, charts, and graphs when they read. Examine with them the illustration in selection 27. "Transparency Masters: Reading Illustrations" in the *Instructor's Resource Manual* are also provided for you to help students analyze information contained in this visual. After a survey of the textbook extract from which it is taken, ask students to interpret the illustration as to how it supports the main idea of the chapter. You also might discuss how a visual helps the mind remember because the mind thinks in pictures.

2. **Critical.** Some reading selections in the text are particularly useful in bringing the student beyond only a literal understanding. If the symbolism is not understood, "The Girl with the Large Eyes" could be read as a ludicrous story of a woman marrying a fish. In "How to Stay Alive," the satire must be appreciated to correctly identify the main point. Have the students read each of these essays, and using the questions on page 60 of the text on "Inferences," take students through the process of analyzing the essays to draw valid conclusions.

3. **Analytical.** Engage students in close reading and careful analysis by having them make up their own questions about a reading selection using the question categories in the book, such as Central Theme and Main Ideas, Major Details, Inferences, and so on. Then distribute the questions to the rest of the class for discussion and answering while the "author" of the questions checks the answers. This activity also promotes debate about the questions in the book, and it encourages students to see questions as not merely tests of their understanding, but springboards to further analysis.

4. **Critical and Analytical.** Make students aware of the connotations of words. The readings "Tyranny of Weakness," page 105 or "Out of Their Element," page 329 provide useful practice in eliminating opinionated words. Instruct students to edit the opinionated words, then revise the articles using only factual statements. This helps the student recognize how the author's choice of words may help to persuade the reader.

5. **Critical and Analytical.** Help students become aware that many essays and articles are made up primarily of opinionated statements. Using the guidelines for qualifying a statement as a fact listed on page 67 of the text, have the students look at opening paragraphs from essays that promote a particular point of view. Ask students to make judgments about the statements in those paragraphs. Some useful reading selections for this are "Tyranny of Weakness," p. 105; "Don't Sell Your Ambitions Short to 'Keep It Real,'" p. 113; "Brains the Ultimate Sex Appeal," p. 161; and "Should a Wife Keep Her Name?" p. 299.

Using the same type of analysis, compare the preceding reading selections to the textbook extracts in Part 6 of the text. This helps students clarify the importance of understanding the author's purpose for writing and the techniques he or she uses to develop the work. Help students recognize that if the author's primary purpose is to inform as in a textbook, he or she will use factual statements; if the purpose is to persuade or influence as in an argumentative essay, the author will use opinions as well as facts and choose words that promote a particular point of view.

Objective for the student: To apply a systematic approach to determine central theme, main ideas, and images; identify key details; draw correct inferences; and distinguish fact from opinion.

Here are some strategies, along with sample questions and answers, and brief explanations to help students answer follow-up questions from the reading selections.

I. CENTRAL THEME AND MAIN IDEA

The **central theme** tells what the entire selection is about. In answering this type of question, students should

1. Look away from the text after reading a selection.
2. Write a one-sentence statement that explains to someone else what the selection is all about. (This statement should resemble a movie description in the *TV Guide*.)
3. Compare this sentence with the four options in a multiple-choice question. (The correct answer is probably the one that most closely matches one of the options.)

The **main idea** tells what a paragraph or group of paragraphs is about. Encourage students to

1. Determine the topic or subject.
2. Determine the point the author attempts to make about the subject.
3. Use the process of elimination for multiple-choice options that may be too specific, too narrow, or maybe even false.
4. Analyze the paragraph. Many of the multiple-choice options for these questions are often sentences, or details, taken from the paragraph in question. By taking the paragraph apart sentence by sentence, students can often see the topic as well as the major point unfold.

EXAMPLE: The following brief explanations relate to central theme and main idea exercises from Selection 1, "A Real Loss."

___d___ 1. What is the central theme of "A Real Loss"?
   a. **These are trying times for men. . . .** is incorrect because the story focuses on one man, and not one media account of child molestation is mentioned.

   b. **The author felt sorry. . . .**is incorrect because there is no evidence to support this sentiment.
   c. **Child molesters can find victims everywhere. . . .**is also incorrect because this issue is not discussed. Only two women are concerned here, and the airplane is the only place mentioned where a possible victim could be found.
   d. **Because of her increased awareness that some. . . .**is the correct choice because it more appropriately summarizes the point the author makes. When the man befriended the little girl, the author watched suspiciously to see what his actions would be. Her alarm heightened when the bathroom issue surfaced, and she became even more suspect. Once she saw that his intentions were honorable, she realized that she had missed out on something beautiful, a very special moment.

   When students look away from the text after reading the selection and write as though they are telling someone else what the selection is about, they tend never to mention ideas presented in options a, b, or c.

c   2. What is the main idea of paragraph 6?
   a. **Airplane passengers often listen to other. . . .**This is too narrow a focus to be the point here.
   b. **Becoming suspicious, the author leaned far. . . .**This is another detail, not the paragraph essence, leading to the main idea.
   c. **As she waited to see what the man would do. . . .**This is the correct answer because it best makes the author's point and summarizes the key ideas in options a, b, and d.
   d. **The man opened the bathroom door for the little. . . .**This is another detail, which answers "as she waited to see what the man would do."

II. DETAILS

Two of the three types of detail questions will be analyzed in this section: (1) distinguishing between major and minor details and (2) true, false, and not discussed.

A. MAJOR AND MINOR DETAILS

In distinguishing between major and minor details, students might follow these suggestions:

1. Reread the central theme.
2. Determine the following:
   a. If the detail supports the central theme
      ASK: Is the detail an example, a clarifying definition, a fact, a statistic, a reason, or a quotation related to some aspect of the central theme?

b. If a relationship exists between the central theme and the detail
   ASK: Does the detail answer *who, what, when, where, why,* or *how* about any aspect of the central theme?

3. Conclude that if some supporting relationship exists between the central theme and the detail, then the detail is most likely major; if not, then it is minor.

   EXAMPLE 1: This sample major details exercise is taken from Selection 1, "A Real Loss."

   Central Theme: Because of her increased awareness that some people are child molesters, the author now realizes that she has become suspicious of people who are kind to children they do not know.

1. The author was sitting in back of a little girl who was flying alone.
   Major—This identifies the setting and presents a fact about the author (*who*) and her seating (*where*), in a position to observe what was taking place.

2. The little girl's mother placed a Care Bear in the girl's arms.
   Minor—Who cares?—no bearing on the story line—could be omitted.

3. The little girl was going to California.
   Minor—(same as #2)

4. The little girl knew how to adjust her seat belt.
   Minor—(same as #2)

5. The bear's name was Furry.
   Minor—(same as #2)

6. Both the girl and the man's daughter were six years old.
   Major—Because of his experience with six-year-olds, the man knew how to gain the little girl's confidence.

7. The little girl announced that she had to go to the bathroom.
   Major—This tells what aroused the author's suspicion.

8. At that moment, the flight attendants were busy collecting lunch trays, so the man offered to take the girl to the bathroom.
   Major—This tells why the man accepted the challenge.

9. The man showed the girl how the lock worked, and then he waited for her outside the door.
   Major—This is climax, indicating what happened.

10. The other woman sighed in relief.
    Minor—(Same as #2)

11. The author's image of the man and the little girl on the plane left her with a feeling of loss.
    Major—This is the essence of the story, telling how the author felt about her needless suspicions.

12. A new heightened consciousness about child molestation is in itself a good thing.
    Major—The author draws this conclusion from the experience.

EXAMPLE 2: This sample major details exercise is taken from Selection 4, "Darkness at Noon."

Central Theme: People often assume that because blind people cannot see, they cannot hear, learn, or work.

1. The author has been blind from birth.
   Major—This fact provides evidence (credibility) about the author (**who**) and tells why he can attest to the central theme.

2. People often shout at blind people and pronounce every word with great care.
   Major—This example supports the "cannot hear" aspect.

3. Airline personnel use a code to refer to blind people.
   Minor—The emphasis here is on identification of the blind.

4. The author goes out to dinner with his wife Kit.
   Minor—The emphasis here is on dining and socializing.

5. If a blind person and a sighted person are together, other people will usually communicate with them by talking. . . .
   Major—This example supports the "cannot hear" aspect.

6. The author was given a year's leave of absence from his Washington law firm to study for a diploma-in-law degree. . . .
   Minor—This emphasizes his ability, not his disability.

7. The author had to be hospitalized while studying in England.
   Minor—The emphasis here is on health.

8. In 1975 the Department of Labor issued regulations that require equal employment opportunities for the handicapped.
   Major—This is an effect of the "work" aspect of the central theme (cause), which indicates why.

9. On the whole, the business community's response to offering employment of the handicapped has been enthusiastic.
   Major—This fact supports the "work" aspect of the central theme.

10. The author and his father played basketball in the backyard using a special system they had worked out.
    Minor—This is about recreation.

11. The author's father shot for the basket and missed completely.
    Minor—This is about the father's disability.

12. The neighbor's friend was not sure if the author or his father was blind.

Major—This statement ironically summarizes the essence of the selection (the author's hope) and connects the assumption made here (was not sure if) with that (assumed) in the central theme.

B. TRUE, FALSE, NOT DISCUSSED

Close reading requires verifying information. Students may apply the following techniques in answering true, false, and not discussed type questions.

1. If the statement is **True,** verify its validity in the text by locating and reading the supporting sentence(s). (e.g., Paragraph 6, Sentence 2)
2. If the statement is **False,** locate reference sentence(s) in the text. Then, cross out the incorrect part of the sentence(s) and substitute the correct information.
3. If the statement is **Not Discussed,** there should be no reference to the key idea in the text.
4. To verify responses, convert statements into questions and answer them: Yes (same as **True**), No (same as **False**), and Not Sure (same as **Not Discussed**).

   EXAMPLE 1: This sample major details exercise is taken from Selection 14, "Genes and Behavior: A Twin Legacy."

1. Thomas J. Bouchard is the director of the Minnesota Center for Twin and Adoption Research.
   Q: Is Thomas J. Bouchard the director of the Minnesota Center for Twin and Adoption Research?
   Yes/True (Paragraph 1, Sentence 3)

2. The behavior of separated twins is being compared with the behavior of a *group of 25 pairs of twins* raised together.
   Q: Is the behavior of separated twins being compared with the behavior of a group of 25 pairs of twins raised together?
   No/False: The behavior of separated twins is being compared with the behavior of a *comparison group* reared together.

3. Even though many of the separated twins have different jobs, they often share the same hobbies and interests.
   Q: Do separated twins who have different jobs share the same hobbies and interests?
   Yes/True (Paragraph 4, Sentence 1)

4. One pair of identical twins who burst into tears easily both cried *when asked to appear* on a talk show.
   Q: Did one pair of identical twins who burst into tears easily both cry when asked to appear on a talk show?
   No/False: . . . both cried *in response to one of the questions.*

5. Twins who are afraid of water are usually also afraid of the dark and of animals.

Q: Are twins who are afraid of water also afraid of the dark and of other animals?

Not sure—can't find answer in selection/**Not Discussed**

6. One set of separated fraternal twins both had antisocial personalities and grew up to be criminals.
   Q: Did one set of separated fraternal twins with antisocial behavior grow up to be criminals?
   <u>Yes</u>/**True (Paragraph 6, Sentence 3)**

7. *A woman's twin sons* won mathematics competitions. . . .
   Q: Did a woman's twin sons win a mathematics competition in Wyoming and Texas?
   <u>No</u>/**False:** *Two identical twin women* **each had a son who won. . . .**

8. Social closeness is essential for happiness in humans.
   Q: Is social closeness essential for happiness in humans?
   Not sure—can't locate answer in selection/**Not Discussed**

9. *Environmental influences* are the most important shapers of personality.
   Q: Are environmental influences the most important shapers of personality?
   <u>No</u>/**False:** *Genes* **. . . primary shaping forces of personality.**

10. Genes determine *almost all* personality traits.
    Q: Do genes determine almost all personality traits?
    <u>No</u>/**False: Genes determin***e about 11* **personality traits.**

EXAMPLE 2: This sample major details exercise is taken from Selection 19, "Restored to the Sea."

1. Stranded false killer whales are known to attack humans.
   Q: Do *false* killer whales attack humans?
   <u>No</u>/**False: The word** *false* **suggests they are** *not* **killers. (Paragraph 2, Sentence 2)**

2. Volunteers from Seal Rocks rescued 37 of the whales.
   Q: Did volunteers from Seal Rocks rescue 37 whales?
   <u>No</u>/**False: Rescuers from as far as 500 miles from Seal Rocks participated in the rescue. (Paragraph 2, Sentence 4)**

3. One whale was the cause of the stranding of 49 others.
   Q: Did one whale cause 49 other whales to be stranded?
   Not sure—Why the whales ran aground is a mystery/**Not Discussed**

4. Some volunteers traveled great distances to help.
   Q: Did some volunteers travel great distances to help?
   <u>Yes</u>/**True: Some volunteers traveled over 500 miles.**

5. The whales' malfunctioning sonar may have led them astray.
   Q: Did the whales' malfunctioning sonar lead them astray?

Yes/True: Only know that along shallow beaches malfunctioning sonar may lead them astray. (Paragraph 3, Sentence 2)

6. Humans are quick to answer calls to help any animal in distress.
   Q: Are humans quick to answer calls to help any animal in distress?
   *Not sure—Only know that humans responded quickly to this call/***Not Discussed (Paragraph 4, Sentence 1)**

7. The volunteers' previous training prepared them for the rescue attempt.
   Q: Did the volunteers have any previous training to prepare them for this?
   *Not sure—No mention is made of volunteers' previous training to prepare them for this rescue/***Not Discussed**

8. Whales are by nature nervous creatures.
   Q: Are whales nervous creatures by nature?
   *Not sure—Volunteers sought to calm the creatures but no mention is made that whales are nervous by nature/***Not Discussed**

III. INFERENCES

In making **inferences,** students must be able to identify the part of the selection (words, sentences, thought groups) that supports a particular response. To do this, students must also read between the lines and supply information the author assumes they know already. The following steps are useful for students in answering inference type questions:

1. Make sure you understand what is stated on the lines.
2. Find evidence to support your position.
3. Use reasoning and background knowledge to bring it all together.
4. Remember: Your thoughts alone are not sufficient; base your response on evidence from the selection.

   EXAMPLE 1: This sample exercise is taken from Selection 1, "A Real Loss." (There is no evidence to support unlisted distractors.)

1. Why did the little girl's mother tell her to remind Daddy to call?
   b. The mother wanted to know that the girl. . . .
      Evidence: Care Bear—indicates concern for child.

2. Why did the man say Furry was a good name?
   c. He wanted to make her feel comfortable and secure.
      Evidence: "Nodded in approval"

3. Why did the little girl's announcement that she had to go to the bathroom wake up the author?
   d. As a mother, the author was used to listening—even in sleep—for children's calls for help.
      Evidence: "My mother instinct"

4. By saying "Well, you can't be too careful these days" the woman was communicating that she was
   c. slightly embarrassed that she had worried about what the man might do to the little girl.
   Evidence: "sighed in relief"

5. What does the author mean when she says "there is a real loss here for us all when we must always be wary of the kindness of strangers"?
   a. . . .from enjoying some of the pleasanter moments. . . .
   Evidence: "saddens me"

6. The *loss* used in the title refers to the
   a. author's loss of trust of adults who are kind to children.
   Evidence: This is what the selection is about: the author's inability to appreciate the adult (man and stranger) being kind to a little girl.

EXAMPLE 2: This sample inference exercise is taken from Selection 4, "Darkness at Noon."

1. The title of the essay suggests that it is sighted people, not blind people, who cannot "see."
   YES: Darkness at noon (the brightest time of the day).

2. The author feels that he is greatly admired. . . .
   NO: "I have never had the opportunity to see myself and have been completely dependent on the image I create in the eye of the observer. To date it has not been narcissistic."

3. The author feels that he can make his point more effectively with humor than with a stern lecture.
   YES: He gives several humorous examples—in the airport, restaurant, and hospital—related to people's assumptions: can't hear (yell at him, enunciate carefully, and whisper), can't talk and needs an interpreter (communications with wife and orderly), can't work (cum laude graduate with law degree rejected by over 40 law firms and told that he could not practice law).

4. The author often eats in restaurants with his wife Kit.
   NO: Often when he and his wife Kit go out to dinner, the same thing happens.

5. The author was highly entertained by the conversation. . . .
   NO: . . . "even my saint-like disposition deserted me."

6. The author got good grades at Harvard Law School because he was given special privileges reserved for blind students.
   NO: Evidence to the contrary—cum laude degree from Harvard College, a good ranking at Harvard, received a year's leave of absence to study for a diploma-in-law degree at Oxford University.

7. The April 10, 1976, Department of Labor regulations were. . . .
   NO: No evidence to support this.

8. The author's father was a much better basketball player. . . .
   NO: No evidence—they both shot and missed; "Dad missed the garage entirely."

IV. FACT OR OPINION

For *opinions*, encourage students to determine if there are differing opinions in the classroom and if any of the following terms/conditions exist:

1. Possibility words (apparently, appears, possibly, potentially, probably, seems, suppose, think)
2. Conditional words (should, could, may, prefer, might, suppose, if, believe)
3. Abstract terms (exhausted, loyalty, democracy, love, expensive, tentative)
4. Someone is speaking for another (you, they, everybody)
5. Any future reference (will, in the future, tomorrow)

For *facts*, test the statement using the three tests for verification: research, observation, or experimentation.

1. Research requires paying particular attention to references to written record, statistics, and concrete terms.
2. Observation may be anything perceived by the senses: smell, taste, touch, see, hear.
3. Experimentation involves manipulation: testing, weighing, counting, etc.

NOTE: Students are to be reminded that their agreement with a statement only makes it a fact for them but not necessarily for anybody else—and this is the concern. The statement remains an opinion if it cannot be verified.

The following three (3) sample fact or opinion exercises come from (a) Selection 1, "A Real Loss," (b) Selection 2, "Tyranny of Weakness," and (c) Selection 4, "Darkness at Noon." The brief explanations attempt to apply the preceding strategies to show their effectiveness in unraveling this type of exercise. Some of the key words are highlighted in opinion sentences.

EXAMPLE 1: This sample fact or opinion exercise is taken from Selection 1, "A Real Loss."

1. The girl adjusted her seat belt and sniffed back a tear.
   Fact—Observation (see)

2. He asked her how much money the tooth fairy was giving out in New York these days.
   Fact—Observation (hear)

3. She revealed to him the names of her favorite friends.
   Fact—Observation (hear)

4. She *looked tentative.*
   Opinion—Abstraction

5. He became transformed in my eyes.
   Fact—Observation (The author sees and speaks for herself.)

6. The *dark* business suit *looked sinister.*
   Opinion—Abstraction

7. The woman and I sighed in relief.
   Fact—Observation (see)

8. *"You* can't be *too careful these days."*
   Opinion—Someone is speaking for someone else.

9. A new *heightened consciousness* about child molestation is in itself a *good thing.*
   Opinion—Maybe for you but not for the child molester.

10. These are *trying times* for men.
    Opinion—Abstraction (trying times)

EXAMPLE 2: This sample fact or opinion exercise is taken from Selection 2, "Tyranny of Weakness."

1. The most *aggressive,* the *strongest* people *we* know are the *weak* ones.
   Opinion—Abstractions and speaking for someone else.

2. *I suppose* it begins in childhood when a child realizes that *helplessness* is a way of *controlling* parents.
   Opinion—Possibility phrase and abstract terms.

3. The man wanted a quiet, shy, helpless wife because his mother had been aggressive and overpowering.
   Fact—Ask the man; he can verify if this is what he wants.

4. She said she was too tired.
   Fact—The lady is speaking for herself. We hear her voice.

5. A *competent* mother can turn into a *weak, helpless* widow.
   Opinion—A general abstract statement about someone else.

6. *It seemed* to break a pattern that was *bad* for *both of us.*
   Opinion—Possibility phrase with abstract terms and speaking for someone else.

EXAMPLE 3: This sample fact or opinion exercise is taken from Selection 4, "Darkness at Noon."

1. Blind from birth, I have never had the opportunity to see myself.
   Fact—Verifiable (The author speaks for himself.)

2. *They fear* that *if* the *dread word* is spoken, the ticket agent's retina *will* immediately detach.
   Opinion—Speaking for someone else, abstractions and possibility.

3. I had been given a year's leave of absence from my Washington law firm to study for a diploma-in-law degree at Oxford.
   Fact—(same as #1)

4. I was turned down by over forty law firms because of my blindness.
   Fact—The author can verify this with written evidence (rejection letters).

5. By and large, the business community's response to offering employment to the *disabled* has been *enthusiastic.*
   Opinion—general statement with abstract terms.

6. Dad shot [the basketball] and missed the garage entirely.
   Fact—Observable (see)

READER RESPONSE

Objective for the student: To learn to shape an informed opinion and to make valid oral or written judgments about a written work.

Structured Reading makes a point of helping students appreciate why recognizing good writing enhances reading. The text also encourages students to make judgments that go beyond, "I agree or disagree with the author" by providing open-ended questions at the end of each selection for oral or written response.

The appreciation of good writing is sometimes lost on students who struggle with some of the mechanics of the reading process. One technique that often ends in elementary school is reading out loud to students, yet it has validity with older readers as well, as reported by Charlotte Huck in the autumn 1982 issue of *Theory into Practice*. Instructors ask students to follow along as they read out loud. These "read-alongs" help students develop reading fluency, and they provide models that allow readers to hear how fluent readers sound. "Read-alongs" also help readers see writing as live communication, or "talk written down." Students discover the drama in what is being read by hearing the author's voice. Some of the reading selections in *Structured Reading* that particularly lend themselves to "read-alongs" are

> "Don't Sell Your Ambitions Short to 'Keep It Real,'" p. 113; "The Girl with the Large Eyes," p. 169; "The Chaser," p. 391; "Summer," p. 155 and "To Catch a Thief," p. 131.